✧ Susan Glaspell in Context

American Theater, Culture, and Politics, 1915–48

J. Ellen Gainor

Ann Arbor

THE UNIVERSITY OF MICHIGAN PRESS

First paperback edition 2004
Copyright © by the University of Michigan 2001
All rights reserved
Published in the United States of America by
The University of Michigan Press
Manufactured in the United States of America
♾ Printed on acid-free paper

2007   2006   2005   2004   5   4   3   2

A CIP catalog record for this book is available from the British Library.

Library of Congress Cataloging-in-Publication Data

Gainor, J. Ellen.
    Susan Glaspell in context : American theater, culture, and
politics, 1915–48 / by J. Ellen Gainor.
        p.   cm.
    Includes bibliographical references and index.
    ISBN 0-472-10650-3 (cloth : alk. paper)
    1. Glaspell, Susan, 1876–1948—Criticism and interpretation.   2.
Politics and literature—United States—History—20th century.   3.
Women and literature—United States—History—20th century.   4.
Theater—United States—History—20th century.   5. United States—
Intellectual life—20th century.   I. Title.
PS3513.L35Z68 2001
818'.5209—dc21   2001002645

ISBN 0-472-03010-8 (pbk : alk. paper)

✧ Acknowledgments

A number of individuals, institutions, and scholarly services helped make this work possible. A year-long National Endowment for the Humanities Fellowship for University Teachers enabled me to conduct the initial research for the book. The Department of Theatre, Film and Dance at Cornell University granted me leave time and supplied additional funding for this research. The assistance of Cornell's Hull Fund, supporters of an earlier book project, helped secure my ongoing relationship with the University of Michigan Press. A grant from the President's Council of Cornell Women enabled me to include the photographic illustrations of Glaspell productions. Elaine Showalter arranged for my status as a Visiting Scholar through the Department of English at Princeton University, a residency that granted me access not only to their facilities but also gave me close proximity to the primary Glaspell materials in various collections in New York City. The curators and reference staff of the Berg Collection at the New York Public Library, the repository of the papers of Susan Glaspell and George Cram Cook, were extremely efficient and helpful throughout the writing of this book. I would also like to acknowledge the research assistance of Marty Jacobs of the Theatre Collection of the Museum of the City of New York, and the reference staffs of the Billy Rose Theatre Collection of the New York Public Library at Lincoln Center and of the Library of Congress. The interlibrary loan divisions of Princeton's Firestone Library and Cornell University's Olin Library were invaluable partners on this project.

The world of Glaspell scholarship is small but extremely dedicated and generous. I would particularly like to express my thanks to Veronica Makowsky for her insightful assistance with late drafts of the manuscript. Linda Ben-Zvi, Marcia Noe, Gail Cohen, Arthur Waterman, and Kathy Rodier provided assistance with answers to specific queries and through their general engagement in dialogue about Glaspell and her work. Stephen J. Bottoms and Judith C. Milligan merit commendation for their organization of the first international meeting of Glaspell scholars at the University of Glasgow in May 1996; the research and artistic work presented there provided me with many new insights on

Glaspell and her contemporaries. Colleagues in American Studies assisted my efforts to establish Glaspell in broader historical, sociopolitical, and artistic contexts. In particular, I would like to thank Harvey Teres, Joel Porte, and Allan Hepburn for their bibliographical assistance and Richard Sewall for his conjectures on Glaspell and Dickinson. Conversations with Michael Goldman spurred my earliest thoughts on Glaspell. I am also grateful for the ongoing mentorship of Sandra Gilbert in matters of feminist scholarship and the profession. Patricia Schroeder and Jeffrey Mason provided very helpful feedback on early chapter drafts. I am also grateful to the graduate students in the doctoral program in Theatre Arts at Cornell, especially Kornelia Tancheva, who assisted my research.

A study of this kind could not appear without scholars' ability to incorporate material held in special collections. I am extremely grateful to the estate of George Cram Cook for granting me full access to and permission to reproduce from the works and archives of Glaspell and Cook. I would like to thank the Theatre Collection at Harvard University, the Beinicke Library at Yale and the Barrett Collection of the University of Virginia Library for granting me permission to quote from materials in their holdings. I am similarly indebted to the Berg Collection and the Billy Rose Theatre Collection of the New York Public Library, as well as to the Museum of the City of New York, for granting permission to reproduce photos of Glaspell and her plays in production. I also acknowledge the *Journal of American Drama and Theatre,* which originally published my work on *The Verge,* part of which is included here.

The patience, enthusiasm, candor, and guidance of LeAnn Fields, my editor at the University of Michigan Press, are immeasurable. I am grateful to her assistant, Abbey Potter, and to the production and copyediting staff at the Press for their shepherding of my work into print.

Words cannot express my gratitude to my family and friends, whose ongoing support buoyed me throughout the research and writing process. My profoundest thanks go to my husband, David, my in-house editor and helpmeet at all times, and to our son, St. John, and daughter, Loie, who add joy to each day of our lives.

✧ Contents

Introduction

I first stumbled across the work of Susan Glaspell in the mid-1980s while reading a brief discussion of her impact on women in the London theater of the early twentieth century, which was the focus of my research at that time. Theater historian Julie Holledge's description of Glaspell's play *The Verge*, in *Innocent Flowers: Women in the Edwardian Theatre*, proved tantalizing; why hadn't I encountered this writer before? After a quick survey of Glaspell scholarship, I realized I was not alone. From the early 1970s on, a number of feminist scholars had been slowly rescuing Glaspell's writing from a comparatively long oblivion. Mary Papke's *Susan Glaspell: A Research and Production Sourcebook* (1993) allows us to trace the history of the dismissal and subsequent disappearance of Glaspell from the canon of American drama. Beginning around 1940, derogatory remarks by such influential theater commentators as George Jean Nathan and Burns Mantle appear to have had a significant impact on Glaspell's standing; the Gelb biography of Eugene O'Neill (1960), which helped cement his placement as *the* American playwright of the early half of the century, "cast Glaspell as a very secondary character in that drama," in the words of Papke's apt summary (212).[1] Such criticism quite radically overturned earlier opinion. At the height of Glaspell's theatrical creativity she was held to be one of the American theater's leading figures, if not its shining light. Ludwig Lewisohn wrote in 1932: "Susan Glaspell was followed by Eugene O'Neill. The rest was silence; the rest is silence still" (*Expression* 398).

The unintended irony of Lewisohn's sense of "silence," in terms of her elimination from the rankings of major American dramatists less than a decade after his *Expression in America* appeared, resonates with the fate of any number of women writers recently rescued from obscurity. In the case of Glaspell we can trace the resurgence of interest in her writing in major part to the scholarship of Mary Anne Ferguson, who reprinted Glaspell's short story "A Jury of Her Peers" in her extremely influential anthology *Images of Women in Literature* (1973), which was one of the early key texts for feminist criticism in the United States. Ferguson's collection prompted seminal critical writing on Glaspell by Judith Fetterley and Annette Kolodny, among others. Sandra

Gilbert and Susan Gubar then chose to include the one-act *Trifles*, the drama Glaspell wrote about the same murder case a year before the story version appeared, in their *Norton Anthology of Literature by Women* (1985), a text that, like all Norton editions, serves as a vehicle for the canonization of both writers and individual works. Within the field of feminist theater studies Helen Krich Chinoy and Linda Walsh Jenkins accomplished a similar goal with their groundbreaking *Women in American Theatre* (1981), which featured several essays focusing on Glaspell.[2]

Although Papke's *Sourcebook* documents a steady stream of published references to Glaspell from the 1910s forward, my concern here is to highlight those works and commentators who may have had the most significant influence on the overall standing of Glaspell in the theater and in the academy. One of the noticeable trends in writing on Glaspell since the 1970s is the predominance of scholarship emanating from the field of women's studies. While feminist criticism has unquestionably rescued Glaspell from literary and theatrical obscurity, its success is double-edged. With Glaspell, as with many artists championed by criticism grounded in the politics of identity (African American studies, queer theory, Asian American studies, to give just a few other examples), a tension lingers between her status in the field that rediscovered her and in the academic mainstream. The latter has been slower to embrace such figures. When it does so, their location within fields of inquiry often remains linked to their positionality, as token representatives of their group, or their work is compared to that of canonical figures.

While, for example, C. W. E. Bigsby's widely known *Critical Introduction to Twentieth-Century American Drama* (1982) has helped introduce Glaspell to an entire generation of students and scholars alike, the way Bigsby positions her speaks volumes about the (re)placement of women writers in the canon:

> Besides Eugene O'Neill, the Provincetown Players produced one major talent in Susan Glaspell. Her work is in many ways more controlled than O'Neill's. Her style is more reticent. . . . Yet she shared her husband's visionary drive, his sense of a Nietzschean life force operating as a counterweight to a tragic potential. And this breaks through on occasion in lyrical arias, apostrophes to the human spirit, at times unbalancing and sentimental, at times affecting in the simplicity of their expression. (25)

Bigsby's situating of Glaspell in contrast to O'Neill and in juxtaposition to her husband establishes a context that gives her little autonomy and even less status in her own right as an important artist. His commentary repeatedly calls into question the aesthetic merits of Glaspell's writing. Yet Bigsby must be commended for his commitment to Glaspell, in this study and especially as the editor of the selected *Plays of Susan Glaspell* (1987), which brought back into print some of her more innovative and influential works, making them available to a wide audience of students, teachers, scholars, and theater practitioners. While the following chapters will detail the highly problematic nature of much of Bigsby's analysis, he ironically remains the scholar more responsible than any other for a renewed awareness of her theatrical career.

Arthur Waterman's volume on Glaspell (1966) presents comparable difficulties but remained the only biographical and critical overview of Glaspell until Marcia Noe published her 1983 monograph, *Susan Glaspell: Voice from the Heartland*. Despite an appreciation of the work of Bigsby and Waterman, my critical appraisal of Glaspell's writing differs significantly from theirs; this study will challenge a number of their interpretations and conclusions. Ironically, moreover, the failure to explore Glaspell's work in its contemporary context may have allowed these and other critics to misestimate her writing even in purely aesthetic terms, for the aesthetics of Glaspell's moment differ from those of the 1960s or 1980s. It should also be obvious that such scholarly explorations, my own included, are inextricably linked to contexts that merit as close scrutiny and understanding as the texts they consider.

This study explicitly avoids making determinations about the "quality" or aesthetics of Glaspell's writing as its prime objective. Such dicta can lead us to dismiss work that may hold great interest for other reasons. To give just a few examples, Glaspell's dramaturgy is compelling for its experimentation with form, its cogent engagement with social and political issues, its central concern with the role of women, its humor.

This work is entitled *Susan Glaspell in Context* precisely because it seeks to introduce and explore a number of the historical, social, political, literary, and theatrical contexts that informed Glaspell's dramaturgy. It is this close engagement with her culture that makes Glaspell's theatrical work important historically, creatively, and intellectually. As Liza Nelligan has observed, Glaspell was "historically situated in a major transformative moment for American women" (85). Nelligan suggests that

> it might be worthwhile to examine her plays through the lenses of Glaspell's own historical context to illuminate . . . what Glaspell's drama meant to the audiences of her time and to complicate, and cross-pollinate, our own readings of her work. (86)

Nelligan's essay on *Trifles* and *The Verge* focuses on the context of Glaspell's feminism, drawing important connections to a panoply of movements that affected women, including socialism, suffrage, and the shifting ideologies around "separate spheres." Establishing this broad historical context for understanding Glaspell's feminism is necessary and cogent. Yet each of her plays also requires distinct analysis grounded in the nuances of the work. My engagement with

Glaspell's plays takes its cue from the scripts themselves, shifting among considerations of dramatic form, theater history, literary themes, characterization, dialogic style, cultural and political forces, and performance issues, among others.

This study focuses on the body of her dramatic writing not only because to date there is no full-length examination of it but also because in her plays Glaspell undertook her strongest, widest social commentary and artistic experimentation.[3] Her drama then, provides the most apt point of entry for a critical analysis that seeks to move beyond traditional criteria of artistic value.

Such an initial study, moreover, has the responsibility to provide an overview not only of the work itself, and what holds it together, but also some detail of its creation and reception. Those of us who work on Glaspell have eagerly awaited the publication of Barbara Ozieblo's and Linda Ben-Zvi's biographies of Glaspell. The former appeared just after this study went to press, and thus, unfortunately, I could not consult it. These biographies will no doubt discuss in much greater detail than is possible here the background to all her work. Still, as Ben-Zvi herself has observed, it is a mistake to read Glaspell's writing primarily through her biography.[4] Moreover, the contested role of biography in contemporary literary criticism has prompted a growing body of revisionist biographical theory. The work of Alison Booth and Cheryl Walker in this field has particularly influenced the way that I use biographical detail in exploring Glaspell's theatrical writing. Booth advocates "the inclusion of the author's biography and of historical context(s) as contributing, unfolding *texts,* not reified entities, in an alert intertextuality" (89). Similarly, Walker champions "persona criticism," which "allows one to speak of authorship as multiple, involving culture, psyche, and intertextuality, as well as biographical data about the writer" (109).

The chapters that follow frame each play with essential information on Glaspell's activities around the moments of composition and initial production(s) as well as with a sampling of the critical response to her New York (and, where possible, British) premiers. Like other twentieth-century dramatists in the United States, such as Arthur Miller, Glaspell's journalistic reception abroad was often more enthusiastic than that on the home front; over the past two decades a number of her plays have also been revived in England (primarily by the now-defunct Mrs Worthington's Daughters and more recently by the Orange Tree Theatre), whereas productions in the States are infrequent and almost exclusively campus based. The 1983 revival of *Inheritors* by the Mirror Theater and the 1999 revival of *Alison's House* by the Mint Theater, both in New York City, are rare exceptions.

Theater scholars often draw upon reviews of performances for information about production details and the historical reception of dramatic texts. Frequently, these brief articles are the only records available to us on the stage work of actors, directors, designers, and playwrights. Yet dramatic criticism—even well-informed reviewing—is, almost by definition, a highly subjective mode of appraisal and performance documentation. We must take care to look at who is reviewing (when the critic can be identified), where that review is being published, and for what imagined audience that review was written. The fact that many of Glaspell's first critics were men who spent the majority of their time covering the commercial theater in New York and London must be taken into consideration.[5] Providing brief analyses and contexts for the criticism itself may therefore help to "place" historically the moments of Glaspell's first performances. Theater historian Ronald Wainscott articulates well his decision to use such materials for his study of the American stage from 1914 to 1929:

> If we are to understand the significance of the artistic experiences both when they occurred and today, we must understand the critical responses to the plays and productions when they were new. Even reactionary and misinterpretive reviews are helpful; sometimes they are more representative of popular responses to difficult and challenging events than more insightful articles. (x)

Glaspell's plays almost always prompted widely diverging critical opinion, which ranged from adulation to flat dismissal. Trying to understand her reception is thus one of the challenges Glaspell scholarship must tackle.

The main thrust of each chapter, however, is a discussion of some primary contexts through which to consider the given play(s). My choices are designed to provide points of entry to the works and are not intended to limit subsequent examination or exclude any other approach. In general my modes of analysis fall into two main categories: making social/political/historical connections with the plays and discussing issues of literary form or subgenre and theater history that they represent.

One of the benefits of a synthetic study of Glaspell's writing may be the identification of overarching dramaturgical techniques, elements of her style that one can trace across her more than three-decade-long career in the theater. A few of these deserve particular note. One is Glaspell's ability to interlace her writing with humor, perhaps to relieve some of the legitimate seriousness of the issues she confronts, perhaps because she attempted truthfully to capture the oscillations from comedy, to pathos, to everything in between she saw in her world. Glaspell's colleague Eugene O'Neill called her in 1920 "the only true writer of real comedy in this country" (qtd. in Wainscott 114). It is therefore intriguing that some of her critics responded immediately to this quality; others seem to have missed it entirely. Some reviewers of *The Verge,* for example, saw nothing funny in the play, whereas others quickly grasped its almost farcical antics with gunplay as well as the subtler ironies of its dialogue. Much the same could be said of the response to *Chains of Dew*. Obviously, senses of humor vary, and the culturally specific nature of some forms of comedy must be acknowledged; similarly, we cannot ignore the impact of performance and direction on the perception of a work's wit. Nevertheless, the disparity between the evidence of Glaspell's comic technique and the vagaries of its reception remains unresolved.

In a 1951 overview of American comedy that traced its twentieth-century development to that date, the revered drama scholar Alan S. Downer points to vaudeville and burlesque and their representations of "the American character and customs and ways of looking at things" as the "roots" of the form (113). Downer identifies the wisecrack as "the heart of American comic dialogue" and farcical and slapstick action as equally essential (119), often with a touch of sentimentality for balance (121). Downer quotes the British critic and theater manager J. T. Grein, whom he feels has perfectly captured the spirit of American comedy:

> [The actors] give us no time to think, to analyze or to criticize; somehow they laugh and will make us respond—and the result is that people on the stage and people in the house let themselves gayly go, both parties really full well aware that they are "dashed" if they know what it is all about. (131)

As the discussions of Glaspell's comic plays will show, however, her humor was all about making her audience think. This may in part account for the comparisons of her work to such dramatists as Shaw, Ibsen, and Chekhov, especially by British critics. It may also have contributed to American critics' confusion over her style, which did not conform to the patterns and techniques subsequently identified by historians such as Downer.

More recently, feminist critics have recognized that women's humor, like many forms of female creativity, may differ from canonical (usually male-authored) examples and may not be appreciated by critics who take this tradition to be definitive. Nancy Walker notes that "in virtually every culture, cultural prohibitions curtail women's participation in humor; just as in American culture, male dominance extends to a control of the expression of humor" (65). Judy Little observes further:

> Women's peripheral yet invested position[s] within a male-dominated culture have given their sentences the license of carnival, a license to overturn, to mimic, and to "deconstruct." Especially in the sentences of women who write comedy, there is a double-voiced tension or "dialogic imagination," to use Mikhail Bakhtin's term, which immerses the piece in a subtle rebellious mockery. (19)

This dialogic tension—the practice of writers both invoking and mocking convention—demands that an audience recognize both the allusions to the dominant codes and their upheaval if the humor is to work. Alice Sheppard posits that women humorists need a like-minded "social group" to serve as both "a reference point and a source of identity" (40). Developing this idea further, Walker maintains that humor can be used to build a sense of community. Significantly, she identifies Heterodoxy, a Greenwich Village women's club of which Glaspell was an early member, as filling this role and fostering the work of women humorists, including cartoonist Lou Rogers, the poets Alice Duer Miller and Florence Guy, and the political speech writer Marie Jenney Howe, founder of Heterodoxy (Walker 69–70).[6] This reciprocity between a woman humorist and her community suggests that Glaspell's location within her Greenwich Village milieu is integral to the genesis and understanding of her comedy.

While her humor has received comparatively little scholarly attention, many writers on Glaspell have observed her repetition of the device of an absent central figure, a hallmark of such plays as *Trifles, Bernice,* and *Alison's House.*[7] While the most obvious instances of this device are indeed the missing female characters at the heart of these three plays, critics who extrapolate from this a message about the marginalization of women, for example, miss a larger implication of this stylistic trait because they ignore her absent men. *Suppressed Desires* revolves around an offstage male psychoanalyst who literally controls the action of the play; *Trifles* makes as much of the dead Mr. Wright as it does of his wife Minnie, incarcerated on suspicion of his murder. A key motivating figure for Madeline Fejevary in *Inheritors* is her friend Fred Jordan, jailed for his stance as a conscientious objector to the war; Claire Archer's dead son haunts her memory in *The Verge* and calls into question assumptions one might initially make about her as a mother. The relative critical blindness to these male characters suggests that a broader view of Glaspell's dramatic writing can both highlight her feminist concerns and demonstrate how she integrates feminism with other political convictions and social issues in her theatrical writing.

Over the years Glaspell's critics have consistently argued about whether her prose or plays were more significant. What such commentary rarely considers is Glaspell's sensitivity to the nuances of genre; she exploits each medium for its greatest impact, revealing a keen understanding of what narratives are well served by theatrical representation. One key achievement of her drama is her ability to make the stage environment come alive as another player in performance. The vibrancy of place in such works as *Trifles, The Outside, Bernice, The Verge,* and *Alison's House* literally makes the sets she envisions function as characters—not backdrops to the action but central parts of it. It is, of course, impossible to determine exactly how Glaspell developed her feel for the theater, but one biographical detail may help account for her seemingly intuitive understanding of the power of performance. A select number of reviews and memoirs of Glaspell's contemporaries allude to her work as an actor—a function she rarely assumed but apparently one at which she excelled. Her Provincetown colleague artist William Zorach recalls:

> Susan Glaspell . . . was a marvelous actress. Acting played a minor part in her life, but she had that rare power and quality inherent in great actresses. She had only to be on the stage and the play and the audience came alive. (47)

It is tantalizing to wonder what impact Glaspell's work onstage, beginning with her appearance as Henrietta Brewster in the premier production of her first play, *Suppressed Desires,* may have had on her as a dramatic writer.

Other more "literary" techniques also enrich her dramaturgy. Foremost among these may be her vibrant and complex symbolic networks: image clusters that give cumulative force to her themes. In *Trifles,* for instance, the way Glaspell uses the quilt, the canary, the cherry preserves, and all the details that surround these evocative objects illustrates her skill at weaving complex and multivalent imagery into the larger fabric of her drama. One could build a similar argument around the use of the lifesaving station, the dunes, the trees, and the geography of Cape Cod in *The Outside.*

Just as this study opposes a critical tradition that seeks to establish the "greatness" of a writer or (most often) "his" individual works, it also resists scholarly inclinations to account for a body of writing under one theoretical rubric or to generate hermetic readings that attempt to account for a writer's concerns with all-encompassing syntheses. The reader will find no one theme, for example, traced throughout Glaspell's dramaturgy here nor one critical form employed as an interpretive strategy. Although many readers come to Glaspell originally through a profound interest in gender studies and feminist criticism, I hope they will recognize that to analyze her work only, or even primarily, through such lenses would be to do her and her work a disservice. As the following chapters show, Glaspell was dedicated to a number of social issues and wrote from a commitment to multiple political beliefs, feminism prominently, but not exclusively, among them.

Glaspell made an important statement to journalist Alice Rohe, another member of the Heterodoxy Club, in a rare published interview she gave in 1921:

> Of course I am interested in all progressive movements, whether feminist, social or economic . . . but I can take no very active part other than through my writing. . . . When one has limited strength one must use it for the thing one feels most important. (4)

It seems obvious from this quotation that Glaspell saw her writing as political activism; establishing Glaspell as a political writer and her plays as the site for her strongest political statements is central to this study.

The timing of Glaspell's career, spanning the era between the two world wars, probably influenced her more profoundly, and affected her dramaturgy more significantly, than any particular political affinity. References to war appear in almost every play she wrote, whether as passing allusions or as central themes. Her dramas reflect the impact of the wars on a specifically American milieu: on the individual character, on social morality, on the commitment to action, and on a sense of national history and its foundational principles. If it has one overarching agenda, this study hopes to convince its readers that the most compelling way to approach Glaspell is as an American writer.

The One-Act Play in America

The one-act play was central to the development of both Glaspell's dramaturgy and twentieth-century American drama in general. The theatrical longevity and favorable critical reception of Glaspell's first two dramatic efforts, *Suppressed Desires* (written with her husband George Cram Cook in 1915) and *Trifles* (1916), attest to her quick mastery of the one-act form of dramaturgy. She followed these two works with five additional one-acts produced in 1917–18, one of which (*Tickless Time*) was again a collaboration with Cook. Glaspell's writing in the one-act form did more, however, than serve the immediate production needs of the Provincetown Players, the company that Cook, Glaspell, and a number of their friends formed in 1915. Her status as one of the key figures in the burgeoning Little Theatre movement also positioned her playwriting within an active critical discourse on the development of American drama.

A part of this debate looked to the one-act as the dramatic mode par excellence for experimentation, innovation, and ultimately the foundation of a national theatrical culture. The identification of this form as a vehicle for innovative aesthetic expression provided a convenient artistic alibi for the early technical limitations of the Provincetown, which at first found one-acts as much as they could tackle. Moreover, this critical discourse lent authority to the group's nationalist mission: to found a theater committed to the development of American playwrights and dramaturgy. In the 1917–18 subscription circular Cook reminded his audiences of the need for "one little theatre for American writers," and by 1920–21 he felt confident to claim, "The Provincetown Players have become a national institution."[1]

Between 1912 and the late 1920s numerous essays, and even entire volumes, were written on the one-act play: its history, strategies for its composition, and its relationship to extant and emerging American and European drama. Glaspell's work, as well as that of her Provincetown colleagues, soon became an exemplar of the form. These essays' repeated citations of Glaspell's work as a model for the new dramaturgy reinforce the sense of her prominence and her critical standing as a leading dramatist in this period.[2] Her one-act contributions to the Provincetown repertoire not only reflect her particular thematic, social, and stylistic concerns; they also resonate with the broader issues of community and nation central to those who championed the one-act play. Thus, we can examine Glaspell's one-acts within this critical tradition that was striving to make the drama and theater part of the development of a national literature and performance culture. The work of the Players reflects the creative synergy between them and their bohemian communities of Greenwich Village and Provincetown, Massachusetts. Similarly, there appears to be an implicit dialogue developing between these critics of the one-act form and the American artists engaged in its development. While Eugene O'Neill came to the group with his legendary trunk-full of plays already composed, most of the dramatists connected with the Players wrote specifically for the company, and the pieces had an immediacy that reflected their creators' interest in the latest stylistic trends, local events, or political issues.

Although some of the contemporary critical analysis was written by theatrical commentators such as John Corbin of the *New York Times,* other pieces were produced by prominent figures in the American theater who were early champions of the form, playwrights such as George Middleton (1880–1967) and Percival Wilde (1887–1953). One noteworthy feature of these articles is their remarkable homogeneity; one could hypothesize that Middleton's essay of 1912, "The Neglected One-Act Play," served as a blueprint for the commentary of the next fifteen years. This essay, published in the New York *Dramatic Mirror,* outlined the history and evolution of the form, explored issues of its production within the commercial theater, and established its connection with the Little Theatre movement in America.

Middleton explains that the one-act has been looked down upon, especially by theatrical managers who assume it will not be considered serious drama and thus will not sell seats. While short comic or melodramatic plays—skits, essentially—were mainstays of the vaudeville stage, Middleton sees the dramatic one-act as a "waif" that needs the right home (13). Middleton makes a serious plea for greater consideration and creation of the form and juxtaposes it to "the morass our drama is in at present," suggesting the one-act as a potential "partial cure" (14).

Middleton feels audiences today "resent the small return for capital invested. . . . The drama should not be the luxury it has become, but a necessary social commodity—and that's not theory, but good business and accurate sociology combined" (13). Middleton and his colleagues were beginning to articulate here the concepts that would eventually lead to the creation of the not-for-profit theater in America, a structure built on the idea that there was an audience for a different kind of theater than that currently dominating commercial stages, especially on Broadway. They contrasted images of the mindless entertainment they saw there to the potential for a drama with real significance and impact, regardless of its style or structure.

The palliative force the one-act might exert on the American stage surely must have appealed to many of the artists connected with the rise of the Little Theatres, who perceived the artistic, social, and practical viability of the form.[3] The appearance of Middleton's piece in 1912 coincided with the founding of two of the most important early Little Theatres: Mrs. Lyman Gale's Toy Theatre in Boston and Maurice Brown and Ellen Van Volkenburg's Chicago Little Theatre. Equally, if not more significant, was the tour of the Irish Players: the group founded in 1904 by W. B. Yeats, John M. Synge, and Lady Gregory, among others, which later became the Abbey Theatre. Seeing their American tour in 1911–12 (Flannery 360–61) was an event that seems to have profoundly influenced many artists, including Cook. In *The Road to the Temple*, Glaspell's biography of him, she speaks of the impact of the group on her husband, who was doing journalistic work with Floyd Dell in Chicago at the time:

> There were excitements in Chicago just then. The Irish Players. Quite possibly there would have been no Provincetown Players had there not been Irish Players. What he saw done for Irish life he wanted for American life—no stage conventions in the way of projecting with the humility of true feeling. (167)

One of the details of the Irish Players' tour that captured the attention of American reviewers, and probably fostered the Americans' subsequent creativity and critical analysis, was the group's production repertoire, which featured "no less than thirty-four" one-acts (Hamilton 187), performed in bills of three per evening. This kind of production schedule, which soon became standard in the early years of such groups as the Provincetown and the Washington Square Players, was at that time quite new for the American stage. Performances of shorter works were becoming known elsewhere in Europe through the writing of August Strindberg and Hermann Sudermann (to name just two); the producers of the Grand Guignol in Paris and the experimental stages in that and many other cities embraced the form. The status of the one-act in the American theater prior to about 1913, however, was decidedly low.

In his 1913 essay "The One-Act Play in America" Clayton Hamilton spells out the only accepted production options for writers of a one-act: either as a curtain-raiser or after-piece to a full-length drama or as part of a vaudeville bill's continuous performance (184). Hamilton feels neither option is likely "to encourage sincere artists to write for these theatres," since the pieces have to be either "comic skits" or "mechanical melodrama." In fact, Hamilton believes, "No experience could be more depressing to any intelligent person [interested in the one-act form] than to spend six successive evenings in six different vaudeville theatres in New York. The experiment, if attempted, would probably result in suicide on Sunday" (185). It took the demonstrations of the innovative European artists touring the States for American writers and audiences, but also producers, to see the great potential of the one-act medium.

Middleton, Hamilton, and Clayton Gibbs, some of the earliest commentators, all discuss the one-act primarily with regard to its future in the commercial theater, as a form with legitimate artistic and financial promise. Hamilton provides a detailed explanation of the one-act in the London theater in particular, pointing explicitly to the separate practices of different classes of theatergoers. While the aristocracy would typically dine late, those who took seats in the pit might have already stood in line for hours simply to gain admission. These patrons needed to be entertained between eight and nine o'clock (185–86). Such short dramas traditionally had been "placed before *the* play of the evening in order to amuse that part of the audience which was waiting for the remainder to finish its dinner" (Goodman). In Gibbs's words, such dramas were "addressed primarily . . . to pit and gallery" and thus "never reached a high quality" (143). But, as Hamilton points out, the fault lay not with this segment of the public but with management, which had erroneous ideas about the interests and capacity of this audience: "The hardest thing to teach any theatrical manager is the advisability—from the standpoint of mere business—of looking up to the public instead of down upon it" (185).

The history of the curtain-raiser in the commercial theater, then, merits study for its class implications, but it is also closely linked to the development of the form as an alternative to commercial fare within the Little Theatres. For such groups as the Provincetown, an avowedly amateur enterprise that rejected the standards and practices of the commercial stage, the class implications accompanying the reception of the one-act form would also have been untenable, as these amateur groups envisioned a democratic theater affordable and available to all.[4] The one-act form presumably promised to the amateur theaters a convenient marriage of form and philosophy for artistic as well as social ends. Taking the form the critics had identified as originally for the "masses" would have been fitting for artists dedicated to socialism, at the same time as one-acts served their performance needs.

In his 1917 piece "Why the One Act Play?" Edward Goodman, director of the Washington Square Players, opens with a discussion of the financial and artistic distinctions between commercial enterprises and the Little Theatres, which "have been less restricting both in their seat charges and in the subject-matter of their plays" (327).[5] As evidence of the general popular appeal of this theatrical format, Goodman cites one recently concluded bill of one-acts produced by his company that ran for 106 performances (327). For him these figures testified to the suitability of this new kind of stage offering for an audience consisting of individuals from many different class positions.

In addition to the financial argument, another historical obstacle to the sponsorship of one-act dramaturgy came from the negative preconceptions the managers held about the artistic quality of the form. As theater commentator Montrose Moses observed in 1925, "The habit of not regarding the one-act-play form as worthy of the highest creative ingenuity . . . has handicapped its development." He relates an anecdote concerning the producer Charles Frohman, who supposedly felt James Barrie's one-act *The Twelve-Pound Look,* cited by many critics as a landmark of the form, was "a waste of good material in small space, and he begged the author to make it into a big play" (397). Part of the agenda of the critical discourse on the one-act was to dispel notions of the artistic inadequacy of the medium.

Some critics took a conciliatory tone, suggesting that shorter genres might serve as creative stepping-stones; they suggested writers develop expertise in the short forms and then progress to the full-length novel or play. Such an apologetic view, of course, only reinforces the sense that the one-act is a "minor" or "secondary" form. Frank Shay, a publisher of numerous collections of one-acts who was closely connected with the Provincetown, embraced this critical position and felt the short drama met both artistic and practical needs:

> The shorter form served both the playwright and the producing group as a vehicle to get where they were going. It was a means to an end: they found their wings or cut their eye-teeth on the dwarfed drama and went on to greater heights. Now, after many years of experience they have large theatres where they produce the long plays of those writers who formerly wrote short plays. ("Introduction" vi)

Most of the commentators on the form compare the negative attitude toward short stage pieces, represented by Frohman, to similar discussions over the relative merits of the short story and the novel, although the short story had, they felt, garnered a certain literary stature yet to adhere to the one-act drama. As Goodman remarks:

> To call a one-acter a "playlet" is to imply that when it or its author grows up it will become a "full-length drama." . . . But if this is so, then the best work of Maupassant and Poe and O. Henry must be relegated to the class of interesting promises unfulfilled. . . . Only—we have realized that the short-story is an art form in itself, not a novel unfortunately stunted in its growth. And we must learn that the one-act play bears an analogous relation to the longer form. (327)

John Corbin concurred, editorializing on the need for theatrical producers to foster the form, much as magazines had served as a necessary outlet for the development of authors' craft in the short story ("One-Act Play" 8).

The repeated critical juxtaposition of short story and one-act resonates with Glaspell's own career, as she followed exactly the trajectory laid out in these essays: she started her creative activities as a short story writer in the early 1900s then attempted her first novel, *The Glory of the Conquered*, in 1909. The close connection between her skill as a writer of short fiction and her early success with one-acts is hardly surprising; one need only look to the plot she conceived in both genres, *Trifles* and "A Jury of Her Peers," to see how the forms complement each other. That she then moved from the one-act to the full-length drama (*Bernice* in 1919) just as her theatrical home, the Provincetown, was expanding its production capacities and gaining greater prominence as a Little Theatre would seem to exemplify publisher and critic Frank Shay's sense of the "natural" evolution of such groups.

From 1919 onward, however, the Players presented bills featuring either a full-length piece or ones composed of multiple one-acts in the same season. The balance shifted more toward full-length works by 1921–22, their last year under Cook's leadership. That the Provincetown continued to produce one-acts, even while expanding its repertoire to include full-length pieces, suggests that its members found merit, aesthetically and politically, in the short form. Clearly, Glaspell's colleagues did not necessarily embrace the idea that it was a lesser means of theatrical expression. In Glaspell's case, then, we should not regard her move to full-length dramaturgy as grounds for dismissing or demeaning her one-acts; rather, we should look to questions of theme, character, and plot to account for her choices of dramatic form and structure.

Nevertheless, in the early years of the Provincetown Players the group adhered to the production schedule of exclusively one-act bills that all these critics endorsed. As Edward Goodman succinctly stated, "The little play fits the little theatre" (327). And just as these Little Theatres gained attention in the rhetoric of theatrical contributions to cultural nationalism, so the one-act, as the form central to this theater, also became linked to the burgeoning of a distinctly American aesthetic. The one-act took its place among the media that came to represent the growth of American artistry as a component of the broader culture. Clayton Gibbs maintained that "the one-act play is . . . especially suited to our national temperament," because it provides exactly what the public craves: the "tenseness of interest at an emotional height, an irresistible focusing of interest and emotion upon a particular situation" (143). Gibbs describes a flabbiness in the full-length drama of his day and asserts that these playwrights need to "vitalize their exposition and psychological explanation" (156) as the one-act dramatists have. Walter Prichard Eaton further asserts in 1916:

> The one-act play in America, as a serious art form, will be cultivated by the experimental theatres, the so-called "Little Theatres," and by the

more ambitious amateurs. As our experimental theatres increase in number . . . it will probably play its part, and perhaps no insignificant a part, in the development of a national drama. ("Introduction" xv)

Montrose Moses reflects: "The movement became an epidemic. . . . [T]he people were . . . using something which was fundamentally important to the future life of the theatre in America. They were utilizing something out of which a national development might arise" (*American Dramatist* 403). Seeing the form as a "great thing" (391), Moses clearly believes in an American theater central to its culture and the one-act form as the linchpin of that theater.

Moses links these developments explicitly to the sense of "community feeling" that surrounded such groups (403). A fine example of such community is provided by the production of *Suppressed Desires,* which directly addressed interests and personalities of the Greenwich Village community. B. Roland Lewis, in his *Technique of the One-Act Play,* goes to considerable length to analyze the relationship of author to audience, suggesting that he may be both part of it and distinct from it; this anomalous position will have a salutary impact on his craft, however, precisely because it will allow the writer to "provoke the very response that he desires to get" (28–29). The particular knowledge Glaspell and her colleagues had of their audience is highlighted in an informative essay from 1918, "How Experimental Theaters May Avoid the Pitfalls of Professionalism." This unsigned essay, published in *Current Opinion,* observed, albeit wryly:

> The audiences come, seven nights every month, and continue to come— the same audiences. The Players know them, and have them classified like beetles in a case. (29)

Having a loyal, stable, and known audience not only insured a certain financial stability; it also allowed the Players to hone their writing toward the goal of calculated viewer impact that Lewis outlined. Glaspell identified strongly with her audience. *Woman's Honor* and *The Outside* demonstrate her sensitivity to gender and feminist issues, while *The People* dramatizes Village professional life. *Tickless Time* presents tensions over industrialization and modernity—a variation on the ambivalence toward the new sexual freedom of *Suppressed Desires.* Moreover, Glaspell had clearly made a commitment to the drama as part of a nationalist aesthetic. By setting plays in various parts of the country and by creating American characters from different walks of life and political points of view, she used the stage as her canvas for representing the United States she knew. She contrasts the midwestern provincialism of *Close the Book* to the bohemian Cape Cod of *Tickless Time.* She explores comic and dramatic tones, mystery, expressionism, and slice-of-life realist forms. Not only does she use the one-act as a place for developing her dramatic voice, but she also reveals through this dramaturgy all her major concerns as a writer of drama and fiction—issues such as women's roles in patriarchal society, the true meaning of democracy in the United States, and the difficulty of maintaining openness and trust in interpersonal relationships.

Because the one-act did not continue to represent the hallmark of American dramaturgy beyond the Little Theatre era, it became all too easy for critics subsequently to dismiss short pieces as juvenilia or as dramatists' trial efforts before tackling "real" (meaning full-length) plays.[6] Thus, it becomes all the more important to consider Glaspell's one-act dramaturgy within this complex discourse on the form, written before, during, and after her composition of seven short dramas between 1915 and 1918. The plays resonate with this critical writing in each of its primary foci: the artistic potential of the form, its connection with broader social concerns, and its suitability to American culture. From gestures toward Village radicalism to adaptations of European expressionism to representations of the antitechnological movement in America to statements of concern over government suppression of free speech, Glaspell's one-acts explore and expand the parameters of the form, exemplifying the idea of a theater in dialogue with evolving critical and social discourses. An important part of the context for Glaspell's theatrical career, then, is the history of the one-act play. This foundational narrative underlies the specific thematic and stylistic elements of each short work.

Glaspell's participation in the Little Theatre movement and her part in the development of the one-act form as an American dramaturgy reflected not only her ties to the critical establishment; her writing must also be seen as evolving within the dynamic theatrical environment in which her work was initially produced. Although subsequent narratives of early-twentieth-century American theater history slighted many dramatists, including Glaspell, in favor of O'Neill, more recent studies present a different perspective. Scholars such as Linda Ben-Zvi and Ann Larabee have demonstrated the strong links, both biographical and stylistic, between Glaspell and O'Neill, and Larabee also notes parallels to other writers such as Djuna Barnes.[7] Gerhard Bach has also shown the strong stylistic and thematic ties among the dramatic works produced by the Playwright's Theatre (the name O'Neill coined for the performance space on MacDougal Street in Greenwich Village used by the Provincetown Players that became synonymous with the group itself) in his analysis of the three phases of its production efforts from 1915 to 1922.[8] While a detailed comparison of Glaspell's plays with those of her Provincetown colleagues lies outside the scope of this study, it is important to acknowledge that such a comparison would enhance an understanding of all the writers concerned. The Provincetown presents an unusually strong example of artistic collaboration among its members, who worked together to design, direct, and

act in one another's plays as well as to evaluate scripts for possible production.[9] Such intimate living and working conditions make it unsurprising to
find close connections among the works the Players staged. The Provincetown
repertoire of one-acts notably exemplifies these associations.

Many of Glaspell's pieces helped define the evolving form of modern
American realism, along with those of her Provincetown colleagues John Reed,
Wilbur Daniel Steele, Pendleton King, Louise Bryant, Neith Boyce, and others.[10] These writers' dramas often depicted their immediate environment or
the communities in which they matured (e.g., Glaspell's midwestern settings).
Whether portraying the darker side of bohemian culture (King's *Cocaine*) or
gently spoofing their circle's morals and manners (Steele's *"Not Smart"*—a euphemism for pregnancy), these realist works strove to make their audiences
more aware of, thoughtful about, or amused by their culture. By embracing
stylistic and thematic innovation, these dramatists endeavored to wrest the
one-act from its maligned status to a place of aesthetic and political import in
the new American theater.

Although realism dominated at the Provincetown, the group welcomed
other forms and stylistic experiments, especially poetic drama and symbol-
ism/expressionism.[11] Alfred Kreymborg led this movement, which coincided
with his dedication to American poetry in his editorship of *Others,* a magazine
of verse. Kreymborg, Edna St. Vincent Millay, Cloyd Head, Floyd Dell, Wallace
Stevens, and Mary Caroline Davies, among others, created this kind of work for
the theater. Some of their pieces tended toward allegory, while others appeared
closer to folk plays. Glaspell's *The Outside* and many of O'Neill's sea plays reflect a blurring of forms; they use expressionist, symbolist, and poetic images
and language to create their distinctive theatrical atmosphere.

Significantly, both realist and poetic dramas at the Provincetown were
used to carry strong social and political messages. Millay's *Aria Da Capo*
(1919), a piece critical of World War I, stands out in this regard, as does Kreymborg's *Vote the New Moon* (1920), an indictment of certain forms of mass political behavior. Irwin Granich (later known as Mike Gold) and John Reed
created equally cogent realist pieces. While Glaspell's strongest political engagement emerges after she moved to full-length plays, it is clear from a reading of her colleagues' short pieces that her work fit well within this aspect of
the Provincetown agenda.

Glaspell's feminist concerns, already highly nuanced by the time she
wrote *Trifles,* also resonated with the work of her fellow dramatists. The
Provincetown produced the drama of a number of women who would become prominent American literary figures: Millay, Barnes, and Edna Ferber
among them. Scholars such as June Sochen, Judith Schwarz, Leslie Fishbein,
and Christine Stansell have analyzed the feminist climate in Greenwich Village
in this era. Most of these women writers knew one another and one another's

work; many belonged to the feminist organization Heterodoxy as well. Feminist concerns reflected in their dramaturgy included critiques of patriarchal culture, especially as it affected personal relationships, the social construction of gender, and inequalities in opportunities for women and men under patriarchy. Ferber's *The Eldest* (1920), for example, details the plight of first-born daughters, destined for spinsterhood and virtual enslavement within the family, a theme also depicted in Glaspell's later full-length work *Alison's House*. Rita Wellman's *Funiculi Funicula* (1917) chronicles a brief, tragic episode in the life of a woman torn among her roles as mother, artist, and lover, which resonates with Glaspell's portrait of Claire Archer in *The Verge*. In *An Irish Triangle* (1920) Barnes contrasts the lives of two women, one married and one unmarried, and uses these characters to analyze women's internalization of gender norms within their culture, paralleling the narrative arc in *Bernice.*

Glaspell's remarkable productivity and creativity during the period of her involvement with the Players may well be the result of her close connections with these other artists. They may have inspired, influenced, and assisted one another in all phases of the creative process. Glaspell's subsequent removal from this environment in 1922—she and Cook left New York for Greece, resulting in her loss of colleagues as well as a stage—seems to have had an equally strong, but opposite, impact: her dramatic productivity sharply declined, and she seems to have abandoned her sense of stylistic experimentation and thematic risk taking.

It appears that Glaspell was a writer more than usually sensitive to her environment. While all artists' work, of course, reflects their times and their culture, Glaspell actively made cultural exploration and commentary a part of her creative agenda. Identifying some of the contexts that informed her writing thus emerges as the starting point for appreciating her work for the American theater.

Suppressed Desires

In the winter of 1914–15 Susan Glaspell and her husband, George Cram ("Jig") Cook, had settled into life in bohemian Greenwich Village. They had moved to New York following their marriage in 1913, eager to join a community of like-minded individuals, many of whom, like themselves, had come back East from other, more conservative parts of the country.[1] The couple was surrounded by the rapidly shifting artistic, social, political, and cultural climate of their new home, and this milieu soon influenced their work. Among other innovative movements Freudian psychoanalysis was spreading across the United States at this time. The Greenwich Village community quickly adopted its concepts, refracted through the lectures of its adherents as well as through journalism.[2] Glaspell recalls the moment in her 1927 biography of her husband, *The Road to the Temple:*

> Those were the early years of psycho-analysis in the Village. You could not go out to buy a bun without hearing of someone's complex. We thought it would be amusing in a play, so we had a good time writing "Suppressed Desires." Before the grate in Milligan Place we tossed the lines back and forth at one another, and wondered if any one else would ever have as much fun with it as we were having. (192)

The one-act comedy, which most critics deem an inconsequential spoof on the psychoanalytic craze, synthesizes with notable economy the trends in the popularization of psychoanalysis early in the twentieth century. Set (lightly) against the background of World War I,[3] the comedy explores the cult of psychoanalysis through its primary object of study, human sexuality.

Suppressed Desires critically examines contemporary marriage and heterosexual relationships—some of the dominant interests of the Provincetown Players and their dramas to come—and reveals the tension between the lingering Victorian values of monogamous marriage and the emerging bohemian code of free love. Ann Larabee and Leslie Fishbein have admirably explored the nuances of gender roles and the struggles to create and define intimate relationships in this Village milieu, Larabee focusing specifically on Cook and Glaspell, while Fishbein looks more broadly at the community as a whole.[4] Numerous other plays produced by the group in its early years reflect a similar preoccupation with personal relations. Neith Boyce's *Constancy* (1915), Boyce and Hutchins Hapgood's *Enemies* (1916), and Eugene O'Neill's *Before Breakfast* (1916) are just a few examples of the Players' dramatizations of relational conflict. *Suppressed Desires* stands out from them, however, for its pinpointing of the psychoanalytic craze as the specific cause of its characters' problems. The play not only echoes the journalistic representation of the psychoanalytic movement but also epitomizes the remarkable synergy between the arts and the culture at large in Greenwich Village at this highly charged time.

Much of the literary criticism of Cook and Glaspell's farce has been lightly dismissive, based on a view of the play as amusing but not aesthetically substantive. This position is epitomized by the commentary of one of the most prominent contemporary Glaspell scholars, C. W. E. Bigsby:

> *Suppressed Desires* marked a somewhat curious beginning to this brave theatre. This first play of the Provincetown Players was an inconsequential comic satire in two scenes. . . . Seen in the context of the Players' later work, it is a very slight piece, distinguished only by its humour. (*Critical Introduction* 11)

Quite to the contrary, "seen in the context of the Players' later work," not to mention the Village and Provincetown bohemian contexts, the piece is extremely revealing and important and sets the tone for many of the group's subsequent theatrical interests. This chapter will describe those broader social contexts and their relationship to the play by documenting the evolution of psychoanalytic discourse of the era and by demonstrating its direct connections to both Cook and Glaspell's community and to their comic drama. While other scholars have previously identified the obvious links between the play and its cultural context, most notably Fred Matthews, here I will explore these ties in greater detail and also situate them in relation to Glaspell's and the Provincetown's subsequent work.

Cook and Glaspell first submitted their play to the Washington Square Players, which had formed in 1914 as an outgrowth of dramatic activity at the Liberal Club, a Village institution frequented by many in their circle. The Washington Square Players, one of the first important Little Theatres to emerge in New York City, initially included a number of individuals later affiliated with the Provincetown Players, including Ida Rauh, John Reed, and Robert Edmond Jones. According to Glaspell herself, however, the members who voted on productions "thought 'Suppressed Desires' 'too special'" for them to perform (*The Road to the Temple* 192). This verdict, quoted in virtually all scholarly commentary on the farce, is tantalizingly vague. Perhaps the Washington Square Players felt that the subject was too contemporary and "specialized," even for their enlightened Village audiences. According to their Provincetown colleague Edna Kenton, the piece was deemed "Too 'scientific', too 'psychologic'" by the other company (4). Yet their 1915–16 season reflects a range of theatrical styles and current topics, including eugenics, extramarital pregnancy, and gender identity amid which psychoanalysis hardly seems out of place.[5] Regardless of the rationale, the rejection was ultimately fortunate, for it contributed to Cook and Glaspell's idea of forming their own theater group to produce the kind of work they championed, rather than looking to place their scripts on others' stages.

In the summer of 1915, while vacationing in Provincetown on Cape Cod, the couple decided to produce the play within their own close circle of friends. Neith Boyce and her husband, Hutchins Hapgood, were staying in Provincetown as were John Reed, Mabel Dodge, and others. At the Hapgood home, at 621 Commercial Street, a group of friends gathered to see their "half improvised" entertainment.[6] Glaspell describes the event:

> Well, if no one else was going to put on our play, we would put it on ourselves. Neith Boyce had a play—"Constancy." We gave the two in her house one evening. Bobby Jones was there and helped us with the sets. He liked doing it, because we had no lighting equipment, but just put a candle here and a lamp there.
>
> A few minutes before it was time to give our play, Jig and I took a walk up the shore. We held each other's cold hands and said, "Never mind, it will be over soon."
>
> But when it was over we were sorry. People liked it, and we liked doing it. (*Road to the Temple* 193)

This now legendary evening, the first performance for the group that was to evolve into the Provincetown Players, has been chronicled by Robert Sarlós in his history of the company, *Jig Cook and the Provincetown Players*. According to Sarlós, "The first play was done on the balcony; for the second, the audience moved out onto the former 'stage' and looked into the living room—in an unconscious experiment with interchangeable performer-spectator space" (14–15). One might question whether the group was really as "unconscious" of their experimentation with audience and space as Sarlós suggests.

Given their record of theatrical innovation, one could just as easily speculate that the group was highly aware of the relationship between the plays and those who viewed them and sought to foreground this dynamic through the (fortuitous) staging limitations under which they performed. In contrast to the conclusion presented in the purely aesthetic criticism of C. W. E. Bigsby,

we can see that the interchangeable spaces exactly captured the relation of audience to production. These first two dramas established one of the central,
but unstated, production criteria for the Provincetown Players: a concern with
issues close to their lives and experience, whether personal, political, artistic,
or social. Thus, the seamlessness, or exchangeability, of the actor-audience
roles perfectly exemplifies the creative milieu for the group. They wrote and
produced their work by and for one another, first within their close circle and
later for an expanded community of like-minded individuals.

The response was so favorable that many others in the community
wanted to see the plays, and in August 1915 a second showing was arranged,
performed this time in a fish house on Lewis Wharf owned by Mary Heaton
Vorse and her husband, Joe O'Brien, which the group had roughly modified
as a theater to accommodate the larger audience. The success of these performances must have cleared the way for the comedy's reception in New York, for
it was performed at both the Liberal Club and at the studio of Ira Remsen in
March 1916 (Sarlós, *Jig Cook* 209–10 n. 39). *Suppressed Desires* proved such a favorite that it was repeated in the theater on Lewis Wharf the following summer; it formed part of the first New York season of the Provincetown Players
in November 1916 and was on the review bill in the spring of 1917 (Sarlós, *Jig
Cook* 169–70).

The Players initially followed a policy of refusing to grant free press seats
to theater critics, because they rejected the financial exchange the practice
implied. Edna Kenton recalled that their decision several years later to give
the critics free tickets and to seek more publicity for their work indeed
marked the first death throes of the Players (117). As a result of their initial
policy, there are comparatively few reviews of the early New York productions of their plays.[7] The first London productions of *Suppressed Desires*,
however, generated a body of journalistic response, all of which quite consistently found the piece witty and creative. The *Spectator* deemed it "exceed-
ingly funny . . . a thoroughly high-spirited farago [*sic*] of good humour and
absurdity" (Tarn. 495).[8] This sentiment was echoed in *Stage*, which pronounced it "merry and clever" ("Everyman" 16). The *Times*, moreover, felt it
was "brilliantly written" ("Everyman" 4).

Glaspell and Cook situate the play within the immediate physical world of
their community but also in a context of rich journalistic debate, popularization, and parody of psychoanalysis current at the time. *Suppressed Desires* opens
on a set that would become a mainstay of Provincetown Players' productions:
"A studio apartment in an upper story, Washington Square South" (233), a set
reflecting the prototypical home environment of many in their circle.[9] A large
table near a window holds architectural drawings at one end and heavy books
and journals such as the *Psychoanalytic Review* at the other.

At a smaller breakfast table Henrietta and Stephen Brewster argue about

Henrietta's craze for the New Psychology; Stephen balks at her insistence that he visit her psychoanalyst, Dr. A. E. Russell.[10] Cook and Glaspell immediately establish the contemporaneity of their comedy by peppering Henrietta's speech with the latest psychoanalytic jargon, including references to the "subconscious," to "complexes," and to the titular "suppressed desires" (233–35). Henrietta's sister Mabel soon enters, having arrived from Chicago for a visit the night before. *Suppressed Desires* revolves around Mabel and Stephen's attempts to cope with Henrietta's mania for the new "science," which soon threatens not only their ability to interact comfortably with one another but even Henrietta and Stephen's marriage itself.

Although the references appear to be no more than locally allusive, the names Henrietta and Mabel would have been extremely resonant for Village and Provincetown audiences. Henrietta Rodman, a high school teacher and Village resident, was an outspoken feminist and "the moving spirit of the Liberal Club" (Dell, *Homecoming* 247), while Mabel Dodge had already become a central figure through her salons, her patronage of the arts, and her notorious affair with John Reed. In fact, many cultural historians attribute the first discussion of psychoanalysis in Greenwich Village to Dodge's legendary evenings at 23 Fifth Avenue.

The reference to the *Psychoanalytic Review* would have been equally resonant. This new scientific journal had been championed only a few months before by Max Eastman, editor of the radical Village newspaper the *Masses:*

> All men and women interested in science—and particularly the sciences of human life . . . may congratulate themselves upon the appearance in this country of a new journal . . . We refer to the Psycho-Analytic Review. . . . If you wish to understand the daring ideas of Sigmund Freud and his disciples . . . you can do no better than buy this first number and begin. But it is not a "popular" magazine. ("New Journal" 9)

Suppressed Desires bristles with other allusions its first audiences would surely have recognized and enjoyed. More important, however, Glaspell and Cook used this first dramatic effort to show how the theater could engage with the latest ideas and events. The dramatists saw in their subject an opportunity to comment on not only psychoanalysis itself but also its connection with larger social issues confronting their own community. Moreover, *Suppressed Desires* exemplifies the way that Greenwich Village life became the source for its artistry, as its residents wrote, painted, composed, or danced their often thinly disguised experiences into the artifacts now revered from the era.

Some background on the advent of psychoanalysis in the United States will help to illuminate its depiction in the comedy. In the fall of 1909 Sigmund Freud arrived at Clark University in Worcester, Massachusetts, having been invited to deliver his *Five Lectures on Psychoanalysis* (Hale 3). According to Sanford Gifford, "For psychoanalysis, Freud's Clark lectures were the equivalent of the 1913 Armory Show for the history of modern painting in the United States" (128). Psychoanalytic historian Nathan Hale explains that in his talks

> Freud emphasized the practicality, the optimism, the comparative simplicity of psychoanalysis, and he included one of his few discussions of sublimation. . . . He condensed almost to the point of caricature the major theories he had worked out in his first great works, *The Interpretation of Dreams, Three Contributions to a Theory of Sex, The Psychopathology of Everyday Life,* and *Studies in Hysteria.* (4–5)

Hale's 1971 analysis of the Clark lectures neatly conveys both their impact and the form of their popularization in the ensuing few years—a history reflected by creative and journalistic writing of the era, including *Suppressed Desires.* Very much like the lay press's representations of the new science, the play reproduces the condensation, caricature, and ambiguity of the popularized American version of psychoanalysis. Information about Freudian psychoanalysis spread widely, but not always accurately, throughout America. Hale notes that within a year of the Clark conference scientific articles were appearing regularly, and such popular magazines as *McClure's* and *Cosmopolitan* published essays on Freudianism in 1912 and 1913, respectively (397–98). In 1913 the *New York Times* "announced 'new hope' from the 'remarkable studies of Sigmund Freud'" (qtd. in Hale 402). And in 1914 the *New Republic* printed Alfred Kuttner's explanation of the Freudian conscious and unconscious, read through Abraham Arden Brill's recent translation of *The Psychopathology of Everyday Life.*[11] Edna Kenton, a close friend of Glaspell and Cook put her spin on the craze in her unpublished history of the Provincetown Players:

> Freud and Jung and the minor psychoanalysts were just then being translated in great segments of their total works, and Washington Square and its many radiating little streets bloomed into a jungle of misunderstood theory and misapplied terms. (4)

Hale attributes the quick dissemination of Freudian concepts in America in part to "the connections between professional and popular culture," which he feels "were unusually intimate in the United States." Hale believes the "most important single reason for popularization was the growing interest of physicians" (398).

Perhaps an even more compelling case can be made for the interest of American literary intellectuals, who read Freud and other theorists and then wrote about the phenomenon in the popular press, spreading the idea of psychoanalysis (as well as of the troubled condition of the American psyche) to the public at large. Two figures important to Cook and Glaspell personally, as well as to the Greenwich Village community, Floyd Dell and Max Eastman, were among the better-known writers to publish on psychoanalysis; their interest in the movement coincides precisely with the period of composition and initial production of the play. In fact, *Suppressed Desires* directly echoes their writing as much as it reflects the general interest in the field within their community.

Dell clearly attributes the spread of psychoanalysis to intellectuals but also suggests why it may have captured the interest of the Village:

> Psycho-analysis is the greatest discovery made by intellectual conversationalists since Bergson and the I.W.W. Nothing quite so provocative of argument has happened since Nietzsche....
>
> There are many reasons for this, aside from the fact that it is new, and that the war has temporarily interfered with the supply of novel ideas from abroad.... It has perhaps the most charmingly recondite technical vocabulary ever invented. It enables people, through the medium of that terminology, to talk about morbid states of health without seeming to indulge a vulgar predilection.... And above all it veers, in its innocent, scientific way, perpetually round and about the subject of sex. ("Speaking of Psycho-analysis" 53)

Dell's sense that sex was central to popular interest in the New Psychology neatly dovetails with Glaspell and Cook's placement of sexual dreams and conflicts at the core of their drama's action. Its appeal to intellectuals may also account for the frankness about sexual desire found in other works produced by the Provincetown group.

Such frankness stirred many an "intellectual conversationalist." In his *Memoirs* Sherwood Anderson remarks on Dell's early discussion of Freud in Chicago (probably in 1912–13), when he was the editor of the *Friday Literary Review* and Cook served as his associate editor (Watson 20). Anderson reminisces:

> I felt then as I am sure most of the men of the time did feel that writing, the telling of tales, had got too far away from life as we men of the time were living and what was so wonderful to me, in the new associates I had found, was a certain boldness of speech.
>
> We were in fact wallowing in boldness. At the time Freud had just been discovered and all the young intellectuals were busy analyzing each other and everyone they met. Floyd Dell was hot at it. (338–39)[12]

Dell left Chicago in 1913 for Greenwich Village, where he became Max East-man's associate editor on the *Masses*. Eastman had undergone analysis in 1913–14 with Smith Ely Jelliffe (Gifford 138), another New York physician and colleague of A. A. Brill, who had become "a convinced Freudian" in 1910 (Jel-liffe, qtd. in Hale 385). Jelliffe was also Mabel Dodge's analyst. Brill had been invited to speak at one of Dodge's "Evenings," events regularly attended by the artists and intellectuals of the bohemian community (Watson 137). Brill re-called the soiree many years later:

> Another interesting group before whom I spoke during the winter of 1913 was at Mabel Dodge's salon. . . . There I met radicals, littérateurs, artists, and philosophers, some of whom have influenced the trends of our times in no small way. . . . My talk aroused a very interesting and lively discussion. ("Introduction" 322–23)

Brill's account of his visit to Dodge's home confirms the dynamism, but also hints at the hermeticism, of the community; his narrative suggests how a provocative topic such as Freudianism could be refracted through the lenses of Village politics, philosophy, criticism, and art.

Village fixture Bobby Edwards posited another source for Freud's entry into their lives: the Washington Square Book Shop, which would have stocked the latest periodicals and full-length studies (Hoffman 60). Near the end of the first scene of *Suppressed Desires*, in fact, Henrietta breezes out for "a com-mittee meeting at the bookshop," probably an allusion to this establishment (251). The shop adjoined another favorite local institution, the Liberal Club, for which Henrietta is preparing a lecture on psychoanalysis at the opening of scene 2.

Floyd Dell and Max Eastman published popular essays on psychoanaly-sis in 1915, Dell in *Vanity Fair* and Eastman in *Everybody's Magazine*. In East-man's series of articles, which appeared in the June and July issues and thus coincided with the premiere of *Suppressed Desires*, he traces the basic tenets of Freudian psychoanalysis as well as its impact on contemporary culture. East-man and Dell both explain that in the New Psychology mental disorders can be traced to the suppression of desires and that the uncovering of these hid-den wishes lies at the center of the recuperative process. In Eastman's words:

> The theory of it [psychoanalysis] is that countless numbers of diseases that we call nervous, or mental . . . *are caused by desires which dwell in our minds without our knowing they are there; and that if we can be made clearly aware of these desires, their morbid effects will disappear*. ("Explor-ing" 742)

He subtitles his last sections of the June piece "The Menace of Submerged Desires" and "How Dreams Help the Doctor" (748–49); in them Eastman lays out
the essential components of Freud's diagnostic and therapeutic process, including the identification of repressed wishes, often aided by the analysand's
narration of remembered dreams.

The play reflects with considerable precision the language and tone of
journalistic descriptions, particularly with regard to the central therapeutic
technique of dream analysis. Shortly after the play opens, Henrietta begins to
question Mabel on her dreams. Stephen warns her not to reveal them: "If you
do, she'll find out that you have an underground desire to kill your father and
marry your mother" (237). Stephen's malapropism *underground* for unconscious or subconscious suggests that he is less engaged with the craze than his
wife; moreover, Glaspell and Cook seem to be using Stephen to exemplify the
linguistic slippage that was also explored in psychoanalytic sessions. Stephen's
offhand remark similarly reveals Cook and Glaspell's acquaintance with the
"Oedipus complex," which Freud had elucidated in 1900 in *The Interpretation
of Dreams* and in 1905 in *Three Essays on the Theory of Sexuality* (Hoffman 17).

Despite the warning, Mabel recounts her strange dream of the previous
night:

> I was pushing along through a crowd as fast as I could, but being a hen I
> couldn't walk very fast—it was like having a tight skirt, you know; and
> there was some sort of creature in a blue cap—you know how mixed up
> dreams are—and it kept shouting after me, "Step, hen! Step, hen!" until I
> got all excited and just couldn't move at all. (237–38)

The sexual intimations here are remarkably strong, indicative of the relative
frankness the authors must have considered acceptable to their Provincetown
circle. The dream also points toward the dramatists' awareness of the specifically sexual character of repressed thoughts and images in Freudian theory.
The creature in the blue cap seems almost a parody of a phallic image. The
woman confined by her own symbol of sexual allure, a tight skirt, is both distressed and "excited" by her predicament, the symbol and situation fusing to
create the temporary immobility of climax. An early critic of the play, Joseph
Wood Krutch, called it "naughtily Freudian" (8). The three characters never
analyze these details very deeply, however, focusing instead on the strange lo-
cution, "Step, hen!" repeated in Mabel's dream. Glaspell and Cook thus establish an interesting performance dynamic in the play, one in which they position their audience in a potentially superior intellectual and interpretive
position to their characters, precisely because of the authors' sense of the former's understanding of the tenets of psychoanalysis.

Indeed, Henrietta soon asks Mabel if she "know[s] anything about psychoanalysis," to which Mabel replies, "It's something about the war, isn't it?" (238). This is the only overt reference to contemporary political events abroad, a passing allusion to a topic that would come to play a much more important role in Glaspell's later dramaturgy.[13] Like other subtle, if throwaway, moments in the play, however, it demonstrates both the timeliness of the writing and the playwrights' assumptions about their informed and perceptive audience. In the play, in fact, Mabel is figured as the outsider, the sweet but naive midwesterner who would not yet have access to the latest trends. The playwrights use her character as the rationale for any explication they felt the farce required. Mabel's dream about "Step, hen!" thus provides the narrative center for *Suppressed Desires*, and Henrietta's familiarity with all the latest writing on psychoanalysis serves as a through-line for the comedy.

Although Henrietta extols the benefits of psychoanalysis, Stephen interjects stories of the results of being, in the preferred bohemian phrase, "psyched": the breakup of their friends Helen and Joe Dwight and "the case of Art Holden's private secretary, Mary Snow, who has just been informed of her suppressed desire for her employer . . . [which] was on the point of landing . . . [her] in the insane asylum" (242–44). This anecdote bears striking resemblance to one of the examples of psychosis related by Eastman in his June 1915 article "Exploring the Soul and Healing the Body." Eastman describes the analysis of a young woman who "had become desirous of the love of her employer, but *refused to acknowledge* this even to herself; refused to *face* it, deeming it a shameful and impossible thing . . . [which] conspired . . . against her sanity and health" (742; my emph.). In the play Henrietta concurs: "Your mind protects you—avoids pain—by *refusing to think* the forbidden thing" (241; my emph.).[14] Like all good satire, Glaspell and Cook's spin on psychoanalysis accurately captures but also exaggerates its doctrines, creating a context that shows how ludicrous they can become if taken too seriously.

The plot develops this satiric point further even as it draws upon specific journalistic popularizations of Freudian theory. Mabel, increasingly distraught over the possibility of her own approaching insanity, begins to make classic "slips," substituting her own name for that of *Mary* Snow and dropping a Spode plate (246–47). These are precisely the kind of everyday psychopathological details catalogued by Eastman:

> Freud proves the existence of repressed desires in many ways besides curing nervous invalids. A thousand little *everyday* symptoms or "peculiarities" . . . reveal the pressure of these unconscious passions. Absentmindedness, laziness, forgetfulness, awkwardness, stuttering, biting one's nails, losing things, slips of the tongue, slips of the pen—all these and others are in many cases attributable to passionate wishes of which one is totally unconscious. . . . When you can not [*sic*] recall a name that you

"ought to remember," it is a sign . . . that this person *is associated in your mind with something you do not want to think of.* . . . Those who find this explanation of every-day slips and accidents difficult to accept will be still more astonished to know that Freud believes that there are frequently unconscious motives in such trivial things. ("Mr.—er—er" 98)

Mabel follows her sister's advice that she seek professional help for her condition; in the comedy's second scene, set two weeks later, we learn that Mabel has been seeing Dr. Russell and that his diagnosis is imminent. Henrietta believes that his examinations of Mabel will confirm her theory about Mabel's "Step, hen!" dream. Henrietta believes it was triggered by Mabel's desire for a friend of hers (but not her husband's), Lyman Eggleston. Henrietta, by word association, has found significance in the *hen* and *egg* portions of the names. Despite Stephen's suggestion that these terms "suggest rather a maternal feeling" (254), Henrietta extrapolates a complicated love relationship surrounding Mabel and her dentist husband, Bob. Henrietta maintains that Bob will simply have to accept Mabel's attraction for Lyman, given the extremes of Henrietta's views, which present no alternatives between "the insane asylum . . . [and] unconventionality" (265).

With this fanciful conclusion Glaspell and Cook provide an illustration of what Village curmudgeon Hutchins Hapgood recalls from the summer of 1914:

Psychoanalysis had been overdone to such an extent that nobody could say anything about a dream, no matter how colorless it was, without his friends' winking at one another and wondering how he could have been so indiscreet. Freud's scientific imagination certainly enriched the field of psychology and was a great moment in our knowledge of the unconscious. But every Tom, Dick, and Harry in those days was misinterpreting and misapplying the general ideas underlying analysis. It was a typical case of the natural exaggeration of a new set of thoughts, making them often ridiculous. (382–83)

The play find much of its comedy in such half-informed exaggeration.

Henrietta reiterates her wish for Stephen to see Dr. Russell; much to her surprise, Stephen reveals that he already has. Stephen, an architect, had been dreaming "that the walls of his room melted away and he found himself alone in a forest" (245–46). But Dr. Russell has interpreted this dream quite differently from Henrietta, who believes it "symbolizes his loss of grip in his work" (246). Dr. Russell has informed Stephen that the dream has a more sexual, relational explanation, that it "indicates a suppressed desire . . . to be freed from . . . marriage" (257). Henrietta, much distressed at this revelation, nevertheless accepts its validity, despite Stephen's rejoinder that Dr. Russell "must be wrong." She exclaims dramatically, "If you are going, I wish you would go tonight!" (259–60). One could hypothesize that, with the introduction of this "expert" reading, Cook and Glaspell might be suggesting the possibility of a problematic outcome for even professionals' forays in this new analytic arena, especially if the analysis causes the patient to take drastic action.

Mabel then returns, full of excitement at the result of her analysis. Again, contrary to Henrietta's hypotheses, Dr. Russell has formed a quite different opinion of the meaning of her dream, proving that "the living Libido [is] in conflict with petrified moral codes" (267). This is one of the playwrights' signal gestures toward the shifting conventions of the time. Cook and Glaspell use Russell's reading to foreground the new sexual consciousness of their era, with its attendant atmosphere of comparatively greater sexual openness. Having delved into the details of Mabel's childhood, Russell has discovered a reading pattern of phonetic syllabification. He thus concludes that "Step, hen!" in fact refers to her brother-in-law Stephen, whose last name, Brewster, is of further significance when read as "Be Rooster" (267). Russell has also established a connection between Mabel and her sister, "*Hen*-rietta," whose place she wants subconsciously to fill (266). In the words of another of the journalistic explicators, Edwin Tenney Brewster, "Every dream . . . in the Freudian formula, is the more or less disguised fulfilment of a suppressed wish" (716).[15]

Both Henrietta's amateur reading and Dr. Russell's professional interpretation of Mabel's dream appear to derive from the practice of word association, central to the new psychoanalytic technique. As Eastman describes it, the analyst says a word and the analysand responds with the first word she associates with the word provided ("Mr.—er—er" 100–2).[16] Throughout this dream analysis section Cook and Glaspell also echo the tone and rhetoric of Freud's *Interpretation of Dreams,* translated by Brill and published in New York in 1913. Freud's notions here of dreams "as a conglomeration of psychic images" that must be analyzed "piece by piece" (86–87), or word by word, as well as the concept of dreams as "wish-fulfillment" seem particularly relevant for the comedy (104).

Yet the revelation of Dr. Russell's interpretation and its significance for the characters—the "*Deus ex Clinica*" (Sievers 95)—prove too much for Henrietta. She immediately decides to abandon psychoanalysis to preserve the decencies of marriage and family life. Glaspell and Cook's coda for the play perfectly illustrates a key component of the therapeutic process, as detailed wittily by Dell:

> There is sex, for instance, which has been repressed as a matter of custom because there seemed to be nothing else to do with so much of it. Repressed, it may lead to neurasthenia, insanity, and what not; but let

loose—well, it does seem as if that would not quite do; at least not without a mighty overturning of institutions in which most of us are fairly comfortable!

Is there no alternative?

There *is*, as the psycho-analysts point out. There is the happy alternative of what they call "sublimation." ("Speaking of Psycho-analysis" 53)

The playwrights close their farce in analogous fashion, by punning on their title and its psychoanalytic significance:

Steve: My dear Henrietta, if you're going to separate from psychoanalysis, there's no reason why I should separate from *you*. (*They embrace ardently.* Mabel *lifts her head and looks at them woefully.*)
Mabel: (*Jumping up and going toward them*) But what about me? What am I to do with my suppressed desire?
Steve: (*With one arm still around* Henrietta, *gives* Mabel *a brotherly hug*) Mabel, you just keep right on suppressing it!

(271)

Their whimsical curtain line points to the sense of measure suggested by many of Glaspell's subsequent plays; in serious as well as comic works Glaspell carefully evaluates both traditional and contemporary cultural perspectives, and seeks to expose and question extreme or unexamined adherence to social trends.

Commenting on the significance of the play and its relationship to the New Psychology, historian Fred Matthews observes that the comedy is "of special historical value because of an unusually direct therapeutic element." Matthews, alluding to Bigsby, remarks:

> While it is difficult to disagree with a recent description of this play as "an inconsequential comic satire," the aesthetic judgment should not obscure its historic importance. Through its use of popularized Freudian mechanisms, and its pungent satire on their effortlessness and futility, the play offers evidence for the power of the psychoanalytic cult among intellectuals. . . . Cook and Glaspell were not ridiculing the New Psychology as such, but rather the pseudo-liberation of talk therapy and the dangers of liberation carried into narcissism. Indeed, its real originality may lie in its presentation of the easy use of pop Freud as a new kind of self-imprisonment, a voluntary entrapment of intellectuals in conceptual cages of their own construction, which could be as confining as the Victorian conventions. (150–51)

In other words, the importance of a piece like *Suppressed Desires* cannot be measured by aesthetic criteria alone; in fact, to do so would result in a critical misprision that ignores the work's broader historical and cultural significance. Moreover, Matthews's conclusion is not unique to this Glaspell-Cook collaboration. His sense of how to position an analysis of the one-act play within its social milieu echoes the strategy of this study with regard to all of Glaspell's dramaturgy.

The microcosm of the Provincetown circle mirrored the larger bohemian community particularly closely in its efforts to find workable solutions to the complexities of modern relationships. In *Suppressed Desires* Henrietta is a conventional woman at heart, despite her outward drive to be modern. As Sanford Gifford has noted, "The motive to unmask hypocrisy is prominent" in the play (123). Many subtle clues underscore the conventionality of the play's world, not the least of which is its construction of gender roles. It may be significant that the two characters most engaged with the practice of "psyching" in the play are female. Drawing on the rhetoric of hysteria, but not explicitly referring to it, Peter Macfarlane wrote in *Good Housekeeping* magazine in 1915:

> Here is hope for every woman . . . who because of the pressure of unconscious forces is living less than a full, free life. . . . Women, who are perhaps the chief sufferers, are here for the first time offered a readable analysis of the new science. Yes, actually! And of faults of character as well as of disease. (125)

Macfarlane charts the new therapy with regard to its significance for modern marriage, for sexuality, and for the sanctity of home life. While the sexist tone of his essay is unmistakable to readers today, it represents the thrust of "serious" journalism targeted at American women of the time, displaying none of the tongue-in-cheek skepticism or whimsy found in the writing on the topic by Villagers Floyd Dell or Max Eastman. Although many radical Village women earned their own living as writers or artists, neither Henrietta nor Mabel works professionally, despite Henrietta's writing and research connected with psychoanalysis. Stephen is an architect, Bob a dentist, Lyman Eggleston a writer, and Dr. A. E. Russell, whose initials seem to suggest a parallel to Dr. A. A. Brill, is a physician—all professional men.

Given the clear sexual division in the play, Arnold Goldman's 1978 essay "The Culture of the Provincetown Players" merits close examination for his analysis of gender in a number of plays and events from 1915 to 1923. Goldman feels that *Suppressed Desires* seems "conservative" in its mocking of Henrietta's "obsession with Freudian psychology." He believes that "the wife's attraction to

Freud . . . is merely a front for her feminist ideology" and wonders if Stephen's undermining her interests "is the subject of the play or simply a lesson that there are lengths to which intellectual wives should not go." He concludes:

> It is not that the play synthesizes the interests and even fears of the Provincetown group, but it touches on them, and even the feminist might just rejoice in the exposure of the pretender to feminism. (298)

Although Goldman has effectively isolated the nature of the conflict in the drama, his analytical strategies strike me as problematic at best. The text simply does not substantiate his identification of Henrietta as a "feminist." We can only guess at his definition of *feminism;* perhaps he equates it solely with a woman's intellectual independence and a willingness to explore sexual freedom. But, rather than "rejoice in the exposure of the pretender to feminism," we might more profitably explore why and how a character with Henrietta's intellectual curiosity, in that particular setting, might be manipulated by Cook and Glaspell.

Henrietta appears as the first in a series of Glaspell's female characters who embody extremes. As such, she is the forerunner of Claire Archer (*The Verge*), Nora Powers (*Chains of Dew*), and Mrs. Patrick and Allie Mayo (*The Outside*), all of whom must learn to temper their zeal or, like Claire, suffer equally strong consequences. This characterological trope in Glaspell should be interpreted as neither antifeminist nor anti-intellectual; rather, Glaspell (here with Cook) sets up extremism as behavior that invites examination and concern. Through the portrayal of these characters and their obsessions, Glaspell demonstrates the need for a balanced perspective in both comic (*Suppressed Desires, Chains of Dew*) and serious (*The Verge, The Outside*) contexts.

In *Suppressed Desires* Freudianism becomes the extreme through which commitments to marriage and fidelity are explored. These same questions simultaneously arise in Glaspell's 1915 novel, *Fidelity,* and recur as late as 1930, in her Pulitzer Prize–winning drama, *Alison's House,* both of which explore the dynamics of relationships threatened by extramarital love. Goldman seems to suggest that feminism—genuine or ersatz—is the real issue: that Stephen's antagonism to Henrietta's compulsion with psychology is a front for his feeling threatened by her feminism, which is equated with her intellectual curiosity and its potential to disrupt their marriage. This interpretation seems to read meaning into the drama, rather than account for the characters and events as written.

A more persuasive analysis of the significance of the New Psychology for the bohemian community comes from Leslie Fishbein, who has established the relation among Freud, gender, and sexuality for the Village radicals at this time: "Longing for sexual liberation, they embraced Freudian psychology in the mis-

taken belief that it condoned sexual experimentation. . . . [In fact,] Freudianism merely reinforced Victorian stereotypes of womanhood" (277). *Suppressed
Desires* strongly conveys the tension between the lingering Victorian conventions of domestic fidelity and the new creed of unconventionality, particularly
with regard to the open marriages and sexual freedom many Village residents
professed. This theme, shared by *Constancy* and *Enemies,* as well as many of the
memoirs of individuals connected with the bohemian culture at this time,[17]
emerges as a major concern for these artists and intellectuals.

Fishbein suggests an alternative cultural reading appropriate to the
specifics of Glaspell and Cook's comedy. Radicals' embrace of the New Psychology exemplified their need for an ideology that would help them resolve
the conflict between the Victorian and the modern, specifically their resistance to the strictures of marriage and monogamy. Within this context one
can understand Stephen's negative response to, Mabel's naive conversion to,
and Henrietta's untested fervor for a science that, at least in its popularized
form, promised resolutions to deep-seated psychic and interpersonal conflicts. The same issues confronted the Villagers in their own relationships. As
memoirs from the era repeatedly attest, couples flailed about, trying to find
workable solutions for their personal dilemmas. Some chose open, or companionate, marriage; others preferred serial monogamy with no legal ties; another option was free love. Under the guise of openness many couples acted
upon their extramarital attractions; as the plays and personal writings reveal,
however, these choices often led to jealousy and recrimination, as one member of a couple, more often than not the female, only professed openness to
appease the other.[18]

Interestingly, *Suppressed Desires* presents no real struggles of this kind.
We know that Stephen does not really want to leave Henrietta, and Mabel's enthusiasm about her analysis does not disguise our awareness that any real sexual intrigue is notably absent. Mabel, the only character for whom there is a
physical description, is depicted as "plump" (235); this detail may have been
included to manipulate the reader/audience's perspective on the psychoanalytic analyses that emerge by the play's conclusion. If Mabel's size is taken as
detracting from her sexual appeal (however misguided the stereotype)—and
there is no other apparent reason for its inclusion—then we have an early sign
of the implausibility of a relationship between her and Stephen. Thus, the
comedy does not veer too close to the more painful realities of the bohemians'
lives, although other pieces produced by the Provincetown Players, such as
Constancy and *Enemies,* do, albeit comically.[19] We might read this avoidance
on Cook and Glaspell's part as a refusal to confront issues in their own relationship that other artists felt willing to take on.

What emerges as the most intriguing element of *Suppressed Desires,*
however, is the enigmatic figure of Dr. Russell, the first in a series of "absent

centers" in Glaspell's dramaturgy. Minnie Wright (*Trifles*), Bernice (*Bernice*), and Alison (*Alison's House*) are the characters most often discussed in this group; however, Fred Jordan (*Inheritors*) and John Wright (*Trifles*) are also significant, unseen figures. Although we never meet Dr. Russell, he is clearly the pivotal force in the drama, controlling the actions and responses of the other characters. When Henrietta realizes that psychology, in the person of Dr. Russell, has betrayed her, her chagrin is clear:

Henrietta: Stephen, are you telling me that Dr. Russell—Dr. A. E. Russell—
    told you this? (Steve *nods*). . . . Did he know who you were?
Steve: Yes.
Henrietta: That you were married to me?
Steve: Yes, he knew that.
Henrietta: And he told you to leave me?
Steve: It seems he must be wrong, Henrietta.
Henrietta: (*Rising*) And I've sent him more patients!

                                                          (258–59)

Thus, the New Psychology, represented by the appropriately unseen Dr. Russell, causes more problems than it solves, perhaps as does this new science's revelations of the unconscious and, by extension, its concomitant push to be modern.[20] The fact that a female character felt the greatest pressure to embrace these new concepts should not surprise us either.

    In the transition from the Victorian to the modern, women had to overcome their images of purity and sexlessness in order to achieve any degree of sexual equality, yet Freudianism actually did little to aid women's emancipation. *Suppressed Desires* seems to embody these ironies and resolves the conflict with a rejection of free love, which turned out to be a prescient solution, given the choice for monogamy made by some Villagers (although apparently not Cook) later in the era.[21] Although this conclusion could be viewed as "conservative," as Goldman observes, it is dramaturgically fitting, as classical comedy renews the heterosexual union, often through marriage. Reassuring rather than threatening for its audience, *Suppressed Desires* resolved, albeit superficially, one of the dilemmas shared by the Provincetown group and allowed them the therapeutic outlet of laughter at their own sexual and emotional machinations.

Trifles

After the success of their first dramatic efforts, several members of the Provincetown group, with Cook in the lead, were eager to stage more plays when they returned to Cape Cod in the summer of 1916. Cook saw them as "a whole community working together, developing unsuspected talents" (Glaspell, *Road* 251). This enterprise exactly captured the spirit of the burgeoning community theater movement that was spreading across the country. Having renovated the Wharf Theatre early that season, the transplanted Greenwich Village bohemians were ready to put on their first bill in mid-July: a revival of *Suppressed Desires* and two new plays, Neith Boyce's *Winter's Night* and John Reed's *Freedom* (Sarlós 20–21). A second bill followed in late July, which included their first Eugene O'Neill production, *Bound East for Cardiff,* Louise Bryant's *The Game,* and Wilbur Daniel Steele's "*Not Smart*" (22–25).[1] Cook then publicly announced that a third bill, in early August, would include a new play by Glaspell.

Glaspell's published account of the genesis of this new work, *Trifles,* has been widely quoted from *The Road to the Temple:*

> "Now Susan," [Jig] said to me, briskly, "I have announced a play of yours for the next bill."
> "But I have no play!"
> "Then you will have to sit down to-morrow and begin one."
> I protested. I did not know how to write a play. I had never "studied it."
> "Nonsense," said Jig. "You've got a stage, haven't you? . . . What playwrights need is a stage . . . their own stage." (196–97)

This dialogue, smacking as it does of condensed theatricality, conveys a strange aura of the backstage world of amateur theater later romanticized in Hollywood, mixed with a version of Virginia Woolf's *A Room of One's Own* designed for a woman playwright. Yet Glaspell wrote another, testier account of these events later in her life, around the time of the publication of her last novel, *Judd Rankin's Daughter* (1945):

> I began writing plays because my husband . . . forced me to. "I have an-
> nounced a play of yours for the next bill," he told me, soon after we
> started The Provincetown Players. I didn't want my marriage to break up
> so I wrote *Trifles*.[2] (Glaspell Papers, Berg Collection)

Taken together, these two narratives suggest that Glaspell's playwriting career
was not originally her idea, regardless of her ultimate success as a dramatist.[3]
It is impossible for us to know what she really intended to convey with the later
remarks; she may have been bristling at the memory of Cook's interventions
in her creative process, or she may have still felt the need to mask her own am-
bitions by placing the impetus for the work on him.[4] Her calculated use of the
verb *forced*, however, suggests resistance to her husband, despite her acquiescence. Glaspell's competing accounts of the genesis of *Trifles*, one for public
consumption, the other contained in her private, unpublished drafts, resonate
with the tensions embodied in the work itself. With techniques foundational
to feminist writing, she inscribes into the play's subject, form, and composition the paradox of "resistant compliance" that she herself experienced in its
creation.

At the time she was drafting *Trifles*, Glaspell still thought of herself primarily as a fiction writer, with three novels and numerous short stories to her
credit.[5] When "forced" to come up with a play, Glaspell used an idea she "had
meant to do . . . as a short story" (*Road* 197), whose plot derived from a murder trial she had covered as a young reporter for the *Des Moines Daily News* in
1900–1901. Linda Ben-Zvi has thoroughly researched the origins of *Trifles*. She
uncovered the background story, "the murder of a sixty-year-old farmer
named John Hossack on December 2, 1900, in Indianola, Iowa" that served as
Glaspell's inspiration ("Murder" 21). According to Ben-Zvi, Glaspell "filed
twenty-six stories on the Hossack case" with the paper (23). She summarizes
Glaspell's coverage of the wife Margaret Hossack's arrest, imprisonment, and
trial as a mix of "fact, rumor, and commentary, with a superfluity of rousing
language and imagery" (24).

Glaspell reworked her evocative columns to produce a theatrical murder
mystery. Taking the basic outlines of the Hossack case, she crafted the story of
Minnie Wright, arrested on suspicion of the murder of her husband, John.
Trifles dramatizes the actions of five characters—three men and two
women—who are attempting to uncover the background to the killing. While
the men explore primarily offstage sites for evidence, the women remain onstage and uncover a number of details that not only may be evidence of a motive for murder but that also link Minnie's life to theirs and profoundly alter
their perspectives on the suspect and the crime. *Trifles* and its short story
counterpart, "A Jury of Her Peers," have since their creation prompted a considerable volume of criticism. Surprisingly, however, these responses have

largely neglected a crucial literary-historical context for the works: detection. The complex, overdetermined political implications of Glaspell's choice to employ this (then) emergent subgenre may be sought in the remarkable analogies between her method of composition and the process of detection she employs within her narrative.

Glaspell wrote *Trifles* very quickly. After just ten days it was put into rehearsal and was ready for production by 8 August 1916. Both Glaspell and her husband appeared in the first performance, in the roles of Mr. and Mrs. Hale, the neighboring farm couple. Glaspell's often-quoted description of her composition process reveals how she was still grappling with a new form of writing that forced her to think about the interplay of acting and staging with a dialogic text. She clearly struggled with the fundamentals of writing for the stage. She had to create language and stage directions that actors could perform and that would convey her meaning without her complete narrative control. Her description of the scripting resonates deeply with both the collaborative process of community theater she was coming to know and of the mode of detection she was developing:

> So I went out on the wharf, sat alone on one of our wooden benches without a back, and looked a long time at that bare little stage. After a time the stage became a kitchen—a kitchen there all by itself. I saw just where the stove was, the table, and the steps going upstairs. Then the door at the back opened, and people all bundled up came in—two or three men, I wasn't sure which, but sure enough about the two women, who hung back, reluctant to enter that kitchen. . . . I hurried in from the wharf to write down what I had seen. Whenever I got stuck, I would run across the street to the old wharf, sit in that leaning little theatre under which the sea sounded, until the play was ready to continue. Sometimes things written in my room would not form on the stage, and I must go home and cross them out. (*Road* 255–56)

This remarkable passage provocatively suggests that dramaturgy for Glaspell was only possible as a form of spectatorship—that only when Glaspell placed herself in the spectatorial position could she effectively become a writer of dramatic texts.

While authors' statements about their process abound, the example of Luigi Pirandello's famous preface to his play *Six Characters in Search of an Author* (1925) may throw into relief the distinctions of Glaspell's technique and its theoretical implications for her playwriting. In Pirandello's essay he uses the trope of parturition, identified early by feminist critics as the patriarchal appropriation of female creativity, to describe his artistry: "What author will be able to say how and why a character was born in his fantasy? The mystery of artistic creation is the same as that of birth" (364). Pirandello talks of the characters that emerge from his fantasy in virtually demonic terms, as they materialize before him in the privacy of his study, "tempting" him and persuading him to do their bidding (365).

Glaspell's description of her process overlaps with Pirandello's in terms of the autonomy she grants her characters, but their actions and the stage world they occupy appear more independent of her creative agency. Moreover, they provoke none of the thinly veiled misogyny of Pirandello's depiction. Glaspell avoids the conventionalized birthing trope, replete with its subtext of battle for dominance over the artistic product. Rather, she emerges as a self-aware and critical conduit for character, action, and narrative. Her distance from her stage figures opens a space for resistance and critique more familiar to the discourses of reception theory than to statements about artistic production.

Feminist theater criticism in particular has privileged the spectatorial position as a site of feminist agency. Reworking Jill Dolan's idea of the "feminist spectator as critic," we might ponder the feminist potential emerging from the notion of Glaspell the spectator as playwright. Dolan compares her feminist critic to a "'resistant reader,' who analyzes a performance's meaning by reading against the grain of stereotypes and resisting the manipulation of both the performance text and the cultural text that it helps to shape." Dolan continues: "By exposing the ways in which dominant ideology is naturalized by the performance's address to the ideal spectator, feminist performance criticism works as political intervention in an effort toward cultural change" (2).

Applying these concepts dramaturgically, we might posit that Glaspell is presciently aware of both the theatrical traditions that such feminist critics would later oppose and her own role as a dramatist in resisting them. Moreover, we should consider the idea that Glaspell's connection of spectatorship with her creative process makes her acutely conscious of both the audience and the concept that the spectator is the force somehow allowing or driving action, the unfolding of character, the revelation of meaning. When Glaspell remarks, "sometimes things written in my room would not form on the stage, and I must go home and cross them out," she is suggesting that writing without spectating may not work theatrically. She implies that seeing things onstage first facilitates the creation—as well as the criticism—of that which is to be scripted. She must then transcribe what she sees so that it can be seen again as she has seen it; she writes her play in order to allow her audience to experience as closely as possible her perception of what she has witnessed (for example, the "reluctant" women). Glaspell's analysis of spectatorship and dramaturgy must have been so compelling that it not only guides her playwriting, but it also becomes a major theme of the play. Observing and interpreting are, indeed, the main activities of the two women. The men are off seeking evidence to confirm their assumptions; they are writing a script for a different play than the one the women, Glaspell, and her audience see. Glaspell seems to have intuited that her creative process was akin to detection, and this may have suggested to her the overarching form that shaped the scripting of what she saw onstage. The ingenious leap that she made was to connect her realizations about watching and writing with ideas about gender and the process of investigation. The empathic responses of the two women replace the traditional male assumption of detached, panoptical knowledge, just as Glaspell came to understand that she could not impose behavior on her characters or totally control their narrative; in order to represent them, she had to work collaboratively, observing, analyzing, and letting them perform for her. Feminist collaboration with a narrative thus succeeds where the attempt toward patriarchal mastery of it fails.

Widely regarded as the most tightly structured and thematically compelling of Glaspell's dramas, *Trifles* has been repeatedly anthologized and produced, standing as an exemplar of the one-act play form in numerous studies of the genre.[6] Early reviews of the play glimpsed the radical possibilities liberated by Glaspell's method. Heywood Broun, who would soon become a strong supporter of the Provincetown Players, first developed his positive opinion of Glaspell's writing when he saw the November 1916 production of *Trifles* by the Washington Square Players. In his theater column for the *New York Tribune* Broun grasped both the stylistic advances and the thematic significance of the work. Commenting on her "indirect" method and her use of offstage characters and late point of attack, he remarks:

> No direct statements are made for the benefit of the audience. Like the women, they must piece out the story by inference. . . . The story is brought to mind vividly enough to induce the audience to share the sympathy of the women for the wife and agree with them that the trifles which tell the story should not be revealed. ("Best Bill" 7)

Broun's review synthesizes Glaspell's interweaving of gender roles and the detection process. He grasps the empathic process central to the women's growing understanding of Minnie and her presumed actions. Arthur Hornblow, the critic for *Theatre Magazine*, praised the production more succinctly as "an ingenious study in feminine ability at inductive and deductive analysis by which two women through trifles bring out the motive for a murder ("Mr. Hornblow" 21). These reviews point to the levels on which the play works: as an engrossing murder mystery and as a more personal study that allows audiences to discover, along with the characters, the harshness of contemporary rural life as well as to see important contrasts of gender roles and gendered behavior. The journalists also understand two distinctive elements of Glaspell's dramaturgy. Her vivid use of offstage characters in *Trifles* will become a hall-mark of her playwriting, recurring in *Bernice, Inheritors,* and *Alison's House,* among others. Mysteries and the process of deduction also recur throughout her plays, making *Trifles* both a representative work and one that adumbrates the themes and methods of many of her subsequent dramas. Moreover, with *Trifles* she develops her technique of conscious manipulation of audiences' perspectives, so that they can see as she has done, which then allows her fem-inist and other progressive political views to come to the fore.

Subsequently, however, adverse theoretical judgments about the political relationship between gender and detection, spectatorship, and mimetic repre-sentation in the theater have arisen that complicate a feminist analysis and re-ception of *Trifles.* Moreover, the critically contested terrain surrounding real-ism, murder mysteries, and feminist writing suggests a formal analysis of *Trifles* and "Jury" is in order precisely because they are Glaspell's best-known works, the discussion of which usually invokes one or more elements of these triangles. Glaspell's resistant compliance to the project that became *Trifles* fa-cilitated her creation of a text that reflects the way women subvert dominant forms and authority, working within yet against such strictures.

Ironically, some of the broader critical regard for the play derives from the fact that Glaspell soon followed her original intent and published the work in short story form within a year. "A Jury of Her Peers" appeared in *Every Week* on 5 March 1917 and was republished in the *Best Short Stories of 1917.* Indeed, one of the keys to the popular success of *Trifles* and "A Jury of Her Peers" may well have been her choice to rewrite the plot as prose. Both before and after her most active period of playwriting, Glaspell was known primarily for sto-ries aimed at women readers, particularly within the "local color" subgenre of works detailing a specific, domestic milieu. "A Jury of Her Peers" originally had a significantly larger audience than the drama, which was not widely available until Glaspell published her collected drama to date, *Plays,* in 1920.[7]

The critical analysis of this one Glaspell product (in two genres) out-weighs commentary on any other of her works. Much of this response can be attributed to the rediscovery of "A Jury of Her Peers" in the early 1970s by fem-inist critics such as Annette Kolodny and Judith Fetterley, committed to a re-examination of forgotten or undervalued women writers. Mary Anne Fergu-son's inclusion of the story in her influential collection *Images of Women in Literature* (1973) was central to this reemergence of Glaspell. Ironically, how-ever, a full appreciation of *Trifles* has also been slightly hampered by the prominence and influence of "Jury" in feminist reader-response criticism. The subsequent appearance of *Trifles* in Sandra Gilbert and Susan Gubar's *Norton Anthology of Literature by Women* (1985) helped redress the balance of Glaspell studies to promote consideration of the dramatic version of the story, but its republication did not dispel the feminist critical skepticism of realist drama.

That *Trifles* is still central to this critical debate will become evident later in this chapter.

Still, the outpouring of critical writing on the short story and one-act attests to the power and creativity of these pieces. Responses to "Jury" in particular exemplify the trajectory of Anglo-American feminist criticism from the 1970s forward. When examined as a body, these commentaries emerge as an evolving dialogue among theorists of gender, fiction, and performance. Yet, despite the panoply of analytic approaches to these works, their failure to scrutinize Glaspell's form and its relationship to her theme, characterization, symbolism, and plot stands out. This chapter, then, aspires to insert a detailed formal consideration of detection into this critical conversation on Glaspell, precisely because in the intersection of considerations of form, content, and performance lies the potential for *Trifles* to emerge as a feminist drama.

While it is not possible to do full justice to the insightful and provocative criticism of the two works here,[8] the responses of Annette Kolodny and Judith Fetterley merit close attention for their points of intersection with the nexus of feminist spectatorship and dramaturgy. In their influential essays on "Jury" Kolodny and Fetterley draw on the methodology of feminist reader-response criticism to analyze how other women readers interpret such texts. Speaking both of Glaspell's story and of Charlotte Perkins Gilman's "The Yellow Wallpaper" (1892), Kolodny explains that even though neither work

> necessarily excludes the male as reader—indeed, both in a way are directed specifically at educating him to become a better reader—they do nonetheless insist that, however inadvertently, he is a *different kind* of reader and that, where women are concerned, he is often an inadequate reader. (57)

In intuiting this difference, Glaspell's spectatorial dramaturgy seeks not only to make these distinctions concretely visible but also to demonstrate the alternative collaborative, empathic reading processes employed by the women. Kolodny and Fetterley's compelling explications of Glaspell's text are particularly relevant to the formal analysis of detection in this chapter. The initial success and ongoing fascination of *Trifles* and "Jury" derive precisely from the relationship between the way Glaspell writes these texts and the pedagogic strategy Kolodny identifies. Why Glaspell might have chosen the detection genre for this work thus remains *the* surprisingly underexamined element of these pieces that have otherwise prompted such intense scholarly interest.

The burgeoning popularity of the murder mystery throughout the twentieth century makes it easy to forget that the genre was still comparatively new when Glaspell selected it in 1916. Mystery writing did not attain its "greatest heights of production and consumption" until the 1920s and 1930s, the "Golden Age" of detective fiction (Grella 84). One might ask, then, why Glaspell opted for this still-evolving form to depict her version of the story she had covered journalistically. Separating out fundamental components of the form reveals how its structure enabled Glaspell to develop her themes of justice, female bonding, and gender ideology in early-twentieth-century America.

The mystery subgenre consorts intimately with Glaspell's spectatorial conception of her dramaturgy. Indeed, detective fiction relies centrally upon active audience involvement in the investigative process. The reader/viewer engages with the text or production through her interest in solving the same mystery as that confronting the sleuth(s) created by the author. The renowned literary critic Jacques Barzun captures the essence of the form's appeal:

> It is not enough that one of the characters in the story should be called a detective—nor is it necessary. What is required is that the main interest of the story should consist in finding out, from circumstances largely physical, the true order and meaning of events that have been part disclosed and part concealed. (144)

Understanding this process of engagement, Glaspell created two deceptively simple amateur investigators through whom the audience is directed to see the evidence and reach conclusions.

Trifles depicts the aftermath of the death of John Wright, a midwestern farmer known for his hard, parsimonious demeanor. All the action takes place in the kitchen of the Wright home, following the arrest of Minnie Wright on suspicion of her husband's murder. Two officials, Sheriff Peters and the county attorney, question Lewis Hale, the Wrights' neighbor who has discovered John's corpse upstairs while Minnie rocked in a kitchen chair. As the men search elsewhere around the house and grounds for clues to the killing, Peters's wife and Hale's wife remain behind to collect some items that Minnie had requested be brought to her in jail. Working in the kitchen, these women piece together the story of Minnie, just as Minnie was "piecing" the quilt that becomes an all-important clue for them. They recreate the history of a pretty young woman with a lovely voice, shut up in an isolated farmhouse with a husband who forbids her to sing or communicate by telephone. The discovery of a broken birdcage ultimately allows them to construct a narrative about the canary whose neck John may have wrung; the bird is taken by the women as a symbol of Minnie's virtual incarceration in a life of privation and hardship. Such insights profoundly affect the women's view of Minnie's alleged action, and they decide to keep the most damning evidence they have found—the dead bird wrapped in quilt pieces—to themselves, enacting their own judgment. The "trifles" they uncover and discuss, over-looked by the men, become the keys to our understanding the characters and the world of the play.

Glaspell recognized the potential of detection radically to transform audience perceptions of women's identities and their working lives. Glaspell guides her audience to see John and Minnie Wright as do Mrs. Hale and Mrs. Peters. But she also directs her viewers toward another level of perception: seeing the two women onstage as she herself does as author, which in turn may make us question the story they construct of the absent couple. She pushes the audience toward feminist spectatorship by using the detective form in the service of her broader political goals; she accomplishes this more succinctly and effectively through detection than she could have done with any other available structure.

In "The Women's World of Glaspell's *Trifles*" Karen F. Stein makes one of the first gestures toward a consideration of the drama within the subgenre of detection. This essay is contained in the theatrical reference work *Women in American Theatre,* which was as influential in its field as Ferguson's was to literary studies. Stein calls the play "an anomaly in the murder mystery genre, which is predominantly a masculine tour de force" (251). Stein's conclusions are perplexing; neither is the work anomalous within its genre, nor has mystery writing historically been a male-dominated field, although Stein's common assumption may help account for the neglect of a formal analysis amid the other kinds of readings of the play and story. In fact, in an essay on the origins of detective novels in America B. J. Rahn identifies two women, Anna Katharine Green (*The Leavenworth Case* [1878]) and Seeley Regester (*The Dead Letter* [1867]),[9] as the authors of the first full-length works in the category (49). Rosalind Coward and Linda Semple point to these and to two works by British writers, Mrs. Henry Wood's *East Lynne* (1861) and Mary Braddon's wildly popular *Lady Audley's Secret* (1862) as some of the earliest women's detection literature (42). Critics do, of course, unanimously trace the development of detective stories to Edgar Allan Poe, whose "The Murders in the Rue Morgue" (1841), "The Mystery of Marie Roget" (1842), and "The Purloined Letter" (1845) initially defined the mystery subgenre. Still, women's subsequent prominence in the field, as writers of both stories and novels, remains unique. The subgenre of detective fiction is "read equally and heavily by both men and women and [is] perhaps the only one in which women have excelled as writers of a form *read regularly by men*" (Bargainnier 2).[10] Earl F. Bargainnier, in the introduction to *Ten Women of Mystery,* expands upon this phenomenon:

> For centuries there have been women writers of all sorts whose writings have been almost totally read by other women, but mystery writing is a unique area of popular fiction in the widespread success of women

writers, the widespread use of women as important characters and the widespread occurrence of *male* readers. (2)

Marilyn Stasio, in her analysis of the subgenres of detective fiction, identifies several that are dominated by women writers. The "Village Mystery" form is particularly relevant for Glaspell, as her midwestern farm community setting establishes *Trifles*/"Jury" within this category. Central to the "Village Mystery" is its placement "in a self-contained society whose way of life is threatened by . . . a major disruption of the social order" (70). Glaspell's orchestration of events exemplifies the fixed order of life within the farm environment and portrays social issues encountered in such communities. In both versions she emphasizes the routines of rural women's existence and the domestic activities and problems they all share, although her characters do not initially realize how much they have in common. Such yearly rituals as canning, as well as group participation in the church choir or the Ladies Aid Society, come to define their lives; Mrs. Hale and Mrs. Peters further realize in the course of the play that partaking in these activities is expected for women in their community. Thus, Minnie's enforced inability to join in them stands out in its fuller implications of sexual politics. While Stasio singles out the forms of mystery writing dominated by women writers, she does not essentialize the creative process by claiming to extract from them a recognizably "feminine" writing style. But neither does she push her analysis toward a political reading of this female authorship or a sense that these women writers had revisionist or other feminist goals for their works, as Glaspell clearly did.

Maureen Reddy goes further by citing notable differences between male and female writers of the genre. In "the most interesting mysteries" by women, for Reddy, the solution to the crime often "lies in character, with its revelation depending upon the investigation of personality and on the conjunction of the personal and the social" (5), in contrast to the straightforward discovery of physical clues or the recreation of a series of events common to many mystery narratives. Following such feminist theorists as Carol Gilligan and Nancy Chodorow, Reddy hypothesizes that, by exploring this conjunction,

> a woman detective might read clues differently than a male detective would and [thus] her relationship to the problem presented would differ from the male detective's. The detective, whether male or female, is primarily a reader, but a reader more than ordinarily sensitive to nuances of meaning and to implications. (10)

Reddy goes on to suggest that "women writers, and especially feminist women, might be expected to play around with the issue of narrative authority and to be at least somewhat distrustful of authority generally" (10). In other words,

Reddy points toward both the women writers' consciousness of stylistic conventions of the subgenre and the female authors' potential to manipulate these conventions in keeping with their politics as feminists. Additionally, Reddy asserts, "Readers of detective fiction and fictional detectives have learned . . . reading strategies in a system that teaches everyone to read as men," but she also acknowledges that "some crime novels teach us how to read as women by focusing on a female detective's thought processes" (12–13). Thus, not only does the feminist detection writer subvert generic conventions, but she also calculatedly transforms the reception and interpretation of her work through encouraging audiences' connections with her female protagonist(s). Glaspell's careful focus on scripting what she has seen, such that her audience may see the stage as she has, defines and enables this process of teaching and connecting.

Glaspell refines these strategies through her *Trifles*/"Jury" narrative. She overtly establishes tension between male and female modes of interpretation and ties this tension to larger questions about social codes of law and justice. The fact that Mrs. Peters is the sheriff's wife figures largely in the conflict between, on the one hand, her allegiances to the men's futile attempts to discover a detached "truth" and, on the other, her dawning realization that an alternative code of justice exists based on women's empathic understanding of one another's lives. Moreover, Glaspell actively involves her audience in these debates, placing the work within the analytical arena of theories of reading. She overtly draws our attention to the different interpretations the male and female characters may make of the same bits of evidence, such as the state of the kitchen or the method Minnie was using to piece her quilt. The early exchanges between the county attorney and Mrs. Hale illustrate Glaspell's efforts to show men's and women's competing interpretive strategies:

County Attorney: (*. . . He goes to the sink, takes a dipperful of water from the pail and pouring it into a basin, washes his hands. Starts to wipe them on the roller-towel, turns it for a cleaner place.*) Dirty towels! (*Kicks his foot against the pans under the sink.*) Not much of a housekeeper, would you say, ladies?
Mrs. Hale: (*Stiffly*) There's a great deal of work to be done on a farm.
County Attorney: To be sure. And yet (*with a little bow to her*) I know there are some Dickson county farmhouses which do not have such roller towels. . . .
Mrs. Hale: Those towels get dirty awful quick. Men's hands aren't always as clean as they might be.

(9–10)

Mrs. Hale's resistance to the attorney's efforts—first, to convince her to join in his criticism of Minnie, then to be swayed by his flattery to condemn her—

exemplifies how Glaspell opposes the interpretive strategies of her male and female characters. Neither party disputes the evidence; the crucial distinction lies in the interpretation of the details. Mrs. Hale's empathic understanding of the domestic conditions of Minnie's life both precludes her making the same assumptions as the attorney and motivates her to analyze the environment differently.

S. E. Sweeney expands upon Reddy's assertion that some detective works both teach feminist reading strategies and prompt identification with female protagonists. She moves her discussion into the area of narrative theory, pointing out that within the mystery subgenre the reader and the act of reading are reflected in and by the text (12–13). Sweeney explains:

> The detective story . . . not only presents the most basic elements of narrative [sequence, suspense, and closure] . . . in their purest form, but also explicitly dramatizes the act of narration in the relationship between its narrative levels and its embedded texts. In other words, the detective story reflects reading itself. (7)

Sweeney's choice of the verb *dramatizes* unintentionally explains the success of Glaspell's work in two distinct categories, fiction and drama. While "A Jury of Her Peers" engages its armchair audience in issues of gender and reading, *Trifles* actively involves its theater viewers in the detection process. It should come as no surprise that detection drama has had a long and successful presence in the theater. Indeed, the relatively newer subgenre of audience-involvement theatricals such as *The Mystery of Edwin Drood* and *Shear Madness* is only a logical extension of the desire of the viewer to be involved in the solution of the mystery.[11]

Structurally and methodologically, there are many parallels—as well as some significant deviations—between Glaspell's work and the mainstays of the detection genre. Many critics of detective fiction point to Britain's Detection Club Oath (1928) as the simple yet definitive code for such writing:

> Do you promise that your detectives shall well and truly detect the crimes presented to them, using those wits which it may please you to bestow upon them and not placing reliance on nor making use of Divine Revelation, Feminine Intuition, Mumbo-Jumbo, Jiggery-Pokery, Coincidence or the Act of God? (Qtd. in Brabazon 197–98)

This vow suggests that detective characters must rely on their interpretive faculties brought to bear on the external evidence alone and not on inspiration or guidance that skips the analytic process. The preclusion of "feminine intuition" stands out, however, as a notably gendered warning to creators of female sleuths. Assuming reasoning to be a masculine process, this edict points toward the fluidity of interpretive strategies that may describe the female detective's ways of knowing. Glaspell highlights this assumption precisely in order to critique such detached male ratiocination. She juxtaposes the ineffective technique of the male investigators to the perceptiveness of Mrs. Hale and Mrs. Peters precisely by placing the women's examination of all the evidence they have in a liminal space between the use of purely externalized logic and empathic (intuitive) understanding.

Other critics like B. J. Rahn identify a more elaborate system for the creation of mysteries than that suggested by the oath. Such a structure sees the narrative move inexorably from the occurrence of a murder through the detection process to the denouement (49–50). Admittedly, Rahn analyzes retrospectively a body of increasingly codified writings. Nevertheless, it is instructive to see how Glaspell's early contributions resonate with such formulas. Glaspell's departures from some of these structural principles correspond to two groupings of narrative elements in Rahn's schema. These deviations illustrate key principles of Glaspell's feminist detection as well as the power of revisionist writing to affect audience perception. In elements 3 and 4 in Rahn's outline the gifted and knowledgeable (male) amateur detective arrives on the scene, after the authorities have failed to solve the mystery satisfactorily. He proceeds to deduce a logical hypothesis from his extensive examination of the evidence. Nearly any Sherlock Holmes story might serve as a model here. Yet, rather than have the detection occur in two stages, with incompetent police consulting the detective(s) after their own process stalls, Glaspell has the official and amateur investigations happen simultaneously, to dramatize concretely the limitations of the authority figures and the inadequacy of their methods. Glaspell's men never learn what the women learn because that would undermine the reversal of competence at the heart of the story. Both male and female viewers must learn to see as the women do, to become feminist spectators, and realize that this kind of seeing is different from, and in this case superior to, the men's way. The secret's staying with the women gives them an authority denied to the men in the narrative, although the potential capacity to read and see as women is, in Glaspell's pedagogical strategy, conveyed to both men and women of the audience. If "Jury" teaches the reader to read "differently," as a woman, then *Trifles* teaches how to spectate as a woman, by teaching how to detect as a woman.

Although the women in the play are amateurs, their knowledge is limited, unlike that of Rahn's usual amateur male detective. Glaspell, however, turns this limitation into a strength: knowledge of their "women's sphere" (that is, of "trifles"), rather than the men's "public sphere," is exactly what enables Mrs. Hale and Mrs. Peters to feel they have solved the mystery. Their identification with the absent Minnie allows them to envision what may have occurred. By portraying their epiphany with such nuanced pain, Glaspell distinguishes their process from the feminine intuition later proscribed by the Detection Club. Mrs. Hale exclaims:

> I might have known she needed help! I know how things can be—for women. I tell you, it's queer, Mrs. Peters. We live close together, and we live far apart. We all go through the same things—it's all just a different kind of the same thing! (27)

In the story version Glaspell adds the following lines to the end of Mrs. Hale's speech: "If it weren't—why do you and I *understand?* Why do we *know*—what we know this minute?" ("Jury" 384). In performance the connection between the actresses should clearly establish this shared understanding for the audience. Mrs. Hale senses that all the women she knows live in relative isolation, despite the fact that all their lives proceed along parallel paths. Mrs. Hale gropes toward an understanding that (patriarchal) social forces prevent women from acquiring this knowledge and keep them from forming the alliances that could change the course of their lives. Glaspell makes the women realize the similarity of their existence to Minnie's at the same time as she directs the audience to come to that understanding.

Glaspell's other deviations from classic generic patterns of detection also express a transformative political agenda. In steps 5–7 of Rahn's breakdown the detective "tests his hypothesis by reconstructing the crime and confronting the villain," "moral and civil order [are] restored," the "comic worldview" is preserved, and any lingering questions about the crime are resolved (49–50). Glaspell's decision to make both the criminal and the victim offstage characters means that no direct confrontation or confession can occur. Although the evidence seems to point to Minnie as the murderer, she never admits her guilt, nor is the case fully resolved. The "worldview" of the community—the patriarchal order—is exactly what is being questioned in Glaspell's narrative, not only by the women but also through the depiction of the crime and its probable motives. Glaspell develops a resolution wherein that worldview must be radically changed. Although a semblance of order will return, we know that the community will never be quite the same as it was before. While many critics assume that Mrs. Hale and Mrs. Peters have uncovered the "truth," Glaspell in fact gives us no definitive textual evidence to support this assumption. The women have constructed a plausible narrative, but we as the "jury" should ponder whether the criteria of evidence "beyond reasonable doubt" have been met.

The ending of the play and story suggests that Minnie could well be released from jail for lack of motive or conclusive evidence, although what her life in the community—or what the community itself—will thereafter be like remains unknown. Additionally, we must ponder what the impact of their realizations and choices will be for Mrs. Peters and Mrs. Hale. Now that their lives are linked (and linked to Minnie Wright's), what will this mean for them, especially given their difference in class position—a sheriff's wife and farmer's wife would not often travel in the same social circles, after all—that the events of the story temporarily elide? Robin Woods provocatively argues that the process of ratiocination separates the detective from society, simultaneously condemning this figure to a life of crime (16). In Glaspell's narrative the women become accessories after the fact, and, to the extent that we identify with them, so do we. Surely, Glaspell is asking her audience to ponder the implications of her work for such broad ideological formations as gender, class, and the legal structure of American society.

Despite the play's gesture toward narrative closure, as I have suggested, Glaspell leaves us with a number of questions. The women who act as amateur detectives now know much more, from a sharply critical standpoint, about themselves and the world they inhabit. Glaspell thus makes the drama more than a mere murder mystery by giving herself the flexibility to use the detection subgenre as the springboard for a wider exploration of character and society. S. F. Sweeney discusses Poe's "The Murders in the Rue Morgue" as "a theoretical discourse on the nature of 'analysis' in general" (11); Glaspell has added the key filter of gender to such discourse. Her particular indictment of the judicial system can be seen through her ironic titling of the story version, "A Jury of Her Peers." Indeed, Sally Munt sees juridical concerns as one of the hallmarks of feminist detection: "As the feminist author expresses her own fantasies of justice, her reader temporarily and figuratively gains membership to the law-making elite" (197). Since only men could serve on juries at that time, Glaspell foregrounds the fact that women could not be tried by their peers. This irony emphasizes how the particular circumstances of a woman like Minnie reflect women's lives throughout the country, regardless of their class position or geographical location.[12]

In connecting some of their feminist concerns with the detection subgenre, Karen Stein and Karen Alkalay-Gut make two important observations about Glaspell's technique. Alkalay-Gut remarks, "While the standard polarization of human beings in a crime story is normally determined by dividing law abiding citizens from the criminal, the characters here are . . . divided on the basis of sex differences" (4). This movement helps Glaspell develop her theme of the "law" versus "justice" that shapes the conflict of the women's initially divided loyalties. Near the end of the play Glaspell catches her audience in a moment of dramatic irony. Revealing no concern about what the women have gathered to bring to Minnie, the county attorney explains: "Mrs. Peters doesn't need supervising. For that matter, a sheriff's wife is married to the law. Ever think of it that way, Mrs. Peters?" Mrs. Peters, who has already determined to protect Minnie by hiding the evidence the women have found, responds cryptically, "Not—just that way" (29). Stein argues that the detection process Mrs. Hale and Mrs. Peters experience is highly unusual for mysteries, in that

> they do not remain objective observers; they become personally involved, and, through their successful investigations they gain human sympathy and valuable insights into their own lives. This growth, rather than the sleuthing process, is the play's focal point. (252)

Whereas detectives such as Sherlock Holmes usually depart the narrative frame fundamentally unchanged by the mystery they have solved, Glaspell's women undergo genuine transformation.

Another way to think of this profound characterological impact is that the women's process of investigating Minnie is integral to their own personal growth. As several critics note, the key symbol connecting the women's daily lives with their role as detectives is the unfinished quilt, which also serves as the central metaphor in the play. Through the recurrent questioning that drives the play Glaspell leads her audience to recognize the interdependency of detection and the women's arrival at self-knowledge. Mrs. Hale and Mrs. Peters reach their conclusions about Minnie's probable actions by observing and then questioning such evidence as her sewing, which has gone from "so nice and even" to "all over the place" (18), indicating her distressed state of mind. Shortly thereafter, they discover the use of the quilt pieces as a burial cloth for the dead canary, whose neck may have been wrung to silence its singing. They see the canary as symbolizing Minnie's voice, which has been silenced by a life with John that allows no place for her former activities, such as the choir (23). Alkalay-Gut aptly describes the women's detection as quilt making—piecing together the clues to the mystery (2)—while Annette Kolodny sees the character of Minnie herself (as well as the tattered clothes she wears) as "a pieced quilt" (56). Elaine Showalter views the quilt as "a hieroglyphic or diary for these women who are skilled in its language" (241–2). Thus, just as Glaspell crafts her drama through observing and questioning, so she makes her characters piece together a narrative about Minnie via their spectatorship of an environment as contained as any within a proscenium arch.

With this image of the quilt the connection of detection and reading— particularly reading as women—has emerged as *the* critical nexus for analysis of both story and play. Judith Fetterley and Annette Kolodny have figured the act of reading prominently in their commentary on the story. Their essays also open the prospect of quilting as a metaphor for the spectatorship and audience collaboration that Glaspell builds into her script. Kolodny suggests that "Glaspell's narrative not only invites a semiotic analysis but, indeed, performs that analysis for us." Kolodny maintains, however, that "only the women are competent . . . 'readers' of her 'message'" (56). Fetterley contrasts the women's success as readers to the men's failure:

> The reason for this striking display of masculine incompetence . . . derives from the fact that the men in question can not imagine the story behind the case. . . . They spend their time trying to discover their own story, the story they are familiar with . . . and know how to read. (147–48)

Fetterley explains Mrs. Hale's and Mrs. Peters's success simply—"Women can read women's texts because they live women's lives"—and expands upon the men's failure:

> It is not simply the case that men can not recognize or read women's texts; it is, rather, that they will not. . . . For the men to find the clue that would convict Minnie . . . they would have to confront the figure of John Wright. (149–153)

In other words, the men would have to acknowledge the male brutality that may have motivated the woman's response. One could argue that Glaspell's revision of the detection subgenre prompts her spectators to do just that.

The sardonic humor of Minnie's having married "Mr. (W)right" (Gubar and Hedin 788) cannot mask the harsh reality of his treatment of her. Playing further with these homonyms, Veronica Makowsky observes, "Minnie . . . now 'writes' the script for her life according to what [John] considers 'right.'" ("Susan Glaspell" 52). As Joan Radner and Susan Lanser explain, Minnie has no means of directly conveying her plight, which results in her creation of a range of semiotic codes the other women must decipher:

> By coding, then, we mean the adoption of a system of signals . . . that protect[s] the creator from the dangerous consequences of directly stating particular messages. . . . Minnie Wright did not deliberately encode her murderous rage and despair into the chaos of her kitchen and sewing basket, but she nonetheless left a message. (414–15)

And Mrs. Hale's and Mrs. Peters's reading of that message—what Minnie *Wright* crafted—is, in Glaspell's schema, an echoed response of righting/wrighting/writing.

One of the ironies of *Trifles*/"Jury" is that, had Minnie enjoyed the friendship of other women, she might not have generated these signs. Another, of course, is that the misanthropy of her husband compelled her to avoid such companionship. Her isolation, in fact, creates the context for the reading of her codes, particularly the quilt. Analogously, Glaspell's actual writing, like

Minnie's quilting, is a solitary process. Yet the ability to understand such creativity, or even to generate it successfully, Glaspell suggests, mandates collaboration. As Alkalay-Gut has noted, the distinction between *quilting* and *knotting*
has great significance for the plot. Toward the middle of the play Mrs. Hale
mentions that Minnie "didn't even belong to the Ladies Aid," as she "couldn't
do her part" (in terms of making financial contributions) and felt "shabby"
and therefore was incapable of enjoying the women's group (14). This information is strategic for the women's later discovery of Minnie's method of quilt
making. When they reveal that they "think she was going to—knot it" (24),
they are not only referring to their conclusion that Minnie indeed tied the knot
that strangled her husband but also to their understanding of her isolation:

> Patchworking is conceived as a collective activity, for although it is the in-
> dividual woman who determines the pattern, collects, cuts the scraps, and
> pieces them together, quilting work on an entire blanket is too arduous for
> one person. Minnie's patchwork would have been knotted and not quilted
> because knotting is easier and can be worked alone. (Alkalay-Gut 8)

Another ironic element of the quilting image is its connotations for the
Wright home. Physical as well as spiritual cold permeates the play; Mrs. Hale's
memory of John Wright prompts a "shiver" as she describes him: "Like a raw
wind that gets to the bone" (22). Cold and hard, Wright seems unlikely to have
been affected by the warmth of Minnie's quilting efforts. Playing on Minnie's
maiden name, Foster, Veronica Makowsky points to Glaspell's development of
Minnie's frustrated efforts at "nurturing domesticity" ("Susan Glaspell" 52).
The women perceive the loneliness behind Minnie's use of the scraps of cloth,
initially intended for the quilt, as coverings for the last bit of warmth in her
life, her strangled canary.
    Neither of the women dwells upon the absence of children in the house-
hold, but this lack raises questions about sexuality in the play, especially given
the evidence of Minnie's nurturance and John's "frigidity." While a great deal
of critical attention has focused on Minnie and her kitchen, critics do not at
all discuss the other key locus of attention in the narrative, the bedroom. Attention to Glaspell's stage action in *Trifles*, however, should force us to think
about where the men go when they leave the stage and what they are doing
there. Minnie has been widely identified as the first of Glaspell's "absent centers"—female characters who never appear onstage but play important roles
in the dramas.[13] But John, too, is a significant yet absent male character, much
as Dr. Russell is in *Suppressed Desires* and Fred Jordan in *Inheritors*. Furthermore, in *Trifles* Glaspell establishes a noteworthy "absent setting," the room in
which the murder occurred and in which the male characters spend much of
the time in the play. If the kitchen is coded as the women's sphere, then surely

the bedroom must be thought of as the male arena, a place of putative importance, as opposed to the locus of trifles. The bedroom is established, through opposition with the kitchen, as a place of male interest and dominance, just as Wright must have controlled the sexuality in his marriage. It is the room on top; the kitchen lies underneath it. At the very least Glaspell's choice of keeping this an offstage space, and the men's activities there similarly hidden, reverses the invisibility of women and their work in a male-dominated world.

Throughout this chapter, following the critical trends that discuss Glaspell's narrative in two genres, I have primarily considered these works jointly. The analysis of *Trifles* by W. B. Worthen in his *Modern Drama and the Rhetoric of Theater*, however, indicates that it is also imperative to consider *Trifles* and "Jury" as distinct literary works, particularly with regard to the critical nexus of feminism, realism, and the theater.[14] Worthen's arguments are in many cases insightful and compelling. Still, his reading of *Trifles* merits scrutiny precisely because of the general conclusions he draws from it concerning feminism, form, and the modern stage—conclusions that closer examination may render problematic.

Drawing on the reader-response criticism of feminist scholars such as Kolodny, Worthen concurs with their analysis of "Jury," noting that its

> signal narrative strategy . . . requires the reader to criticize the relationship between gender and interpretive authority, for the narrative exposes the operation of patriarchal ideology both in the story and in the reader's interpretive activity as well. (50)

He sees *Trifles* functioning differently, however, precisely because of its theatrical construction: "Staging such a narrative obviously entails a critical refiguring of this process, the replacement of the narrative voice by the mise-en-scène, and of the reader by the spectator" (51). The loss of the narrative voice in the realist theater, for Worthen, precludes the possibility that *Trifles* could function as a feminist work. He argues:

> the play consistently presents the "freedom" and "objectivity" of a spectator's observation as false, irresponsible, and uninformed, not really empowered to resolve the "truth" that realistic dramaturgy promises and withholds. . . . The audience of *Trifles* can observe . . . only from a distance, the explicitly "masculine" distance with which the realistic theater insistently "others" its objects. (52)

Unfortunately, Worthen does not provide textual or performative examples to demonstrate how this happens in the play. But his comments about the

"'masculine' distance" of spectatorship, extrapolated from the concept of the
male "gaze" in feminist film theory, resonate provocatively with Glaspell's
ideas of spectatorship and dramaturgy discussed earlier. Can the spectatorial
position of the feminist woman as writer oppose the hegemony of the male
gaze in a theatrical context? And does not Glaspell's deployment of the detection form, which works explicitly to pull the audience into the action, enable her to resist these conventions of the realist stage?

Worthen places his analysis of *Trifles* and "Jury" in the framework of a
broader consideration of the early modernist theater. He argues convincingly
that realistic theater "casts its audience as absent from the field of representation" precisely because of its reliance upon a verisimilitude that attempts to
mask its own theatricality (15). Worthen's depiction of stage realism is in keeping with the tenets of much feminist theater criticism, which has long posited
mimetic realism as a form antithetical to feminism. In the words of critic Elin
Diamond:

> Realism's putative object, the truthful representation of social experience
> within a recognizable, usually contemporary, moment remains a prob-
> lematic issue for feminism, not least because theatrical realism, rooted in
> part in domestic melodrama, retains the oedipal family focus even as it
> tries to undermine the scenarios that Victorian culture had mythified. (4)

Worthen builds his analysis of the realist theater around an understanding of
the complex social, technological, and artistic moment in the nineteenth century that fostered its rise. Yet the realist theater he describes differs in significant
ways from the modified fish house space of the Wharf Theatre on Cape Cod
that inspired the drafting of *Trifles*, although Worthen lists the work of the
Provincetown Players as part of the tradition he traces (12–19). Worthen's highly
nuanced and theoretically sophisticated analysis nevertheless suffers from its
failure to look at the specific, individual circumstances of this play's creation
and production. A comparison of Worthen's argument with Elin Diamond's recent exploration of theatrical realism and its potential for feminist subversion
may help frame the distinctive position of *Trifles* for this debate.

In *Unmaking Mimesis* Diamond, through a compelling reading of the
1893 play *Alan's Wife*, by Elizabeth Robins and Florence Bell, concludes that
these dramatists "unmake realism" in their drama of a young widow who suf-
focates her deformed infant and is condemned to death for its murder. Robins
and Bell "not only subvert the conventions of realist texts, they insist on the
untranslatability of a woman's . . . language before the law—the law represented by the dramatic fiction and the representational law of realism" (Diamond 37). Diamond's detailed analysis secures a very important critical space
for the consideration of women dramatists predating Brecht as writers of re-

sistant texts. Her invocation of the law, in terms of both plot and mimetic representation, resonates with Glaspell's formal manipulations but, equally significantly, with the playwright's thematics of justice. Diamond identifies a series of nodes of resistance in the writing and performing of *Alan's Wife:* its refusal to recuperate its central character, who remains unrepentant of her crime; its rejection of the "closure of positivist inquiry" despite its use of narrative; and its displacement of the "imaginary wholeness of the actor in realism," specifically through the performative demands the dramatists place upon the actor in the widow's role (37). While *Alan's Wife* serves as an exemplary text for Diamond precisely because its dramaturgy throws into question previous feminist assumptions about theatrical realism and feminism, *Trifles* accomplishes similar ends, albeit through a different plot and especially through Glaspell's strategic choice of the detection form. The open-endedness of Glaspell's drama, which both refuses traditional narrative closure and suggests the ambiguous place her absent protagonist may henceforth occupy in her community, parallels the structural resistance Diamond sees in the Robins and Bell piece.

I want to linger further on Diamond's idea of the displacement of the "imaginary wholeness of the actor in realism." Although Diamond is referring to the performance of *Alan's Wife,* her concept can also be used to challenge Worthen's inclusion of the productions of the Provincetown Players in his critique of realist theater (19). For Worthen the realist mise-en-scène, refined through the development of Stanislavsky's acting and staging techniques in the late nineteenth century, renders the actor's performance "theatrically invisible" (19). Such "invisibility" distinguishes this mode of acting from its most common countertechnique, the Brechtian performance style favored by feminist or otherwise oppositional theater critics and practitioners. This style separates actor from role, allowing the performer to "comment on" the character she portrays, thereby inducing Brecht's famous "alienation effect" between performers and spectators. The audience's distance from the text, including its consciousness of the simultaneous presence of actor and character, prevent both its identification with gender behavior and its acceptance of a mimesis that feminist critics would find problematic.[15] Worthen argues that the Provincetown Players' performances corresponded to an "increasingly subtle reproduction of domestic behavior" that defines realist acting (19). According to Worthen, in realist performance a character necessarily becomes "fully identified with its productive environment" through the erasure of the actor in the work (18–19). But this simply did not happen in the conceptualization and initial performances of the Players' dramas.[16]

Notions of identification and mimesis take on distinctly different resonances in the context of community theater production. By definition community theater is produced by and for a community, a situation epitomized

by the work of the Players. In a community in which the identities of the actors are known to the audience, in which their status as members of the community doubles with their artistic identities as performers, it is impossible for
the audience to "identify" with "real" people onstage or for the production to
convey an unfiltered mimesis in the way that critics have subsequently found
troubling, precisely because the audience will not suspend its knowledge of
that duality. In fact, the refusal to suspend disbelief is integral to the enjoyment of the art. Any time an actor is known to the audience, either personally
or as a recognized figure (for example, a movie star), the seamless fusion of the
actor with her role becomes impossible.[17] Although this is not at all the same
phenomenon as Brechtian alienation, it may function in a related fashion, creating a heightened awareness in the audience of the mechanics of performance. Audiences may still enact something akin to "identification" with a
character, but that process cannot happen independently of their simultaneous awareness of the actor in the part, which in turn may well affect the reception of character. The key distinction is that the performative structure described here operates regardless of the style of work being produced—and
moreover, that the Players' repertoire in fact embraced not only realist but also
expressionist, symbolist, and other dramaturgies.

Details of the production environment in community theater further
work against blanket concepts of the realist form propounded by such theorists
as Catherine Belsey (whom Worthen also cites). Belsey believes that in "classic
realist" drama "the author is apparently absent from the self-contained fictional world on the stage (68)." On the contrary, in the Provincetown context
the authors' identities and proclivities, known equally well to the audience
as the actors', would preclude the suspension of authorial consciousness even
within a realist production. This revised construction of realist performance
and dramaturgy is significant, moreover, to the reception of the Players' productions within their community as political drama.

Still, the preceding objection to Worthen's analysis has a comparatively
limited scope. Even if we do not "know" the actors in a given performance, we
do need to be aware that the term *realism*, like the term *feminism*, in the manner used by Worthen, has come to be seen by theorists as too broad. In identifying multiple forms of realism, as well as feminism, critics have realized that
such designations require specific contextualizing. Thus, a more telling coun-
terargument resides in the formal analysis of detection and its relationship to
realism and feminism.

Glaspell, we may assume, must have hoped that her works would find
production beyond her immediate community. Thus, particularly in the case
of *Trifles*, her choice of the detective form is key to this analysis. The play calls
for both our empathic identification with the women's realizations and the
relative detachment the process of ratiocination requires. Glaspell's subver-

sions of both early-twentieth-century American realism and detection create an important space for feminist resistance. To pursue this final line of inquiry we must return to criticism of the murder mystery subgenre, which, significantly, shares similar concerns about the potential for feminist intervention with writings on feminism and realism in the theater.

In a well-known essay from 1975 the prominent literary critic Geoffrey Hartman questions the "realism" of detective fiction, even though his discussion is not concerned with feminist intervention per se. Hartman notes that the subgenre's "voracious formalism dooms it to seem unreal, however 'real' the world it describes" (218). Hartman believes that in the American context, in particular, the success of the subgenre has more to do with its "social, or sociological [content], than with its realistic implications" (219). Feminist critics have expanded on Hartman's observations in their specific inquiries into women's writing in the subgenre. While this scholarship takes fictional work as its object of inquiry, the issues it raises about realism and detection are equally valid for a dramatic context. These theorists are concerned with detection as a form of writing but not the genre in which it is developed per se. We can thus apply their findings equally to both Glaspell's story and her play. The issue of form, then, transcends the distinctions between fictional narrative and the theatrical mise-en-scène on which Worthen focuses.

In her study of "feminists re/writing the detective novel" Barbara Godard, quoting theorist Tzvetan Todorov, explains:

> the murder mystery is imbricated in an antagonism between truth and verisimilitude. . . . In the codes of the genre . . . are to be found the subversive potentials of feminist murder mysteries. Challenging verisimilitude, they "discover the laws and conventions of the life around us" and expose the sexism of these conventions, all the while finding themselves constrained by the constitutive law of narrative discourse. (47)

Godard hypothesizes that writers use "this margin of escape" to "challenge generic laws through contesting social laws" (47). We might extend this argument, by analogy, to Glaspell: employing the detective form, Glaspell creates within her feminist, spectatorial dramaturgy just such a margin of escape.

In their study *Detective Agency* Priscilla L. Walton and Manina Jones layer their consideration of detective fiction with an exploration of the impact of feminist intervention on its extant subgenres. They argue that "feminist appropriation . . . can redefine textual and cultural boundaries precisely because it comes into intimate contact with them." They maintain that such co-optation "is an extremely important revisionary gesture that may work to alter the paradigms of both genre and gender" (87, 89). Walton and Jones posit that Michel Foucault's concept of "reverse discourse," which "repeats and inverts the ideological imperatives of the dominant discourse in order to authorize those marginalized by it" applies to feminist detection (92). They suggest, however, that "the effects of reverse discourse depend on the reader's ability to recognize difference between *this* particular performance of the genre and those it both repeats and counters" (96).

In other words, women's use of detective fiction as a site for literary resistance or social critique cannot, tout court, overthrow the subgenre, including its links to realism. But such appropriation, through its audience's recognition of the key points of departure from convention, can still underwrite subversion. We may recall Glaspell's signal departures from the structuring elements of the detection narrative identified in the schema of B. J. Rahn. It is through just such an examination of her divergences from standard detective form, coupled with our understanding of her breaks from traditional stage realism through her employment of detection and critical spectatorship, that we can identify specific dramatic moments of resistance. Glaspell's staging of simultaneously ineffective male and insightful female detection activities, her refusal of narrative closure, and her repeated questioning of both the social order and its gender codes all hold such subversive potential. These ruptures suggest that *Trifles* may indeed be seen as a feminist play.[18] Glaspell's narrative of spectatorship implies that watching and thinking prompt doing. Just as Glaspell herself "hurried in from the wharf to write down what [she] had seen" onstage, so her female characters respond decisively to their discoveries in Minnie's kitchen. Writing for a community of activists and artists poised to change the entire shape of twentieth-century America, Glaspell surely also worked to galvanize her audience for *Trifles* into thought and action.

Other One-Act Plays: *The People, Close the Book, The Outside, Woman's Honor,* and *Tickless Time*

The People

The People is Glaspell's homage to the *Masses,* the radical magazine that was central to Greenwich Village culture as well as to the Provincetown Players, envisioned as having the reach and impact of print journalism. According to historian William O'Neill, the *Masses* "was not only a national magazine for the radical intelligentsia but also a local institution reflecting some of the idiosyncrasies of the pre-war Village" (*Echoes* 20). As such, it became, along with the Players and such other events as the Armory Show and the Paterson Strike Pageant of 1913, "a leading expression and symbol of the 'little renaissance' of the prewar years" (Leach 28). Glaspell's decision to depict theatrically a periodical engaged with issues of national culture allowed her to make these concerns lively. Moreover, her dramatization facilitated debate on nationalism and culture on two levels (or in two media) simultaneously.

The *Masses* had been founded in 1911 by Piet Vlag but did not find its voice until Max Eastman took over as editor in December 1912. He appointed Floyd Dell as his associate editor in 1913, and contributors to the magazine included Glaspell, Cook, Dell, Mary Heaton Vorse, John Reed, Harry Kemp, Wilbur Daniel Steele, Djuna Barnes, and William Carlos Williams, among others, many of whom also wrote for the Players. Glaspell highlighted the overlap in the two organizations' memberships by establishing numerous parallels between the world and characters depicted in the play and that of the Provincetown group; years later, when she wrote about the genesis of the theater, she revealed her wish that "the Provincetown Players had been a magazine" (*Road to the Temple* 218). She does not explain whether the motive for this desire was personal, professional, political, or some combination thereof; she may have been alluding to the ephemerality of theatrical, as opposed to journalistic, endeavor. The theater's penchant for self-dramatization seems partially to have motivated some of Glaspell's thematic, dialogic, and production choices for

61

The People. The play reveals the connections Glaspell saw between these two distinct but related enterprises.

There are numerous similarities in the institutional structure of both the *Masses* and the Provincetown Players. The Provincetown's script selection process by committee mirrors the format for evaluating contributions used by the *Masses.* Moreover, a struggle for balance between authoritarian leadership and the need for a semblance of democracy haunted both Cook and Eastman. Cook appears to have been, however, a much more forceful figure than Eastman. Each organization also had two salaried workers with volunteer contributions by the rest of the membership.

Eastman's statement about the journal, printed on each issue's masthead, expresses its spirit and energy:

> THIS MAGAZINE IS OWNED AND PUBLISHED COOPERATIVELY BY ITS EDITORS. IT HAS NO DIVIDENDS TO PAY, AND NOBODY IS TRYING TO MAKE MONEY OUT OF IT. A REVOLUTIONARY AND NOT A REFORM MAGAZINE; A MAGAZINE WITH A SENSE OF HUMOR AND NO RESPECT FOR THE RESPECTABLE, FRANK, ARROGANT, IMPERTINENT, SEARCHING FOR THE TRUE CAUSES; A MAGAZINE DIRECTED AGAINST RIGIDITY AND DOGMA WHEREVER IT IS FOUND; PRINTING WHAT IS TOO NAKED OR TRUE FOR A MONEY-MAKING PRESS; A MAGAZINE WHOSE FINAL POLICY IS TO DO AS IT PLEASES AND CONCILIATE NOBODY, NOT EVEN ITS READERS
> —There is a field for this publication in America. (Eastman 421)

This proclamation also reveals similarities in both tone and content to the annual subscription announcements drafted by Cook for the Provincetown that combined a sense of their artistic mission with a call for the audience to participate in their theatrical experiments. The financial independence and nationalistic sense of the organizations' places in American political and cultural life are but two key elements of both tracts.

Glaspell set her play in the office of the *People,* subtitled "A Journal of the Social Revolution" (48). The phrase pays homage to both the subheading for the *Masses,* "A Monthly Magazine Devoted to the Interests of the Working People," and to the title of Eastman's monthly editorial column, "Knowledge and Revolution." The scene evokes the feisty spirit of the journal: "On the wall are revolutionary posters ... [This is] the office of a publication which is radical and poor" (33). The time is the present, March 1917.[1] With Aristotelian economy of time and place Glaspell depicts a day in the life of the *People,* a day fraught with financial, personal, and social conflict but also highly representative of the chaotic world that Eastman and Dell inhabited until the end of 1917.

The plot of *The People* pulls together three areas of controversy: fund-raising and subscription problems; internal disputes over content and editorial philosophy; and legal complications stemming from the journal's radical focus. On the day in question Glaspell depicts the editor, Edward Wills, having just returned from a fund-raising trip. As Veronica Makowsky observes, his name is ironic, for he "has lost his will to persevere" ("Susan Glaspell" 55). Depressed about whether he can continue to publish amid all these competing pressures, he is buoyed by the belief of three loyal readers, who have traveled to New York from across the country to show their support. Despite the carping of contributors, each of whom insists that the publication move in another direction, these unwitting ambassadors of the people whom Wills is trying to reach reinvigorate him, and he vows to go on with the magazine once again.

Glaspell seems to have modeled Wills fairly closely on Max Eastman. In his biography of Eastman, *The Last Romantic*, William O'Neill explains the kinds of financial difficulties the editor confronted. While he built up the subscriber base from five thousand to a peak of twenty-five thousand, "the magazine was expensive to print and always lost money. To be self-supporting, it needed a wide audience that it never got, despite, and possibly even because of, considerable notoriety" (41). Yet Eastman had "a gift for raising money" (31), an activity he himself wittily described as his "career in high finance" (Eastman 455). In *The People* Glaspell depicts the magazine at a financially precarious point. The printer, Tom Howe, is threatening to take a job on the *Evening World*, and the associate editor, Oscar Tripp (the Floyd Dell character), informs the others that Wills has not been financially successful this time, a fictional departure from Eastman's record of comparative success on such trips. In fact, soon before the premier of the play Eastman had returned from a "two-months' lecture and money-raising tour across the country to San Diego" (Eastman 538). Glaspell's plot, however, facilitates the somewhat melodramatic denouement as well as neater narrative closure in Wills's vow to continue publishing despite setbacks.

In the play the financial problems bolster the contributors' sense that, if the magazine were only produced their way, all the issues would be resolved. Glaspell presents a humorous gallery of allegorical figures who freely share their opinions with Wills. The Earnest Approach maintains, "*The People* has been afraid of being serious." The Light Touch asserts, "A lighter touch—that's what *The People* needs." The Firebrand calls out, "Too damn bourgeois! You should print on the cover of every issue—'To hell with the bourgeoisie!'" And The Philosopher opines, "The trouble with this paper is efficiency. . . . It should be more carelessly done, and then it would be more perfectly done" (41–42). Wills, barraged by these competing voices, deftly avoids committing to any of their proposed courses of action.

Glaspell closely captures here the atmosphere of struggle Eastman faced in confronting the ranks of the contributors to the *Masses*. While she does not slavishly duplicate the battles Eastman endured between his artists and his writers, she conveys the fraught environment surrounding the publication. Dell saw the journal as embracing elements of all these individuals' perspectives: "It stood for fun, truth, beauty, realism, freedom, peace, feminism, revolution" (qtd. in Eastman 559). But the artists and writers seem consistently to have disagreed over its form and content. The conflict peaked in March 1916 and became "a war of the Bohemian art-rebels [the writers] against the socialists who loved art [the visual artists]" (Eastman 548). While the *Masses* gained much respectful attention for its balance of artwork, literary content, and nonfictional essays and reports, some of the artists "pressed for greater aesthetic freedom and a purer devotion to art" (O'Neill, *Echoes* 17–18). A group led by the socialist artist John Sloan confronted Eastman about his editorial policies; Eastman in turn offered his resignation, although a vote by the full membership strongly endorsed him as editor (Eastman 548–54). A significant difference, however, between Eastman's career and that of Wills in the play lies in the link that Glaspell establishes between editor and magazine. While Eastman clearly put his mark on the *Masses,* he never projected a life-or-death hold over its survival. More than once he expressed a resolve "to bring out one more number and quit" (Eastman 406), but this threat never meant the simultaneous demise of the journal. The editor of the *People,* however, holds its fate in the balance, so that much of the dramatic tension—as well as some humor—derives from Wills's diatribe on the forces working against the publication.

It is not, perhaps, a great coincidence that Cook played the role of Wills in the first production nor that the part conveys at least as much of Cook's personality as Eastman's, if not more so. The impassioned rhetoric Glaspell gives Wills indeed sounds more like Cook:

> We are living now. We shall not be living long. No one can tell us we shall live again. This is our little while. This is our chance. . . . Move! Move from the things that hold you. If you move, others will move. Come! Now. Before the sun goes down. (49)[2]

For the 1917–18 season circular, for example, Cook had written:

> This season too shall be an adventure. We will let this theatre die before we let it become another voice of mediocrity. If any writers in this country—already of our group or still to be attracted to it—are capable of bringing down fire from heaven to the stage, we are here to receive and help.

Eastman's voice was equally intense but far less spiritual:

The end we have in view is an economic and social revolution, and by revolution we do not mean the journey of the earth around the sun, or any other thing that is bound to happen whether we direct our wills to it or not. We mean a radical democratization of industry and society, made possible by the growth of capitalism, but to be accomplished only when and if the spirit of liberty and rebellion is sufficiently awakened in the classes which are now oppressed. (Eastman 402)

The messianic fervor Cook felt for the theater comes through more clearly in Wills's speeches about the *People* than in Eastman's editorial pronouncements. Thus, one is tempted to see the play both as a dramatization of the *Masses* and as an analogy to the Provincetown Players and its own internal and financial struggles.

Luckily for the playwrights, aside from early citations for building code violations, the authorities never threatened to close the theater, whereas Anthony Comstock's censorship of the media had legal and financial consequences for the *Masses*.[3] One of the great ironies for today's readers of *The People* derives from the knowledge that, soon after Glaspell's play dramatized the potential cessation of the journal, the government forced the *Masses* to shut down. The November–December 1917 issue was its last. Controversy had surrounded the content of the *Masses* for some time, however, and Glaspell richly alludes to such problems in the play. What William O'Neill has termed the "strongly anti-clerical" bent of the magazine caused considerable public outcry (*Echoes* 19), and Oscar's "Talk with God" column in the play (43) directly corresponds to the "Heavenly Dialogue" section in the *Masses* (O'Neill, *Echoes* 31–32). The most financially damaging situation arose, however, with the 1916 publication in the *Masses* of "A Ballad," a poem with a distinct spin on the tale of Mary and Joseph:

The Biggest man in creation?
    It was Joseph the Nazarene.
Joe, the Yiddisher "carpenter stiff,"
    The husband o' Heaven's Queen!
Joe, that was smitten o' Mary,
    Joe, that was game as grit—
When she came weepin' to 'is arms,
    Needin' a father for it.

Joe was as right as the compass,
    Joe was a square as the square.
He knew men's ways with women,
    An' Mary was passin' fair!

Passin' pretty an' helpless,
    She that he loved th' most,
God knows what he told th' neighbors,
    But he knew it warn't no Ghost.
        (Qtd. in Eastman 592–93)

Publication of this verse, which went on for five additional stanzas and a coda, led to a ban on the sale of the *Masses* in New York's subway newsstands (O'Neill, *The Last Romantic* 43). Glaspell incorporates this outcome into her dialogue in *The People*. A boy from Georgia arrives to announce that he has left school for "something different and bigger," which he believes the magazine represents. He cries, "I heard about your not being able to sell your paper on the newsstands just because lots of people don't want anything different and bigger, and I said to myself, 'I'll sell the paper! I'll go and sell it on the streets!'" (50–51), even though he will probably risk arrest for doing so (55).

The unwavering commitment of the readership to the magazine and the ideals it represents come through most strongly in the character of The Woman from Idaho, played by Glaspell in the first production. The Woman tells Wills that his words are "like a spring breaking through the dry country of my mind," and how those "great words carried me to other great words." Invoking Lincoln (as Glaspell will again in *Inheritors*) for his dedication to the philosophy of freedom for all, she speaks of the wonders of riding "across the county and see[ing] all the people. . . . and I said to myself—This is the Social Revolution! . . . *Seeing*—that's the Social Revolution" (57). One is tempted to associate Glaspell with this character through her performance, as if the playwright had created a role that would allow her to give voice to the fervent views she could not speak in her own persona. Veronica Makowsky maintains that, through this character and Glaspell's performance in it, she was claiming that "life is an art, so that women who work in this medium, rather than paint or pen, may be those who most fully express themselves and inspire others" ("Susan Glaspell" 57).

The critic Heywood Broun viewed Glaspell's performance as having "depth and spirit" and claimed she "has done more for American drama than any playwright of the year," as *Trifles, Suppressed Desires,* and *The People* were all produced in New York during the 1916–17 season (*Suppressed Desires* and *The People* by the Provincetown; *Trifles* by the Washington Square Players). Broun felt *The People* "needs condensation and simplification, but . . . it is built upon a gorgeous plan and developed with humor and telling eloquence, despite a trace of an intrusive literary quality" ("In Wigs and Wings" 3). While Broun said nothing about the real-life parallel to the *Masses,* he conveyed in detail the social spirit of the drama and the importance of the titular publication to the readership characterized in the play. He even expressed the hope that he could print the lengthy impassioned speech of the editor's (quoted earlier in part) as a "capital piece of writing."

Broun's and the play's emphasis on "the people" served by the magazine sets up an ironic contrast with the *Masses,* however. In his history of Village life, *Garrets and Pretenders,* Albert Parry questions,

> But then, was the magazine really for the masses? It was not. It was by the radical petit bourgeois for the liberal petit bourgeois. Yet, though the working classes almost never read the *Masses,* the magazine did, in the long run, help the working classes. (281)

Glaspell's most strategic divergence from her model, then, comes in her characterization of a range of individuals touched by the publication, some of whom were left out of the *Masses'* orbit. The Woman from Idaho, wearing "plain clothes not in fashion" (34), the Boy from Georgia "dressed like a freshman with a good allowance" (43), and the Man from the Cape [Cod], "a mute, ponderous figure" who cultivates oysters by trade (45), represent a spectrum of America by age, sex, geography, and class. All are equally affected by the rhetoric of the journal, however, and feel drawn irresistibly to its home. Glaspell created a magazine whose title truly reflected its mission; the *Masses* in some ways did not. While capturing the general feel and structure of her model, Glaspell was able to make her fictional journal the publication she may have wished the *Masses* genuinely to be.

Especially through the character of The Woman from Idaho, we sense that Glaspell had a vision of journalism and theater that will not only reach across America but that will help realize social change. While deeply appreciating the work of her colleagues and the closeness of her bohemian world, she depicts a moment when their talent, idealism, and energy can transcend their immediate confines; *The People* conveys hope for their achieving the impact that seemed perpetually to elude them in real life, despite their dedication to advanced political and social principles. It would appear that for Glaspell the key lay in a kind of egalitarianism and nationalism that in some ways was antithetical to the concept of the "beloved community" that typified her milieu and fostered its productivity. *The People* only revealed that irony, however; no group ever fulfilled those goals.

Close the Book

Questions of race rarely surface in discussions of the Provincetown Players. When the issue does arise, it is most often broached in connection with the work of Eugene O'Neill (particularly *The Emperor Jones* [1921] but also such one-acts as *The Dreamy Kid* [1919]). As early as 2 November 1917, however, with the premiere of Glaspell's *Close the Book,* the company began its exploration of American attitudes toward the ethnic and racial Other. It was, then, a logical progression for the group to move on from this initial foray to the production of O'Neill's plays with nonwhite characters centrally featured.[4]

Close the Book concerns the relationship of Jhansi, a student at an Iowa university, and her fiance, Peyton Root, an instructor at the school whose family is powerful and influential in the community. Believing herself to be an orphaned Gypsy, Jhansi actively opposes the social mores and restrictions of her midwestern environment both on principle and as a gesture of solidarity with her ethnic roots. She quickly emerges as the image of a liberated, free-thinking modern young woman who wishes to share equality and openness with her husband-to-be. As she tells him with Whitmanesque fervor early in the scene, "I should take you by the hand and you and I should walk together down the open road" (66). Such phrases emblematize the freedom she envisions in their life together and reflect her romanticized image of her migratory ancestry. The fact that one version of Gypsies' origins connect them with the Central European region known as Bohemia, conceptualized as a locus of antibourgeois sensibility later adopted by the Village, may also have informed Glaspell's creation of the play (Stansell 17). Ironic reversals of expectations about racial identity drive the denouement, however: during the course of the play we learn Jhansi's true, white Protestant identity, and the conflicts surrounding her and the potential marriage are resolved when a genealogical treatise exposes skeletons in all the characters' closets.

While critics noted the satire upon conventionality in *Close the Book,*[5] they chose to treat the play dismissively, rather than to look beyond the plot and the most accessible themes to its more serious social content. From a current critical perspective the drama merits closer analysis on narrative, characterological, and structural levels for its complex and even contradictory treatment of race, ethnicity, and the perceived threat of miscegenation.

Racial and ethnic difference is just one of several themes linking *Close the Book* to Glaspell's 1921 play, *Inheritors,* although the latter focuses on Native American and Asian Indians instead of Gypsies. Details of character, setting, and plot also link the two works. In each play Glaspell creates an older female character (here Mrs. Root) who voices many racist opinions, as this dialogue from *Close the Book* illustrates:

Mrs. Root: (*In great distress*) Mother, how would you like to see your grandson become a gypsy?
Grandmother: Peyton a gypsy? You mean in a carnival?
Mrs. Root: No, not in a carnival! In *life.*
Grandmother: But he isn't dark enough.

Mrs. Root: And is *that* the only thing against it! I had thought you would be
a help to me, mother.

Grandmother: Well, my dear Clara, I have no doubt I will be a help to you—
in time. This idea of Peyton becoming a gypsy is too startling for me to
be a help instantly. In the first place, could he be? You can't be anything
you take it into your head to be—even if it is undesirable.

(69)

The age and familial status of these characters presumably suggest older social
attitudes; Glaspell often opposes such women to younger figures who express
conflicting views. She imbues the grandmothers in each play with down-to-
earth common sense, however, and they emerge as pragmatic individuals
unswayed by others' more emotional positions. By speaking their minds, they
practice a form of "free speech," the pattern of free expression that historians
such as Christine Stansell believe define this era.[6]

The Grandmother in *Close the Book* continues her train of thought by
questioning her daughter's mission to "civilize the young woman" (71) and
proceeds with a comparison between ethnic and racial difference:

Grandmother: I wonder how it is about gypsies. About the children. I wonder if it's as it is with the negroes.

Mrs. Root: Mother!

Grandmother: It would be startling, wouldn't it?—if one of them should turn
out to be a real gypsy and take to this open road.

Mrs. Root: (*Covering her face*) Oh!

Grandmother: Quite likely they'd do it by motor.

(71–72)

Within the context of the midwestern setting the frank prejudice of these ideas
seems intended to appear humorous. Grandmother's linkage of *negroes* and
gypsies, however, also underscores the construction of Jhansi as a nonwhite
woman and suggests that Glaspell was aware of the historical persecution of
Gypsies as a dark or black race (Singhal 21–22). While Mrs. Root (played by
Glaspell in the original production) represents a social tradition wherein race
is simply not discussed in polite circles, Glaspell also uses her to express what
we might now identify as a "politically correct" (albeit hypocritical) position
about the progress of society. She tells her mother that men no longer just fall
in love with such women; "they marry them now. (Both sigh.) Of course, it's
very commendable of them" (71).

With the arrival of Uncle George, the "president of the board of regents"
of the university (65),[7] however, the conversation begins to take on more serious and troubling overtones beneath the veneer of comedy. Glaspell starts to

make the connections between private and public concerns more weighty, precisely by invoking the term *free speech* and showing how easily the right to speak may be assumed by some and taken from others:[8]

Mrs. Root: I am prepared to speak freely with you, Uncle George. The matter with Peyton is this girl. Well, they're going to be married . . . and I think it's a good thing. She won't be in a position to say so much about freedom after she is married.
Uncle George: But they say she's a gypsy.
Mrs. Root: She won't be a gypsy after she's Peyton's wife. She'll be a married woman.
Uncle George: Yes, but in the meantime we will have swallowed a gypsy.
Grandmother: And I was just wondering how it would be about the children.
Mrs. Root: Mother, please don't be indelicate again.

(73–74)

The perspectives expressed here are startling. Not only will marriage act as a silencing force, compelling Jhansi to accept the strictures of society, but it will also erase difference, at least to the outside world. While the family will have to internalize ("swallow") her Otherness, their external representation will be one of social conformity. In Mrs. Root's worldview not only does the younger character lose individual identity as a woman through marriage, but she also actually loses her visible ethnicity altogether. Marriage to a white man, she implies, is powerful enough that it can overwhelm alterity, replacing it with a signifier of social position. Thus, Glaspell combines concerns with ethnic and gender identity. She creates parallels between these markers of a woman's individuality through their erasure in matrimony.

Glaspell frequently critiques the Midwest and its narrow social codes in her novels, plays, and stories by juxtaposing characters with unacceptable, provincial views to those figures superior to their neighbors' limited perspectives. If the theme of prejudice had operated exclusively on the level of dialogue, we might suppose that Glaspell was intentionally distancing her setting and characters from the world of her eastern, urban(e) audiences. Had she generated a plot that neatly separated the overall action from this reactionary dialogue, the level of critique identifiable in the play could have become clearer. Such a story line might have bracketed the views of characters like Mrs. Root much in the same way that we come to understand the perspectives of the men in *Trifles,* for example. Yet the narrative resolution of *Close the Book* complicates the analysis of the play's thematics, rendering the treatment of race and ethnicity much more problematic.

Near the end of the play Peyton's sister Bessie enters, a character whose arrival has been heavily foreshadowed. Bessie proves a *dea ex machina,* for not only does she come to resolve the conflict, but she does so accompanied by a book that holds the truth value of a family bible, complete with genealogical tables. She also brings witnesses with her, the formidable Senator Byrd and his wife, to attest to her discoveries and add valuable details to her story. Bessie, a spunky young woman who has taken it upon herself to uncloak the mystery of Jhansi's parentage, discovers by looking through county records that her "father was Henry Harrison, a milkman in the town of Sunny Center—an honorable and respected man," and that her "parents were married in the Baptist Church" (80). The senator and his wife, cousins of Jhansi's mother, provide the additional information that her parents died of typhoid, orphaning her at an early age. Bessie deals the ultimate blow to Jhansi's fantasy of alterity by observing that her adoptive mother "never told you you were a gypsy either, did she? No; she just wanted you to think you were their own child. And then I suppose you heard some foolish tale at school" (82). The final irony for Jhansi comes when it is revealed that her "outlandish" name is not ethnically derived but, instead, is the name of a town in India where her mother's church had a missionary interest (84).[9] Bessie triumphantly proclaims to her future sister-in-law: "You must not stand outside society! You belong *within* the gates. You are one of us!" (79). Glaspell further uses the book Mrs. Byrd carries, entitled "Iowa descendants of New England families" (83), as a comic prop holding undesirable secrets about both families' ancestors. This leveling device undermines the note of class difference (cf. a milkman and a senator) that has come to replace racial or ethnic distinction to wrap up the action. Yet this comic denouement, with a socially acceptable marriage as the conclusion, radically disrupts the more progressive tension between social convention and personal freedom introduced in the first half of the play. This conclusion may also remind one of the sidestepping of unconventional sexual morality in the resolution to *Suppressed Desires*.

Glaspell's elimination of Jhansi's Otherness suggests a conservatism that cannot be reconciled with the political liberalism suggested in the play's opening scenes. While Jhansi's extremes of "non-conformity" (63) establish her as a figure open to Glaspell's critique (as she critiques all types of extremism), the treatment of Jhansi's ethnicity might seem, for a more recent reader, to be a separate issue immune from compromise. Yet the possibility of miscegenation appears to have been more than Glaspell could face theatrically. The play's narrative resolution indicates the drive for sameness on both authorial and characterological levels. Glaspell's preclusion of a plot resolution that incorporated a "mixed marriage," in essence, closes a book above and beyond those figured within her drama.

Ironically, however, her other genuinely radical political view is presented uncompromised in the play. One of Glaspell's and her Greenwich Village community's major concerns in the period immediately before and during

America's involvement in World War I was the protection of the constitu-
tional right to freedom of speech. Safeguarding this right was of particular
interest to those whose public speaking and journalistic writing became the
target of government prosecution under the Espionage and Sedition Acts of
1917–18, especially staff members of the *Masses*. While Glaspell treats the issue
in greater depth and detail in *Inheritors*, it is a strong undercurrent for *Close
the Book* as well.

Glaspell introduces the specifically political component of the theme
offhandedly early in the play. Peyton remarks that he and Jhansi must "finish an
article on Free Speech which must get to the Torch [*sic*] this evening" (68).[10]
Grandmother is dismissive: "Free Speech? How amusing," but Peyton's come-
back is serious: "You may be less amused some day, Grandmother" (68). After
Mrs. Root rules out the discussion of race as unsuitable, Grandmother broaches
free speech as an alternative topic, reminding the others that Peyton and Jhansi
are writing on it: "Well, if there's nothing else we may speak of, let's talk about
free speech" (74). The irony of this remark is brilliant, as Glaspell uses it to expose how conservative characters like Mrs. Root and Uncle George apply such
principles hypocritically and unthinkingly, in essence allowing freedom of expression only to those whose views match their own. Uncle George bristles: "I
don't know what this university is coming to! An institution of learning! It isn't
that I don't believe in free speech. Every true American believes in free speech,
but—" (74). Uncle George's comments reflect the burgeoning conservatism and
narrowly defined nationalism on university campuses at the time, particularly
virulent with regard to any statements of opposition to American involvement
in the war.[11]

Peyton's distressed mother remarks on the future of her son's career at
the university:

> I don't know how much longer he'll teach it. He said the other day that
> American literature was a toddy with the *stick* left out. Saying that of the
> ·very thing he's paid to teach! It got in the papers and was denounced in
> an editorial on "Untrue Americans." (69–70)

The accusation of national disloyalty, emblematic of the rhetoric of the Espionage and Sedition Acts, links this moment in the play with its other concerns
about identity. The acts, much like Peyton's family, represented a value system
that attempted to expunge difference—to eliminate any force or figure that attempted to break through its hermetic boundaries. Again ironically, however,
at the same time that Glaspell criticizes such enforced conformity thematically, she enacts it narratively, precisely by appealing to "roots" (genealogy).

Peyton, echoing the Declaration of Independence, reminds his family of
the founding principles of the country, in much the same way that Glaspell will

invoke this heritage and the words of Lincoln in *Inheritors*. Glaspell connects the traditions of freedom and democracy on the national and familial levels, linking Peyton's ancestors to both the signing of that historic document and the establishment of the university in a similar spirit of academic freedom. The truthful revelation of family history—both the heroes and the ne'er-do-wells—through the printed word mirrors this theme of openness on a narrative level.

Interestingly, however, this free speech context does not extend in the play to any mention of the war itself, perhaps because Glaspell felt it lay outside the comedic world she was creating. This omission causes characterological problems: other than Jhansi's mistaken notions of her ancestry, there is little to support her political convictions of nonconformity and free expression and nothing other than Peyton's love for her to explain why he has joined her in her crusade. It is in this regard that she differs markedly from Madeline in *Inheritors,* who has ample personal and political motivation for her beliefs. In the comedic drama Glaspell seems to walk a tightrope between two extremes: between the parody of Jhansi's naive desire for the freedom of the open road and a gypsy meal of "berries and nuts" (67), on the one hand, and a more serious discussion of the issues of personal and political freedom that Jhansi introduces, on the other. In this work Glaspell's better-established, longer-standing (proto)feminist sensibilities, evident even from her early fictional writing,[12] seem to give way to the dramaturgical force of the well-made comedy. She replicates this structure with the marital resolution and the restoration of social order, yet another ironic "closure" she may not have intended her title to suggest.

It can be tempting to join early reviewers in dismissing *Close the Book* as an inconsequential comedy, a piece whose classic dramaturgy is much like that of its predecessor, *Suppressed Desires.* We might also take *Close the Book* as an anticipation of *Inheritors,* as Glaspell explores themes and character types she would expand and refine in the later work. Perhaps most interestingly, however, *Close the Book* exemplifies the curious blend of conservatism and radicalism that characterizes much of Glaspell's writing. Such contradictions were in fact endemic to the era, especially within Glaspell's circle, in which her fellow bohemians' lives and work reflect vestiges of Victorian morality appearing side by side with the latest progressive politics. Such inconsistencies remain part of the fascination of this one-act in particular and Glaspell's period more generally.

The Outside

Coming midway through the Provincetown's second full New York season (1917–18), *The Outside* was produced at a pivotal moment for the group. Theater

historian Gerhard Bach has identified three phases of dramaturgic development for the Players:

> the initial phase of social realism, leading to the phase of realism vs. sym-
> bolism (or the realistic prose play vs. the symbolistic verse play), leading
> again into the last phase of renewed social realism interspersed with ex-
> periments in expressionism. ("Susan Glaspell" 36)

A number of the verse plays Bach associates with the second phase were
mounted in 1918 and 1919. These productions were spearheaded by the efforts
of Alfred Kreymborg, who sought a home for verse drama in the American
theater. The "Other Players'" bill at the Provincetown, named for the poetry
magazine *Others* founded by Kreymborg, came just two months after the production of *The Outside*.[13] While Bach makes a clear distinction between the
forms and modes of the drama in this period, I would argue that the divisions
were not so neat, particularly with regard to the "prose plays," a number of
which share elements of form, style, and poetic language with the verse pieces.

The bill comprising the three prose plays *The Outside,* Floyd Dell's *The
Angel Intrudes,* and Irwin Granich's *Down the Airshaft,* performed 28 December–3 January, is a case in point.[14] Robert Sarlós calls the entire program
"mildly poetic" (84); I would extend this designation to suggest that Glaspell's
one-act occupied a liminal space dramaturgically. Hovering among the divisions of modernist form Bach identifies, as well as between prose and verse, it
conveyed a heightened realism that bordered on the symbolic. Indeed, C. W.
E. Bigsby disparagingly refers to Glaspell as a "patent symbolist" for this work
(Plays 14), as if to suggest that the accessibility and clarity of her image clusters were somehow an artistic flaw. Yet these very stylistic choices perfectly illustrate why her work was identified by so many earlier commentators as exemplars of the one-act form. Percival Wilde, who cites Glaspell on a number
of occasions in his 1923 *The Craftsmanship of the One-Act Play,* notes that "the
one-act play is impressionistic, and subjects not susceptible to such treatment
must remain foreign to it. Even its realism is likely to be impressionistic" (37).

In creating a piece blending realism with symbolism and incorporating
poetic language within prose dialogue, Glaspell evinces her clear ties with the
evolution of modern drama in America in this period. As J. L. Styan observes,
symbolism can "exist alongside realism" in the drama (*Modern Drama* 1).
Glaspell's work corresponds to that of other prominent European modern
dramatists for its selection of "more symbolic expression" at a time when her
success as a realist was well established (Styan 2). *The Outside* exemplifies the
unique development of American dramatic modernism, moreover, in its incorporation of multiple stylistic influences. Whereas expressionism and symbolism, to give just two examples, evolved rather distinctly in Europe, these

and other forms of modernist creativity arrived in the United States virtually simultaneously. American artists felt free to explore in combination elements of modernism's signature techniques, a multiplicity Glaspell would later exploit with *The Verge*.[15]

The connection in *The Outside* between symbolism and realism has implications, however, beyond the script itself. Michael Meyer has pointed out the theatrical efficacy of performing symbolism "with the simplest realism" (qtd. in Styan 27); Glaspell's text exemplifies the potential for set and action to reflect this fusion. In this way the script for *The Outside* represents the possibility of holistic artistry in production (*Gesamtkunstwerk*) that critics associate with the calculated theatrical experiments of the modern era. Many of Glaspell's plays reveal an integral, thematic relation between setting and action, as, for example, the kitchen environment of *Trifles* and the almost anthropomorphized homes of Bernice and Alison Stanhope. Yet of all Glaspell's dramas *The Outside* may best represent her ability to create a dynamic correspondence of set, character, and theme. It is within this context of experimental, modernist fusion in American drama that the piece may be most profitably explored.

Set in an abandoned lifesaving station on the outer banks of Provincetown on Cape Cod,[16] the play focuses on two women who have both suffered great loss and who help each other rediscover their connections with life. Mrs. Patrick, who used to summer in Provincetown with her husband, comes to live in the station after her husband has left her. She hires Allie Mayo, the widow of a fisherman lost at sea, to help her keep house. Allie has a reputation for silence: she is described as "somebody . . . that doesn't say an unnecessary word" (107). Allie's return to language is one of the major arcs of the play. Mrs. Patrick has similarly chosen to isolate herself in response to her pain and is thus extremely distressed when she discovers a group of men inside the station, working to save the life of a drowning victim.[17]

As with all her plays, Glaspell takes great care here with the initial set description, providing for artists and readers a full rendering of the environment she envisions. A glance at a map of Cape Cod reveals the exactness of the placement of *The Outside*: a room in a former lifesaving station set on the outer shore at "the point, near the tip of the Cape, where it makes that final curve which forms the Provincetown Harbor" (99). Painted a uniform, dulled gray, the room seems to exist in limbo; no longer of use to the Coast Guard, it "has taken on no other character, except that of a place which no one cares either to preserve or change" (99). Glaspell will waste little time establishing the symbolic link between the transitional nature of her characters' lives and this scenic indeterminacy. The theme of struggle between the sexes, played out spatially as well as characterologically, emerges with similar economy. Glaspell interweaves concerns with gender, space, and loss in a short drama that, like

its themes, embraces liminality.[18] Most strategic to the set is the upstage focal
point: the "big sliding door" that is "about two-thirds open," revealing the
shore and sea beyond, complete with sand, dunes, woods, brush, and beach
grass (99). This unusual upstage environment, which equally quickly comes to
represent all the forms of division in the play, must have posed quite a challenge to the original designers and technicians, as this area needed to be at
least partly practicable (that is, usable in the play's action), according to
Glaspell's stage directions throughout the script.[19] Her focus on the threshold
of the room, the large sliding door in the rear wall, serves to highlight its literal and figurative status as a point of transition: from the man-made to the
natural world, from salvation to danger, from male to female, from "inside" to
"outside." The liminality of this point carries over to the environment beyond,
however, with its concentration on the line separating dunes from woods, a
point of continual struggle that takes on even greater connotative, symbolic
value in the drama.

Glaspell connects the imagery of the station with that of the land beyond
through exposition on the history of the building. Bradford, one of the lifesavers, remarks sardonically that this was "a place that life savers had to turn
over to the sand" after the government decided "to build the new station and
sell this one" (106). He calls the station "an empty house, a buried house . . .
off here on the outside shore" (107). The act of burial by sand, linked to both
the station and the woods beyond, establishes a symbolic continuity, which
Glaspell also ties to the character of Mrs. Patrick. Bradford observes:

> I've seen her—day after day—settin' over there where the dunes meet the
> woods, just sittin' there, lookin'. . . . I believe she *likes* to see the sand slip-
> pin' down on the woods. Pleases her to see somethin' gettin' buried, I
> guess. (105)

Allie Mayo has formed the same conclusion:

> I know where you're going! . . . What you'll try to do. Over there. (*Point-
> ing to the line of woods.*) Bury it. The life in you. Bury it—watching the
> sand bury the woods. (111)

Mrs. Patrick can only see the act of destruction in the struggle between sand
and wood and rejects the significance of the coming spring. But Allie sees the
potential for new life and renewal and affirms the conventional seasonal interpretation: "Vines will grow over the sand that covers the trees, and hold it.
And other trees will grow above the buried trees" (112). The struggle has implications for the survival of civilization, emblematized by the community of
Provincetown, separated from the Outside by the protecting line of woods:

"Dunes meet woods and woods hold dunes from a town that's shore to a harbor" (113).

Glaspell literally embodies this image with Allie's arm gesture—holding it up and curving it around "to make the form of the Cape" embracing its port (113).[20] Glaspell's description of Allie in fact so closely links her with her surroundings that she becomes a virtual mirror of the play's environment herself:

> A bleak woman, who at first seems little more than a part of the sand before which she stands. But . . . one suspects in her that peculiar intensity of twisted things which grow in unfavoring places. (104–5)

Glaspell makes similar symbolic connections among character, objects, and setting in *Trifles* and *The Verge*, but the economy of the matrix here is unparalleled and is reminiscent of the imagist style of poetry, exemplified in the work of Amy Lowell and Ezra Pound, flourishing from about 1910 to 1917.

Glaspell establishes further scenic, characterological, and thematic ties in other components of her dramatic world for *The Outside*. The rest of the room seems to be virtually empty at the play's opening, with the possible exception of a portable stove and bed, which we learn have recently arrived (107), but which may also still be offstage (Glaspell is not explicit on this point). The production might have featured a comparatively shallow downstage area to allow for greater use of the upstage space. Other significant details within the room are a slanting wall and a door in the left wall,[21] through which we can see, at rise, two lifesavers working on a body (99). Glaspell thus ties this corporeal image of the human act of lifesaving to the symbolic matrix of the natural environment, a continual struggle between forces of regeneration and destruction: either between man and his environment or solely within nature.

Glaspell uses the opening moments of the play to establish the theme of gender and space that will evolve during the action. The initial dialogue between the men and their former captain, who enters soon thereafter, reveals through exposition that they have brought the body in from "force of habit" (101), although the space is no longer the official station. The men clearly do not feel welcomed by the new female inhabitants; one of the men mutters that, if the victim "did have any notion of comin' back to life, he wouldn't a come if he'd seen her [Allie Mayo]" (101). Tony, a Portuguese lifesaver who never worked in the former station,[22] observes the room, conveying his stereotypical assumptions about women:

> A woman—she makes things pretty. This not like a place where a woman live. On the floor there is nothing—on the wall there is nothing. Things— (*Trying to express it with his hands*) do not hang on other things. (103)

In addition to the women's "failure" to behave with proper deference (to "hang on" the men)[23] or to convert the space into a feminine sphere—a domestic space replete with ornament and homey comforts—they also refuse the putatively feminine role of nurturance and life giving within the space.[24] As Mrs. Patrick cries out to the men upon her entrance:

> You have no right here. This isn't the life-saving station any more. Just because it used to be—I don't see why you should think—This is my house! And—I want my house to myself!

Glaspell pits Mrs. Patrick's claims for dominance through ownership against the Captain's professional and moral determination:

> You'll get your house to yourself when I've made up my mind there's no more life in this man. . . . If there's any chance of bringing one more back from the dead, the fact that you own the house ain't goin' to make a damn bit of difference to me! (104)

Thus, Glaspell quickly establishes an agonistic dynamic that will operate on multiple levels. A structural balance develops between the status of the space (a station abandoned by its former male inhabitants) and the character who takes it over (a woman abandoned by her husband). The male drowning victim is clearly a lost cause from the start; despite the Captain's tenacious efforts, we sense no hope for his resuscitation. Rather, the ending of the play shows an alternative, symbolic resurrection. Mrs. Patrick and Allie Mayo, both of whom have given up on life, each help to "save" the other, much like Mrs. Hale and Mrs. Peters discover a bond through their examination of "trifles."

Late in the play Glaspell begins to pull the image clusters and themes together as the characters' trajectories move them toward better understanding and narrative resolution. One symbol of personal struggle reflecting the development of the trope of rejuvenation is incorporated in a speech of Allie's that exemplifies Glaspell's use of a quasi-poetic dramaturgy. Tying together men and the literal with women and the symbolic, Glaspell creates a powerful image through the use of a rhetorical strategy bordering on zeugma. Glaspell makes serious use of this device, which more often comically places in a relationship two words found in distinct contexts. Connecting the drowning victim to her husband who died in the frozen waters of the northern Atlantic, Allie gropes toward self-expression:

> That boy in there—his face—uncovered something . . . For twenty years, I did what you are doing. And I can tell you—it's not the way. . . . The ice that caught Jim—caught me. (*A moment as if held in ice . . .*). (109–10)

Thus, Glaspell pits the grittily real against the metaphoric, the male world of literal drowning and rescue against the female process of symbolic salvation. The juxtaposition of these structures gives them a balance of weight significant for the final impact of the play; as the men leave the station with the dead body, the women fully return to life. Looking out at the sand Allie exclaims: "And life grows over buried life! . . . It will. And Springs will come when you will want to know that it is Spring" (117). The spiritual rescue has succeeded, and its triumph seems every bit as critical as the fate of the unnamed sailor.

Given the power and clarity of such imagery, it is rather surprising that C. W. E. Bigsby attributes the tone of rejuvenation with which the play concludes to the male characters:

> At first, then, it seems that death has been triumphant, but the very commitment of the men, and in particular the Captain, serves to transform the life of one of those who had sought to immure herself in this remote house. Thus, in the end, they do, paradoxically, succeed in their efforts. (*Plays* 13)

This reading corresponds to many of Bigsby's thoughts on the play, which reflect a strange overall bias about Glaspell; Bigsby consistently acknowledges her achievement at the same time that he feels compelled to belittle it or cast it as male-determined. We might go so far as to say that Bigsby's reading of *The Outside* ironically parallels the play itself. His attitude toward Glaspell and her work mirrors that of the Captain and his men to Mrs. Patrick and Allie Mayo in both tone and form.

In his comments on the symbolic setting of *The Outside*, for example, Bigsby invokes O'Neill's successes with a similar technique, never acknowledging, as both Linda Ben-Zvi and Ann Larabee have demonstrated, that O'Neill may actually have been indebted to Glaspell for the strategy (*Plays* 12–13).[25] Bigsby's remark, "Outside of O'Neill it is hard to think of anyone in the American theatre who would have been prepared to take the risks which Glaspell does in *The Outside*" (*Plays* 14), exemplifies the hierarchy of comparison that always serves as his filter for analyzing Glaspell's plays. Bigsby uses male points of reference and assumes male authority, just as Glaspell's Captain assumes control over space and action without hesitation, "hurrying" onstage and commanding, "I'll take this now, boys" (100). The phallocentric rhetoric of Bigsby's dramaturgical analysis may even unwittingly mirror his critical perspective: "The play's dramatic tensions are discharged in a flood of language whose abstractions diffuse the clarity of the play's own symbolic system" (*Plays* 14).

Bigsby's critique of the "feminism" he sees in the play is equally narrow:

> The feminist dimension of the play lies in the extent to which the two
> central characters have allowed their lives to be drained of meaning when
> abandoned by their husbands. . . . The male life-savers have a simple de-
> termination lacking in the two women, whose story this nonetheless is as
> they stumble towards the realisation that their own relationship itself
> constitutes the beginning of the meaning which they fear but which co-
> heres even as they contend. (*Plays* 14–15)

By seeing the feminist implications of the play in terms of the hackneyed notion of women's lives revolving around men, Bigsby has missed most of the
work's nuances. Tony's observation that "things . . . do not hang on other
things" in the station corresponds to the women who no longer see themselves
as adjuncts of their husbands (103), a fact neither Bigsby nor the men seem to
perceive. It is clear that Glaspell wants her audience to think about the way
that men construct female identity and make assumptions about women's
roles. This is also conveyed in Tony's speech about a woman making a home
"pretty" as well as in the wryly comic action surrounding Bradford's sarcastic
request for coffee. Bradford simply assumes it is Allie's job to meet the needs
of the men who have invaded the station. Despite the fact that the Captain has
taken over the lifesaving efforts, he remarks, "Some coffee'd taste good. But
coffee, in this house? Oh, no. It might make somebody feel better" (105). Soon
Allie quietly returns with a fresh pot of coffee, just in time to see the men
leave, having realized their work is futile and having of course forgotten the
woman's work they in effect demanded (108).

Just as the men are oblivious to the women's sense of violation of their
home, Bigsby misses the entire connection between gender identity and
space—the struggle between the Captain and Mrs. Patrick over occupancy of
the station as well as the broader symbolic connections of the space with male
and female versions of salvation and renewal. And, although Bigsby grasps
Allie's inability "to sustain the coherences of language any more than she has
been able to bear the developments of experience" (*Plays* 13), he fails to notice
the way that language in the play is marked by gender, just as it will be to even
greater effect in *The Verge*. Allie's and Mrs. Patrick's fragmented speech, replete with dashes and syntactic gaps, anticipates that of Claire Archer as she
struggles to find expression for her state of mind. Allie's return to language reflects her rediscovery of an independent self and her renewed faith in the
power of life over destruction. Veronica Makowsky calls the women "female
modernist artists-in-life" ("Susan Glaspell" 57), highlighting Glaspell's dramaturgical innovation with dialogue, structure, and characterization in this
short piece.

The women's war with words is a struggle for symbolic dominance—
whose image of the line of demarcation separating dunes from woods, death

from life, will triumph. The Captain's damnation of Mrs. Patrick (104) and his desire to silence her by slamming the door (106) literalize the relationship of male dominance of space to control of language and even modernism itself; Bigsby follows suit by associating the women's "grammar" with "dislocation" (13), reading them and their expression as marginal. The male characters, intentionally, are not part of the symbolic linguistic realm of the play. They neither speak in poetic images nor envision their world through symbolism.

A review of Bigsby's evaluative strategies for Glaspell's work reveals the narrowness of his methodology, derived primarily from traditional New Criticism, which, in Veronica Makowsky's words, valued art that existed "timelessly, for and in itself, with little relationship to the life around it" ("Susan Glaspell" 64). How a given play (or playwright) compares—favorably or unfavorably—with other works (and other, usually male, dramatists) drives and shapes Bigsby's readings. The aesthetic criteria for these decisions are assumed to be known and shared by all his readers. While this phenomenon is hardly new to readers of feminist or other forms of oppositional criticism, it perhaps merits mentioning again here, for two reasons. First, to his credit Bigsby is one of the few scholars to have published extended commentary on Glaspell. The tone of Bigsby's remarks, however, is one that conveys a sense of definitiveness and critical superiority to the works under consideration. Glaspell endeavored to create an organic, theatrical whole, each component of which is structurally and thematically connected with the others. As such, the play represents not only a significant development in her own dramaturgy but also situates the drama within the larger framework of emerging American modernism.[26] Glaspell's exploration of Freudianism in *Suppressed Desires* and her use of expressionist techniques in *The Verge* give further evidence of the range of her engagement with modernist concerns and creative strategies, suggesting the potential for more examination of her work within this context. For the critics of the one-act play Glaspell's employment of these new techniques helped established her as a writer centrally engaged in the revitalization of this form.

Woman's Honor

In *Woman's Honor*, premiered by the Provincetown on 26 April 1918, Glaspell returned to a juridical setting, reminiscent of the murder backdrop of *Trifles* but striking a different tone, if not an altogether new theme. Christine Dymkowski believes the two plays share a concern "with the gulf between female and male experience, centering on the ways men define and limit the world in which both sexes live and the ways in which women challenge those definitions and limitations" (93). Additionally, however, this later play demonstrates not only Glaspell's stylistic range as a one-act dramatist but also her ability to incorporate the thematic concern with gender roles into forms as diverse as docudrama and farce.

Woman's Honor is perhaps the most broadly comic of her plays. It draws on such theatrical devices of French farce as a profusion of entrances and exits, mistaken identity, and repetition of action with minor variation. But, as Edwin Björkman astutely noted in his 1920 review of the published version, the play "is a farce that cuts more deeply than many tragedies" (519). Arthur Waterman dismisses the work in his 1966 analysis, the first book-length study of Glaspell. He comments that a play like Woman's Honor "is quite easy to write and produce" (69). This kind of critique says much about Waterman's refusal to read beyond surface style; the strength of the drama resides in the dexterity with which Glaspell weaves farcical action with serious social commentary.

The play is set in "a room in the sheriff's house which is used for conferences"; at rise we see two characters "in heated conversation," a lawyer, Mr. Foster, and the prisoner, Gordon Wallace, "an attractive young man" (120–21). Wallace has been arrested on suspicion of murder, but he is reluctant to provide an alibi, for doing so will necessitate his compromising the reputation of the woman he was with at the time the crime was committed. Glaspell uses rapid-fire exposition to provide both context and tone. Sternly remarking that "murder is no laughing matter"—a sure sign that, in this case, it will be—the lawyer "shoots" out a line which may well have already become a cliché of the murder-mystery genre: "Where were you on the night of October 25?" (121). He rebukes his client for "having loved a woman who'd let a man face death to shield her own honor," providing the titular phrase that will serve as the theme and variations for the remainder of the play. The woman in question, who has no name and never appears in the play, is yet another of Glaspell's "absent centers," a figure around whom the plot revolves but whose character is constructed totally by the action, description, and inference of others. In an astute reading of the play Susan Kattwinkel concludes that Wallace "insists on the protagonist's [the woman's] absence as essential for maintaining his place of privilege, if not his freedom" (43).

We learn that Foster's defense strategy will be to generate an heroic narrative with Wallace at the center, a story he has already calculatedly released to the press: the chivalric man protecting the woman he loves. He hopes that the image will appeal to the "jurors' wives," as "women just love to have their honor shielded" (123–24; my emph.). As with the title of her short story "A Jury of Her Peers," Glaspell here calls attention to the still all-male composition of juries in America and how this essentially renders impossible the equality and objectivity supposedly built into the trial process. She uses the dialogue of the two men to set up the social conventions that will be exploded later in the play: both the "old-fashioned" values of Wallace (121), who has "respect and reverence for women" (124), and the cynically misogynistic attitude of Foster, who claims women are "afraid they won't be looked upon as the pure noble sensitive souls they spend their lives trying to make us believe they are" (122).

Having fully anticipated that his planted news story will draw out the woman in question, whom he assumes will fulfill his expectations for feminine behavior, Foster displays no surprise at the arrival of the woman he assumes was Wallace's companion and who will confirm the alibi. The "Shielded One," however, is revealed to be someone else, only the first of many women who appear to lay claim to the role of (dis)honor. Glaspell sets this up perfectly; just as Wallace concludes his paean to femininity, expressing his readiness "to die to shield a woman's honor," the "Shielded One" enters with the stirring line, "No! You shall not!" (124). But the lawyer's self-satisfaction is cut short by the realization that Wallace has never met this woman before; the irony deepens when Foster, hearing the approach of someone else, quickly ushers her offstage, inadvertently "protecting the honor," so to speak, of the woman pretending to the pivotal role.

In quick and witty succession Glaspell brings on a series of female types, each identified in the script by a descriptive quality encapsulating her character, such as "the Scornful One" or "the Silly One." She thus repeats here the characterological technique she developed in *The People*, with the figures that arrive from around the country. Dymkowski calls the naming of the female characters in *Woman's Honor* "expressionistic" (93), but to me they also appear allegorical, like the identities of figures from a morality play like *Everyman*. Nothing in the style of *Woman's Honor* otherwise suggests theatrical expressionism, but much in the play mirrors the morality focus of the late medieval form, including the intermingling of humor with a serious message.

Each of the women in turn arrives at the office and settles in to stake her claim as the mysterious, and now notorious, woman. "Placidly" removing her knitting, the "Motherly One" claims that she was with "that young man" from midnight to eight a.m. of the day in question (128). And, as she leaves by another exit to inform her family that she won't be home for lunch, the "Scornful One" enters to begin a similar exchange with the lawyer. Not only does Glaspell wring considerable humor from the repetition of dialogue, but she also creates her first neat twist on the play's theme: this succession of women in fact arrives to "shield" the man, clearly having little concern for the shibboleth of "woman's honor." As Veronica Makowsky observes, the title concept becomes "a euphemism for the sacrifices by women that men need to maintain their self-affirming fictions of themselves and the society that they have created" ("Susan Glaspell" 59).[27] And in her little known "Feminist Manifesto" from the same period as the play Village poet and actor Mina Loy turns such euphemisms on their heads by telling women:

To obtain results you must make sacrifices and the first and greatest sacrifice you have to make is of your VIRTUE. The fictitious value of woman
as identified with her physical purity is too easy a standby. It renders her
lethargic in the acquisition of intrinsic merits of character by which she
could obtain a concrete value. (270)

Loy's challenge is precisely what underlies the discoveries being made by the
women in Glaspell's short comedy.

With the arrival of the "Silly One" we realize that Glaspell is not only
showing up the male characters, but she is also exposing extremes of female
behavior with her dramaturgical trademark of balance for all perspectives.
Throwing her arms around the lawyer, this woman exclaims "hysterically,"
"Darling! I cannot let you die for me!" (131), projecting her complete acceptance of the ideology of chivalric love. Susan Kattwinkel feels this is the character "with which Glaspell had the most trouble" (45), but it is not clear from
Kattwinkel's remark exactly what the dramaturgical or characterological issues here may be. Dymkowski reads the Silly One as a woman who "undermines her position" (93), as a woman we may take seriously, through her exaggerated demeanor. In contrast to these readings, I would say this
characterization is just as calculated on Glaspell's part as all the others. Taken
together, these figures' behavior comes to represent a composite portrait—albeit a virtual caricature—of women in early-twentieth century society who
are trying to fulfill their culture's expectations of them. As Kattwinkel observes, "*Women's Honor* uses stereotypes to engage the debate between life
philosophies," particularly the tension between Victorian femininity and
modern feminism, "in which Glaspell is interested" (47).

Bemusedly resigned to this parade of willing self-sacrifice, the men nevertheless react with "terror" to the news that many more women are now lined
up outside (132), waiting for the opportunity to present themselves as "the
one" (146). The lawyer exits to stem the tide, leaving Wallace with the Scornful One, who voices the first of the serious speeches that undermine the
chimera of honor: "Did it ever strike you as funny that woman's honor is only
about one thing, and that man's honor is about everything but that thing?"
(134). She continues to expose the logic of the very act of shielding, pointing
out that the honor itself has already been lost by the absent, unnamed
woman's actions. Wallace cannot save her honor: "You're dying to keep us
from knowing she is what she is" (135). Glaspell never defines exactly what the
Scornful One—or any of the other women—believe "woman's honor" to be.
Instead, like the expectations for women's behavior she exposes through the
allegorical parade, Glaspell leaves unspoken the specific details of the moral
codes underlying the action. Both are based on assumptions shared by the culture she depicts and the one for which she writes. The very indeterminacy of

these presuppositions allows for critique: the difficulty of pinpointing exactly what the characters intend may prompt us to question the social forces that drive these assumptions about gender roles.

As the women gather in the room, Glaspell creates the opportunity for them to discuss their motives for coming as well as to comment on the broader issues at stake. The Motherly One remarks that the women who "think a great deal about their honor" probably "aren't very well" or "haven't much else to take up their time" (137). The Scornful One, again cutting to the heart of the matter, announces, "Woman's honor would have died out long ago if it hadn't been for men's talk about it" (139). It is here that Glaspell reveals the patriarchal constructs underlying the convention; honor, like other aspects of women's identity, is a male creation foisted upon women but one that they accept begrudgingly or even embrace unquestioningly within male-dominated society.

One of the most interesting scenes in the play begins with the arrival of the "Mercenary One." Glaspell makes her audience think the discussion has reached its most fundamental level, with this character's announcement that "a business proposition is a business proposition. What a man needs and can pay for—" (142), in other words, that Wallace can buy their cooperation for his alibi. The other women roundly reject this idea, assuming the Mercenary One to be a prostitute. Glaspell quickly flips their complacency around, however, by having her state, "I'll have you know I'm an honest working girl! I heard they were going to take on another stenographer down here" (143). This revelation puts into perspective all the hypocritical self-satisfaction inherent in the magnanimity projected by each of the others. Whether money was to be exchanged for their participation in Wallace's case or not, each of the volunteers to the role of the unknown woman was guilty of a form of self-sale, as they quickly realize. Glaspell may have been equally effective in trapping her audience at this moment, forcing them to reassess their own assumptions not only about this particular character but also the other women's points of view.

The "Shielded One" calls on her "sisters" to "work out some way to free us from men's noble feelings" (146), introducing the spirit of female bonding into the play. As with *Trifles*, Glaspell focuses here on women's working together to solve problems facing all their lives. This realization allows them collectively to transcend an interest in which of them might be "the one," and indeed to strip the one of any special status in their campaign, since each is equally affected by the concept of women's honor. As Veronica Makowsky observes, "The women become interested in saving their sisters 'through Gordon Wallace' . . . they are now the subjects and he is the tool" (59). Yet, in keeping with her technique of parodying sensibilities taken to extremes, Glaspell reveals the newly formed ties of sisterhood to be a front for a more self-focused competitiveness among the women for the coveted role—ironically, for the "honor" of being publicly identified as "dishonored."

Ultimately, through the narrative of the last to arrive, the "Cheated One," the other women learn a new perspective on their goal, one motivated by a spirit of retribution rather than the cloak of self-sacrifice. The Cheated One tells the collected group:

> I've been cheated. Cheated out of my chance to have a man I wanted by a man who would have what he wanted. Then he saved my woman's honor. Married me and cheated me out of my life. I'm just something to be cheated. That's the way I think of myself. Until this morning. Until I read about Gordon Wallace. Then I saw a way to get away from myself. It's the first thing I ever wanted to do that I've done. (154)

The story of the Cheated One is remarkably brutal. Being in love with one man, she is sexually "taken" by another; the man she loves then rejects her because she is no longer "pure." She is "saved" by the man who most probably raped her, but this cheats her further by precluding any opportunity for her to have love or desire.

In response to the Shielded One's renewed call for sisterhood and the knowledge of "all those unfortunate women," the Cheated One replies, "The only unfortunate woman I'll think about is myself" (154). Glaspell seems to be suggesting a notion similar to the 1960s concept of "the personal is political" here: that the most compelling motives for action are grounded not in a philosophical idea about humanity but, rather, in the texture of personal experience. Dymkowski sees this debate as a choice "between personal and political objectives" (94), but I would argue for a position more synthetic—one that generates political solutions from personal roots. The Scornful One sees both the Cheated One and Wallace as needing the other women's help, and she calls on the others to "save *both* of them." The final stage directions provide strong semiotic images of how we are to conceive these characters. All the women except the Cheated One are huddled together; she is separate from them, "watching" them plan, and "trying now not to be cheated of what is being said" (155–56). Drawn to their union, she is still distinct from it, just as her personal convictions distinguish her from their philosophical goals, although the two may both soon be combined.

The men, however, have remained strongly separated from all the women's activity. As Dymkowski points out, by the end of the play the prisoner is "both marginal and powerless" (94), literally and figuratively. As he attempts to slip past the Cheated One to reach for the door, it swings open one last time, revealing "a large and determined woman" looming over him. He "staggers back to the Lawyer's arms," exclaiming, "Oh, hell. I'll plead guilty," providing a comic fillip before the final curtain (156). We realize that, for the women, Wallace has become as much of an anonymous symbol as women have allegorically been within the play, not to mention in the male chivalric tradition. Beneath the humor of this foray into the struggle over social roles, conventions, and interpersonal power lies Glaspell's sense, conveyed through the Cheated One, that we must not lose sight of individual experience in the rush toward idealistic action. This final message allows *Woman's Honor* to resonate with other pieces such as *The People,* a play similarly built around representative characters. At a moment when many of Glaspell's colleagues were immersed in ideological debate over politics, society, and other issues, she concentrated on the humanity underlying the rhetoric, a focus often lost in philosophical abstraction.

Tickless Time

In his influential study of technology and the pastoral ideal in America, *The Machine in the Garden* (1964), the literary critic Leo Marx points to *The Education of Henry Adams* (1907) as exemplifying "a sense of the transformation of life by technology" and argues that Adams "regards industrial power as an objective 'cause' of change in American society" (345). Although Marx sees the origins of the tension between technology and the pastoral even earlier in American writing, he traces the theme through Fitzgerald's *The Great Gatsby* (1925), explaining that "the machine represents the forces working against the dream of pastoral fulfillment" in America (358).

Glaspell and Cook's 1918 *Tickless Time* fits squarely within this American tradition; indeed, it is quite literally about machines in the garden, about man's slavish devotion to technology at the expense of natural truth, despite the latter's frustrating inexactness. While Cook and Glaspell may have known Adams's work, it is more likely that they wrote their short comedy as a dramatization of the philosophy of Henri Bergson. His 1889 treatise, *Essai sur les données immédiates de la conscience* (*Time and Free Will: An Essay on the Immediate Data of Consciousness*), "was primarily an attempt to establish the notion of duration, or lived time, as opposed to what he viewed as the spatialized conception of time, measured by a clock, that is employed by science" ("Bergson" 129).[28]

Tickless Time also seems to stand in response to then current concerns with the growth of industrialism in America, very possibly derived in part from Bergson, especially those voiced by the so-called young intellectuals. This group included Randolph Bourne, Van Wyck Brooks, Waldo Frank, and others closely connected with the Village periodical the *Seven Arts,* which flourished briefly between November 1916 and October 1917.[29] In such essays as Brooks's "The Culture of Industrialism" (1917) and James Oppenheim's "Art, Religion and Science" (1917) these cultural critics presented their views on the debate and tried to synthesize the current threads of the argument within a broadly conceived American cultural context.[30]

According to Brooks, "The world over the industrial process has devitalized men and produced a poor quality of human nature" (199), a state he explores in detail within the current American milieu. Oppenheim explicates the tension between the world of art and religion and that of science, specifically linking science with burgeoning technology:

> There is noticeable among many of our American artists, poets and religious-minded men a deep distrust of science, even, at times, an anti-scientific spirit. . . . And for the scientist they [the artists, etc.] have even harsher names: he is a mechanistic intellectual, he is uncreative . . . In short, he is like his offspring, the machine. (229)

And, while Oppenheim later in the essay presents a more balanced perspective, his description nevertheless captures well the spirit of opposition to technology central to the anti-industrial movement.

More recently, Casey Blake has explored this sensibility as depicted specifically by the young intellectuals. Blake maintains that these writers believed "industrialism had manufactured a commercial substitute for America's missing cultural center" and "had widened the gap between culture and practical life that dated back to Puritan New England" (*Beloved Community* 115). Juxtaposed to Blake's analysis, Glaspell and Cook's comedy emerges as being closely in tune with the sentiments of their contemporaries' writing and with Bergsonian theory as well as exemplifying Marx's longer literary tradition.

Tickless Time is set in "a garden in Provincetown," immediately evoking both the Edenic pastoral theme and the geographical connotations of a New England locale. The set pieces include part of a two-story house complete with fence and abundant sunflowers; prominently left-center stands a sundial on a shaft, to which is attached a large diagram of "Shadow Time" replete with numbers, dates, and graph (275–76).[31] We are quickly introduced to the major theme of the play, the conflict between natural truth and industrial progress, through the opening scene's opposition of the sundial ("natural" time) and the mechanical clocks in the home of Ian and Eloise Joyce. Glaspell and Cook quickly reinforce their theme by having Ian call Eloise to come outside "quick or you'll miss it" (276): he is referring to his perfection of the calibration of the sundial, while she thinks an airplane is flying overhead. In the 1910s airplanes had yet to achieve widespread commercial use and had just recently come into prominence as part of military activities of World War I, so the sighting of a plane would represent the latest in technological innovation.

Their dialogue soon pits Ian's new timepiece against the clocks they have been using:

The sun-dial is more than sun-dial. It's a first-hand relation with truth. . . .
When you take your time from a clock you are mechanically getting information from a machine. You're nothing but a clock yourself. (278)

Ian wants them instead to "live by the non-automatic sun-dial—as a pledge
that we ourselves refuse to be automatons" (280). Invoking the spirit of the
current debate, he opines that "it is clockiness that makes America mechanical and mean! Clock-minded! A clock is a little machine that shuts us out from
the wonder of time" (281). Swept up in the fervor of his own rhetoric, Ian decides to bury all the mechanical clocks in their possession and digs their grave
at the foot of the sundial. Certain of the couple's spiritual growth as a result,
he expounds to Eloise (in a line that sounds very much like Glaspell's writing
in plays like *The Outside* or *The Verge*), "You will go out to large things now
that you have done with small ones" (283).

Yet, as much as Eloise is drawn to Ian's commitment to this new way of
life, she is loath to give up the world linked to clocks: "Oh, Ian, *not* the alarm
clock! How would we ever go to Boston? The train doesn't run by the sun. . . .
I wanted to go to Boston and buy a hat!" (285). Beginning to panic, Eloise cries,
"I need a tick! I am afraid of tickless time!" (286).

Strongly echoing the dramaturgical strategy of *Suppressed Desires,*
Glaspell and Cook here duplicate the comedy of philosophical extremes. Henrietta's fervor for psychoanalysis is matched by Ian's devotion to "natural
truth"; the playwrights create a theatrical world where their audience is led to
see the ludicrousness of such fanaticism and to expect a more measured perspective to prevail in the end. The hermeticism of Ian's position indeed begins
to unravel when he explains his "Shadow Time" diagram, which is necessary
to correct for the variations on the sundial. To Eloise's surprise, she learns "the
sun only tells the right *sun*-time four days in the year" (301) and that she will
be reliant on a snakelike graph to help her determine the hour with anything
like accuracy (302). And, of course, the problems presented by sundown, rain,
and other natural phenomena that interfere with the sundial's function only
add to her frustration (303).

Glaspell and Cook also provide a number of secondary characters to the
plot who help them dramatize various contiguous elements of their theme.
Mrs. Stubbs, "a Provincetown 'native'" (288), is a stereotyped figure—unso-
phisticated, uneducated, but warmhearted. When she stops by to see the sundial, Eloise must explain to her that she cannot use it to gauge the proper time
for her husband's dinner: "You see, Mr. Stubbs is coming home by the mean
solar time of Philadelphia" (289). Mrs. Stubbs's inability to grasp the nuances
of the Joyces' new philosophy becomes the butt of the humor, as she takes their
concept of truth literally, assuming they are accusing her husband of mendac-
ity when they say, "How can you live by the truth if Mr. Stubbs doesn't work by

it?" (290). The fact that "the Government" is ultimately responsible for their having to conform to Philadelphia's time, coupled with the Joyces' injunction not to tread on the grave of the timepieces, drives Mrs. Stubbs away in distraction. Through her the dramatists demonstrate the gulf separating the practical matters of time from the Bergsonian abstractions as well as the humor of the catch-all excuse for the bureaucratic obstacles we face in our daily lives, "*them congressmen!*" (291).

Through the characterization of the Joyces' friends Eddy and Alice Knight we see the social implications of their fanaticism. When the Joyces bury the cuckoo clock that had been the Knights' wedding gift to them, they offend their friends deeply. Earlier in the play Eloise appeared smugly annoyed at Alice's gossiping, remarking, "Alice Knight has been here talking to me for an hour. I want to think that something's true" (278). But Eloise soon comes to appreciate the pragmatic grasp the Knights have of the long-term results of following sun time, when everyone else uses clocks. As Eddy comments dryly, "I'm afraid you'll be awful lonesome sometimes" (295).

The drama concludes on a manic note with the introduction of Annie, the Joyces' cook, who tries valiantly to conform to life without a clock in the kitchen. The stage directions describe her as "frantically rushing in, peeling an onion." She announces, "Starting the sauce for the spaghetti. Fry onions in butter three minutes" and then "wildly regards sun-dial—traces curved line of diagram with knife. Looks despairingly at the sun. Tears back into house" (298). Annie repeats her appearances and disappearances several more times as she attempts to prepare dinner, but she finally gives it up and announces she is quitting after the Joyces return her clock, but then change their minds and decide to bury it again (310). At this point Alice attempts to interject "sanity" by conveying an image of life without Annie. Alice tries to impress upon them the dire consequences of the loss of their servant and what it would mean to have to take on working-class activity:

> But you can't get anybody else! . . . What does any of the rest of it matter if you have lost your cook? (*To* Ian) Eloise can't do the work! Peel potatoes—scrub. What's the difference what's *true* if you have to clean out your own sink? (*Despairing of him she turns to* Eloise) Eloise, stop fussing about the moon and stars! You're losing your *cook!* (311)

With this dose of reality the Joyces determine that, not surprisingly, a more balanced perspective is in order, and they decide to live in a world of both truth (keeping the sundial) and social conformity (keeping the clocks). They embody the conclusion James Oppenheim presented (with regard to the perspective of those opposed to technology) at the close of "Art, Religion and Science":

They are looking to the past, they are seeing what once produced art, and they fear that art will die in any other sort of world. What they must do now is to look to the present, face reality as it is, . . . and . . . convert knowledge into vision, and the intangible and abstract into concrete forms. (234)

Heywood Broun's review in the *New York Tribune* indicates that he felt the play "easily the best . . . in the new bill," which also included O'Neill's *The Moon of the Caribbees* and Rita Creighton's *The Rescue*. According to Broun:

A sundial may not suggest all sorts of humorous possibilities, but the misfortunes of a couple who try to live by true time without recourse to machine-made approximations of truth are capitalized most amusingly. The play suffers slightly from being allowed to run just a shade too long, but perhaps it was timed by a sundial rather than a clock. ("Susan Glaspell and George Cook Have Bright One-Act Play")

For Broun it appears that the main theme of the play came through clearly and that the production afforded him the opportunity to show off his own wit in the review. It must be noted, however, that, despite the humor and philo-sophical balance achieved by the end of the play, the world of the drama (as with the worlds of *Suppressed Desires* and *Close the Book*) remains conserva-tive and its hierarchical structures of class and gender undisturbed. Glaspell and Cook create characters conforming to deeply rooted conventions of het-erosexual gender behavior, including an intellectually domineering and con-descending husband who masks his superiority through the guise of protec-tiveness ("I am here, dearest" [305]) and a flighty, shallow, and emotional wife who relies on her husband for guidance. Glaspell explodes such guises in plays such as *Chains of Dew,* in which the conventions of husband and wife roles are exposed as exactly that: poses perpetuated to conform to social pressures that warp the individual.

Cook and Glaspell create a semiotics of class position through dramatic language, characterization, and economic references; substandard English usage, intellectual inadequacy, and occupational status such as fisherman or cook mark the lower-class figures. But in Glaspell's solely authored works, such as *Inheritors,* a more sensitively crafted class consciousness emerges. She makes a point of condemning intellectual and economic snobbery in the young college student characters, for example. By contrast, the general social order in *Tickless Time* is never questioned any more than are the assumptions about what Eloise is (or is not) capable of doing. One is tempted to hypothe-size that Cook's influence may have been dominant in the collaborative process and that this might account for the depiction of gender and class roles.[32] There are discernible differences in the presentation of both gender and class between, on the one hand, Glaspell's own one-acts from this period, whether comic (*Woman's Honor*) or serious (*The Outside*), and those cowritten with Cook, on the other. There is little concrete evidence from their collaboration, however, on which to build any firm theories of influence, dominance, or creative process to account for these distinctions. Cook's own dramas, such as *The Spring*, do convey greater adherence to conventions of gender roles, lending some credibility to the idea that his sensibility prevailed.[33] These two early collaborations also share certain features with Glaspell's later collaborative effort, *The Comic Artist*, which she wrote with Norman Matson after Cook's death.[34] The three joint efforts, taken together, suggest that Glaspell's collaborative voice differed in some significant ways from her voice as a sole author. Future scholarship might explore in greater depth the dynamics of her collaboration within the context of a heterosexual relationship and the influence of that dynamic on the dramaturgy of those plays.

Another area of contention within this collaborative dynamic is the issue of humor. In his discussion of *Tickless Time* Arthur Waterman observes, "The play is very funny; it is as witty in its way as *Suppressed Desires*, which indicates that Cook had a decided flair for light comedy" (72). Why does Waterman conclude, because these two pieces are collaborations, that Cook was the source of the comic "flair"? Surely the broad humor of *Woman's Honor* or the slapstick chaos of the opening act of *The Verge* demonstrate Glaspell's skill in this arena? Waterman's conclusions are troubling, not only as they apply to *Tickless Time* but also to the other one-act pieces from this moment in Glaspell's career.

Thus, we might explore more pointedly some of the assumptions underlying the evaluation of these one-act plays by Waterman, who, along with Bigsby, is one of the few scholars to have commented on them in the aggregate. Waterman's summary of this phase of her dramatic writing is worth quoting at length:

> We might say that in these one-acts Miss Glaspell had not yet found her dramatic voice. Two are collaborations, one is close to the short story, the others try various techniques and attitudes ranging from witty satire to hesitant idealism. She had little difficulty writing satiric sketches, but she had yet to find the techniques that would permit her to say something serious in dramatic form, with dramatic focus. Her idealistic plays stumble into vagueness, and her comedies skim the surface of life. Moreover, these one-acts follow quite consistently the same kinds of plays other playwrights and little theaters were doing. They show, therefore, how dependent she was on her contemporaries; and they also indicate that Miss Glaspell was still looking for a dramatic tradition she could use.

Writing these short plays and also absorbing stagecraft by acting in and directing her own plays and those by others, she was learning to be a playwright in the best way possible. When the Provincetown Players moved to its new theater in 1918 . . . she was ready to write full-length plays. (73)

Waterman's analysis reveals a host of assumptions about dramatic writing, the one-act form, Glaspell's own trajectory as a dramatist, and the history of this theatrical moment. It seems clear that for him a playwright should have an identifiable and static style. Glaspell's having written in a range of forms, from farcical comedy to expressionistic, poetic drama, appears to Waterman to show an instability of technique; one could say with equal validity that these works demonstrate remarkable breadth. It is unclear what Waterman means by *dramatic focus;* perhaps this is a New Critical term that is assumed to be understood by all readers. Waterman appears not to have been able to see the seriousness in Glaspell's comic writing, as a play like *Woman's Honor* so vividly demonstrates.

Similarly, Waterman seems to assume, as does Bigsby, that Glaspell appropriated others' techniques, themes, and style in search of her own, although he brings no concrete evidence for this into his analysis. As mentioned earlier, other Glaspell scholars have more recently shown that the line of influence very likely pointed the other way—that Glaspell's writing was a source of inspiration to O'Neill and possibly others in the Little Theatre movement as well. Furthermore, within the history of modernism instances of collaboration and influence abound. *The Waste Land* suffers little denigration for the fact that Pound worked so closely with Eliot in its composition. Why, in Glaspell's case, should the fact that she participated in and benefited from her community's development of theatrical artistry translate to "dependence" and the absence of a distinctive voice in this criticism? Virginia Woolf explicates brilliantly the problem of women's writing and literary tradition in her essay "A Room of One's Own"; Waterman's sense that Glaspell "was looking for"— and, by extension, needed—a "dramatic tradition" reveals further bias about women dramatists' participation in the American theater, which had very few pre-twentieth-century models for women wishing to express their own concerns on the stage.

Finally, Waterman's closing comments demonstrate the prejudice against the one-act form itself that even the critics of Glaspell's own moment discuss. In using the traditional apprenticeship model to describe the "evolution" of her dramatic writing from the one-act to the full-length play, he perpetuates the sense that a one-act is a lesser work. Such commentary as Waterman's shows that the critical history of the one-act form in America, like the one-acts themselves, stands in need of excavation and recirculation. Moreover, Waterman's condescension, like Bigsby's, ironically mirrors the behavior of domineering men such as the Captain, Ian, and others who will emerge in Glaspell's later works, all of whom consistently belittle women and their creative or intellectual endeavors. The dismissiveness surrounding these first plays creates a critical atmosphere antithetical to their full and objective evaluation.

Glaspell's five solely authored one-acts: *Trifles, The People, Close the Book, The Outside,* and *Woman's Honor* stand as a remarkable group of works that, considered with the two collaborations, *Suppressed Desires* and *Tickless Time,* represent all that the proponents of the new American theater championed. Drawing on topical regional and national concerns, Glaspell explored dynamic combinations of dramatic form, character, and setting in an effort to capture the panoply of theatrical possibilities available to these new American stages. The seven pieces embody Glaspell's conviction that the theater could and should be a place strongly engaged with both intellectual movements and community interests as well as a locus for artistic innovation within the modernist avant-garde.

Bernice

Near the end of her affiliation with the Provincetown Players, Glaspell gave an interview to the *New York Morning Telegraph* about her work as a playwright. During the course of that 1921 discussion with reporter Alice Rohe,[1] Glaspell divulged that *Bernice* was "the only thing [she had] written in New York" (Rohe). Glaspell's early stories and novels were composed primarily in the Midwest; its small-town life informed her writing, often providing both geographical and social settings. After her marriage to Cook and their discovery of the quiet atmosphere conducive to creativity on Cape Cod, she did most of her work there and frequently used the Cape milieu as she had the midwestern one. Yet she also employed city settings, especially Chicago, Paris, and New York, for a number of her short stories and plays. Such stories as "Whom Mince Pie Hath Joined Together" (1913) and "At the Source" (1912) reflect a tension between the urban and the rural and suggest that, in Glaspell's imagination, different codes of behavior and lifestyles inhere to these contrasting regions of the United States.

Glaspell sets *Bernice* in New England, in an unnamed town a few hours outside of Boston.[2] She uses a New England setting, just as she will more explicitly in *The Verge,* to evoke the spirit of social convention and then exerts pressure upon it through the force of her characters' expressions of desire. The play chronicles the immediate aftermath of the death of the title character, as family and friends struggle to understand the significance of their loss. *Bernice* thus becomes the third Glaspell work, following *Trifles* and *Woman's Honor,* built around an absent central female character. The play is also infused with the aura of Manhattan. The city pervades the play through the character of Craig, Bernice's husband, a writer who is often absent because of his work. New York is figured as a center for publishing and as a locus of personal freedom or license—at least for Craig, who takes advantage of his business travel there to conduct extramarital affairs. Through the character of Bernice's close friend Margaret Pierce, however, Glaspell shows the potential for women's impact on urban locales. Margaret's activist work takes her there, and we sense that women's connections with modern, urban life allow for their personal growth in a way that rural life, such as that detailed in *Trifles,* precludes.

Glaspell also develops a subtler character dynamic, perhaps linked to her own experience of New York, within the play that particularly helps her define the relationship between Bernice and Margaret, whom Bernice had sent for right before her death. Glaspell's residence in Greenwich Village and membership in the Heterodoxy Club at the time she was writing the play no doubt influenced its composition, perhaps most significantly affecting the way she dramatized the bond between these two women. Whereas Mrs. Peters and Mrs. Hale form a connection based on temporarily shared experience in *Trifles,* for example, the link between Bernice and Margaret (and, to a less-developed extent, between Bernice and her lifelong caretaker, Abbie) exists on a more profound, nuanced emotional and psychological level. Moreover, although *Bernice* has not received much scholarly attention,[3] I would argue that it is a crucial piece for understanding Glaspell thematically and dramaturgically as well as for grasping some of the theoretical implications of her work.

In *Bernice* Glaspell demonstrates, more thoroughly than she could in her one-acts, how she uses her absent figures to foreground the construction of identity. She grapples with the impact of male infidelity on women more openly than in any of her other plays, joining her Provincetown colleague Neith Boyce, among others, in the dramatization of an issue that touched many Village lives. She highlights the importance of real friendships between women, something she herself cherished as she aged.[4] And she continues here to develop an element of her dramaturgy that is integral to her identification with stage modernism; her conception of the set as a vital part of a play corresponds to the rise of the *Gesamtkunstwerk* in the theater.

Although Glaspell was never explicit about the sources for her writing, she readily acknowledged the general connection between her own life and the work she produced.[5] While even her earliest stories feature friendships between women[6]—particularly those on the verge of adulthood, as were Glaspell and her close friend Lucy Huffaker when both were launching their careers—the bond in the play between Bernice and Margaret exists on a much deeper level. Glaspell describes the characters' relationship explicitly in the draft of a short story, "Faint Trails," which she may have written to experiment with ideas she developed in *Bernice* but neither dated nor finished:

> They had been friends since they were little girls. "Men may come and men may go, but I go on forever," Margaret had said to Craig when, just before he and Bernice were to be married he had said some laughing thing about permitting this friendship to continue. He couldn't have kept it from continuing. He knew that Margaret had had more of Bernice than any one else had had. (3)

The associations Glaspell observed and formed through her affiliation with the Heterodoxy Club, an organization whose members were some of the most educated creative and professional women of the era, may well have influenced her portrayal of the play's female characters.[7] The intensity of Margaret and Bernice's relationship reflects both the playwright's evolving skill in depicting subtleties of women's emotions and a sensitivity to the perpetually shifting dynamic of gender relations in the bohemian Village.

Judith Schwarz, in her study *Radical Feminists of Heterodoxy,* not only provides the history of the group but also demonstrates its members' relationship to the very fabric and ethos of Village life. Drawing extensively on the Heterodites' own writings, Schwarz shows how significant the group was for the formation of bonds among women. Their meetings created a space in which members could air a variety of political, social, and personal views, fostered the development of a sense of community, and called women to action around a number of radical causes. From 1912 to the early years of World War II the club met every other week for lunch, a guest's or member's speech, and discussion (1).[8] Schwarz documents the wide constituency of the organization: women of varying races, ethnicities, class backgrounds, sexual orientations, and professions belonged and came from "three distinctive . . . neighborhoods: Greenwich Village, the Lower East Side, and Harlem" (1). Many members were artists, writers, lawyers, doctors, or political activists. The Heterodoxy roll reads like a Who's Who of now famous women from the era: Charlotte Perkins Gilman, Agnes de Mille, Crystal Eastman, Rose Pastor Stokes, Mary Ware Dennett, Elizabeth Gurley Flynn, Beatrice Hinkle, Marie Jenney Howe, Mary Heaton Vorse, Henrietta Rodman, Mabel Dodge Luhan— one hundred and ten in all (ii). A number of members were closely associated with the theater, including Glaspell, Rauh, Mary Shaw, Zona Gale, Helen Westley, Margaret Wycherley, Edna Kenton, Fola La Follette, Maida Castellun, and others, making it one of the three most represented professions in the club (56).

The profound influence of Heterodoxy's membership on avant-garde American culture makes it all the more likely that it would deeply influence Glaspell's own creativity. Mabel Dodge Luhan, whose volumes of memoirs provide invaluable glimpses into the bohemian life of the era, describes the group as follows:

> There was a club called Heterodoxy for unorthodox women, that is to say, women who did things and did them openly. Women who worked. New York was largely run by women; there was a woman behind every man in every publisher's office, in all the editorial circles, and in the Wall Street offices, and it was the judgment and intuition of these that determined many policies, but they were anonymous women. They didn't

seem to mind being so, for the most part. . . . But the Heterodoxy were composed of women whose names were known. (143)

Dee Garrison, in her biography of Mary Heaton Vorse, makes an impressive claim for the influence of the club on the entire fabric of Village life in the period immediately preceding the writing of *Bernice:*

> Five organized groups gave birth to the prewar Village spirit—the Heterodoxy Club, the staff of the *Masses,* the Liberal Club, the Provincetown Players, and those who met at Mabel Dodge's Fifth Avenue Salon. (63)

Schwarz convincingly counters notions that Heterodoxy was little more than a social organization by documenting how central it was to the lives of its members. As an avowedly feminist group, whose feminism "was the one belief that united every member" (Schwarz 25), it played an important role in the sharing of ideas and information about issues of concern to its affiliates:

> pacifism, birth control, the Russian Revolution as seen first-hand by Heterodoxy women, health issues, infant mortality, anarchism as a political tool for social change, education of women, Black civil rights, disabled women, the Irish independence movement, free love, psychology. (Schwarz 19)

Members gained direct knowledge of the range of lifestyles and personal experiences of other women and developed keen interest in one another's work and achievements.

According to Schwarz, Glaspell joined the group early on (14), and she appears to have maintained her membership throughout her Village residency. In Glaspell's mostly blank diary for 1921 she notes a few significant events: a meeting with the actress Ruth Draper; her appearances in the role of Madeline in her play *Inheritors;* her learning to drive; and, on 19 February, a Heterodoxy meeting.[9] Glaspell's commitment to the club seems to match that of other members, including her friend Vorse. Dee Garrison claims that whenever Vorse was in New York, "she adjusted her schedule in order to attend Heterodoxy meetings." Garrison also adds a significant bit of information about Vorse's membership, however, that may also explain why Glaspell made little mention of her own affiliation: "In observance of her pledge of silence, and with the loyalty shown by almost every Heterodoxy member, she left no evidence of her experience there" (68).

In 1920 many of the members contributed pictures and encomia (frequently witty and personal) to a tribute album for Heterodoxy founder, Marie Jenney Howe, that reflect both their admiration of her and their dedication to the club overall. Glaspell's entry featured a reproduction of her portrait—the cover illustration for this book—and the following passage:

> I am Susan Glaspell. I am from the painting by William L'Engle—a friend. That is why I look so nice and refined. I didn't know when being painted, that I was going into Marie Howe's album. Otherwise I am sure I would have looked happier—she is a woman in whose album I like to be. Greetings! ("Heterodoxy to Marie")

Members attended Glaspell's 1921 play *The Verge,* and discussed the play with much excitement at a subsequent meeting. Glaspell's friend Hutchins Hapgood recalled the event in his autobiography, quoting the dancer Elise Dufour, who had been in attendance:

> It seemed to me, while these women were talking about *The Verge,* that I was in church, that they were worshiping at some holy shrine; their voices and their eyes were full of religious excitement. (Hapgood 377)

Given the club's impressive roster of members, we can assume Glaspell admired her colleagues and their work as much as they did hers.

While *Bernice* has no overt references to Heterodoxy, it is certainly possible to hypothesize that Glaspell's understanding of the range of female experience, reflected throughout her plays but especially strongly here, was informed by her lengthy membership in this organization. *Bernice* is very much a play about the differences between men and women and the way that each sex processes events and forms relationships. The sense of potential for intimacy—intellectual, psychological, and emotional—between women pervades the drama in a manner unique to the Glaspell canon. Furthermore, through the conflicting visions of Bernice presented by Craig and Margaret, Glaspell gives us two profoundly different images of woman: the conventional patriarchal construction of an idealized wife and that of an independent being giving of herself and her love only as she chooses. By juxtaposing these roles, Glaspell foregrounds the social pressure surrounding gender identity and gives her audience alternative perspectives from which to see these constructs.

Glaspell uses the distinctive plot device of beginning the play after the title character's death to facilitate the development of her other figures, who reveal themselves by responding to information about Bernice's demise and by interacting with one another. We learn that on her deathbed Bernice has asked Abbie, the family servant, to tell her husband that she has committed suicide. When Margaret hears this from the husband, Craig, she cannot believe it of her friend, whom she associates with life itself. Eventually, she convinces Abbie to tell her the truth, that Bernice indeed died from natural causes; we have already learned in passing that Bernice had been suffering from stomach ulcers for some time (180). As Veronica Makowsky observes, "she may well have been killed by repressed anger, the good girl's disease" (71). Margaret certainly believes this at first; she thinks that Bernice must have acted out of hate, because Craig had been unfaithful to her. But this, too, runs counter to her sense of Bernice. Eventually, Margaret realizes that Bernice had reason for leaving Craig with a lie, that Bernice left each of her loved ones with a special image of herself that she knew would be of greatest value to them.[10]

Although the production's first critics grappled with Bernice's character, trying to grasp it through her depiction by those who loved her, it eluded the reviewers, in large part because her friends and family speak of her via ephemeral images: "Life broke through her—a life deeper than anything that could happen to her" (173); "Everything about her has always been—herself. That was one of the rare things about her" (183). Bernice, intentionally, I believe, remains a cipher, for who she was is less important than how she affected those around her. In this way *Bernice* prefigures some of the important feminist drama of the 1970s that portrays women's identity only through the language of others. Janelle Reinelt has described these plays, such as Simone Benmussa's *The Singular Life of Albert Nobbs* and Marguerite Duras's *India Song*, as ones in which central female characters as subjects neither "take stage" nor "take place." Glaspell's drama, however, differs significantly from them. Although her title character is similar to what Reinelt calls "a supreme object of desire," her physical absence makes her construction by others all the more apparent (49). Moreover, as Susan Kattwinkel has observed, "with an absent protagonist the spectator's desire to identify is constantly deferred" (51).

Glaspell's repeated use of this device in her realist plays does not make them less realistic; rather, this technique subtly disrupts verisimilitude, creating between the audience and the characters a critical distance distinctive in realist dramaturgy. As the discussion of *Trifles* has detailed, Glaspell's use of realism in the context of the work of the Provincetown Players does not conform to some of the paradigms identified by recent critics in their problematizing of realism and feminism. While Glaspell's disruption of identification with her absent centers clearly predates and differs from Brechtian dramaturgical and performance techniques, it does accomplish related ends: that its audience recognize the ideological constructedness of character. And, once the spectator realizes that she is witnessing the bricolage of absent figures, she may begin to think about the constructedness of all character identity, which is a key part of the political agenda underlying Glaspell's dramaturgy.

In addition to the unusual form of her opening scene, which combines traditional exposition with the destabilizing absence of the title character, Glaspell employed another notable technique in *Bernice* by subtly manipulating the time-honored literary device of the romantic triangle. Most often, this trope depicts the rivalry of two men over the same woman. What distinguishes *Bernice* is Glaspell's decision to build her drama around the fight between Margaret and Craig over the woman they both loved. In other words, Glaspell skews the traditional homosocial relation between two characters of the same sex to highlight the struggle for power in a society deeply conflicted over the changing dynamic of gender relations.

Bernice shares additional dramaturgical strategies with other Glaspell plays, particularly *Trifles*. Like the earlier one-act, the full-length drama places in question the actions and identity of an absent female character. Edna Kenton, a Provincetown member and Glaspell's close friend and Heterodite, wrote in her chronicle of the group that *Bernice* was a "spiritual mystery" (133); like her earlier one-act work in the mystery genre, moreover, Glaspell here makes the discovery of the "truth" about Bernice the throughline for the drama. As Jackie Czerepinski has observed, "ultimate knowledge" in this play, as in *Trifles*, "comes from feeling, from an understanding based on shared experience" (148). Glaspell will use a similar strategy in the exploration of the motives of Alison Stanhope, the dead poet at the center of her Pulitzer Prize drama *Alison's House*.

Bernice also anticipates *The Verge* in its experimentation with fragmented dialogue, a technique that Glaspell had also explored in *The Outside*. As Margaret struggles with her ultimate realizations about what Bernice has meant to those who loved her, Glaspell expresses her thoughts with dashes and imagistic phrases:

> . . . Yes—I know now. I want to know. Only—there are things not for words. Feeling—not for words. As a throbbing thing that flies and sings—not for the hand. (*She starts to close her hand, uncloses it.*) (229)

Margaret here exemplifies the struggle faced by many of Glaspell's female characters to find a language, "outside" of conventional communication, gestural as well as verbal, to capture the complexity and depth of their discoveries.

The first point of contact for an understanding of the central character in each of these plays is the physical environment. We come to know the women through the rooms in which they have lived, rooms that reflect their identities. In fact, as with many of Glaspell's plays, the scenic spaces are virtually anthropomorphized; certainly, they are as important as the characters who inhabit them, becoming a carapace or even a mirror of being:

> *Scene:* The living room of Bernice's house in the country. You feel yourself in the house of a woman you would like to know, a woman of sure and beautiful instincts, who lives simply. (159)

Czerepinski rightly notes that "Bernice first emerges as a palpable and powerful figure through the setting" (146). Bernice's father underscores the relationship between the title character and her environs: "Bernice made this house. . . . Everything is Bernice. . . . You can't get Bernice out of this room" (160).

Like *The Outside, Bernice* visually presents us with liminality—a permeable border between indoors and out, between domesticity and nature. Glaspell describes the rear wall of the set as composed of "French windows lead[ing] directly out of doors. On each side of this door is a window thus opening almost the entire wall to the October woods" (*Bernice* 159). Within the house, however, we confront a very different boundary: the closed door upstage left that represents the barrier between life and death, the door leading to the room in which Bernice has been laid. One by one the characters must interact with this threshold. Significantly, we cannot see through this door; we cannot get even a glimpse into the room on the other side. Bernice's death is initially unfathomable, and the door becomes a projection of Bernice in death—an object approached with conflicting emotions, shrunk from yet reached for. Glaspell writes that Margaret "puts out her hands, but she does not even touch the door and when she cannot do this she covers her face and, head bent, stands there before the closed door" (218–19).

As in *Trifles,* Glaspell sets up the atmosphere of mystery in the opening moments of the play. Even before Margaret arrives at the house, Bernice's father reminds Abbie that his daughter had said, "Margaret sees things." Abbie expresses "apprehension" and "fright" at this, since Margaret Pierce might be able to expose the servant's promise to lie for her mistress (to "pierce" the lie) as well as to unravel the motivation for Bernice's falsehood (161). It may be more than coincidental that Glaspell originated the role of Abbie herself, creating a performative corollary to her authorial negotiations among her characters. Abbie thus generates the suspense of foreshadowing and provides the foil that reveals the other characters.[11]

Glaspell soon introduces these additional figures: first Craig and his married sister, Laura Kirby, then Margaret. Laura, initially described as "sensible" (162), quickly shows herself to be the highly conventional and narrow-minded kind of woman Glaspell depicted in a number of her stories and plays, perhaps most fully and forcefully with Adelaide in *The Verge.* For Laura, Bernice's difference counts against her: "It isn't as if Bernice were—like most women. There was something—aloof in Bernice . . . things that might have hurt another woman—" (177–78). Laura alludes here to Bernice's seeming indifference to Craig's infidelities. She implies that Bernice's love for her brother may not have been terribly strong and later tells Margaret that Bernice herself was responsible for Craig's behavior:

Laura: . . . It's unfortunate Bernice hadn't the power to hold Craig.
Margaret: Hadn't the power to hold Craig!

Laura: She didn't want to—I suppose your scoffing means. Well, she should
have wanted to. It's what a wife should want to do. . . . I don't agree
with you that Craig is especially vain. He's a man. He does want to affect—yes, dominate the woman he loves. And if Bernice didn't give him
that feeling of—

Margaret: Supremacy.

Laura: There's no use trying to talk with you of personal things.

(186–87)[12]

In this scene Glaspell neatly demonstrates how the ideological pressure
to conform to specified gender and social roles comes not only through men
but also through women who have internalized patriarchal views. Laura, on
some level, realizes how her attitudes sound to Margaret, and she sidesteps
further discussion of this issue. Margaret has already heard Craig's version of
this same rhetoric, in a scene that echoes "Faint Trails" in its discussion of
one's grasp of another in a relationship—the sense of having "had" someone,
with its connotations of intimacy, shared understanding, and possession:

Craig: . . . I never *had* Bernice.

Margaret: Oh, wasn't it wonderful to you that beneath what you "had" was a
life too full, too rich to be *had?* I should think that would flow over
your life and give it beauty.

Craig: I suppose a man's feeling is different. He has to feel that he moves—
completely moves—yes, could destroy—not that he would, but has the
power to reshape the—

Margaret: Craig! "Reshape" Bernice!

(173–74)

Glaspell clearly uses Margaret in a classically choric role with these other characters, having her defamiliarize the ideas they present so that the audience sees
that even such conventional attitudes are not universal.

Later in the play, after learning from Abbie the "truth" (i.e., the version
she was ordered to tell him) about Bernice's suicide—which Craig interprets
as a romantic gesture of anguish over his affairs—he returns to this topic:

Craig: . . . Margaret, I wish I could tell you about me and Bernice. I loved
her. She loved me. But there was something in her that had almost
nothing to do with our love.

Margaret: Yes.

Craig: Well, that isn't right, Margaret. You want to feel that you *have* the
woman you love. Yes—completely. Yes, every bit of her!

Margaret: So you turned to women whom you could have.

Craig: Yes.

Margaret: But you "had" all of them simply because there was less to have.
    You want no baffling sense of something beyond you.

                                                                (197)

Through Craig and Margaret, Glaspell dramatizes conflicting images of relationships. She contrasts those adhering to the notion that the woman gives all
of herself to her mate (with, significantly, no mention of what the man gives
in return), to those presenting the idea of equality and the maintenance of independent identity in a partnership between two people who love each other
(notably here with no reference to sexual identity).

    In her later play *Chains of Dew* (as well as in her novel *Ambrose Holt and
Family*) Glaspell develops another man like Craig in the figure of Seymore
Standish. Like Standish (and like Jig Cook), Craig is a writer who has somehow not broken through to a clarity and impact his supporters desire; his
words cannot "pierce," despite the fact that people "continue to look to *writers*" for insight (202). Margaret remarks:

> You write so well, Craig, but—what of it? What is it is the matter with
> you—with all you American writers. . . . A well-put-up light—but it
> doesn't penetrate anything. . . . Craig, as you write these things are there
> never times when you sit there *dumb* and know that you are glib and
> empty? (199)

These real and fictional figures also share male egos that seem to require considerable attention. The men turn to other women to build up their sense of
self, and it is only through the sacrifice of their wives that they have a chance
to achieve greater potential as artists, although, significantly, this potential is
never fulfilled in the works themselves.[13]

    Bernice is unique among Glaspell's plays, however, for acknowledging the
importance of emotional bonds external to marriage. The close, compelling
ties between Bernice and Margaret correspond to the bonds the Heterodoxy
Club fostered among its members. Moreover, the play suggests additional benefits from these associations by recognizing the centrality of sisterhood to personal achievement. Thus, Glaspell puts another spin on conventional literary
tropes through her refiguring of the kind of relationship that prompts individuals to achieve. It is the connection with Bernice that motivates Margaret;
rather than the traditional hierarchy of "behind every great man is a woman,"
a pairing of equals facilitates Margaret's sociopolitical accomplishment.

    Glaspell never explicitly defines the nature of Bernice and Margaret's
friendship. We sense that it is of long standing and that it was extremely important to both. We learn that Bernice has sent for Margaret near the time of
her death but not for Craig, whom "she didn't want to hurry . . . away from

New York" (168). Father remarks that "Margaret will get here the quickest way. She always came to Bernice when Bernice needed her" (161). We also learn from Father an interesting detail, easily passed over, about the house and Bernice's activities in it shortly before her death: "She had done over your [Craig's] room upstairs. And hers too. They both look so nice and fresh. And she was just starting to do some things to Margaret's room" (167). While separate rooms for Bernice and Craig might not be especially noteworthy, particularly given Craig's need for a place to write, it is striking that Bernice maintained in her home a room specifically designated as Margaret's.

It is unclear if Margaret has a home elsewhere; she appears a peripatetic individual, devoted to her work. Perhaps drawing on the strong political convictions of many of the women Glaspell encountered in the Village and through Heterodoxy, she makes Margaret an activist. In *Bernice,* as with the character of Madeline in *Inheritors,* Glaspell shows that she strongly admires women who are committed to democracy and social change. Father has a vague sense that Margaret is involved in "some labor things" in Chicago (167), and Margaret later reveals she is "trying to get out of prison all those people who are imprisoned for ideas" (187). This, too, proves a point of controversy with the conservative Laura, who does not "sympathize" with Margaret's position, although she claims to "see" it. Margaret responds: "If you did see, you would have to sympathize. If you did see, you would be ashamed; you would have to—hang your head for this thing of locking any man up because of what his mind sees" (187).

These details suggest Margaret may be affiliated with the Industrial Workers of the World (IWW), a group with many supporters in the Village, including Glaspell and Cook's friend John Reed, who had staged the Paterson Strike Pageant with the IWW's help in Madison Square Garden in 1913. She might also have been connected with the Free Speech League, an organization that supported writers and public lecturers with legal and financial resources.[14] Many radical activists, as well as the workers they championed, were persecuted under the Espionage and Sedition Acts of 1917, which they believed censored freedom of speech. Craig calls Margaret "a wreck of free speech" (192), and her own brief depiction of her cause bears unmistakable resemblance to this repressive campaign against activists, which would have been fresh in Glaspell's mind from the recent trial of Heterodite Rose Pastor Stokes (Schwarz 40–41) as well as others who were imprisoned for their written and spoken objections to World War I (Schwarz 40–41).[15]

Margaret's description of her life and work shows how important her relationship with Bernice was to her sense of completeness: "It's been the beauty in my life. In my busy, practical life, Bernice—what she was—like a breath that blew over my life and—made it something" (183). She strikes out at Laura for the latter's narrow perception of the emotional loss of Bernice: "Your brother has lost his wife! That's all *you* see in it!" (185). Glaspell describes Margaret's reaction to the news of her friend's death as being "like blood from her heart" (171). In her disbelief at the story of suicide she has heard from Craig, Margaret insists she has "a *right* to know" the truth and turns to Abbie for information (184), crying, "Don't shut me out like this! *She* wouldn't shut me out. Bernice loved me" (181).

These expressions of intense emotion provide a cumulative sense of Margaret's profound love for and attachment to Bernice, which Glaspell contrasts sharply to Craig's more self-involved response. Glaspell also makes it clear, when Craig pumps her for personal information, that Margaret has no other emotional bond in her life:

Craig: You ever wish you had children, Margaret?
Margaret: Yes.
Craig: (*Roughly*) Well, why don't you have?
Margaret: (*Slowly*) Why, I don't just know, Craig. Life—seems to get filled up
     so quickly.

(192–93)

Laura also has questions about Margaret's life choices and speaks allusively of her unconventionality: "You who have not cared what people thought of you—who have not had the sense of fitness—the taste—to hold the place you were born to" (189). Laura is not explicit about this "place" or why Margaret's avoidance of it shows a lack of "taste," and Craig does not push further with his queries about her not fulfilling her maternal interests. Glaspell's ambiguity about Margaret's personal life renders her an enigmatic figure; the one indisputable anchor in her world is her tie to another woman. Thus, Glaspell seems to point toward a personal context for Margaret outside the confines of established heterosexual marriage. We might look to the struggle between Craig and Margaret, who seem throughout the play to be battling over their knowledge of and closeness to Bernice; Margaret's pressing need to resolve the matter of Bernice's death, such that her sense of the woman she loved, and all that means to her sense of self, can be confirmed; and all the veiled comments and provocative scenic detail to support such a reading. Glaspell may have been calculatedly reticent about overtly depicting Margaret as a lesbian, given her sensitivity to dominant cultural views on sexuality beyond the confines of Greenwich Village bohemia; it is equally likely that the indeterminacy creates a greater range of interpretive possibilities for an audience attuned to a panoply of life choices.

Craig believes the suicide "has given Bernice to me" (226), that she has acted totally because of him, and Glaspell hints that this lie will provide Craig with enough emotional support to spur him to greater artistic heights: "Now—

of course it is another world. This comes crashing through my creativity" (227). Yet the fact that Craig remains unenlightened, that he will probably never know the truth about Bernice and her death, is significant. Margaret, after discussing her knowledge of the truth with Abbie, decides not to inform Craig (212–13), as the information will only take something more away from him. In this way Margaret colludes with Bernice, having the superior grasp not only of Craig but also, more important, of Bernice. The bond among women, with its foundation in an innate sensitivity to honesty and "rightness," emerges foremost from Glaspell's drama. As in her earlier work *Trifles,* Glaspell here reinforces the notion of women's shared understanding and communion to support action from within, but still fully aware of, the male-dominated society.

We realize that, almost magically, Bernice has provided the gesture each of the characters needs to go on. In the closing moments of the play she gives the victory to Margaret:

Father: . . . I was all alone in there a few minutes—right at the last. Bernice said one last word, Margaret. Your name.
Margaret: She called to me?
Father: No, I wouldn't say she called to you. Just said your name. The way we say things to ourselves—say them without knowing we were going to say them. She didn't really say it. She breathed it. It seemed to come from her whole life.

(220)

Glaspell also gives Margaret the closing speech: "Oh, in all the world . . . has there been any beauty like the beauty of perceiving love?" (230).

When Margaret grasps the full dimension of Bernice's final choices, it is as if a veil has been lifted. She is able to break through the barrier between herself and her friend, and she opens the door and enters the room where Bernice has been laid. Immediately thereafter, Craig and Abbie set about restoring the living room to its original order. When Margaret reenters the main room, she leaves the door into Bernice open—a gesture that suggests she is again part of and accessible to them all; Father reenters from his study to announce, "Oh, you have given the room back to Bernice" (229). Glaspell includes the physical space as strongly in the resolution of the play as in its opening, with Margaret having made the crucial final gesture.

Writing in Greenwich Village, surrounded by individuals confronting changing sexual codes, Glaspell fashioned a drama to reflect this upheaval. While Craig's infidelities help Glaspell expose the hypocrisy of those familial and social conventions,[16] Margaret's failure to conform to norms of womanly behavior exemplifies the movement toward a new morality. While Glaspell leaves the degree of Margaret's transgression vague, she creates through her a compelling alternative to the traditional dichotomy of women's professional and personal lives. Margaret is neither a wife submerged by her husband's interests nor a pinched, ineffectual spinster but, rather, a fully adult woman engaged in the life of her times.

Most contemporary critics have discussed *Bernice* in only two contexts: historically, as the author's first full-length drama; or stylistically, as her second major work (after *Trifles*) to feature an absent, central female character (Dymkowski 96–98). Bigsby counts it, along with her later play *The Comic Artist,* among her weaker works for "a tendency to a somewhat mawkish sentimentality" (*Critical Introduction* 26). At the time of its March 1919 production, however, the reviewers expressed great enthusiasm for it. John Corbin rhapsodized in the *New York Times:*

> The little play is quite beautifully simple and deft . . . tender and heart-wise as Barrie at his best. . . . If the Provincetown players [*sic*] had done nothing more than to give us the delicately humorous and sensitive plays of Susan Glaspell, they would have amply justified their existence. ("Seraphim")

The *Boston Evening Transcript* deemed Glaspell "the ablest playwright contributing to their [the Provincetown Players'] stage" ("Miss Glaspell's Long Play"). The London production (1925) evoked a similar response. One reviewer called it "exquisite" and added, "Through 'Bernice' runs a streak of rare beauty" ("The Gate Theatre Salon"). Commenting on the published version, Edwin Björkman noted the drama's "haunting atmosphere and the provoking significance of the work as a whole" ("The Theatre" 519).

Interestingly, the only negative commentary from Glaspell's contemporaries came from women, namely Margaret Anderson, editor of the influential Greenwich Village journal the *Little Review,* and her lover and editorial associate, "jh" (Jane Heap).[17] Although she complimented the production itself, Anderson challenged Glaspell to "take up with her" a discussion of the dramaturgical core of the play, which she found wanting ("Susan Glaspell's New Play" 59).

> I sat tense with interest up to the middle of the last act. The alleged drama centers in the husband. *But there is no drama.* That is all I wish to prove.
> You must either work through cause and effect to get drama, or you must present dramatically the foibles of a human being who dramatizes himself with charm, intelligence or power; or a human being who tries to dramatize himself and fails. . . . All playwrights who deal with ideas . . . or with propaganda work in the first realm. Susan Glaspell does. Therefore she must present some intellectual or psychic conflict.

Taking for her hero a man without power she gives him power through the report, carefully arranged for by the wife before she dies, that she has killed herself because she loves him. . . . You can't make drama out of this kind of lie without giving your discriminating audience the feeling that your play is without context. . . . *Some one* must be "on" to what is happening,—either a character in the play or you yourself when you write. (58–59)

Anderson's highly nuanced and sophisticated argument against Glaspell's narrative sparked considerable controversy; in the subsequent issue of the *Little Review* she published four follow-up opinions, including a second of her own.[18]

One of the rebuttals to Anderson, entitled "A Great Drama," indeed deemed the piece "an important play, superbly acted" (Barnes 55) and called it "daring" (53), but the author conceded Anderson's position by acknowledging, "The *denouement* is the weak part of the play if one judges it by the high standards of knowledge and intelligence which the author herself has set and maintained up to that point" (55). Another response, in letter form, came from Philip Moeller, a director and founder of the Washington Square Players. Calling *Bernice* "an important play," Moeller launched forth:

> It is you, Margaret Anderson, who have rushed in fluttering your mental wings into a very hell of theory. . . . I don't think Miss Glaspell has ever written anything but well, and often spendidly [*sic*], and in "Bernice," to my mind, so well and spendidly [*sic*] that her play I think takes rank amongst the pitifully few plays that count done by us Americans. (56)

jh then joined the fray, opening her remarks ingenuously:

> I believe there is a controversy on at present over Susan Glaspell's "Bernice." It isn't a play, it bears no relation to drama as an art. It is quite patent that neither the emotional nor intellectual conception of "Bernice" presented itself to the author in the form of drama but as a psychological problem, a problem to be worked out in words. (63)

Clearly, both Anderson and jh had strong views about what does and does not constitute drama. An analysis of those attitudes, potentially reflective of the feelings of an important group of Village artists and intellectuals, certainly merits further study. For the purposes of the present discussion, however, what appears most intriguing is the way the critics (Anderson in particular) frame their discussion: what they include and what they omit in their analysis of the play. Most notable is the conflict between how they see the play working in performance, on the one hand, and how they analyze its characters and action intellectually, on the other. While each commentator lauds the actress Ida Rauh highly for her portrayal of Margaret Pierce—Heywood Broun called her "magnificent" ("Realism")—each totally ignores the work of James K. Light as Bernice's husband, Craig.[19] Yet the critics' commentary suggests they see Craig as the pivotal character; some leave out discussion of Margaret's role altogether.

In attempting to account for this disjunction, I would suggest that the critics may espouse precisely those conventional attitudes that Glaspell has chosen to expose. Thus, Anderson's inability to see the drama stems from the fact that she could not grasp the irony inherent to Glaspell's denouement. This irony requires the audience to understand the nuances of the triangular character dynamic among Bernice, Margaret, and Craig as well as Bernice's refusal to privilege her husband and her marriage above all other relations in her life. The critics' focus on the husband may betray an unexamined assumption that matrimony trumps all other relationships for a woman and that a male character must be at the center of a drama. Such presumptions preclude their realizing that Glaspell subtly disrupts that premise. There is a direct connection between the impact of Ida Rauh's performance and her role in *Bernice,* just as there is between Light and his: Glaspell wrote Margaret as the strong, pivotal role and made her the character who endures a dramatic crisis, thereby fulfilling Anderson's concept of "real drama." By contrast, Craig is intended to appear vapid and self-absorbed. Precisely because of the tenacious power of conventional attitudes, the critics had to override their own aesthetic response to Craig's vacuousness. Rauh simply, however impressively, fulfilled Glaspell's aim to have Margaret be the most striking presence onstage.

The male reviewers' response to Craig demonstrates their empathic understanding of him; Corbin remarks, "We all of us know—all of us, that is, who know masculine vanity" ("Seraphim"). It is more difficult, however, to explain Anderson and Heap's position. Anderson announces, "The alleged drama centers in the husband" ("Susan Glaspell's New Play" 58), and she focuses her critical attack on Bernice, whom she deems an "uninteresting Pollyanna" ("Neither Drama nor Life" 60). Anderson's admonition to Glaspell that "*Some one* must be 'on' to what is happening,—either a character in the play or you yourself when you write" willfully ignores the character who fulfills that precise function, Margaret.

In her analysis of the *Little Review* and other magazines edited by women earlier in the century Mary Biggs tries to account for the seeming contradictions between the lives of Anderson and Heap—who lived openly as lesbians and embraced some feminist issues of their time—and the positions they often took in print. Biggs believes Anderson's feminism, like her anarchism, was a passing fancy—that she moved from one *ism* to another in rapid succession. Furthermore, Heap's influence, combined with that of Ezra Pound, "probably pulled *LR* further away from social concerns and toward aesthetic issues and innovation" (192–93), thus paralleling the struggle occurring simultaneously within the Provincetown Players between the dramatists favoring the new poetic drama and those who continued to champion social realism.[20] Biggs amply demonstrates, but cannot fully account for, "the odd biases and male-identified character of this . . . major literary journal . . . woman-founded and edited" (193). However perplexing their position on *Bernice,* it appears clear that Anderson and Heap, like Laura in the play, failed to recognize the importance of Margaret—ironically, a character not too different politically from Anderson herself early in her career. They also seem oblivious to the subtle feminist theme of the play. This blind spot may have more to do with their predilections as critics and less with the alleged weakness of Glaspell's dramaturgy. Although Anderson knew and admired such prominent Village feminists as Emma Goldman (Biggs 193), she was not closely associated with feminist activities; tellingly, neither Anderson nor Heap seems to have had any connection with the Heterodoxy Club.

The critical response to *Bernice* seems to indicate that Glaspell's dramaturgy was still too nuanced for some of her audience. Burns Mantle calls the 1918–19 season in the commercial theater "hard" and points to the "many war plays" that helped maintain "the morale of a nation at war" ("John Ferguson" 352). He highlights St. John Ervine's *John Ferguson,* an Irish domestic drama that posed few challenges to conventions of gender or family life, as his play of the year. It ran for 177 performances, securing the future of the fledgling Theatre Guild. *Bernice* was clearly cut from different cloth, but it nevertheless struck a chord with a number of Village patrons.

The space devoted to the play in such a major literary publication as the *Little Review* confirms the growing importance of Glaspell and her writing to her community and, more broadly, to modernist art. Sharon Friedman sees the play as "poised between the feminist awakening in *Trifles* . . . and the modernist revolt in *The Verge*" (156). Thus, this first full-length piece emerges as a watershed for Glaspell's career. Soon to create her most important political and experimental dramas, *Inheritors* and *The Verge,* with *Bernice* she crafted a play that refined her earliest dramatic devices and points toward the drama of characterological and symbolic power to come.

Inheritors

The intellectual, social and aesthetic engagement of Village residents in the early 1910s prompted an unprecedented level of creative and political endeavor, exemplified by the dedication and productivity of the first years of the Players' activities. But the outbreak of global violence and the suppression of free expression in the United States prompted a new kind of commitment from Glaspell and her colleagues. They took action to confront the very real threats to themselves and their livelihoods posed by governmental edicts to curb dissent.

When declarations of war spread across Europe in August 1914, President Woodrow Wilson had officially proclaimed United States neutrality. But by early 1917 a proposed alliance between Germany and Mexico directly threatened the U.S. border, and Wilson decided that the country had to enter the conflict ("World Wars" 961–77). Later that spring, four years before *Inheritors* was staged, President Wilson signed into law a series of executive orders that became the Espionage Act on 15 June 1917. This legislation, aimed primarily at the press, in effect censored their ability to circulate any views in opposition to the official war effort. The key provisions, found in Title I, section 3, stated:

> Whoever, when the United States is at war, . . . shall wilfully cause or attempt to cause insubordination, disloyalty, mutiny, or refusal of duty, in the military or naval forces of the United States, or shall wilfully obstruct the recruiting or enlistment service of the United States, to the injury of the service or of the United States, shall be punished by a fine of not more the $10,000 or imprisonment for not more than twenty years, or both. (Qtd. in Mock 49–50)

Title III of that act prohibited the mailing of any materials that would fall under the restriction of Title I, which essentially prevented the circulation of any periodical with views critical of the government, such as the *Masses*. According to historian James Mock, this "was the first bit of legislation in more than one hundred years that gave officials the statutory opportunity to restrict freedom of speech and the press" (50).

Mock further explains, however, that, "by January 1918, the restrictions upon our liberties already provided were not considered sufficiently stringent to deal with the situation" (53), as they did not cover other forms of public address and oppositional activity. Thus, the Sedition Act was created as an amendment to the Espionage Act:

> Offenses under it included the willful writing, utterance, or publication of any "disloyal, profane, scurrilous, or abusive language about the form of government of the United States, or the Constitution of the United States, or the military or naval forces of the United States, or the flag of the United States, or the uniform of the army or navy of the United States, or any language intended to bring the form of government of the United States, or the Constitution of the United States, or the flag of the United States, or the uniform of the army or navy of the United States into contempt, scorn, contumely, or disrepute." (Mock 53)

The Censorship Board, established by the president (Mock 51), enjoyed full authority to enforce these measures; the leniency or strictness with which they were to carry out their provisions was left undetermined (Mock 54). Although historian Zechariah Chafee dates their repeal to March 1921 (41), a month before *Inheritors* went into production, Kenneth Macgowan's review of the play in *Vogue* indicates enforcement must still have been in practice:

> The night I attended "Inheritors," the United States Marshal of New York and an assistant had come to the play to see if the stories of its "un-Americanism" were true enough to justify its suppression or amendment.

Macgowan uses the marshal's departure from the theater as an opportunity to make a snide remark about the play, but his quip cannot mask the serious threat the official presence posed to the production and to Glaspell herself:

> The marshal went away after the tedious business of sitting through the first act. . . . Had he stayed for the remaining two acts, I wonder what his emotions and action might have been. ("Seen on the Stage" 86)

Thus, at the premiere of *Inheritors* the power of these acts would still have been fresh in the minds of the Greenwich Village audience, many of whom themselves might have faced fines or imprisonment. The questions prompted by the war and its aftermath, particularly questions about national identity and the country's founding principles, provided Glaspell with the primary themes for the work, her second full-length play.

America's involvement in the war in 1917 had quickly become a point of contestation within the Greenwich Village bohemian community. As historian Arthur Wertheim explains, "up to 1916 the question of America's participation was not a divisive issue," as the artists in the New York "Little Renaissance" felt it was their "mission to uphold culture while the Continent was in turmoil" (215). But once America entered the conflict everything changed. Floyd Dell summarized this new situation in *Love in Greenwich Village:*

> The war had scattered and divided us; friend was set against old friend; and even if that had not been unhappily true, the war would inevitably have brought to an end that glorious intellectual playtime in which art and ideas, free self-expression and the passion of propaganda, were for one moment happily mated. (27)

The theatrical community had responded to the war in different ways. The Washington Square Players had suspended operations "because many members were drafted" (Wertheim 217), but the subscription circular for the third season of the Provincetown Players (1918–19) announced that the group would continue production despite the war:

> Seven of the Provincetown Players are in the army or working for it in France, and more are going. Not light-heartedly now, when civilization itself is threatened with destruction, we who remain have determined to go on next season with the work of our little theatre. ("The Provincetown Players: Third New York Season")

Two prominent Village publications, the *Masses* and the *Seven Arts,* opposed American intervention. As a result, the *Seven Arts* lost the financial support of its patron Annette Rankine and had to cease publication, while seven members of the *Masses* staff, including Dell and editor Max Eastman, were prosecuted (Wertheim 219–22). Dell's comments on the end of "free self-expression" defined the era for many in the bohemian community. The persecution and prosecution of numerous individuals who spoke out against the war became a frightening domestic conflict fought in the shadow of the larger military campaign abroad.

As I have already suggested, Glaspell alludes to the battle over freedom of speech in three plays produced between 1917 and 1919: *Close the Book, The People,* and *Bernice.* The struggle to retain the right to free expression during World War I became an increasingly pressing concern for writers, teachers, and political activists. With the passage of the Espionage and Sedition Acts in 1917 and 1918, individuals who spoke out or wrote in opposition to America's governmental activities or policies risked prosecution for their beliefs. The *Masses* trials of 1918 under this legislation had brought the conflict home for many Village radicals, who saw firsthand the force of government repression.

Thus, Glaspell's decision to make the fight for freedom of thought and expression a central theme of *Inheritors* emerges as a logical continuation and expression of her long-held political beliefs. In doing so, she joined her colleagues in political activism, directly challenging governmental repression and risking prosecution for her writing. With its sweeping vision of American history and its pointed examination of the foundational principles of democracy, *Inheritors* stands as a testament to Glaspell's and the Provincetown Players' belief in the power of the stage to express and influence political convictions. Through her central character, Madeline Fejevary Morton, Glaspell depicts the inextricability of the personal and the political for the individual dedicated to the nation as it was originally conceived. Her use of a strong and independent woman to drive home these commitments adds a feminist dimension to her rich, multivalent narrative.

Glaspell probably wrote *Inheritors* during the 1919–20 season, which she and Cook spent away from the Players. At the end of the previous season, they had decided to take a "sabbatical," in part to give them more time for their own writing, in part to give other members of the group the opportunity to lead it (Sarlós 107; Glaspell *Road* 215). They took a trip back to their home town of Davenport, Iowa, which may have prompted them both to think about a midwestern setting for their latest projects (Noe, *Susan Glaspell: Voices from the Heartland* 41). Cook was working on his drama *The Spring*, which Glaspell describes as "a psychic play [with] American Indians as background" (*Road* 222). Presumably, their discussions of the Blackhawk Indians' history proved equally influential on the creation of *Inheritors*. The Players produced *The Spring* as the third bill of the 1920–21 season; *Inheritors* was the fifth bill (Sarlós 178).

Critics immediately saw the link between the works. In *Theatre Arts Magazine* Kenneth Macgowan observed:

> Susan Glaspell's *Inheritors* compares curiously with her husband's *The Spring*. It is laid in the same Blackhawk country. It utilizes a prolog [*sic*] in an earlier day. Its idiom of expression seems almost the same. And in its story of how the people of a Western university met and suffered from the black reaction that has spread over the United States since the war, there is the same radical courage that Cook displays in his handling of the psychic. It does not seem, however, so moving, fine as it is in many respects.
>
> ("Broadway Bows to By-Ways" 183)

Reviewing the London production of *Inheritors* a few years later, N. G. Royde-Smith also compared the works but saw their merits differently:

"Inheritors" . . . is a kind of twin play to "The Spring." Each play begins with the conflict between the white and the red man, and goes on to show a divergence of opinion between the elder and the younger generations in a provincial university. . . . The purpose of each play is identical. Our forefathers, say the dramatists, made steps towards the brotherhood of man. . . . But their aim is still beyond the magnanimity of their descendants, and still the young must sacrifice their freedom for the dream of freedom which each generation inherits only to destroy. . . . The detail varies a little. . . . But the impulse is the same in both plays. So is the material. It is in the handling that the important difference between them shows. . . . It becomes clear that "Inheritors" is a better play than "The Scene" [sic]. ("The Drama: The American Play" 25).

Although neither critic explains his final opinion, reading these two plays now, three-quarters of a century after their composition, one can certainly identify the similarities the critics stressed. The plays' differences, both stylistically and thematically, are, however, much more apparent. Cook's drama, which relies heavily on Nietzsche, psychology (and current notions of insanity), and romantic mysticism, appears melodramatic and contrived. *Inheritors,* through its restraint of emotion, calculated use of offstage action and characters, and emphasis on politics' and history's impact on individuals, remains a more cogent and compelling work. The fact that Glaspell's play was revived both within a few years of its premiere and as recently as 1983 attests to its ongoing relevance. Glaspell's careful connection of issues from America's past to contemporary world political concerns gives her play a weight and value that her husband's effort lacks.

The plot of the first act of *Inheritors* is relatively simple. A young man with the quintessentially "American" name of Smith, a spokesman for a group of investors who wants to purchase the property of Silas Morton for a housing development, arrives at the Morton farm on the Fourth of July 1879 to discuss the matter with Morton. This highly desirable tract of land, situated on a hill above the town, once belonged to the Indians. Silas, however, is off participating in the day's festivities with his friend Fejevary, a refugee from the Hungarian revolution of 1848. Smith chats instead with Silas's mother, Grandmother Morton, until the men arrive. After hearing Smith's pitch, Silas politely declines his offer, intimating that he has other, better plans for his property.

After Smith leaves, Felix Fejevary Jr. enters, having just returned from his college days at Harvard. Silas takes this opportunity to reveal his dream of founding a college on the hill. Silas explains to the son that the influence of his father, Felix Sr., has been integral to his plan, since the Hungarian helped imbue him with an understanding of the importance of education for society. Although Grandmother Morton protests, feeling the hard-earned land should stay in the family, Silas's arguments prevail, and the elder Fejevary agrees to support his vision. Glaspell thus introduces us to the conflicting ideas over "inheritance" that will shape the play.

Glaspell sets the remainder of the action in 1920—her present day—on the fortieth anniversary of the founding of Morton College (118). The descendants of Silas and Felix Sr. are now the central characters: Felix Jr. is a banker trying to support the growth of the college, and Madeline Fejevary Morton, Silas's granddaughter and Felix's niece, is a student at the school. Acts 2–4 revolve around Madeline's struggle to establish her own identity and beliefs when the weight of her ancestry and the pressures of her family and friends pull her in many directions. She befriends a group of Hindu students whose political opposition to the British raj has jeopardized their place at the college. Madeline's support for these foreign students and her growing realization that the quest for liberty and justice they follow is the same as that of her ancestors lead her to question many of the values espoused by those around her who claim to be upholding her forebears' democratic principles. She is forced to choose between the compromised but comfortable morality she perceives within her community and her emerging ideals, the pursuit of which will have serious legal consequences. Glaspell depicts Madeline's burgeoning political consciousness through her realizations about the necessity of free speech for a democratic society, regardless of the consequences for her as an individual through governmental legislation. Through Madeline's quest for a personal truth Glaspell explores the evolution of value systems in the United States and raises important questions about our own national priorities and beliefs.

As many of the critics observed, act 1, set in 1879, serves as a kind of prologue or frame for the rest of the action in 1920. O. W. Firkins of the *Weekly Review* noted distinct changes in tone between each act, calling the first "a pastoral," the second "a satire," and the third "a tragedy of the propagandist order" ("Drama" 344).[1] Glaspell would repeat this dramaturgical technique of tonal variation between acts in her next play, *The Verge*, as well as in *Chains of Dew*. Even more important, she uses the first act to frame the question of inheritance: what property, qualities, and values from our history will be passed on to subsequent generations of Americans, and how will they be appreciated by them? Thus, despite its lighter feel, the first act of *Inheritors* is crucial for grasping the significance of the play. Its very lightness helps to establish the keen irony inherent to the play's treatment of America's philosophical deterioration.

Glaspell's opening stage directions and dialogue deserve attention because of the overarching relationship she subsequently establishes among the play's four acts. First, the physical location of the Mortons' farmhouse, "on the rolling prairie just back from the Mississippi [River]," as well as Grandmother Morton's reference to "the war of 1832" (104) set the play in northwest Illinois, in the midst of territory contested by the Black Hawk War of that year.[2] Such details introduce the theme of Native American dispossession in the play. According to historian Kenneth Walker:

> The conflict had its beginning in a treaty made by a few representatives of the Sauk and Fox Indians at St. Louis in 1823. In return for an annuity of $1,000, they ceded to the United States their claims to fifty-million acres of land. . . . Although Chief Black Hawk denounced this treaty as illegal, settlers moved into western Illinois, put up fences, burned Black Hawk's summer village, and plowed up the Indian burying grounds. (83)[3]

Black Hawk and his people retreated across the Mississippi into Iowa but then tried to return, precipitating a massacre. According to Walker, "Of the 1,000 Indians who had crossed over into Illinois . . . only 150 were left alive" (83). Historian Dan Clark ends his account of the conflict by remarking that the strength of the government troops combined with volunteer militia completely overwhelmed the Indians and "enabled many a resident of Illinois and Wisconsin to tell his children and grandchildren how he fought the redskins" (66–67).

The fact that Glaspell has Grandmother Morton describe how *she* fought the Indians helps establish a motif of female courage and strength for the play that we see carried through each generation and inherited by Madeline. Historian Glenda Riley has specialized in the study of women's frontier experiences;[4] she observes that this aspect of American history has been ignored, as if the westward expansion had been an exclusively male phenomenon (*Female Frontier* 1), despite the depiction of female pioneers in the work of such prominent American writers as Willa Cather, for example. The details of her experiences as a frontierswoman that Grandmother Morton presents expositionally to Smith correspond very closely to the historical records Riley consulted in her research. Particularly relevant is Riley's sense that these women not only "manage[d] their households and families, they were also charged with preserving family, religious, and ethnic traditions; and they served as family historians"(*Female Frontier* 2). Glaspell will show that family history has a particularly strong impact on its female members, in this instance Madeline, who inherits two equally compelling family narratives that influence her character.

Riley also details these women's relations with Native Americans, an account remarkably similar to that depicted by Glaspell:

> In spite of repeated occurrences of violence between settlers and natives, many prairie women had pleasant experiences with American Indians. . . . [W]omen formed friendships with Indians, exchanged medical and child care with them, visited their camps and homes, and hired them as domes-

tic workers. Similar interchanges occurred in . . . embattled prairie areas, including Indiana, Illinois, and Iowa. (*Female Frontier* 45).[5]

Glaspell immediately makes clear that her play will avoid the traditional opposition of Indians and pioneers:

Smith: I guess you believe the saying that the only good Indian is a dead Indian.
Grandmother: I dunno. We roiled them up considerable. They was mostly friendly when let be. Didn't want to give up their land—but I've noticed something of the same nature in white folks. . . . This very land—land you want to buy—was the land they loved—Blackhawk and his Indians. . . . This was where their fathers—as they called 'em—were buried. I've seen my husband and Blackhawk climb that hill together. . . . He used to love that hill—Blackhawk. He talked how the red man and the white man could live together.

(104–5)

Through Grandmother Morton's speeches Glaspell establishes several of her most important themes and plot details. Questions of the land—ownership, use, inheritance—drive the play's narrative. Moreover, issues of race relations between settlers and natives, the history of conflict as well as ideals of harmony, become exponentially complicated through the arrival of immigrants and resident aliens by the twentieth century. Glaspell makes several strategic points here: that these conflicts are not simple, despite our attempts to make them appear clear-cut; that it is imperative to recognize the essential humanity and similarity among people of different races and backgrounds; and that we should respect difference but work toward the ideal of living together peacefully.

Glaspell reinforces these concepts through Silas, who expands on the relation of his family to their Indian neighbors:

Silas: . . . Our honesty with the Indians was little to brag on.
Grandmother: You fret more about the Indians than anybody else does.
Silas: To look out at that hill sometimes makes me ashamed.
Grandmother: Land sakes, you didn't do it. It was the government. And what the government does is nothing for a person to be ashamed of.
Silas: I don't know about that. . . . A seeing how 'tis for the other person—*a bein'* that other person. . . . 'Twoud 'a' done something for us to have *been* Indians a little more.

(111)

Glaspell's sense of perspective here, of seeing situations from the point of view of the Other, reflects not only a racial sensitivity distinctive for her era but also the kind of empathic response such theorists as Carol Gilligan have subsequently identified as distinctive to women's social development.[6] That Glaspell should imbue a male character with this quality stands out, prompting questions about her attribution of gendered behavior. Katherine Rodier, for example, has posited that Glaspell elsewhere "crosses genders" with her exploration of male and female artist figures (211); it could be argued more broadly that Glaspell's most provocative and sympathetic characters often display traits that belie the strict gender codes still lingering two decades after the close of the Victorian era. Silas's sense that the individual may need to act on the guidance of his or her conscience, rather than to follow the dictates of the government, will prove critical to the drama's denouement.

In addition to forging links to the Indian theme introduced in the opening moments of the play, Glaspell ties the issue of individual action to other important elements of *Inheritors* through her use of strategic design and temporal details in the setting. She notes that a picture of Abraham Lincoln hangs on the sitting room wall and that all of act one "was lived" on 4 July 1879. The verb phrase emphasizes the reality behind the action. Grandmother Morton's opening speech alludes to the day's festivities and to the battle at Gettysburg, currently being reenacted by the male characters soon to appear (104). Glaspell designed this conjunction of war references—to the American Revolution and the Civil War—to make her audience think of the various causes of individual freedom (particularly colonization and racial discrimination) they represent. Glaspell quickly establishes an ironic relationship between these wars' commitments to freedom and territory and those fought between the settlers and the Native Americans, whose prior claims were patently ignored or unfairly manipulated.

Glaspell adds one additional conflict, the Hungarian Revolution of 1848, to the group set forth early in act 1. This foreign war is introduced via the character of Felix Fejevary, neighbor to the Mortons and Silas's closest friend. Grandmother Morton explains that the Fejevarys "came here from Hungary after 1848. He was a count at home. . . . But he was a refugee because he fought for freedom in his country" (106). The Hungarian Revolution, like the American, was fought to free the country from imperial domination, in this case by Austria. Louis Kossuth became the central figure in the Hungarian nationalist freedom movement, and many rallied to his side, including those of the nobility who saw that the time had come for a more egalitarian system (Sinor 254–56). A tribute to Kossuth, written in 1854, describes him as a man who "followed the dictates of his conscience" and was "attached to her [Hungary's] constitution and her liberties" (E. O. S. 495). Although Kossuth and his supporters were defeated when Russia joined the Austrian forces to suppress the insurgents (Sinor 267–68), he became a national hero. He and his followers were forced to flee their country to Turkey. They were subsequently received warmly in the United States, which had joined other countries to work for the exiles' liberation (E. O. S. 502–3, 521). According to Václav Beneš, the "Forty-eighters and other groups of political exiles—such as the Polish or Hungarian revolutionaries," although a small portion of the immigrant stream to America— were significant to its "cultural and political development" (124).

The character of Fejevary reflects the principles of Kossuth and the Hungarian Revolution. Marcia Noe notes that "Glaspell used the surnames of two historic Davenport families in this play. The Mortons . . . were . . . pioneer settlers, and Nicholas Fejevary, a wealthy Hungarian nobleman, had fled to Davenport during the 1840s after supporting the revolution in his homeland" (*Susan Glaspell: Voice from the Heartland* 91 n. 32). The fact that he was a former nobleman adds a class dimension to the chronicles of revolution that the first act develops. The friendship of Morton and Fejevary represents the same idealized view of the transcendence of class barriers that is also championed in the harmonious race relations depicted between Blackhawk and Silas's father.

The fact that Morton's sense of the value of education for perpetuating American ideals of freedom and democracy should come from a recent immigrant is an important backdrop to the rest of the action. Yet how Silas envisions the college and his rationales for its construction on the hill are equally meaningful. Glaspell reveals the former through an exchange between Silas and Felix Jr.:

Felix: It—it's a big idea, Uncle Silas. I love the way you put it. It's only that
   I'm wondering—
Silas: Wondering how it can ever be a Harvard College? Well, it can't. And
   it needn't be (*stubbornly*). It's a college in the cornfields—where the
   Indian maize once grew. And it's for the boys of the cornfields—and
   the girls. There's few can go to Harvard College—but more can climb
   that hill.

(113)

George Cram Cook had attended Harvard for his senior year, receiving an A.B. degree in 1893, when he was nineteen. Judging from the frequency of Glaspell's fictional references to the institution, usually through male teacher figures modeled on Cook who were educated there, he must have impressed her with the significance of this period for him. Yet the sense of elitism associated with the college must also have affected Glaspell, for she often contrasts it with other institutions of greater accessibility, particularly for women. Thus, Silas's comment that the school he foresees will be open to men and women is telling.

It is also important that the idea for Morton College develops in the Midwest and as a nonsectarian institution. According to historian Albert Schmidt, many of the liberal arts colleges founded in the Midwest before the Civil War were strongly identified with denominations and were created by the alumni of eastern schools (234–38). Schmidt writes, "Presbyterian Princeton and Congregational Yale took the initiative in fathering western institutions" (238). After that war, however, the trend shifted toward the founding of nonsectarian schools, often with an agricultural mandate.

Glaspell is also historically accurate about the financial difficulties such schools faced. Fejevary remarks: "I fear you don't realize the immense amount of money required to finance a college. . . . You would have to interest rich men; you'd have to have a community in sympathy with the thing you wanted to do" (117). This speech foreshadows the conflict that develops early in act 2 over state appropriations for Morton College; it also echoes the historical realities of college closures in the era. Schmidt presents statistics showing that four-fifths of schools founded before the Civil War failed economically (245), figures that perhaps improved slightly for schools established soon after the war, when the country as a whole began to recover industrially.

Silas believes that using the hill in this fashion, on land that once belonged to the Indians, will be a way to "give it back—their hill. I give it back to joy—a better joy—joy o' aspiration" (118). Marcia Noe explains this resolution as the means by which Silas "assuage[s] his guilt about taking land away from the Indians" (*Susan Glaspell* 42), which is true enough. Still, the line of argument young Felix presents, which Silas accepts in rationalizing his decision, merits closer scrutiny:

Felix: You haven't read Darwin, have you, Uncle Silas? . . . Darwin, the great new man—and his theory of the survival of the fittest?
Silas: No. No, I don't know things like that, Felix.
Felix: I think he might make you feel better about the Indians. In the struggle for existence many must go down. The fittest survive. This—had to be.
Silas: Us and the Indians? Guess I don't know what you mean—fittest.
Felix: He calls it that. Best fitted to the place in which one finds one's self, having the qualities that can best cope with conditions—do things. From the beginning of life it's been like that. He shows the growth of life from forms that were hardly alive, the lowest animal forms . . . up to man.
Silas: Oh, yes, that's the thing the churches are so upset about—that we come from monkeys.

(115–16)

Writing at least five years before the famous Scopes "monkey trial" of 1925, Glaspell presciently incorporated in *Inheritors* an issue of increasing concern in American education. Adding yet another layer to the developing senses of "inheritance" already manifest in the drama (among them property and America's founding ideals), Glaspell adds an evolutionary, quasi-genetic angle that demonstrates the early application of social Darwinism. Glaspell, through Felix, repeats a common mistake of her era (and ours), by attributing this line of argumentation to Darwin, whose *On the Origin of Species* had been published in 1859, when in actuality it was Herbert Spencer who appropriated Darwin's phrase *survival of the fittest* to apply to man in society ("Social Darwinism" 919–20). This application of Darwinian theory then "was used as a philosophical rationalization for imperialist, colonialist, and racist policies, sustaining belief in Anglo-Saxon . . . cultural and biological superiority" ("Social Darwinism" 920).

Felix's argument is essentially that the white's "superiority" is proved by their triumph over the Indians and that this outcome need not motivate guilt; rather, it should be seen as the natural evidence of evolutionary principles at work. Glaspell complicates the argument further, however, through Fejevary's comments:

> Why have we hands? . . . [W]hen you think we have hands because ages back—before life had taken form as man, there was an impulse to do what had never been done—when you think that we have hands today because from the first of life there have been adventurers—those of best brain and courage who wanted to be more than life had been, and that from aspiration has come doing, and doing has shaped the thing with which to do—it gives our hand a history which should make us want to use it well. (116)

Here Lamarckian theory is conflated with the Darwinian and Spencerian discourse to suggest that man's past achievements can be passed along genetically from generation to generation, making the need for man to use his attributes well all the more compelling, given the impressiveness of the process through which those traits were acquired.[7]

These philosophical musings render this section of *Inheritors* one of the most interesting, but also most troubling, in the play. Given Glaspell's sensitivity to racial discrimination in *Inheritors,* that she would invoke this line of argument and have Silas accept it seems perplexing. Furthermore, why does she have the (educated) characters demonstrate such scientific confusion, when she is so historically accurate elsewhere in the play? It is tempting to attribute these slippages to Glaspell's placement within the Progressive era and its belief in the future; we must also remember that concepts of what is "racist" have changed over time. Interestingly, a clearer presentation of plant genetics emerges later in the drama as well as in *The Verge* and other fictional works.[8] Human genetics, however, is not a theme developed elsewhere in Glaspell's writing.

Perhaps more important, this scene adds to the developing sense of midwestern cultural heritage in the play. The values and attributes exemplified by Morton and Fejevary correspond to the emerging image of midwesterners within American culture and corroborate a phenomenon identified by historian James Shortridge (17): the Midwest "quickly came to symbolize Arcadian idealism" (7), or what he calls "an ideal middle kingdom suspended between uncivilized wilderness and urban and industrial evils" (6). As Glaspell will reiterate in *Chains of Dew*, she uses the conceptualization of the Midwest as the idealized heart of the country to her thematic advantage; she exploits the connotations of geography to underscore her action, much as she uses interior settings as corollaries to character in such plays as *Trifles*, *Bernice*, and *Alison's House*. Thus, the land itself and all that has happened on it resonate with the tropes of political, cultural, material, and biological inheritance that emerge in act 1 and will inform the remainder of the play.

Glaspell uses the rest of *Inheritors* to demonstrate the disintegration of the idealism that was profoundly disrupted not only by the arrival of those same "evils" alluded to by Shortridge but also by the cataclysmic events of World War I. Act 2 opens in October 1920, "upon the occasion of the fortieth anniversary" of the founding of Morton College (118). Both acts 2 and 3 are set in the library of the college, a picture of Silas Morton hanging prominently as an echo of the Lincoln portrait in act 1. The act begins with a scene between Felix Fejevary Jr., now a banker and president of the board of trustees of the school, and Senator Lewis, chairman of the state appropriations committee (120). Like the first act, this one quickly establishes a war context, with allusions to America's recent involvement in World War I. Senator Lewis refers to Felix's son, who "stood up and offered his life," and Fejevary responds: "Yes. And my nephew gave his life. . . . Silas Morton's grandson died in France. My sister Madeline married Ira Morton, son of Silas Morton" (121). The two men, however, do not dwell on these details. Senator Lewis is much more concerned about a faculty member at the college, Professor Holden. The Senator identifies Holden as a "radical" and condemns him for his support of a former student, Fred Jordan, who is in prison for conscientious objection to conscription and the war (120–21).[9] Holden makes the legislator "see red" (121), a pun on the anger the teacher's views evoke and his suspected identification with socialist politics; Glaspell's audience might also hear an echo of the first act's concern with attitudes toward Native Americans, whose red skins were the object of scorn from some government officials.

Senator Lewis makes it clear that "this state . . . appropriates no money for radicals" and encourages Fejevary to dismiss Holden if he wants the state's much-needed funding for the college (120). Glaspell thereby opens her second act in an atmosphere of economic and political debate. She echoes act 1's financial arguments for compromise "in the public interest," represented by the proposed real estate transaction. Although Fejevary correctly pegs Lewis as a "reactionary" (131), he feels he cannot afford to antagonize him and agrees to talk to Holden about his views. The Senator insists that "we can get scholars enough. What we want is Americans" for the school—meaning, of course, only those who share his jingoistic views. Glaspell has Fejevary reply in harmony, assuring the Senator that Morton is "a one-hundred-percent-American college" (119).

Such phrases as *one hundred percent American* were common in the period, epitomizing the rapid change in political perspective in the Midwest following the war. According to James Shortridge, by this time "conservatism had begun to replace progressive idealism" (9); Lewis represents an extreme but legitimate version of then current midwestern ideology. Historian William Preston, drawing on the work of John Higham and Oscar Handlin, explains:

> There was "an unwillingness to surrender the psychic gratifications the war had offered." The American people's unabated evangelical fervor might now be satisfied by a proscription of the enemy within. The . . . unexpected survival of 100 percent Americanism indicated the strength of nationalism and nativism in the postwar world. (192)

Moreover, Glaspell's choice of a college setting as the battleground for American values was no doubt as appropriate then as now. Historians H. C. Peterson and Gilbert Fite record an astounding number of incidents like that depicted in *Inheritors,* in which schools responded to both internal and external pressure against teachers who held political views different from those in power. Peterson and Fite detail specific events from schools all across the country, where faculty were dismissed or forced into silence in order to maintain their positions. At Columbia University in 1917, for instance, Professors Henry W. L. Dana and James M. Cattell were both dismissed on the grounds that they "had done grave injury to the University by their public agitation against the conduct of the war" (103).[10] In Nebraska in that same year "the State Council of Defense . . . charged that certain professors at the State University were pro-German." Despite protests, the regents of the university demanded their resignations (104–5). According to Peterson and Fite, the phenomenon spread across the country: "Throughout 1917–18, newspapers continued to report dismissals of professors for disloyalty" in Maine, Michigan, Minnesota, Washington, Missouri, Indiana, and Ohio, and inquiries were held in New York, Illinois, and Pennsylvania (105–8). At the University of Virginia Professor Leon R. Whipple "made a speech entitled 'The Meaning of Pacifism,'" which "declared that to make the world safe for democracy and to insure our own democracy everyone should work for peace." The next day the president of the university received a telegram of complaint from Senator Carter Glass, demanding Whipple's dismissal. The trustees complied and Whipple was discharged (106–7).

Given the extensive press coverage of these events, Glaspell certainly would have had ample factual material for her play. In any case she dramatizes the action surrounding Holden with great authenticity. In order to keep him an important part of acts 2–4, she does not have him fired. Instead, she involves him in a moral dilemma, pitting his principles against the compelling financial pressures of his family situation. Fejevary tells him that, if he speaks out further, he will lose his place, which may result in the death of his wife, who is ill and needs expensive medical care he could not then afford. In this way Glaspell makes concrete—if a bit contrived—the theme of individual responsibility that must answer to conflicting claims. By realistically depicting the struggle Holden confronts between his political beliefs and his personal commitments, she renders tangible Americans' problems with conflicting ideologies that had become simplistically polarized in the context of world war.

Holden's moral dilemma soon resonates with all the other conflicts Glaspell develops. Through the dialogue of Fejevary and the Senator we learn the nature of Holden's protest and the details of Fred Jordan's situation. Jordan has been expelled for his stance as a conscientious objector and subsequently imprisoned for these beliefs (120). Although Holden has protested the expulsion only within the school, he has publicly objected to Jordan's treatment in prison, particularly the fact that he was denied access to books (121). Jordan, we discover, had also been a good friend of Madeline Fejevary Morton, the character who soon becomes the central figure in play. In act 4, set in the same Morton sitting room of act 1, Madeline reads a letter she has received from Jordan, written on a scrap of paper, as he is denied the means of regular correspondence as well:

He's in what they call "the hold" . . . a punishment cell. (*with difficulty reading it*) It's two and a half feet at one end, three feet at the other, and six feet long. He'd been there ten days when he wrote this. He gets two slices of bread a day; he gets water; that's all he gets. This is because he balled [*sic*] the deputy warden out for chaining another prisoner up by the wrists. (143)

In what must have been the most moving physical actions of the play, Madeline takes out some chalk and draws on the floor the dimensions of Fred's cell, placing herself within it (143). Then, a few moments later, she raises her hands up to imaginary bars as if chained to them: "Eight hours a day—day after day. Just hold your arms up like this one hour then sit down and think about . . . detachment" (153).

Christine Dymkowski astutely reads the situation of Jordan and the Hindu students Madeline champions within the context of Glaspell's dramaturgical technique of portraying absent yet central characters.[11] She observes that "those characters with the greatest integrity are the most marginal. . . . [s]een by society as both extremists and outsiders" (99). Glaspell literalizes this marginality by having them never appear onstage. Nevertheless, she forces us to recognize the figures society has ostracized by making them integral, if invisible, to the action.

As with Holden's situation, Glaspell based the details of Fred Jordan's imprisonment on fact. There is an astounding record of the treatment of prisoners jailed for their political beliefs in this era, a sample of which is chronicled by Lillian Schlissel in her documentary history of conscientious objection in America. According to Schlissel:

> The Selective Service Act of 1917 provided exemption for religious objectors, but stipulated that "no persons so exempted shall be exempted from service in any capacity that the President shall declare to be noncombatant. . . ." The effect of this stipulation was to put all conscientious objectors into some form of noncombatant service. (129)

Thus, anyone who refused to participate in this alternative form of service, as did many whose beliefs did not allow participation in any activity related to war, was liable to be prosecuted. Schlissel explains:

> The military courts were severe with "absolutists" who refused all cooperation with the army. . . . There were seventeen death sentences, 142 life terms, and 345 sentences where the average term was sixteen and one-half years.

Although, as Schlissel notes, most of these sentences were later commuted or reduced, "it was not until 1933 that the last full pardon was issued . . . and the last conscientious objector . . . was released from prison" (131). In addition to the personal records substantiating the treatment of Fred Jordan and his fellow prisoners, Schlissel reprints a report published by the National Civil Liberties Bureau, the organization that would later become the American Civil Liberties Union. The report details treatment for "recalcitrant" prisoners consisting of "solitary confinement in dark cells, manacling and a diet of bread and water" (150).

The profoundly disturbing details of Jordan's situation are not the only contemporary issues of political persecution depicted in *Inheritors*, however. Glaspell used the specific situation of prosecutions under the Espionage and Sedition Acts of 1917 and 1918, as well as the impact of this legislation on individuals who opposed government practices more generally, to structure the main conflict of the last three acts of the play. Above all, she complicates the narrative with a range of moral debates that both link the current setting to that of the 1879 prologue and portray the complex array of ideological positions inherent to the current political concerns she raises.

On the day of the Senator's visit in act 2 and the anniversary festivities (which echo the July Fourth events of act 1), some Hindu students stage a protest in response to the school's "not fighting the deportation" of one of their fellow students and countrymen (122).[12] Horace Fejevary, son of the board president and also a student, indignantly comes to the library to look for the speeches of Abraham Lincoln, whom the Hindus have been quoting in support of their position. The richly ironic scene is worth quoting at length:

Horace: I want the speeches of Abraham Lincoln.
Senator: You couldn't do better.
Horace: I'll show those dirty dagoes where they get off! . . . I'm going to sick the Legion on 'em.[13]
Fejevary: Are you talking about the Hindus?
Horace: Yes, the dirty dagoes.
Fejevary: Hindus aren't dagoes you know, Horace.
Horace: Well, what's the difference? This foreign element gets my goat.
Senator: My boy, you talk like an American. But what do you mean—Hindus?
Fejevary: There are two young Hindus here as students. And they're good students. . . . But they must preach the gospel of free India—non-British India.
Senator: Oh, that won't do.
Horace: They're nothing but Reds, I'll say. Well, one of 'em's going back to get his (*grins*).
Fejevary: There were three of them last year. One of them is wanted back home.
Senator: I remember now. He's to be deported.
Horace: And when they get him—(*movement as of pulling a rope*) They hang there.
Fejevary: The other two protest against our not fighting the deportation of their comrade. They insist it means death to him (*brushing off a thing that is inclined to worry him*). But we can't handle India's affairs.
Senator: I should think not!

Horace: Why, England's our ally! That's what I told them. But you can't
argue with people like that.

(122–23)

Into this short scene between the men Glaspell packs a wealth of political positions and historical references, emblematic of her dramaturgical technique
in this play. She uses the Lincoln allusions as an ironic indicator of the perversion of the causes of liberty currently supported in the United States. The
Hindus, who read passages from his "first inaugural address to Congress" of
1861 in support of their own revolutionary movement against British imperial
domination in their country (123–24), receive no recognition of the legitimacy
of their belief. Here, too, Glaspell demonstrates the breadth of her political
understanding, by weaving into her narrative the story of these foreign na-
tionals who sought opportunities for education and professional success in
North America.

The history of South Asian political activity in the United States is complex, and Glaspell's references are understandably tangled. Historian Christine
Stansell claims that around 1916 Indian radicals in New York were "plotting
various revolutions" (314), but she is not specific about this insurgency. A
closer link to the student activity Glaspell depicts can be found in the history
of the Sikhs, an Indian people from the Punjab. According to Darshan Singh
Tatla, over five thousand Sikhs had come to the United States and Canada between 1903 and 1909. Between 1913 and 1919 an activist group called the
Ghadar movement arose within this community, particularly its educated
members. They perceived parallels between the discriminatory immigration
laws and other restrictions they experienced in North America and the imperialism dominating their native land and advocated "a revolutionary struggle
against British rule in India" (Tatla xiii–xiv). By contrast, Hindus and other
Indian groups in this period were just coming under the pacifist influence of
Gandhi. The 1919 Amritsar massacre in the Punjab, where Hindus had gathered for a festival and were attacked by the British ("India" 101), no doubt
spawned Western confusion around distinctions between Sikhs and Hindus
or the nuances of Indian politics at the moment.

Able to think no more deeply or historically than the most recent alliance
of England and the United States in the war will allow, Horace and the Senator cannot see the connection between America's own revolutionary struggle
against imperial England nor the racial domination behind the Civil War that
also applies to the Hindus' position. Furthermore, America's own comparatively recent territorial acquisitions in the Spanish-American War made many
in the United States more supportive of other imperialists' positions.[14] Lastly,
recent ideas of racial (i.e., Anglo-Saxon) solidarity underlying the alliance between America and Great Britain—the "white man's burden"—preclude the

historical vision that would allow Horace or the Senator to see the Hindus'
perspective.

The attribution of the term *Reds* to the foreigners is linked to the imminent possibility of their deportation as well as to another event Glaspell mentions immediately following this scene: Horace's involvement with other
"boys" at the school in breaking a strike at the local steel mill is an activity that
cements his identity as "one hundred per cent American" (123). William Preston, drawing on the work of fellow historians Robert K. Murray and Daniel
Bell, observes, "The United States witnessed 'an eruption of mass strikes on a
scale never before seen in American society'" immediately following the war:
"Over four million workers walked out in protest before 1919 came to an end"
(192). Much of this labor unrest was attributed to the agitation of the Industrial Workers of the World (IWW), nicknamed the Wobblies, whose radical
politics and association with the socialist and communist parties were well-
known. The IWW also became closely linked with foreigners and recent immigrants, many of whom worked in the factories and responded to their pro-
labor agitation.[15] Preston describes the conflict this unrest presented to the
government: "Devotion to America's revolutionary ideals and to its historic
career as an asylum for Europe's oppressed clashed with the equally intense
distaste for domestic radicalism" (78). Although Glaspell does not have the
Hindus involved with the strike put down by Horace and his cronies, their
identity as activist foreigners proved them guilty by association with other
"un-American" radicals. In the simplistic parlance of the time Hindu anti-
imperialists could therefore only be seen as "Reds." Furthermore, historian
William Tuttle actively links racial prejudice at this time to a broader-based
political conservatism. He makes a direct association between the "Red Summer" of 1919—so named for the race riots that bloodied the streets—and the
"Red Scare" of the same era (14).

The threat of political persecution of the Hindus, which Glaspell aligns
with other forms of reprisal in the play, has a factual foundation as well, revolving around techniques developed by the government to suppress dissent.
During the war radicals speaking out against the United States involvement
were subject to prosecution under the Espionage and Sedition Acts. After the
war, however, these same statutes could not be applied so easily. Since many of
the activists were of foreign origin and linked to the IWW, the government
sought fresh ways to quell unrest by eliminating radicalism. In February 1917
Congress passed a new immigration bill, which included the following clause:

> Any alien who at any time after entry shall be found advocating or
> teaching the unlawful destruction of property, or advocating or teach-
> ing anarchy or the overthrow by force or violence of the Government of
> the United States or of all forms of law or the assassination of public of-

ficials . . . shall, upon the warrant of the Secretary of Labor, be taken into custody and deported. (Qtd. in Preston 83)

The rapid and widespread enforcement of this law accounts for Fejevary's close questioning of his son on the Hindus' quotation of Lincoln:

Fejevary: Look here, Horace—speak accurately. Was it in relation to America they quoted this?
Horace: Well, maybe they were talking about India then. But they were standing up for being revolutionists. . . . Lincoln oughta been more careful what he said. Ignorant people don't know how to take such things.

(124)

Horace's jingoistic condescension to the Hindus, coupled with his and his friends' distaste for Eben Weeks, a student ridiculed for "trying to run a farm and go to college at the same time" (125), are pointed examples of the class and race prejudice as well as the political myopia that Glaspell sees emerging in postwar America.

Madeline Fejevary Morton is the character through whom the audience learns the realities of the current, disturbing political climate. Her awakening to the seriousness of the issues confronting her generation, and the connection of those concerns to America's past, make of her story a theatrical bildungsroman. *Inheritors* becomes a play showing her growth and development from naive and carefree coed to thoughtful and principled activist. Barbara Ozieblo discusses Madeline in the context of Glaspell's feminism, the aspect of her writing that has unsurprisingly received the most critical attention. Ozieblo asserts that, although *Inheritors* "is the least overtly feminist of Glaspell's plays, the surface plot thinly disguises her disappointment with patriarchal society, with man's weakness and his readiness to forego his ideals under pressure." She sees the work mocking "several male myths," including "the frontier" and "male superiority" (68), and believes Madeline is integral to this process. While Ozieblo's reading shows that *Inheritors* conforms to feminist principles Glaspell dramatizes more fully elsewhere, a reading of Madeline from this perspective alone defines her characterological significance too narrowly. Glaspell's politics embraced but exceeded sexual politics. Rather, it is the *connection* between feminist beliefs and other social and moral convictions that make *Inheritors* a complex and important political drama.

Glaspell's depiction of young characters who must learn from the actions of others becomes a metaphor for the development of America itself, the upstart nation evolving from a multiethnic, geographically diverse past. Actress and director Eva Le Gallienne, who staged a 1927 revival of the play and who would premiere the Pulitzer Prize–winning *Alison's House* three years later, saw the significance of the piece for America's youth. In her memoir, *At 33,* Le Gallienne observed that the play was "all too little known" and intimated that if she were in charge, she would "make a rule that all young American people be forced to read it—that is, if they could not see it played" (205), in order to guarantee that all the country's children would be exposed to the play's vital lessons.

Madeline's emotional and intellectual maturation occur as she comes to recognize her relationship to American history. When she first meets Senator Morton, she does not express the reverence for the vision and memory of her grandfather the legislator expects. Madeline maintains that she hasn't "any idea what he really was like" and hates "to be the granddaughter of a phrase" (127). Soon afterward, however, Madeline's inheritance of his ideals comes to the fore, in the offstage conflict involving the Hindus. At the end of act 2 Horace comes racing onstage to announce that Madeline has been arrested in the melee:

> Awful row down on the campus. The Hindus. I told them to keep their mouths shut about Abraham Lincoln. . . . We started—to rustle them along a bit. Why, they had *handbills* . . . telling America what to do about deportation! . . . So we were—we were putting a stop to it. They resisted—particularly the fat one. The cop at the corner saw the row—came up. He took hold of Bakhshish, and when the dirty anarchist[16] didn't move along fast enough, he took hold of him—well, a bit rough, you might say, when up rushes Madeline and calls to the cop, "Let that boy alone!" Gee—I don't know just what did happen—awful mix-up. Next thing I knew Madeline hauled off and pasted the policemen a fierce one with her tennis racket! . . . I could have squared it, even then, but for Madeline herself. I told the policeman that she didn't understand—that I was her cousin, and apologized for her. And she called over at me, "Better apologize for yourself!" As if there was any sense to that—that she—she looked like a *tiger.* (129)

Glaspell closes the act with a note of wry irony in this exchange between Horace and the Senator:

Senator: If she had no regard for the living, she might—on this day of all others—have considered her grandfather's memory (raises his eyes to the picture of Silas Morton).
Horace: Gee! Wouldn't you *say* so?

(129)

Of course, Madeline has uncalculatedly done just that by championing the Hindus' fight for freedom of expression as well as her own right to a voice and opinions her male cousin tries to disparage.

Their struggle, like that of their real-life counterparts in journalism, labor, and education, was essentially a fight against censorship and for their right to state their views, even in opposition to those in power. We can see in the narrative of the Hindus Glaspell's reflections on the events she had so recently witnessed that connected her bohemian world to the world of the play. The failure of two juries to convict the *Masses* staff of violating the Espionage and Seditions Acts was attributed particularly to a defense on First Amendment grounds (Chafee 78–79). Glaspell dramatizes the importance of these rights in the aftermath of the melee. When Madeline is released from jail later in the afternoon, her uncle confronts her:

Fejevary: May I ask why you have appointed yourself guardian of these
    strangers?
Madeline: Perhaps because they are strangers. . . . They're people from the
    other side of the world who came here believing in us, drawn from the
    far side of the world by things we say about ourselves. Well, I'm going to
    pretend—just for fun—that the things we say about ourselves are true.
. . .
Fejevary: (*Trying a different tack, laughing*) Oh, you're a romantic girl, Made-
    line. . . Rather nice, at that. But the thing is perfectly fantastic. . . . You
    are going against the spirit of the country. . . .
Madeline: (*In a smoldering way*) I thought America was a democracy.
Fejevary: We have just fought a great war for democracy.
Madeline: Well, is that any reason for not having it?

                                                    (139–40)

Suddenly, the noise of a new dispute is heard offstage, and Madeline races to the window of the library to see Horace and his cohorts confronting Atma, the remaining Hindu. Fejevary takes a firm stance:

Fejevary: . . . If you go out there and get in trouble a second time, I can't
    make it right for you. . . . You don't know what it means. These things
    are not child's play—not today. You could get twenty years in prison for
    things you'll say if you rush out there now. . . . Do you know that in
    America today there are women in our prisons for saying no more than
    you've said here to me!
Madeline: Then you ought to be ashamed of yourself!
Fejevary: I? Ashamed of myself?
Madeline: Yes! Aren't you an American?

                                                    (141–42)

Turning the rhetoric around to her new understanding of what it really means to be "American," Madeline dashes off to aid the Hindu Atma, which leads to her second arrest and the crisis of act 4. Through the escalation of the moral dilemmas and conflicts she dramatizes Glaspell tries to show how governmental restrictions were affecting a broad spectrum of society, not just the extremists one could imagine would take a radical stance. By creating a sympathetic heroine on a collision course with the legal system, Glaspell wants her audience to think carefully about the implications of such legislation, now and for the future.

Although the final act opens with Madeline temporarily back at the Morton homestead, we learn that she will soon have to appear in court before Judge Lenon, who is "one fiend for Americanism," like many real judges of this era. Her friend Emil Johnson, who works for the court, remarks to her, "Guess you don't know much about the Espionage Act or you'd go and make a little friendly call on your uncle" (145). Emil's comment is the first overt reference to the legislation that has lain behind all the attacks on freedom in the play. His suggestion, aimed to help Madeline, is just one of the play's multiple references to Fejevary's ability to circumvent the judicial system in his community. Such details point to the subtlety of Glaspell's indictment of the workings of American systems of power.[17]

Throughout act 4 Glaspell introduces various rationales and inducements for Madeline to consider in order to avoid legal proceedings, complicating her ethical quandary even further. Her Aunt Isabel, Madeline's surrogate mother since the death of her own, urges her to think about the family she will hurt and disrupt if she continues in this activist vein. Glaspell will strike a similar note around the nonconformism of extramarital relations in *Alison's House*. To Isabel's mind all Madeline need do is "say you felt sorry for the Hindu students because they seemed rather alone; that you hadn't realized—what they were, hadn't thought out what you were saying" (149). She tells her niece "these are the days when we have to stand together—all of us who are the same kind of people must stand together because the thing that makes us the same kind of people is threatened" (147).[18] Isabel's speech reflects both her jingoism and her ability to manipulate the facade of innocence that corresponds to stereotypes of politically naive womanhood. That Glaspell should give such an ugly, scapegoating speech to an otherwise sympathetic and loving character perfectly exemplifies her careful avoidance of diatribe or agitprop dramaturgy in her portrait of a complex political moment.

The pressure on Madeline mounts: Fejevary asks Professor Holden to speak to her, to try another approach to dissuade her from taking an irrevocable step. Holden asserts:

You do this thing and you'll find yourself with people who in many ways you don't care for at all; find yourself apart from people who in most ways are your own people. You're many-sided, Madeline. . . . I don't know about its all going to one side. I hate to see you, so young, close a door on so much life. I'm being just as honest with you as I know how. I myself am making compromises to stay within. I don't like it, but there are—reasons for doing it. . . . It's not a clean-cut case—the side of the world or the side of the angels. I hate to see you lose the—fullness of life. (152)

Holden, who has chosen to silence himself in order to retain his job at the college and thereby care for his wife, hopes that Madeline will understand and appreciate his own example enough to emulate it. He explains, "If you sell your soul—it's to love you sell it." Madeline perceives the irony in this for the realization of the political goals they share: "It's love that—brings life along, and then it's love—holds life back" (153).

Two examples from Madeline's own family and their ways of loving, however, finally cement her resolve. Her decision turns on yet another question of the inheritance of a spirit peculiar to her family—specifically its women—yet somehow wholly American. She asks her father, Ira, a recluse since the death of his wife, to tell her about her mother and how she died.

Ira. . . . Then *she* came—that ignorant Swede—Emil Johnson's mother—
    running through the cornfield like a crazy woman—"Miss Morton!
    Miss Morton! Come help me! My children are choking!" Diphtheria
    they had—the whole of 'em—but out of this house she ran—my
    Madeline, leaving you—her own baby—running as fast as she could
    through the cornfield after that immigrant woman. She stumbled in the
    rough field—fell to her knees. That was the last I saw of her. She
    choked to death in that Swede's house. They lived.
Madeline. (*Going to him*) Oh—father. (*Voice rich*) But how lovely of her.

(154)

Madeline's mother's sacrifice, for those new to America and different from herself, is juxtaposed to her father's protectionist and isolationist attitudes, the result of his suffering from his wife's loss. Glaspell metaphorically presents this through his depiction of his corn, the object of all his attention since her death:

Why can't I have my field to myself? Why can't I keep what's mine? . . .
Plant this corn by that corn, and the pollen blows from corn to corn . . .
like a—(*the word hurts*) gift. . . . I want it to stay in my field. It goes
away. The prevailin' wind takes it on to the Johnsons—them Swedes
that took my Madeline! . . . I want my field to myself. What'd I work
all my life for? . . . No! The wind shall stand still! I'll make it. I'll find a
way. (155)[19]

The lesson Ira unwittingly gives his daughter makes her realize "The world is all a—moving field. . . . Nothing is to itself. If America thinks so—America is like father." She chooses to "be the most you can be, so life will be more because you were" (156), an acknowledgment of the need for each individual to achieve and give of herself to the betterment of all, as opposed to the selfish view of taking all you can and protecting what is yours, the view endemic to postwar America.

Writing for the *Nation* in 1921, Ludwig Lewisohn produced one of the strongest supporting evaluations of *Inheritors:*

> If the history of literature, dramatic or non-dramatic, teaches us anything, it is that Broadway and its reviewers will some day be judged by their attitude to this work. . . . It is the first play of the American theater in which a strong intellect and a ripe artistic nature have grasped and set forth in human terms the central tradition and most burning problem of our national life quite justly and scrupulously, equally without acrimony or compromise. ("Drama: 'Inheritors'" 515)

The play may not have proved to be the benchmark Lewisohn predicted. But the reviews of its first productions—its 1921 New York premiere, the 1925–26 British productions, and its 1927 and 1983 New York revivals—tell a great deal not only about critics' and audiences' artistic and political views but also about how quickly American political opinions shift. Within the space of a few years issues of burning concern during wartime were all too quickly assumed to be nonissues for the future. Only recently have critics been able to see the ongoing relevance of Glaspell's themes.

In 1921 the critic for the *New York Evening Post* opened one review by stating, "There is still hope, even promise, for the theatre of ideas in this country while such as Susan Glaspell continue writing for our stage" (P. F. R. 9). Alexander Woollcott of the *New York Times,* frequently hard on Provincetown productions, was true to form; he damned the play theatrically but acknowledged its political and literary force:

> Its material is a contribution to the literature of radicalism, the expression of a genuine social spirit and an earnest, patiently reasonable mind, which makes doubly regrettable the fact that the play itself is painfully dull, pulseless and desultory. ("Second Thoughts about First Nights" 1)

The reviewer for the *Christian Science Monitor* pointed more kindly to the "burning" nature of "the problem which the author undertakes," contrasting Glaspell's handling of "economic issues" to the "quenched and perfectly safe" concerns "so often . . . on the stage" ("'Inheritors' by Susan Glaspell" 12). These first reviews conveyed the political urgency of Glaspell's moment, weighing the play's thematic significance against the (by this point) well-established complaint that Glaspell's dramas were overly "literary."

The reception in England was equally enthusiastic. The Liverpool Repertory Company premiered *Inheritors* in September 1925, following the success of the March 1925 British opening of *The Verge*, which was produced by the Pioneer Players and starred Sybil Thorndike. The *New York Times* reported that the English critics found the new work "even a more gripping play" ("*Inheritors* a Triumph in Critics' Opinion" 24), and *Inheritors* was reopened in London in early 1926. R. Ellis Roberts, writing for the *Guardian,* waxed rhapsodic: "Miss Susan Glaspell is the greatest playwright we have had writing in English since Mr. Shaw began" ("A Great Playwright"). In his piece for the *English Review* Horace Shipp called the play "a noteworthy contribution to contemporary drama, and something for which we may give America thanks." He deemed it one of the "plays of broad vision and big human purpose; it gives a trumpet call to all that is great in us; it projects big ideas" ("Language of Drama" 268). The reviewer for the *Era,* who had read the play in its published version first, agreed: "After seeing Miss Glaspell's epic-like theme vitalised into throbbing life on the stage, we realize how much greater is the play than a single reading made apparent" ("Inheritors"). N. G. Royde-Smith provides a clue to the British audience's emotional reception of the play, alluding to "the tears 'Inheritors' draws from its spectators in the last act" ("Drama: The American Play" 25). This commentary suggests that, at least for London critics and audiences, *Inheritors* indeed conveyed the national flavor and emotional force that Glaspell must have hoped this play would carry.

Notably absent from these British reviews, however, is commentary on the political background to the play. Although we might not expect British critics to have access to the full range of sources from which Glaspell constructed her work, it is surprising that the recent war seems to have no bearing whatsoever on their interpretation of the play. Furthermore, none of the British critics chose to engage with the debate on England's imperial role incorporated into the plot. The critic for the *Stage* catalogues the range of issues the play encompasses but makes no further comment upon them:

> So many points of interest—metaphysical, sociological, political, and racial—are raised in Susan Glaspell's arresting play that it is as difficult to appraise it within the limits of an ordinary notice as it has apparently been for the author herself to crowd all her dramatic material into three closely packed hours. ("Inheritors")

The *Times* of London simply remarked that "the problem with which it deals is more familiar to American audiences than to our own" ("Inheritors" 12),

while the *Spectator* observed the play's "extensive criticism of American mental limitations" ("Anarchist of the Spirit"). The *Weekly Westminster* interpreted
the play as "an exposition on the effect of the war upon America" (Farjeon
242). *Inheritors* appears to have been seen in England as a drama about the pioneer heritage, a history play grounded in the tradition of the farms of the
Midwest as well as in the philosophical tradition stretching from the Puritans
through Emerson, and into the anarchism of the present. The *Spectator* maintains Glaspell is the first dramatist "effectively to dramatize their [these Amer-
icans] creed" ("Anarchist of the Spirit"). One can only speculate about why
the London critics turned a blind eye to Glaspell's pointed extension of her
native theme to international affairs, specifically England's imperial stake in
India. Obviously, it was much easier and more comfortable to take the play as
being only about the United States. Ironically, a number of American critics
would take a related stance toward the 1927 revival. They assumed that its historical remove (like its geographical remove for the British) meant that *Inheritors* was not relevant to their lives.

Yet some New York reviewers, and of course the revival's producer, Eva
Le Gallienne, perceived the continued cogency of Glaspell's drama. Le Gallienne had founded her Civic Repertory Theatre in New York in 1926 and selected *Inheritors* as the eighth and final play for her first season. Glaspell's
drama was the first American piece the company produced. It opened 7 March
1927 and played for thirty-three performances at the Fourteenth Street Theatre (Le Gallienne, *At 33* 200, 261). In her memoir, *At 33*, she explains the rationale for this selection:

> "Inheritors" is not perhaps a "good play," but it is a burning challenge to
> America, full of indignation against the results of a too rapid, too greedy
> prosperity, in which the material has become the ultimate goal in com-
> plete disregard of spiritual and ethical values. . . . Miss Glaspell, in words
> which reveal her clear and gallant spirit, does not spare America, but only
> because she loves America so much; she can't bear to see it fall so lamen-
> tably short of the ideals it was founded upon. The play is a tonic, and I
> heartily recommend it as an antidote to incipient smugness! (205–6)

Acknowledging that Glaspell's writing may not conform to critics' conventional notions of "good" playwriting, she highlights the dramatist's commitment to America as her protagonist and shows that that conviction gives
the work its theatrical structure and power. Le Gallienne speaks presciently
here of the economic theme of the play, a warning that unknowingly foreshadowed the financial catastrophe of 1929. Her remarks point to the complexity of Glaspell's drama, with its incorporation of both topical political
concerns and larger ideological issues. While the immediacy of certain events

connected with the war may have faded by 1927, the broader questions about America's development still emerged strongly for her from Glaspell's text. Thus, Le Gallienne, and some of the more perceptive reviewers, understood that Glaspell's themes transcended the specificity of her setting. While the Espionage and Sedition Acts had been left behind, questions of governmental repression remained. While the chaos from the war was receding, its underlying causes still percolated around the world. And, while the United States was enjoying prosperity, it still needed to keep sight of its founding principles of democracy and tolerance.

The play's ongoing relevance became a point of clear division among the critics of the Le Gallienne production, most of whom believed strongly either that the play was dated or that it still presented an important lesson for its audience. Charles Brackett was one of the few reviewers of the 1927 revival to hedge his bets in the *New Yorker* by defending the play's "essentially chaotic subject matter" and "interesting factual background," rather than stating an opinion on its current thematic value ("Theatre" 33). R. Dana Skinner of the *Commonweal* called the drama "perhaps a few years out of date in its external form, but none the less timely in its deeper implications," and pointed to "its sharp and often scathing social analysis" ("Play" 582–83) Skinner astutely identified the problem with producing *Inheritors* at that moment:

> The play is distinctly not a plea for pacificism, but it is a flaming protest against limiting the convictions and speech of those living in a democracy. Unfortunately, it already seems like a distant flame. It is not old enough to be historical; and not fresh enough to be timely. (583)

David Carb wrote in *Vogue* that the play "has not dated" ("Inheritors" 138), while Arthur Ruhl in the *New York Herald Tribune* asserted Glaspell's theme cannot "evaporate overnight with changes of scene and general mood" ("Audiences Stirred by 'Inheritors' at Civic Repertory" 17). The critic for the *New York Evening Post* maintained:

> [the] passions and prejudices which brought intolerance and approval of the torturing of conscientious objectors and the suppression of liberty of speech and thought are still rampant in other forms, but . . . they seem a little stale and unimpressive on the stage. ("Another Play" 14)

John Mason Brown, writing for *Theatre Arts Monthly*, stated unequivocally:

> When Susan Glaspell's *The Inheritors* [*sic*] was first mounted at the Provincetown Theatre during the stress of war time, it must have flamed

with a greater vehemence than it can today. Its issues were of the immediate present. . . . Today . . . in the cold light of peace it can not but be ad-
mitted that it was Miss Glaspell herself who was too close to her causes
to weld them into a play that would outlast their topicality. ("This Bad
Showmanship" 327–28)

J. Brooks Atkinson of the *New York Times* wrote two pieces about the Le Gallienne revival, each of which humorously, if a bit snidely, tackled the question
of the play's ongoing relevance. Atkinson suggested that "probably Miss Le
Gallienne selected this outdated play . . . because of its honesty, its idealism
and its Americanism in the eclectic meaning of that word" but found that
"what it had to say about" a range of political issues from the Red scare to political prisoners "leaves us rather cold today" ("Pioneer Traditions" 1). He intimated that Glaspell's "attack . . . was perhaps sharper in 1921 . . . than in this
serene era when every one knows, the American Government has not committed a single act of injustice nor a single stupid blunder for at least five
years" ("Play" 23).

It would appear that some of the critics of 1927 did not have sufficient distance from recent historical events to realize the lasting import of Glaspell's
themes. The reviews also reflect the ongoing public division of opinion on the
war and its impact on the United States, some wishing to put it behind them,
while others felt it was critical to keep such events alive in the collective consciousness of the nation. Those who dismissed the relevance of the piece reflected the feeling of many Americans at the time who saw the postwar years,
especially in terms of governmental behavior, as completely different from the
preceding era of international conflict. Atkinson's humorous exaggeration of
the state of affairs in Washington only lightly masks the sense that the country
was on the upswing, with a focus on the bright future ahead. Skinner's comment that the revival appeared before the nation had had sufficient time to
achieve historical perspective on recent events may well account for the tenor
of the more dismissive commentary. Glaspell must have been struck by this opposition, for she builds it into her last play, *Springs Eternal,* which reflects on
World War I in the midst of the second.

On other issues the critics of each production were virtually unanimous.
They uniformly felt the play was too long, and many expressed dissatisfaction
with the blatancy of the social and political content as well as the dialogue. On
the other hand, most praised the characterizations, and in each production the
actress playing Madeline Fejevary Morton received raves, indicative both of
strong casting and a well-written part.[20] Glaspell's dramatization of the American pioneer spirit received many enthusiastic comments, and both the New
York and British critics observed the emotional impact of the play's conclusion on the audience. Chronicling the opening night enthusiasm for the Civic

Rep production, the *New York Herald Tribune* reported the audience "inter-rupted the action with little bursts of applause," and at the curtain calls "Miss Glaspell was lifted from her orchestra seat and . . . escorted to the stage" (Arthur Ruhl, "Audience Stirred" 17).

The reviews suggest that *Inheritors* may have appealed more to audi-ences than to critics, especially in New York.[21] This will also prove true for Glaspell's Pulitzer Prize play, *Alison's House,* which the Civic Rep would pre-miere in 1930. It would appear that the viewers responded positively to the plot, characters, and emotional tone of *Inheritors,* caring little for the critics' concerns with literary style or their perceptions of aesthetic or sociopolitical merit. The fact that some writers responded only to the questions of imme-diate connection to World War I, while others identified only the broader themes, indicates that Glaspell may have packed too much social commen-tary into the work for audiences to grasp at a single performance. Anticipat-ing the contemporary criticism of Glaspell editor C. W. E. Bigsby, one re-viewer maintained the play featured "too many parallels and coincidences" (R. Dana Skinner, "Play" 582).

Indeed, Bigsby finds "the moral symmetry" Glaspell develops among the play's acts "all too pat" (*Plays* 17) and a "rather too adroit irony" (*Twentieth Century American Drama* 28) and deems the play overall "deeply conven-tional" (*Plays* 16). Specifically, Bigsby is responding to the linking of Native American Indians with Hindu Indians, of "reds" with "Reds," and of battles fought here and abroad for native land and culture against colonizers.[22] Bigsby's emphasis on dramatic form and genre (here the realist history play) may, however, have overwhelmed his sensitivity to the play's content and the dexterity and impressive grasp of history Glaspell demonstrates in her weav-ing of complex and varied social and political allusions. Clearly, Glaspell made a series of calculated choices about which wars, political movements, and groups of peoples to use in *Inheritors.* These choices obviously generate the symmetry Bigsby finds objectionable, but, as he acknowledges, other critics, including Ludwig Lewisohn and James Agate, saw them as dramaturgical strengths (Bigsby, *Plays* 16–17). Glaspell's ability to identify correspondences between discrete historical events and to link a range of social phenomena with changes in the American ethos represents an astounding grasp of Amer-ican culture and history that, as Lewisohn observed, was unparalleled in the drama to date. One could argue that only Tony Kushner's two-part *Angels in America* (1991–92) has since attempted the scope, sweep, and political force of Glaspell's writing in this play.

The reception of the 1983 revival of *Inheritors* by the Mirror Theater in New York, however, presents an interesting contrast to Bigsby's roughly contempora-neous appraisal.[23] Writing for the *New York Times,* Herbert Mitgang called the play's warnings "relevant" and states "the play holds up well as political and

moral history." He draws explicit parallels between the 1980s and the 1920s, sum-
marizing the play's concerns with an intentionally updated spin:

> protecting the environment from greedy real-estate developers, profes-
> sors who give up their principles under pressure from administrators,
> dark-skinned people who are harassed because they are "foreigners," the
> rights of Indians to their traditional lands, Federal vigilantes who exer-
> cise control and conscientious objectors who oppose war.

As Mitgang concludes, Glaspell's themes "still go in 1983" (26). His notice suggests that, despite its "fault" of length, *Inheritors* indeed transcends the specificity of its original moment to convey its larger political meaning in the theater.

    Inheritors stands as Glaspell's strongest ideological drama. Some critics
see her next play, *The Verge*, as Glaspell's best for its dramaturgical and thematic experimentation, poetic dialogue, and feminist orientation. Her own
comments on the importance to her writing of "all progressive movements,
whether feminist, social or economic" (Rohe) suggest that content as well as
form merit equal consideration in the evaluation of her drama and make *Inheritors* her most important overtly political work. Given the urgency of the
debates on freedom she presents in *Inheritors*—concerns still bequeathed to
us in the new millennium—this play maintains its status as "a deed of national
import" (Lewisohn 395).

The Verge

The Verge stands second only to *Trifles* as the Glaspell play that has stimulated the most lively, sophisticated, and varied contemporary critical responses, recent scholarship that contrasts intriguingly with the bewilderment reflected in many of the reviews of its original productions in New York (1921) and London (1925). What connects these two bodies of criticism are writers' attempts to provide a totalizing explanation of the play, to bring to it a coherence and sense of containment that the play itself continues to evade. While their bafflement tended to make the journalists either flatly dismissive or unquestioningly reverential toward the play, its complexities have prompted scholars to approach it from multiple perspectives, perhaps in the hope that some combination of methodologies would ultimately explicate the drama's nuances of character, language, imagery, and narrative.

The plot is relatively simple: Claire Archer, an unconventional woman married to a rather conventional man, attempts to find outlets for her creativity and intellect through horticultural experimentation. She eschews the traditional outlet for women, motherhood, by openly rejecting her daughter from her previous marriage; Claire's son from her second marriage has died in infancy. The daughter, Elizabeth, has instead been raised by Claire's sister Adelaide, one of Glaspell's quintessentially conservative, conventional female characters. From Claire's perspective Elizabeth appears to be growing into the image of her aunt. The action of the play concerns the culmination of Claire's most adventurous experiment to date: the flowering of a plant she has bred called "Breath of Life." Glaspell intertwines and juxtaposes Claire's botanical work with her human interactions, particularly those with the men in her life: husband Harry, lover Dick, and confidante Tom.[1] Claire's growing dissatisfaction with human relationships and disillusionment with her scientific work coalesce in her mental breakdown and the destruction of what she has cared for most.

Drawing on multiple senses of a "verge," Glaspell constructs her drama around transitions and contrasts: between characters' beliefs and actions, botanical forms, and states of mind, among others. Claire Archer is a woman on

the verge of insanity. Her social and familial behavior teeters on the edge of pro-
priety. Her horticultural experiments bring plants to their biological limits,
thrusting them toward an evolution into new species. And Glaspell's dramaturgical form echoes this indeterminacy: the play appears at times to be on the
brink of farce; at other moments it mirrors a Strindbergian development from
problem play to expressionism and symbolism. Glaspell represents the disintegration of Claire's world through a complex network of poetic language, floral
and religious imagery, and experimentation with theatrical form that continues
to challenge and perplex. Glaspell takes as her very subject the impossibility to
contain or fully to explain; critics' efforts to do just that, in the case of *The Verge*,
are thus doomed from the outset. If we simply accept this calculated opacity,
that may enable us to probe the connections among Glaspell's dramatic obscurity, her thematic and structural experimentation, and the contexts of the
work's creation, however inconclusive those explorations must remain.

During the 1919–20 theater season Glaspell and Cook took a "sabbatical"
from the Provincetown Players, in order to replenish their own creative ener-
gies, to step back from the artistic and administrative tensions that were
mounting among various factions within the Players, and to give other members of the group the opportunity to pursue their own vision for the theater.[2]
The couple spent much of that period at their home on Cape Cod, where Cook
worked on his play *The Spring* and Glaspell drafted *Inheritors* (Noe, *Critical Biography* 109) and may also have worked on *The Verge*.[3] Although it is difficult
to date Glaspell's exact period of composition for the latter, its links to *The
Spring* and to some of Cook's other writing are intriguing.[4] On the levels of
plot, setting, and form *The Spring* and *Inheritors* appear to have the stronger
ties: both feature narratives involving Native Americans; both take place in
Black Hawk territory; and both utilize a historical prologue, followed by the
main action. But Glaspell's writing about *The Spring* in *The Road to the Temple*
reveals other, subtler connections between Cook's play and *The Verge*.

According to Glaspell, *The Spring* developed from earlier ideas for a play
based on the alchemist Paracelsus. In Cook's words, "Paracelsus is one of the
flaming minds of the world—his soul a crucible in which the elements of nature are transmuted into a new form of existence" (*Road* 294). Glaspell also includes in her husband's biography selections from his verse, including a passage from his poem about a greenhouse he had built:

> No mere Wordsworthian guest of Nature be,
> Spectator and not sharer of her life,
> But her co-worker, with selective art
> Prescribing form to her wild energies:
> Saying, "Thou shalt be!" and "Thou shalt not be!"
> (*Road* 202)

The greenhouse as setting and symbol, replete with its connotations for growth, experimentation, and new life, seems to have been conceived similarly for both authors.

One overt link between Glaspell's 1921 play and Cook's notes for the Paracelsus drama is their central characters' Faustian thirst for knowledge; Glaspell combines the vegetative creativity of the greenhouse lyric with the alchemical, Nietzschean compulsion to make superior life forms. One can also see in Cook's poetic discourse here a resemblance both to Glaspell's diction and to her elusive style. Compare, for example, Claire's passionate exclamations at the close of act 1, in her frenzy to uproot the experimental "Edge Vine":

> Why did I make you? To get past you! Oh yes, I know you have thorns! The Edge Vine should have thorns. Oh, I have loved you so! You took me where I hadn't been. (78)

These stylistic and thematic similarities among *Inheritors, The Verge, The Spring,* and Cook's notes as transcribed in *The Road to the Temple* suggest a creative synergy at work in the couple's writing. Linda Ben-Zvi and Ann Larabee have discussed the associations between Glaspell's and O'Neill's work during this period;[5] it seems equally plausible that a similar dynamic existed between Cook and Glaspell, especially given their history of dramatic coauthorship. It would be impossible and counterproductive, however, to atomize their collaborative process. Rather, we might see in these resonances Glaspell's distinctive positioning of motifs and concerns she shared with her husband within a decidedly different critical and cultural matrix, one that raises questions about gender, modernism, and history. Veronica Makowsky argues that "through Claire Archer . . . Glaspell explores the causes and the tragic consequences of the high modernist's alienation from the life around her" ("Susan Glaspell" 62).

One of the intriguing passages from the section of *The Road to the Temple* devoted to the this same period is a note by Cook that Glaspell includes, but does not comment upon, for another never-written drama:

> Play of Madame Curie and her husband—she discovering radium through the guidance of his superior sources of knowledge, he having sunk back into the unconscious. She tapping the sub-conscious mind of the whole world through her belief in the vitality of his dead mind. (293)

It is tempting to read such material (auto)biographically. One might infer an even more direct connection between the marriage and Glaspell's writing than the sharing of creative stimuli that nevertheless resulted in very different aesthetics. Such an analysis might posit a link between the experiences of Glaspell's marriage and her depiction of women's lives in her drama and fiction; it might map the trajectory of Glaspell's career as an ongoing reaction to the concerns and actions of her husband. Certainly, a passage such as that on Madame Curie could foster a theory that Cook fantasized that he was responsible for her creativity, that he was the real source of her gifts. We might also see it as Glaspell's gesture, albeit a conflicted one, acknowledging her husband's intellect and talents. Yet, as Linda Ben-Zvi has persuasively argued, to read Glaspell's work biographically through her relationship with Cook, particularly as it is documented in *The Road to the Temple,* is a risky venture at best. Ben-Zvi maintains that Glaspell's self-portrait in the biography is as much a construct as are her fictional characters and that her complex agenda in writing the biography renders analysis based on its narrative highly problematic.[6] The links between the couple's writings at this time form an interesting backdrop to, but not a full explanation of, the creation of *The Verge.* The well-established pattern in her work of responses to her social environment, to political events, to her observations of the American character, and especially in this instance to aesthetic and formal issues of modernism deserves more detailed scrutiny.

In this regard we might productively compare Cook's construction of Madame Curie with that of the modernist poet Mina Loy, who saw her as an iconic figure for creativity and experimentation. Loy and William Carlos Williams, both of whom also acted with the Players, incorporated Curie into seminal verse: Loy in a tribute to Gertrude Stein written in this same period; Williams years later in his epic *Paterson,* most likely influenced by Loy's verse (Conover 324). It is doubtful that Glaspell knew Loy's poem, and yet the resemblances between the poetic image of Stein and the characterization of Claire Archer are striking:

> Curie
> of the laboratory
> of vocabulary
> she crushed
> the tonnage
> of consciousness
> congealed to phrases
> to extract
> a radium of the word.
> ("Gertrude Stein" 26)

Loy captures here the sense that Stein's poetry transcended rhetorical form and extracted from the morass of language the means of pure expression. Loy uses the metaphor of the laboratory for its connotations of significant, life-changing, but also dangerous exploration and discovery. These images not only convey a feeling for Stein's creative process; they also give it the weight and value that the modern age attributed to science. Glaspell draws upon these same images and resonances in creating her new drama for the modernist stage.

Moreover, *The Verge* stands as one of many American literary works, written soon after the end of World War I, that reflects the era's profound response to the chaos and destruction of this cataclysmic event. As cultural critics such as Loren Baritz and Frederick J. Hoffman argue, much of the writing from the 1920s, the "postwar decade," shares sensibilities shaped by the war and its aftermath.[7] It is not so much that these works are about the war per se but that they depict its impact on countless aspects of postwar life. Baritz summarizes the ethos of the era for exactly the kind of individual Glaspell represents through her central character, Claire Archer:

> For intellectuals and artists, the brutality of the war . . . together with the political prominence of provincial America, seemed to force them into themselves. . . . [T]hey tended to withdraw from society, actually to become exiles . . . perhaps anti-social, and probably alienated strangers at home. The lost generation was created by the war and non-urban America. (xxx–vii)

While *Inheritors,* the play that immediately preceded *The Verge,* traces some of the most serious and overt political consequences of war, especially jingoism and censorship, the latter play is primarily a character study, an exploration of how one life mirrors what we have later come to recognize as the profound malaise of a large sector of the population at this moment.

Glaspell's emphasis on individual psychology and psychosis also ties *The Verge* to her first play (cowritten with Cook), *Suppressed Desires.* A comparison of these two works graphically illustrates the differences between the dark vision of the 1920s and the lighthearted era when, with the war a distant European conflict, Mabel could "feebly" guess that psychoanalysis is "something about the war, isn't it . . . [perhaps] the name of a new explosive" (*Suppressed Desires* 238). This was the moment when being "psyched" was a bohemian pastime; all too soon thereafter, clinicians began to observe the devastating impact of the war on the psyche and saw cases of real neurosis and hysteria burgeon. Glaspell's creation of the "hysteric" Claire shows the dramatist's understanding of the rapid evolution of psychology and psychiatry and her timely sensitivity to the manifestations of neurosis in the postwar period. Glaspell refracts the chaos of war's aftermath through the wild emotional arc of Claire's character, through her language and imagination, and in the very form of the drama itself, which careens from farcical comedy to the borders of melodrama and tragedy.

As Elin Diamond explains in *Unmaking Mimesis,* one can trace a complex relationship between the medical understanding of hysteria and women's writing for the modernist theater through characterization, corporeal figuration, dialogic experimentation, and action that disrupts stage conventions.[8] Diamond contrasts the "unmaking of realism" evidenced by Elizabeth Robins and Florence Bell in their play *Alan's Wife* (1893) to conventions of the "'sex-problem play,'" exemplified in the realist dramaturgy of Henrik Ibsen. Through an analysis of the dramatists' divergent representations of woman as hysteric, Diamond concludes:

> In deciphering the hysteric's enigma realism celebrates positivist inquiry, thus buttressing its claims for "truth to life." In effect, hysteria provides stage realism with one of its richest and, ideologically, one of its most satisfying plots. (4)

Diamond points to such dramatic techniques as Robins and Bell's creation of a heroine who murders her child, frankly expresses her sexuality, and refuses to participate in the conventions of realist dialogue, as examples of the playwrights' subversion of dominant dramatic forms. For Diamond *Alan's Wife*

> refuses to allow the "hysteric" to become recuperated as the necessary stake in realism. It does not abandon narrative, but it refuses the closure of positivist inquiry. It does not dismantle the text as a unique source of meaning, but it destabilizes the relation between text and performance, each contaminating the other. (37–38)

The overt similarities between *Alan's Wife* and *The Verge* are most likely coincidental, in that we have no evidence that Glaspell knew the British play. But the characterological, thematic, dramaturgical, and even narrative parallels between the dramas suggest that Glaspell was participating in a similar enterprise: the manipulation of form, the refiguring of female characters, the unmasking of theatrical conventions. Glaspell positions *The Verge* within the revisionist project of feminist playwrights from the late nineteenth century forward. Moreover, she makes these links overt by tying her characterization of Claire explicitly to the "symptoms and etiology of the hysteric" through the specific contexts of the war and its psychoanalytic framework (Diamond 4).

Act 1, set in Claire's greenhouse, begins on a deceptively comic note. With snow and wind whirling outside, Claire has switched all the heat from the main house to the greenhouse to protect her plants. In retaliation her husband, Harry, has ordered breakfast to be served there for himself and their guests, Tom Edgeworthy and Richard (Dick) Demming. The connotative value of a "hothouse" may also underlie the first act's exposition; we soon sense the intimacy Claire shares with each of the three men. The action soon begins to resemble French farce, with characters blowing in and out of the door, eggs rolling about the stage, double entendres in the dialogue, and stage business revolving around the need for someone to fetch the salt.[9]

But Glaspell's early stage directions suggest other simultaneous nuances at play. She describes Claire as "disturbed . . . from deep" within herself (61). Claire makes jokes that betray a dangerous edge, as, for example, her comment to Dick about trying his egg without salt: "You must have tried and tried things. Isn't that the way one leaves the normal and gets into the byways of perversion?" (63). One senses that she may also be referring to herself with this remark; Glaspell consistently juxtaposes Claire, her unconventional behavior, and her unusual use of language to the "refined" mode preferred by Harry. We can also see that Glaspell is setting up the patriarchal critique of independent women such as Claire; the traditional behavior insisted upon by Harry is also preferred by the "American mind" that evolved from the same New England roots that bred Claire but from which she is desperately trying to escape (64).

Claire soon connects madness to the recent war, as a moment when America could have escaped its narrowness and puritanism but failed:

Claire: . . . But the war didn't help. Oh, it was a stunning chance! But as fast as we could—scuttled right back to the trim little thing we'd been shocked out of.
Harry: You bet we did—showing our good sense.
Claire: Showing our incapacity—for madness.
Harry: Oh, come now, Claire—snap out of it. You're not really trying to say that capacity for madness is a good thing to *have*?
Claire: (*in simple surprise*) Why yes, of course.
Dick: But I should say the war did leave enough madness to give you a gleam of hope.
Claire: Not the madness that—breaks through. And it was—a stunning chance! Mankind massed to kill. We have failed. We are through. We will destroy. Break this up—it can't go farther. In the air above—in the sea below—it is to kill! All we had thought we were—we aren't. We were shut in with what wasn't so. Is there one ounce of energy has not gone to this killing? Is there one love not torn in two? Throw it in! Now? Ready? Break up. Push. Harder. Break up. And then—and then— But we didn't say—"And then—" The spirit didn't take the tip.

(70)

Veronica Makowsky astutely observes that "for Claire the war itself was not responsible for her incipient madness, but its failed aftermath was" ("Susan Glaspell" 62). Moreover, this section of dialogue encapsulates many of the dynamics that shape *The Verge:* the intertwining of images that characterizes Claire's mental process, her fragmented and evocative use of language, and Glaspell's own symbolism that links the madness of the war to Claire's neurosis and to her metaphoric connection to her plants.

Harry, ever the voice of traditional decorum, attempts to reinstate an atmosphere of geniality, but Claire continues to make unconventional, disturbing associations:

Harry: Claire! Come now (*looking to the others for help*)—let's talk of something else.
Claire: Plants do it. The big leap—it's called. Explode their species—because something in them knows they've gone as far as they can go. Something in them knows they're shut in to just that. So—go mad—that life may not be prisoned. Break themselves up into crazy things—into lesser things, and from the pieces—may come one sliver of life with vitality to find the future. How beautiful. How brave.

(70)

The metaphoric link between horticulture, neurosis, and the war had already gained currency in the medical community. In their famous *Studies on Hysteria* (1895) Freud and his collaborator, Josef Breuer, called hysterics "the flowers of mankind" (2:240), while a 1919 article from the *Long Island Medical Journal* suggests more pointedly that practitioners "consider the problem [of war neurosis] biologically, likening the growth of a neurosis to a healthy plant" (Nichols 257). Harry specifically describes Claire as "hysterical" (72), introducing a term that would have resonated with Greenwich Village audiences. In the time between the production of *Suppressed Desires* and the premier of *The Verge* New York had become a center for the study and practice of psychoanalysis in the United States, and Glaspell's colleagues Max Eastman and Floyd Dell had published influential essays on their experiences with analysis.[10]

The impact of the war on the individual psyche, especially that of soldiers, focused public attention on a precise application of psychoanalytic technique. Harry confides to Dick:

I'd like to have Charlie Emmons see her—he's fixed up a lot of people shot to pieces in the war. Claire needs something to tone her nerves *up.* (65)

Early in act 2 Harry explains to Claire that Emmons, whom he's invited for dinner, is "a neurologist" whom he hopes can help her, as her "nerves are a little on the blink"—this in the interest of her being made "happy again" (83). As Sanford Gifford notes in his discussion of the reception of psychoanalysis in the United States, Americans had what Freud called a "medical fixation" that only physicians were capable of psychoanalytic training and practice (139). As with her presentation of the "New Psychology" in *Suppressed Desires,* Glaspell demonstrates in *The Verge* her clear understanding of the latest trends and theories in psychoanalysis. Her depiction of Claire and her symptoms, as well as Dr. Emmons and his diagnosis, closely mirrors the descriptions of traumatic disorders brought on by the war, documented in both the medical literature and memoirs from the era.

What is fascinating about Glaspell's drama, however, is her prescient understanding of the gendered significance of Claire's psychosis. As cultural historians have more recently concluded, this era was the first that aligned a particular class of male psychiatric disorders with the condition previously coded as almost exclusively female, namely "hysteria."[11] In his 1979 study *No Man's Land* historian Eric J. Leed explains that

> the symptoms of shell-shock were precisely the same as those of the most common hysterical disorders of peacetime, though they often acquired new and more dramatic names in war. . . . [W]hat had been predominantly a disease of women before the war became a disease of men in combat. (163)

That Glaspell should have Claire treated by a clinician who has worked extensively with those whom Harry calls "shot to pieces by the war" shows her unusual awareness of the parallels psychiatrists and psychologists had just begun to draw between certain male and female neurotic conditions. The *Long Island Medical Journal,* for example, with its groundbreaking 1919 article comparing "War and Civil Neurosis," concluded that "without question . . . the war neuroses are identical with the civil neuroses as to etiology, symptomatology, course, treatment, and prognosis" (Nichols 257).

Equally important is Glaspell's construction of Claire's behavior as part of a thematic matrix; through Claire the playwright brings together the war and American culture, madness and its treatment, and a feminist sensibility. As Elaine Showalter has noted, it was not until such pioneering clinicians as W. H. R. Rivers (who had worked extensively with male shell-shock victims during and immediately after the war) hypothesized parallels between male and female hysteria around notions of gender anxiety, that any opposition to the long-standing theories of sexually separate mental disorders arose ("Hysteria, Feminism and Gender" 325–26). The fact that Rivers's work was not published until 1922 makes Glaspell's sensitivity to this correspondence of gender and neurosis all the more striking. Although "immediately after the war" a number of women writers had "appropriated the theme of shell shock" (Showalter, *Female Malady* 190), examples of this work, such as Rebecca West's novel *The Return of the Soldier* (1918), usually featured a male shell-shock victim. These female authors "made explicit connections between psychiatric therapies and the imposition of patriarchal values insensitive to passion, fantasy, and creativity" (Showalter 190). In their deeply conflicted male characters they found corollaries to the repression women experienced. Showalter credits Virginia Woolf and her 1925 novel, *Mrs. Dalloway*, with finally making the connection between "the shell-shocked veteran . . . [and] the repressed woman of the man-governed world through their common enemy, the nerve specialist" (192). Yet Glaspell's 1921 play had already established this linkage: Claire rejects Dr. Emmons's attempt to mollify her at the close of act 2 and subsequently recognizes that Emmons and those who agree with him will only "pull [her] down" (97); she refuses to be drawn away from the madness that to her is the only release from the confinement she sees in every aspect of her life. As Christine Dymkowski has observed, for Claire "madness *is* liberating" (101).

Although Claire never says so explicitly, part of her resistance to Emmons may stem from an intuitive understanding that the rest he recommends for her thinly masks yet another form of containment. After a short conversation with her in act 2, he insists, "Oh, we've got to get you rested" (91), and her husband echoes this sentiment in act 3: "Emmons says you need a good long rest—and I think he's right" (96). By suggesting this therapy for Claire, Glaspell invokes the best-known treatment for hysteria, the infamous "rest cure" in use in the United States since the 1870s. Following his experiences with "malingering soldiers in the Civil War," Dr. Silas Weir Mitchell developed a therapy for female patients of six weeks' duration in which

> the patient was isolated from her friends and family, confined to bed, and forbidden to sit up, sew, read, write, or do any intellectual work. . . . Mitchell was well aware that the sheer boredom and sensory deprivation of the rest cure made it a punishment to the patient. (Showalter, "Hysteria" 297)

The goal, of course, was for the woman to return to her former life with the understanding that it was indeed preferable to the treatment, despite the fact that nothing about that life and what had led to her symptoms would have been addressed. Variations on the rest cure were also the initial treatment of choice for officers suffering from shell-shock in World War I (323), an interesting, if ironic, full-circle revival of the therapy initially derived from a war context by Mitchell.

In addition to this recent resurgence of the rest cure technique, however, the fact that one of Mitchell's patients had been Charlotte Perkins Gilman may also have been significant for Glaspell's conceptualization of Claire's condition. Gilman was not only a Heterodite, and one of the subjects of Floyd Dell's study, *Women as World Builders* (1913), but was also an author of considerable standing, perhaps best known now for her story "The Yellow Wall-paper" (1892), which had just been reprinted in a 1920 collection entitled *Great Modern American Stories* (Gilbert and Gubar, *Norton Anthology* 1147). Gil-man's harrowing experiences with Mitchell's rest cure formed the basis for "The Yellow Wallpaper." Her narrative and Glaspell's share many elements, in-cluding their central characters' movement from sanity to madness. In each the protagonist approaches a madness integrally connected to feelings of en-trapment within patriarchal structures, especially the traditional maternal function; each desires to escape to a realm of alternate self-definition. Both works feature woman's critique of conventional gender roles and the knowl-edge that they must be subverted through female creativity. Both works depict central male characters whose well-intentioned yet obtuse behavior causes more harm than good. The works also share with other texts that have become central to feminist criticism the structural nexus of a "madwoman in an attic": here Claire's "thwarted tower" room (*Verge* 79), which is the setting for act 2 and is Claire's refuge within her home.

Sandra Gilbert and Susan Gubar, the feminist scholars who have ex-plored this "madwoman" trope most extensively, discuss the connection of women writers to World War I in the second volume of their later study, also entitled *No Man's Land*. Quoting Malcolm Bradbury, they observe that "many critics have seen the war as . . . the apocalypse that leads the way into Mod-ernism" but that these critics were really only talking about male modernists (260). Thus, Gilbert and Gubar take as one of their goals in this later work the exploration of women as modernists equally, if not identically, influenced by the "Great War."[12] Critics of *The Verge* invariably point to its stylistic innova-tion, its fragmented dialogue, its tension between realism and other dramatic forms such as symbolism and/or expressionism, in short, its status as a mod-ernist work. With this one piece Glaspell not only joins the ranks of other emerging female modernists but reveals her remarkable sense of the nexus of madness, modernism, and war that is a touchstone of some of the major artis-tic and literary works from the era.

Gerhard Bach, one of the foremost historians of the Provincetown Players, has analyzed the group's dramaturgy as a reflection of the tensions between the sociopolitical agenda of Cook, exemplified by their realist productions, and the modernist aesthetics of some of the other members, such as Alfred Kreymborg, who favored a poetic, symbolist, or expressionist sensibility.[13] But to pit aes-thetics and stylistic experimentation against social goals is to suggest that these are mutually exclusive dramaturgical possibilities. In fact, in the seasons before the Players produced *The Verge* they had presented other works demonstrating clearly the political force of the newer dramatic forms, especially the poetic, symbolist plays of Edna St. Vincent Millay, whose *Princess Marries the Page* (1918) confronts questions of class; her *Aria Da Capo* (1919) was universally recognized as a blatant critique of the rationales for World War I and the callous responses to it by some members of her own Greenwich Village community. Glaspell scholarship has not often sought explanations for her dramaturgical innovations beyond the influence of her theatrical colleagues. If we widen our analytic perspective, however, we may also see Glaspell's participation in the larger modernist movement that attempted to represent perceptions of chaos and social struggle with the latest experiments in form, theme, and character.

Criticism of *The Verge* frequently looks at its scenic environment, especially the act 2 set, as the key indicator of its expressionist leanings. Glaspell describes it as

> a tower which is thought to be round but does not complete the circle. The back is curved, then jagged lines break from that, and the front is a queer bulging window—in a curve that leans. The whole structure is as if given a twist by some terrific force—like something wrong. (78)

Distinguishing Glaspell's play from the older German theatrical tradition in the form, Ronald Wainscott nevertheless believes *The Verge* predates all other American "dramaturgical attempts" at expressionism (114). W. David Sievers observes that the setting of *The Verge* "apparently marks the first expressionistic distortion of scenery in our [American] theatre for a subjective effect—that of unconscious 'regression to the womb'" (71). Sievers's psychoanalytic reading is, of course, only one of several interpretive possibilities (even within psychoanalytic interpretation) for Glaspell's scenic intent; other readings might include the physical projection of Claire's mental state or the broader symbolic representation of the self as a skewed version of traditional form.

An analysis of the set sensitive to gender concerns might posit a relationship between the "thwarted tower," with its warped phallic imagery, the terrific impact of the war, which "unmanned" soldiers both literally and figuratively, and female modernists' associations of these dynamics with their own cultural positions. It is important to remember that one of the hallmarks of Glaspell's dramaturgy, regardless of dramatic form as such, is the integral relationship of, and mirroring between, scenic environment and character. Bernice's home, Alison Stanhope's bedroom, and the lifesaving station favored by Mrs. Patrick in *The Outside* each exemplifies this notable element of Glaspell's theatrical creativity. Glaspell surely wants us to see direct connections between Claire and the space within her home she views as most completely her own.

In addition to this linkage of stage design with expressionism, critics also point to the cumulative effects of Claire's character, her language, and the symbolism of her representation through botanical and religious imagery as endemic of American expressionism. Arthur Waterman, for example, concludes that "it weaves the design of the set into the meaning of the play, and it forsakes realism in character, dialogue, and staging to achieve Expressionistic effects" (*Susan Glaspell* 83). Reviewers at the time of its premier also saw stylistic resemblance in the scenography to recent developments in expressionist film technique, especially *The Cabinet of Dr. Caligari*.[14] Yet to extend Glaspell's artistic choices with regard to her scenic environment and central character to encompass the entire play—in other words, to label the whole drama as expressionist—is to miss a strategic tension in the work that operates on formal, characterological, and thematic levels. Claire is at war with her family but not only in terms of the play's basic action. Glaspell stages this conflict dialogically and stylistically, such that we can actually see the battle operating in the movement between opposed poles of value: between realism and expressionism, between straightforward prose and poetic language, between the new and the traditional, between patriarchal condescension and feminist struggles toward release, as well as among the various scenic environments of each act. Glaspell introduces these tensions early in the play, as she works to establish the distinctions between Claire and those around her.

Claire: . . . We need not be held in forms molded for us. There is outness—
    and otherness.
Harry: Now Claire—I didn't mean to start anything serious.
Claire: No; you never mean to do that. I want to break it up! I tell you, I
    want to break it up! If it were all in pieces, we'd be (*a little laugh*)
    shocked to aliveness . . . wouldn't we? There would be strange new
    comings together—mad new comings together, and we would know
    what it is to be born, and then we might know—that we are. Smash
    it. . . . As you'd smash an egg. . . . You think I can't smash anything? You
    think life can't break up, and go outside what it was? Because you've
    gone dead in the form in which you found yourself, you think that's all
    there is to the whole adventure? And that is called sanity. And made a
    virtue—to lock one in. You never worked with things that grow! Things
    that take a sporting chance—go mad—that sanity mayn't lock them
    in—from life untouched—from life—that waits. . . . (*she exits*)
                                                              (64–65)

Claire's extended speech here demonstrates how she connects the events around her, from the sublimity of the war to the inconsequentiality of a smashed egg, with her overarching sense of the need to transcend strictures of all kinds to achieve a truer connection with life. The newness Claire calls for also reflects the revolutionary force of modernism itself, with its upheaval in theatrical, literary, artistic, and other cultural forms that rejected the stasis and torpor in dominant modes of expression.

Glaspell oscillates between Claire's elevated and evocative language and her husband's pragmatic transparency. This movement is echoed in Claire's realizations about Harry's profession as a pilot. While "Claire hoped that this modern technology would change man's perspective" (Makowsky, "Susan Glaspell" 62), liberating him from tradition, she discovers that flight always devolves to his return to earth (69).

Harry: Oh, I wish Claire wouldn't be strange like that. (*helplessly*) What is it? What's the matter?
Dick: It's merely the excess of a particularly rich temperament.
Harry: But it's growing on her. I sometimes wonder if all this (*indicating the place around him* [the plants in the greenhouse]) is a good thing. It would be all right if she'd just do what she did in the beginning—make flowers as good as possible of their kind. That's an awfully nice things for a woman to do—raise flowers. But there's something about this— changing things into other things—putting things together and making queer new things—this—
Dick: Creating?
Harry: Give it any name you want it to have—it's unsettling for a woman. They say Claire's a shark at it, but what's the good of it, if it gets her? What *is* the good of it, anyway? Suppose we can produce new things. Lord—look at the ones we've got.

(65)

Glaspell juxtaposes the infinite potential Claire sees in her work with the quotidian conclusions Harry reaches about Claire's horticultural pastime; she pulls her audience back and forth between the imagistic realm of Claire's mind and the everyday reality of Harry, Dick, and their breakfast chat.

As Cynthia D. Smith observes,

In order to fully appreciate Glaspell's attempt at de-essentializing the feminine roles assigned to women through Claire's uninhibited nature, one must evaluate the male identities within this text as possible hindrances to that attempt. (61)

Smith reads the constructions of Tom, Dick, Harry, and Claire's assistant, Anthony, through recent writing on male identity that builds upon some of the foundational work of feminist gender theory. Smith rightly notes that most critical (and I would add the early journalistic) discussion of the play focuses on Claire. Smith's comment, however, that Glaspell should not have allowed the men "to disappear into the background" displays a perplexing disregard for the work as a play to be performed (77), with much of our understanding of Claire coming precisely through her interactions with them and dialogic opposition to their concepts of her.

Surprisingly, Smith says nothing of Claire's construction of the play's fifth male—the absent son, David, who died as a child. Although Adelaide accuses her of never having "known the faintest stirrings of a mother's love," Harry insists "Claire loved our boy," so much that, in the chaos and failure of the world she sees around her, Claire asks, "Why should I want him to live?" (84). In one of the play's most vivid and poignant moments Claire shares with Tom her memory of David's last night:

> In his short life were many flights. I never told anyone about the last one. His little bed was by the window—he wasn't four years old. It was night, but him not asleep. He saw the morning star—you know—the morning star. Brighter—stranger—reminiscent—and a promise. He pointed— "Mother," he asked me, "what is there—beyond the stars?" A baby, a sick baby—the morning star. Next night—the finger that pointed was—(*suddenly bites her own finger*). But yes, I am glad. He would always have tried to move and too much would hold him. Wonder would die—and he'd laugh at soaring. (87)

The intensity of love and loss Glaspell conveys in this speech must be kept in perspective when considering Claire's attitudes toward the life around her and what it means to exist in a moment that she sees as having failed to fulfill its promise. Glaspell brilliantly captures here Claire's rationalization of the loss of her son, her preference that he die rather than lose the potential and wonder of a childhood that had to give way to adulthood in a debased culture.

Smith concludes that Glaspell's "feminist viewpoint . . . falls short" in *The Verge* because the male characters are objectified, constructed, and victimized by Claire and are not given independent agency (61). While it is true that the men in the play function as foils for Claire, they also serve a purpose subtler than, though related to, Glaspell's goals for understanding gender construction and theatrical conventions in *Trifles*. By putting Claire at the center of the play and by highlighting her construction of male identity, Glaspell is again turning the tables on a dramaturgical tradition that enables male characters to define and objectify female identity. Through this technique Glaspell creates a binary that posits her adult male characters as traditional, conformist, and static, while Claire emerges as the force striving toward the experimental, the transgressive, the modern. Claire's modernity is fierce and wild, but it is productive, unlike Dick's modern art, his "lines that don't make anything" (*The Verge* 65).

Glaspell would have been well aware of the male domination of modernist movements in the arts.[15] *The Verge* both participates in the call for a female/feminist modernism and recognizes, precisely through the struggle and extremity of Claire, how great a challenge it is. Liza Nelligan neatly summarizes this conflict in her critique of Claire:

> *The Verge* anticipates a feminist audience that fully expects to find a character with whom they can sympathize by giving them Claire Archer, a heroine who privileges her right to self-development over maternal and wifely devotion, articulately demands satisfying and egalitarian relationships with men, and is committed to exposing and destroying the conventional social boundaries that crush her individuality. At the same time, Glaspell gives them an unquestionably disturbing character: a mad, inchoate, unsympathetic woman who rejects her daughter, abuses her sister, betrays her husband, and murders one of her lovers because he wants to "save" her from madness. (91)

In short, as a figure who has taken on male privilege and rejected the conventions of feminine behavior, Claire fits the model of the high modernist who scorns and transvalues traditional expectations.

Glaspell makes Claire's language mark a range of issues linking madness, modernism, and feminism. Claire sees a direct connection between words and plants, identifying herself as both botanist and poet. Her act 2 conflict with her sister Adelaide metaphorically ties language to horticulture:

Adelaide: Come, come now—let's not juggle words.
Claire: (*springing up*) How dare you say that to me, Adelaide. You who are such a liar and thief and whore with words!
Adelaide: (*facing her, furious*) How *dare* you—
. . .
Claire: Yes, I do dare. I'm tired of what you do—you and all of you. Life—experience—values—calm—sensitive words which raise their heads as indications. And you *pull them up*—to decorate your stagnant little minds.

(82–83)

Glaspell manipulates Claire's speech to demonstrate her more rational and hysterical phases. Claire, always reaching toward escape from form, finds herself in a "prison house of language." She discovers that words cannot permanently transcend form any more than her Breath of Life can. Glaspell plays on the irony swirling around the very name *Breath of Life* and the idea of "inspiration." Claire cannot exist without her creative outlets, and yet her genius is tied to structures as fundamental and inescapable as the constant need for us to breathe to live.

Claire breaks away from sentences into verse, in the hope that she will come closer to what she wants to express, but she finds poetry equally confining:

> Let me tell you how it is with me;
>   I do not want to work,
> I want to be;
> Do not want to make a rose or make a poem—
> Want to lie upon the earth and know. . . .
> Stop doing that!—words going into patterns;
> They do it sometimes when I let come what's there.
> Thoughts take pattern—then the pattern is the thing.
>   (88)

Like Virginia Woolf's women writers in *A Room of One's Own*, Claire finds that extant forms of expression cannot meet her needs. She actively seeks "some new vehicle, not necessarily in verse, for the poetry in her" (Woolf 80). With this short lyric Glaspell demonstrates how difficult it is to achieve the freedom high modernism promises, how surreptitiously such "hardened and set" structures "made by men" as rhyme and meter pull the female artist back to convention (Woolf 80). Glaspell fills Claire's dialogue with dashes and syntactic gaps, illustrating both her mental distress and her recognition that language is yet another structure she must deconstruct to make her own.

In this regard Claire resembles one of Breuer's most famous patients, "Anna O.," the first of his and Freud's case histories documented in their *Studies on Hysteria*. The clinicians record the breakdown of Anna O.'s use of language; Breuer explains his patient was first "at a loss to find words. . . . Later she lost her command of grammar and syntax . . . [and] in the process of time she became almost completely deprived of words" (qtd. in Showalter, *Female Malady* 155–56). Feminist critic Dianne Hunter has subsequently read these "linguistic disorders" as a "rejection of the patriarchal orthodoxy" of the patient's familial and social environment.[16] Hunter's reading of the case of Anna O. through the writing of the French psychoanalytic theorist Jacques Lacan resonates with responses to *The Verge* in terms of French feminist discourse, itself closely tied to the French psychoanalytic tradition. As I observed in my 1989 essay, "A Stage of Her Own: Susan Glaspell's *The Verge* and Women's Dramaturgy," parallels emerge between the play and the more recent writing of such French feminist critics as Luce Irigaray and Catherine Clément. Glaspell's use of terms such as *outness* and *otherness* finds echoes in these writers' subsequent depictions of female alterity; Claire's linguistic experimentation and hysteria correspond exactly to critiques of the impact of patriarchal culture on women as presented by the French scholars. Marcia Noe makes a similar argument in her 1995 article, "*The Verge: L'Écriture Feminine* at the Province-town," which extends the correspondences between Glaspell and the French feminist tradition to include the work of Hélène Cixous. Elin Diamond, through the use of these French feminist and other critics, explores the provocative possibility that the modern realist theater is itself "a form of hysteria" (7). Glaspell's creation of a hysteric as the centerpiece of *The Verge*, a text whose formal moves among realism, expressionism, and symbolism evoke other perspectives on hysteria, resonates with Diamond's thesis through its multiple scenic and linguistic enactments of the condition.

Through Claire's exploration of language Glaspell overtly calls attention to the traditional orderliness and form of dramatic writing and experiments tentatively with a new style, one that more closely represents the female expression she is trying to convey. While Katharine Rodier has observed the important links between Claire's syntax, especially its disjunctions and use of dashes, and the work of Emily Dickinson,[17] Claire's language is equally closely related to emerging conventions of American expressionism. These theatrical experiments took shape in such texts as Elmer Rice's *The Adding Machine* (1923) and especially Sophie Treadwell's *Machinal* (1928), which is also centrally concerned with the strictures on women's lives and expression. Still, Claire's rejection of *all* form, as represented by her experiments with language, should not be overlooked. Through Claire, Glaspell may be suggesting that any single dramatic style, whether expressionist or realist, can constrict the artist and that only through continual experimentation with multiple forms, as she has done with *The Verge,* can truly innovative creativity begin to emerge. Linda Ben-Zvi alludes to this interpretive possibility, suggesting that Glaspell may have had literature in mind as well as plants when she has Claire remark, "'We need not be held in forms molded for us'" ("Introduction" 6). Isaac Goldberg expressed a similar view more evocatively in 1922, when he deemed Claire's struggle "the brave protest of an artist-soul against the cramping patterns of existence," likening Glaspell's work to that of the American imagist poet Amy Lowell (481).

The experimentation with form indeed has its most specific application within the world of the play in Claire's horticultural work. The Edge Vine's reversion to original form and Breath of Life's stasis in its new form both distress Claire enormously and serve as catalysts for her hysteria. Most critics of *The Verge* see Claire's plants as symbolic images of herself and her creativity. Karen Malpede, for example, states baldly, "The plant, of course, is a metaphor for self-creation" (124); Marcia Noe extends the symbolic network of Claire and her plants to include her attraction to the new architecture represented by her unusual tower's design ("*The Verge*" 136). Glaspell may also have had some contemporary reference points in mind; she may have been alluding specifically to the well-publicized botanical and genetic experimentation of Hugo de

Vries (1848–1935), whose work with the evening primrose flower has many points of tangency with Claire's own discoveries, or the career of Luther Burbank (1849–1926), famous for his successes with plant hybridization and grafting techniques.[18]

Other scholars have placed Claire's compulsion to create new life within the literary tradition that spawned such figures as Faustus and Frankenstein. Julie Holledge astutely reads this impetus to creativity as a challenge to God (147). Although Holledge does not explore this angle further, her observation directs attention to the unusual (for Glaspell) presence of Christian imagery in the play.[19] One of Glaspell's earliest stage directions describes the Edge Vine from this perspective:

> At the back grows a strange vine. It is arresting rather than beautiful. It creeps along the low wall, and one branch gets a little way up the glass. You might see the form of a cross in it, if you happened to think it that way. (58)

At the close of act 1, when Claire realizes the vine, which through her ministrations was to have transcended its initial genetic structure, has reverted to its original form, she uproots the plant and flings it at her daughter Elizabeth, another failed experiment she violently rejects. At this moment Claire experiences what might be called a "crisis in faith," and Glaspell problematizes the religious symbolism in her hysterical allusions to Christianity, patriarchy, and conventional womanhood. Her helper Anthony remonstrates:

Anthony: Miss Claire! Miss Claire! The work of years!
Claire: May only make a prison! . . . You think I too will die on the edge?
   (*she . . . is now struggling with the vine*) Why did I make you? To get
   past you! . . . Oh yes, I know you have thorns! The Edge Vine should
   have thorns.

                                                                    (78)

The linkage of the cross and thorns with Claire's potential death suggests she may see herself as a Christ figure, a sacrificial victim of the ruling order. Glaspell's having named the dead son David surely resonates in this context as well; there can be no salvation if the forefather of Christ has been lost. Claire asks Tom to "say something pleasant—about God." But she immediately admonishes, "But be very careful what you say about him! [*sic*] I have a feeling— he's [*sic*] not far off" (78). These lines, which close the first act, clearly foreshadow the play's final moments, although we do not anticipate that Tom, rather than Claire, may be moving "nearer, my God, to Thee."

Glaspell builds upon the religious theme early in act 2, when Claire's sister Adelaide suggests that she "come and hear one of Mr. Morley's sermons" as an antidote to her strangeness and isolation. Claire asks Adelaide if the hymn "Nearer, My God, to Thee" is still sung at their family's church and requests that she sing it to her. Adelaide refuses, claiming, "It would be sacrilege to sing it to you in this mood." Claire counters: "Oh, I don't know. I'm not so sure God would agree with you. That would be one on you, wouldn't it?" (80–81). The sisters' struggle over a vision of God and His ways mirrors all the other levels of conflict in the play, but Glaspell also uses religion metaphorically as perhaps the most complex, and ultimately inexplicable, image of conformity in the play. Claire's repeated calls for "outness" and "otherness" throughout the drama culminate in her strangulation of Tom, the figure who seems to represent her last hope for transcendence but whom she perceives as ultimately also failing her.

The final lines of the play are Claire's faltering, truncated rendition of the first verse of the hymn she has mentioned in act 2:

> Nearer, my God, to Thee
> Nearer to Thee,
> E'en tho' it be a cross
> That raises me;
> Still all my song shall be,
> Nearer, my—
> (100–101)[20]

This enigmatic conclusion is, I believe, intentional. Arthur Waterman insists that "we must realize that Claire has gone too far" and that Glaspell "was making her an extreme case for dramatic purposes and was acknowledging the limitations that have to be placed on aspiration, the boundaries beyond which no one may go" (81). Barbara Ozieblo, however, maintains a different perspective:

> The play ends on a savagely ironic note. . . . Claire . . . is now her own God and cannot be reached by societal structures and compunctions; she has broken out and is existentially free, alone in the transcendental beyond. (116)

Ozieblo's description recapitulates the ideal image of the high modernist artist, detached and godlike. Christine Dymkowski offers a third view, that the ending represents "a personal triumph" for Claire "but one to be understood symbolically rather than realistically" (101), like the conclusion of Gilman's "The Yellow Wallpaper."

The very indeterminacy of the ending has allowed for this range of critical responses, some of which point toward a feminist liberation for Claire, while others see Glaspell's intent as a movement away from an endorsement of extremes of any kind. Critics must also try to grapple, however, with the significance of Christianity as a religion and as a social practice with specific historical structures and concepts of women's lives in order to begin to parse its meaning for Claire as well as for Glaspell. I would argue that this ending is indeed deeply ironic but not exactly for the reasons that Ozieblo proffers. Rather, Claire's final evocation of an emblem of the Protestant Church points toward the ultimate inescapability of patriarchy, much as Treadwell's *Machinal* soon would similarly show the ongoing power of male social systems, including the church, over the central female character, even at the moment of her death. Glaspell's struggle throughout this text to negotiate dramatic form also seems presciently to anticipate feminist theater theory's recognition that "realism operates in concert with ideology" and "surreptitiously reinforces . . . the arrangements of that world" (Diamond 4–5).

Sybil Thorndike, the actress who originated the role of Claire in England in 1925, intuited the conflicts at the center of the drama. Vividly recalling Glaspell's script, Thorndike reminisced in 1962:

> That play also dealt with the dangers of conformity, something that I've always tried to fight. Once you give an idea a name and you pin it down, you deep-freeze its vitality. You may have made it comfortable to live with, but you've drained it of all meaning; you've lost the chance of making a real leap forward. (Qtd. in Morley 83)

Thorndike's elucidation of this central theme in the play extends alike to the character Claire and to Glaspell's dramaturgy. But many reviewers made a point of separating Thorndike's (and her New York counterpart, Margaret Wycherley's) brilliance in performance from the work itself, giving the credit to them, rather than to the dramatist who, with the actors and other artists, created the production. Ironically, Thorndike's remarks are equally applicable to the opinions expressed by many of the play's original critics, especially some of the prominent New York journalists, who dismissed the play's adventurousness and refused to see the work as an important step in the development of American dramatic modernism.

The *New York Herald* took a sarcastic approach, titling its review "What 'The Verge' Is About, Who Can Tell?" and opening its commentary thus:

> The extraneousness of dissonance as compared with the perfume of a periwinkle in reduced circumstances, the whole [of which] is enclosed in a barbed wire fence and labelled, "The Verge," was presented last night to an audience which filled to capacity the commodiousest stable of the Provincetown Players. (15)

The *New York Times* lead critic, Alexander Woollcott, was equally snide, calling the play one that "can be intelligently reviewed only by a neurologist or by some woman who has journeyed near to the verge of which Miss Glaspell writes. And by the same token, only those would enjoy it" ("Play"). In his follow-up commentary, "Second Thoughts about First Nights," Woollcott calls Glaspell's language "rubbishy" and derisively critiques her rhetorical choices (1). These dismissals both hark back to the rejection of *Suppressed Desires* as "too special" and anticipate the (male) critical view of Marsha Norman's Pulitzer Prize drama *'Night, Mother* (1983) as a tragedy with no universality or breadth of interest because it was about women.

Writing for the *Nation*, Ludwig Lewisohn, an avid supporter of Glaspell, attempted to put a different spin on his colleagues' response, explaining that *The Verge* "is known in New York as an incomprehensible, ultra-esoteric play." But, he concludes, the vituperation says more about the critics than the play:

> Miss Glaspell's dramaturgic structure is clear and clean and firm. The dialogue is delicately and precisely wrought. She has used a few uncommon words, but they are quite simple in themselves. Considering the intricacy of her theme the speech of her people is extraordinarily direct and lucid. Other American dramatists may have more obvious virtues; they may reach larger audiences and enjoy a less wavering repute. Susan Glaspell has a touch of that vision without which we perish. Those who desire to share it will gather about her. (709)

Stark Young assumes a similar position in the *New Republic*, subtly taking his colleagues to task for their hypocrisy:

> No play of Susan Glaspell's can be passed over quite so snippily as most of the reviewers have done with The Verge. . . . Art forever dilates its being with new matter, new life. And this in time finds its right form. . . . Prattling about new forms in the theatre and then fighting any attempt at new material is a poor game. We shall never have new form without having first the new matter, of which the soul becomes at length the form. (47)

Young has astutely grasped the connection in the play between Claire's botanical experiments and Glaspell's interest in new dramatic form, but he takes the connection further, exposing his colleagues' hypocrisy in calling for theatrical innovation while rejecting artists' attempts to answer that call.

A few other critics noted and applauded her innovations. Maida Castellun, who often reviewed productions by the Provincetown for the *New York Call*, noted the "fascinating, even thrilling" quality of the work (4), and Kenneth Macgowan, who was otherwise ambivalent about the play, acknowledged that "for the tiny audience of the keen, the sensitive, the genuinely philosophic, here is the most remarkable dramatic document that they have ever come across" ("New Play").

The official journalistic responses to the London premier in 1925 closely echoed the range of sentiments expressed by the New York critics. Cicely Hamilton, writing for London's *Time and Tide,* suggests that Glaspell belongs to a "class" of playwrights "whose gifts lie in cloudy impressiveness, not in clear-cut statement and idea," and that only an actress as gifted as Thorndike can make the play appear to be great, when in reality it has "not proven" itself to be so (379). Yet Herbert Farjeon countered in the *Weekly Westminster,* claiming such writers as Hamilton had "done their best to throw water on a dramatic masterpiece of the first class" (708). Other British critics fell into these same opposing camps. The London *Observer* called Glaspell's writing "pretentious" (Griffith 11), a sentiment stated even more baldly in the *New Statesman* by J. F. Holms, who believed the piece to be "a pretentious travesty of emotion and truth" (746); another article maintained Glaspell's dialogue was "choked by symbolism" ("Last Subscription Performance"). By contrast, the *Daily London Telegraph* called both the acting and the writing "well-nigh perfect" ("Pioneer Players"). Moreover, the *Times,* while quibbling a bit with the dialogue, acknowledged, "There is something in this play, something of fire and air, a rare quality of intellect and spirit in common attack, which makes its verbal blemishes unimportant" ("Verge"). Another London-based reviewer tried to put all the disputes in perspective, while insisting *The Verge* is "a great play":

> *Of course* the play has crudenesses and violences as well as surpassing beauties. Nobody whose genius was less than Ibsen's could have hoped to tackle this theme at all; and the essentially critical thing, I repeat, is to compute the play's virtues from the ground-level up rather than calculate by how much they decline from the top of achievement. ("Verge")

Perhaps even more significantly, the critic for *The Lady* chose to reproduce audience commentary, quoting a remark "overheard as the crowd left the theatre": "'I don't know what it was all about, but it was the most thrilling thing I have ever seen'" ("Last Week's Theatrical Hurricane"). Ironically, the critics echo the play's own contrast between Claire's sublimity and Harry's commonsense pragmatism. It is perhaps too easy to summarize this divergence of critical opinion by invoking the historical reception of the avant-garde: some critics and patrons embraced it, while others retreated from its challenges and innovations. The record of similar responses to modern art, music, and dance of the time, however, presents compelling evidence for the consideration of *The Verge* within the paradigms of modernism.

While it is always tempting to attempt to glean audience response through such critical comments as those in *The Lady,* in this instance we have a record of viewers' own statements about the play that actually corresponds to the journalistic debate. A number of New York patrons of *The Verge* chose to register their reactions to the play themselves in public forums. Like Glaspell's earlier work *Bernice, The Verge* prompted extended commentary within her community that even moved beyond the confines of the reviewers' appraisals. Over the space of four issues, from 16 November to 3 December 1921, the weekly newspaper the *Greenwich Villager* ran six pieces on the production. The 16 November issue, which must have been put to bed before the play's opening on the fourteenth, predicted that "no matter how many gaudy and expensive shows blossom next week on Broadway, the most significant dramatic event in the city, bar none, will be the opening of . . . 'The Verge'" ("Drama" 7). The *Villager* ran two pieces the following week, the first a cover story detailing the controversy the play had prompted:

> Some said the play was too bad to roast, even. Others insisted that it was a work of genius, but too great to be written about on short notice. This wasn't getting copy in. We flew to the phone, called up philosophers, and hustled them off . . . to the Playwright's Theatre. . . . As the Villager goes to press the philosophers are still philosophizing and will not turn in their story until next week. ("Philosophers Wrestle" 1)

Yet the paper did run Frank Shay's review the week of the twenty-third, which was a thundering endorsement of the work: "It is without question the finest piece of dramatic craftsmanship placed on the boards this season. The Verge definitely places Susan Glaspell alongside Strindberg, Tchekoff and about three notches above Shaw" ("Drama" 7).

The "philosophers" produced a preliminary report for the 30 November issue, another front-page feature printed as a debate among the viewers. A "poet" responded to the aesthetics of the production, likening them to Maeterlinck. The "feminist philosopher" concluded that "Miss Glaspell is saying something to us, and we'd better listen," after which she went on at some length about the "unsatisfactory males" Glaspell depicts. An "anarchist philosopher" was struck by the true-to-life issues, themes, and characters; the conversation then turned to the mix of realism and symbolism in the piece that some found confusing ("Claire" 1, 4). The editors seem to have opted to let the debate remain unresolved, printing a follow-up letter to the Frank Shay review in the 3 December issue as well as a final occasional piece by Harry Godfrey in his column, "The Mews." Godfrey, who makes no pretensions of being a theater critic, nonetheless goes on to comment on the professional journalists' responses and to present his own subjective views:

We've been screwing our courage up to say that we liked it just because we liked it. We went there expecting not to. . . . We dunno why [we did like it]. Maybe we're neurotic. (3)

The reports of the "philosophers," coupled with that of Godfrey, of course, touch on all the critical elements of the play's themes as well as its reception: its poetic diction, its feminist politics, its references to current social debates, its exploration of dramatic form, its theme of madness. One is tempted to think, given the aptness and fullness of the coverage, that the philosophers' views were actually penned by a single author anxious to convey the force and breadth of the work's impact.

In his autobiography *A Victorian in the Modern World* Hutchins Hapgood records another segment of the Greenwich Village community's response to the play, that of the Heterodoxy Club's membership, who seem to have reacted with similarly collective fervor.[21] Hapgood's antagonism to the politics of the club comes through clearly in his references to the "passionate excesses of feminism" he believed the group espoused (377), and he used their endorsement of Glaspell's play as ammunition for his rejection of what he saw as their unfounded assumptions about patriarchal society. Nevertheless, his recording of most of the members' attitudes toward the play is historically significant, especially when juxtaposed to that of the unnamed philosophers who praised the work in the *Greenwich Villager.* Hapgood narrates:

> When Susan's *Verge* appeared, I had a healthy instinct of passionate reaction. At the next meeting of Heterodoxy, the subject for discussion was this play. One of my friends in the club, Elise Dufour the dancer, who had never succeeded in getting away from what those women called the mere man's psychology, describing the meeting to me, said, "It seemed to me, while these women were talking about *The Verge*, that I was in church, that they were worshiping at some holy shrine; their voices and their eyes were full of religious excitement. I was, I think, the only woman not under the spell. I tried at first to say a few things about the play that were in the line of ordinary dramatic criticism, which I thought had a reasonable basis; but when they all glared at me, as if they thought I should be excommunicated, I spoke no further word." (377)

In her history of the Heterodoxy Club, Judith Schwarz contextualizes this reaction, explaining that the members' response in part stemmed from the fact that "so many Heterodoxy women were so deeply involved in the theater" and that this may well have been "one of the first feminist plays they had seen" (3). Heterodite Ruth Hale shared her views of the play directly in a letter to the editor of the *New York Times:*

I admit that much of the play was unfortunately overwritten. This, I thought, was not that there was actually so much talk, but that Miss Glaspell had overtalked the importance of her background. . . .

Miss Glaspell is the only playwright I ever knew who can tell a story like this. If the surface of life changes by a hair's breadth, she not only knows it, but can convey it in words. She is the painter of those wisps of shadow that cross the soul in the dead of night. She can write great horrors in the terms of little ones—come to think of it, of course, she wrote "Trifles." (1)[22]

Hale's even-handed response confirms the admiration noted by Hapgood and Schwarz but also shows that Heterodoxy's membership could indeed be objective about their colleagues' work.

The groundswell of feminist response to *The Verge* within Glaspell's community resonates with contemporary critical commentary on the play; since the early 1970s a number of scholars have explored the drama and its connections with a range of feminist literary concerns and theoretical positions.[23] Indeed, a survey of the writing on the play since its initial production reveals feminist critical readings as one of three main categories for its analysis; the other two are either relatively straightforward discussions of the piece within the Glaspell or Provincetown oeuvre or the more nuanced controversy over the form of the play, with its tension between realist and expressionist dramaturgy and staging.

It was fascinating to see how these three critical groupings still dominated discussion of the play at the first international meeting of Glaspell scholars, sponsored by the University of Glasgow in May 1996. At this conference considerations of *The Verge* prompted very lively discussion, particularly as two radically different recent productions reinforced the controversy over the form of the work. One staging, mounted by the conference organizers, brought a postmodern sensibility to the piece, extending our feel for the play's experimentation with style and form. The other, a production of London's Orange Tree Theatre (a company known for its revivals of works from this period), chose a more realist approach that reviewers found static. It appeared that neither performance was able to convey fully the tension between forms integral to the drama.

In his director's notes for a recent professional reading of *Trifles* at the Shaw Festival in Canada, Denis Johnston makes a cogent observation on that play equally relevant for *The Verge*. In Johnston's interpretation, Glaspell "seem[s] to be saying, mad behaviour might just be sane behaviour in mad circumstances: understand the circumstances, and you will understand the behaviour." From the earliest days of the Great War critics had deemed the conflict madness and found it impossible to account for the governmentally

sanctioned sacrifice of so many lives. The postwar era was one of greater political and social conservatism in the United States; the sense of oppression,
containment, and stricture that pervaded American culture finds expression
in the dramaturgy of *The Verge* and in the character of Claire *Archer,* who, like
Margaret *Pierce* before her, seeks to puncture the enclosures of pretense and
convention. As Ronald Wainscott observes, Claire, with her clarity of vision,
"personifies the struggle of modernism with tradition in the postwar world"
(28). The moment Glaspell depicts in *The Verge* reflects the madness Johnston
encapsulates and forces us to question our assumptions about sanity and hysteria, just as the wealth of response from Glaspell's audiences demonstrated
once again how compelling her work was for her community and how powerful the theater must have been for her cultural moment. Feminist critic Toril
Moi has suggested that "the *reason* why the neurotic fails to produce coherence
is that she lacks the *power* to impose her own connections on her reader/lis-
tener" (82). We may never be able to account for the madness of war, murder,
and the plethora of social ills plaguing Glaspell's time or our own. But *The
Verge* haunts us with the possibility that alterity holds truths just out of our
reach. As Heterodite Ruth Hale concludes in her letter on *The Verge* to the *New
York Times,* even "if we cannot always quite understand her, it would be smart
of us to try" (1).

Chains of Dew

In February 1922 Cook, Glaspell, their loyal supporter Edna Kenton, and the rest of the executive committee met to decide on the future of the Provincetown Players. O'Neill's success had greatly strained relations in the group, and Cook no longer felt they were in control of their work. Cook wanted to suspend group activities for a while and fulfill his own ambition of exploring Greek civilization, with the thought of perhaps returning in the future to reconstitute and renew the organization. Glaspell makes no mention of her response to Cook's announcement, "It is time to go to Greece," in her biography of him, *The Road to the Temple* (240). She may, however, have felt some understandable ambivalence about leaving New York midseason, with her play *Chains of Dew* announced as the sixth bill offering, scheduled for an April opening. Glaspell entrusted Kenton with overseeing the production of her script. Fortuitously, she also sent the manuscript to the Library of Congress to secure the copyright; this version is now the only extant copy of the play. On 1 March, after setting the affairs of the Provincetown in relatively reasonable order, Cook and Glaspell set sail for Greece, where Cook unexpectedly died in 1924.

The script Glaspell left for her colleagues to stage incorporates many of her familiar tropes, including the opposition of midwestern to eastern American culture and the exposé of assumptions about gendered behavior. She builds *Chains of Dew* around the highly topical campaign for birth control, allowing this issue to prompt the larger ideological and character conflicts of the drama. The play opens in the New York office of the Birth Control League. Nora Powers, secretary of the league, is a young, energetic, and attractive woman, committed to her cause. She is soon joined by her slightly caustic friend Leon Whittaker, the associate editor of the *New Nation,* a literary and political journal, and James O'Brien, an Irish writer visiting the States. Whittaker and Powers exemplify East Coast "progressiveness" (political liberalism and/or activism, bohemian lifestyle, etc.). Glaspell explores this ideology from the perspectives of both the foreigner O'Brien and the midwestern poet, Seymore Standish, whose work Whittaker admires (and publishes) and who is in New York for one of his periodic visits.

Standish presents himself as a man trapped by the conventions of his life in the Midwest and bound to the demands of a job, family, and civic obligations. Seymore declares that he would like to be free of these burdens, but, when his New York friends unexpectedly arrive at his midwestern home to help him achieve this goal in act 2, they discover a very different situation from the one he has presented. Seymore's wife Dotty (Diantha) is lively and bright, his mother wise and vital. Nora, who has traveled to Seymore's hometown to bring the birth control campaign to the Midwest, quickly befriends the other women, and, much to Seymore's dismay, converts them to her cause. The women, in their effort to help Seymore, actually start dismantling the cloak of self-sacrifice that he perpetually wears, until his mother realizes that his martyr complex is actually central to his life and work as a poet. She makes Diantha see that, in order to help Seymore, they must continue to allow him the saintly role he has played for so long, actually becoming the martyrs themselves by sacrificing the freedom from midwestern conventions they so recently enjoyed. The women's willed return to conventional morality seemingly "suppresses" their "desires" for a different life, "closing a book" on modern, independent womanhood.

Following the dramatic arc of other Glaspell works such as *The Verge, Chains of Dew* progresses from light comedy in act 1 to a darker conclusion. As with *Inheritors,* she develops both political and geographical milieux to underscore her themes. Like the one-acts *Woman's Honor* and *Trifles, Chains* explores a range of gendered roles within society. The play also uses multivalent symbols, as do *The Outside* and *Trifles.* By examining familial interactions, particularly marriage and the parent/child dynamic, Glaspell continues to focus on concerns evident in *Close the Book* and *Bernice.* Thus, *Chains of Dew* exemplifies many of the devices evident in her previous plays. With its extended scrutiny of the Standish family and their social environment *Chains* also looks forward to her more intimate dramas of the 1930s and 1940s and inaugurates the in-depth exploration of the connection between an artist's life and work that will dominate *Alison's House* and *The Comic Artist.*

Although she may not have known it would be her last work for the Provincetown Players, *Chains* nevertheless brought to a close the most active phase of Glaspell's dramatic career. Perhaps most significantly, it is the last of her works driven by a political concern. While her final play *Springs Eternal* is informed by World War II, it is not a play about the war so much as a play about the war's impact on family dynamics. All three of Glaspell's last plays: *Alison's House, The Comic Artist,* and *Springs Eternal* are family dramas in the American tradition that blossomed between the wars. Like the best-known works of that period, Glaspell's final plays are informed by the American sociopolitical milieu but reflect and comment on society and culture exclusively through an intimate, familial context.

By contrast, Glaspell's use of the birth control campaign as the backdrop and central plot device for *Chains of Dew* positions the comedy amid the very real political debates of its day. The play also belongs to a subgenre of dramatic works, written between 1914 and 1922, that explore the birth control movement and its links to issues of race, class, and gender.[1] Some of these pieces were produced by the Provincetown Players, the Washington Square Players, and other theatrical groups in the Village, while others were published in journals with a large bohemian readership. Together, they testify to the seriousness with which this movement was viewed within Glaspell's community. Moreover, the plays demonstrate once again the strong, symbiotic relationship between political and aesthetic debates within Greenwich Village society and artists' direct incorporation of these concerns in their work. *Chains* exemplifies how Glaspell mined her environment to provide both character portraits and compelling, timely narratives for her dramaturgy. As with *Inheritors,* Glaspell here reflects an intimate understanding of both the politics and history of the issues she dramatizes as well as the more personal, individualized dimensions of the birth control movement's supporters and antagonists. An excavation of the ground supporting this campaign should help illuminate Glaspell's deployment of its rhetoric and tactics; a comparison of *Chains* and the other birth control dramas will show how Glaspell moves from the blatancy of their concerns to her own subtler fusion of political and personal themes.

By the early twentieth century in America an organized movement for the legalization of, and dissemination of information about, birth control had begun to take hold, particularly in urban areas where rapid population growth strained the limited resources of immigrant and working-class communities. Over less than a decade, through the tumultuous, war-torn 1910s and into the 1920s, the artistic and journalistic responses to the campaign mirrored the growth of the battle for birth control, reflecting its rapid evolution from its roots in anarchism and socialism to its endorsement by bourgeois America. Greenwich Village quickly became the center of the struggle, with such well-known figures as Emma Goldman, Mary Ware Dennett, and Margaret Sanger spearheading the movement, backed by the active support of such periodicals as the *Masses,* the *New York Call,* and Sanger's own journals, the *Woman Rebel* and the *Birth Control Review.* Glaspell's *Chains of Dew* reproduces this evolution, with its cast of bohemian eastern journalists juxtaposed to staid midwesterners, its setting moving from New York City to the nation's heartland, and its plot tracing the expansion of the campaign across the country.

Although the birth control movement in America is now associated closely with the work of Margaret Sanger, many other individuals were already active in the campaign before Sanger's commitment to the cause. In the late nineteenth century the "voluntary motherhood" movement was well under way, having evolved from the earlier radical utopian movements that fostered notions of perfectionist eugenics.[2] By the early twentieth century the notion of voluntary motherhood had spread enough to cause alarm in the government, and in 1905 President Roosevelt joined the attack on women who wanted small families, appropriating the phrase *race suicide* to describe their behavior. Between 1905 and 1910 birth control became "a public national controversy" (Gordon 133–34). As the movement's historian Linda Gordon points out, "the race-suicide alarm did not emerge out of the imagination of Roosevelt . . . , but was a backlash, a response to actual changes in the birth rate, family structure, and sexual practice" (134). The deeper meaning of this reaction related to a number of other issues, including concern over women's rejection of their primary role of motherhood, the sense that America needed a growing "indigenous" population (i.e., descendants of original WASP settlers), and the related fear of an immigrant, poor and/or nonwhite takeover of the Yankee race (Gordon 134).

Around 1910 leading American intellectuals and those favoring voluntary motherhood began to be influenced by European theorists of sexuality such as Edward Carpenter. Carpenter had established a connection between sexual oppression and other forms of economic and imperial oppression (Gordon 183–84), thus helping to form a stronger link between issues facing the working class and population concerns. These new lines of argument influenced many who believed that birth control education for the poor was essential: prosperous Americans were using contraception anyway, and thus keeping it from the poor was socially destructive (Gordon 186).

In 1914 Sanger had just begun her work for birth control, having started publishing her first periodical, the *Woman Rebel,* in March of that year (Kennedy 22). Sanger biographer David M. Kennedy explains: "The *Woman Rebel* discussed and advocated contraception—the June issue for the first time called it 'birth control'" (23). It was not until 1915, however, during her "self-imposed exile" in Europe following her arrest for violation of the Comstock laws (Kennedy 72),[3] that Sanger's fame as a birth control reformer began to spread. During this period the birth control movement underwent a number of rapid and radical transitions, complicated by its connection to other pressing social and financial issues. Many of the early activists were socialists. Within this group the need for contraceptive education was perceived as a working-class, not a feminist, issue—part of, but subordinate to, larger questions of class economics. Activist, labor leader, and Heterodite Rose Pastor Stokes became one of the more outspoken socialists to support birth control reform. With filmmaker Alice Blaché, Stokes drafted an unproduced "propaganda film" (Blaché 89), *Shall the Parents Decide?* (1916), which positions the issue squarely within the larger concerns of labor and economics.

After the war Sanger intentionally guided the birth control movement in an "antipolitical" direction, however (e.g., away from socialism), which allowed it to become a free-standing issue that could be embraced by many individuals or groups with other positions potentially in conflict.[4] Historian Christine Stansell sees the campaign as "the greatest practical demonstration of the vanguard role of feminists," deeming it "perhaps the clearest political articulation of sexual modernism and a lasting achievement of the cross-class coalitions of the teens" (234). Sanger also made a significant shift away from the working class and toward the growing middle and upper classes as the targets of her campaign, particularly with respect to her expanding need for fund-raising. She began to attract "professionals" to her cause, not only those in medicine but also in other occupations that could prove influential within their communities or on a national scale. According to Linda Gordon, this transition radically altered the entire structure of the movement. The professionals' influence "transformed birth-control leagues from participatory membership associations into staff organizations" (249), with the predominantly male professionals in advisory capacities and their wives and other women maintaining "amateur" status in the organization, primarily in staff positions (251). This is the precise moment Glaspell depicts in her play; Nora's involvement in fund-raising, her decision to travel to the Midwest, her attempt to enlist Seymore Standish as a spokesman for birth control, and the references to a staff and a well-orchestrated campaign all reflect Glaspell's understanding of the nuances of Sanger's tactics. Glaspell's selection of an initial Greenwich Village setting, with its journalist-activist milieu, provides historical traces, the echoes of the earlier phases of the campaign that would underlie its later permutations.

This activist dynamic informed the group of birth control plays written and produced in the period. Glaspell's longtime friend and colleague Lawrence Langner, one of the founders of both the Washington Square Players and the Theatre Guild, wrote his first drama in this vein. *Wedded: A Social Comedy* (1914), a one-act set in a "cheap district" of Brooklyn (8), depicts the dilemma young Janet Ransome faces when her fiancé dies, leaving her an unwed mother-to-be. The family tries to convince their minister to attest that the marriage occurred before the death, a prevarication he ultimately agrees to, after voicing platitudes on the problem of premarital sex and its consequences:

> I'm sorry to see a thing of this sort happen—and right in my own congregation, too. I've expressed my views from the pulpit from time to time very strongly upon the subject, but nevertheless it doesn't seem to make much difference in this neighborhood. (12)

Janet, in turn, serves as the mouthpiece of the campaign for contraceptive education:

D'ye think I wanted a baby? I didn't want one. I didn't know how to stop it. If you don't like it—it's a pity you don't preach sermons on how to stop havin' babies when they're not wanted. There'd be some sense in that. There'd be more sense than talkin' about waitin'—an waitin'—an waitin'. There's hundreds of women round here—starvin' and sufferin'— an' havin' one baby after another, and don't know the first thing about how to stop it. (15)

Janet's outcry epitomizes the socialist rhetoric of many birth control advo- cates who condemned the financial and social inequities such women faced.

Sada Cowan's 1915 drama *The State Forbids* strikes similar notes, pinning blame squarely on the medical profession in its collusion with governmental regulation. Impoverished Mrs. Nash confronts her physician when she gives birth to an unwanted, deformed child:

Doctor: I warned you when Harold came not to have another baby.
Mrs. Nash: (bitterly) You warned me! But How?
Doctor: I told you . . .
Mrs. Nash: (passionately). You DIDN'T tell me. You hinted! You gave me vague advice that left me as blind as I was before.
Doctor: You are ungrateful. I told you all I dared. It is against the law to tell a woman ways and means to prevent conception. Perhaps you didn't know this. But it is against the law.

(196–97)

Cowan's piece, like Langner's, uses a melodramatic plot and urgent tone to drive home her class and gender concerns.

Mary Burrill added the strategic issue of race in her 1919 birth control play *They That Sit in Darkness: A One-Act Play of Negro Life.* This short work, published in Sanger's *Birth Control Review,* dramatizes the tragedy of the Jaspers, a poor black family in the rural South. Lindy Jasper is a promising young woman who is about to leave her home for a college education in Tuskegee when her mother dies, the victim of repeated childbearing. Lindy must abandon her hope of a bright future to stay at home to care for her im- poverished and bereft family. Like Cowan, Burrill uses a health care practi- tioner as the voice of state regulation. Although the nurse Miss Shaw wishes she could help, the law precludes her assisting the family:

I wish to God it were lawful for me to do so! My heart goes out to you poor people that sit in darkness, having, year after year, children that you are physically too weak to bring into the world—children that you are unable not only to educate but even to clothe and feed. Malinda, when I took my oath as a nurse, I swore to abide by the laws of the State, and the law forbids my telling you what you have a right to know! (7)

These pieces all reflect the heavy-handed approach and rhetoric favored in the initial years of the campaign.

Early in *Chains of Dew* Glaspell has her heroine Nora Powers echo some similar sentiments to those found in these birth control dramas. The setting for act 1 clearly derives from the ambiance of this phase of the movement, but Glaspell strategically avoids both melodrama and agitprop to represent a more balanced and ultimately more provocative examination of how the campaign affected both individuals and the culture at large. The play's final triumph of tradition, perceived as an almost tragic conclusion for Dottie and Mother, extends beyond the characterological level; the irony of the play's ending comes when we juxtapose the fate of the female characters with the success of the strategic turn toward convention for the campaign itself.

Glaspell opens *Chains of Dew* on a light note, however, easing her audience into her serious concerns. Glaspell's Birth Control League office in New York City is cluttered with pamphlets and papers, closely resembling how Sanger biographer Madeline Gray depicts her office near Union Square in the Village (142–43). Interestingly, Glaspell carefully avoids naming the group either the *National* Birth Control League (the rival group to Sanger's run by Mary Ware Dennett) or the *American* Birth Control League (Sanger's organization, founded in November 1921 [Kennedy 94]). The details of Glaspell's depiction, however, strongly indicate Sanger's as her model. An "'excess family' exhibit" and posters of undesirably large and desirably small families hang on the set's walls; these duplicate the photographic spreads in the *Birth Control Review* that featured images of large, poor families with headlines proclaiming, "Shall Women Have Families like These—or Shall We Let Them Control Births?" (April 1919, 10–11; see figs. 1–2). Just as in *Inheritors* and *The Comic Artist*, *Chains of Dew* deploys graphic images prominently center stage to convey visual synecdoches of Glaspell's larger narrative themes. But, unlike these other pieces, *Chains* allows these tangible symbols to contribute to the comic, yet still political, tone of the play.

By way of the initial banter between Nora and Leon, Glaspell quickly establishes several nodes of conflict. She introduces the major issue of birth control but also the debate between aestheticism ("art for art's sake") and activism that plagued the bohemian community and affected the artists and intellectuals who grappled with the best means to have both political and creative impact on American society.[5] The entrance of the foreigner James O'Brien provides Nora with an opportunity to present the leading arguments in favor of legalization. Glaspell represents the other struggle through the friction between Nora and Leon, as she tries to pay attention to both birth control and poetry.

Leon is trying to read her the latest poem by Seymore Standish, but Nora's fight with a cantankerous and noisy mimeograph machine disrupts his reading. Leon suspends his recital, commenting huffily, "Since you care more about birth control than you do about poetry—" to which Nora responds, "I thought I could do both" (1.3). The links and struggles between art and politics reverberate throughout the play, tantalizingly suggesting Glaspell's consciousness of these concerns both for her own work and for her community. Through the character of Leon Whittaker she evokes the same journalistic environment that she had used earlier in *The People*. Leon's publication, the *New Nation*, suggests several prominent magazines of the period, including the *Nation*, the *New Republic*, and the *Liberator*, the journal that succeeded the *Masses*. All these publications strove to achieve a balance between the competing agendas of art and politics.

Glaspell handles the introduction of the main topic of birth control straightforwardly. In the following dialogue from early in act 1 she synthesizes the main tenets of the debate at that time, echoing the rhetoric found in many of the birth control publications as well as the other dramatic works created around the movement.

O'Brien: (*Brightly*) Tell me, what is birth control? (As they look at him, he grows confused.) Oh, yes—yes, in a way, I know, to be sure. But why— (*looking around the room*)—all this demonstration about so personal a matter?
Nora: (*now on her job*) I'll tell you why the demonstration. Because our laws are so benighted and vulgar that they do not permit a personal matter to be carried on in a personal way.

With deft comic balance Glaspell avoids letting these early moments of *Chains of Dew* degenerate into agitprop drama by maintaining a humorous distance from all the characters.

Nora: The demonstration is to demonstrate the stupidity of the law. The cruelty. The vulgarity. The brainlessness. (*With growing excitement, personally directed against the young man*) Do you wish to give birth to seven children you cannot feed? Have you no respect for children? A child has a right to be wanted. You bring into this world an impoverished, defective, degenerate—But here. I will give you our literature.
Leon: (*with relief*) Yes, that will be better.

(1.9–10)

Nora's zealousness is as gently satirized as the artistic narrowness of Leon, who believes that "every time we get down to essentials . . . we're choked off by birth control" (1.13).

Glaspell makes clear that birth control is perceived by Leon, James, and Seymore as primarily a women's issue, one that makes the men uncomfortable and that they prefer be "spoken of—somewhat sparingly" (1.11). Leon's view of "essentials" as not including birth control can be seen as patriarchal: to him the most important matters do not include this central concern of women's lives. When the men in the play insist on the separation of art and politics, Glaspell shows that this debate is based in gender difference, since, for all the creative women in the drama, they are invariably interconnected activities.

Moreover, Glaspell uses this debate as a subtle marker of poetic aptitude and achievement. Lesser poets, we come to understand, insist on the separation while greater ones see art and politics as inextricable. Seymore's sense of poetry as distinct from politics comes through strongly in his narrow and in-accurate vision of the Romantic poet Percy Bysshe Shelley, to whom he has dedicated his recent work. Seymore sees Shelley as a "pure" artist rather than as one whose creativity is integrally tied to his political views:

Seymore: . . . I'm not a propagandist. I'm a poet.
Nora: What is it you admire about Shelley, Seymore?
Seymore: His poetry.
Nora: But what made him the kind of poet he was?
Seymore: (*Jauntily*) God.

(1.29–30)

Seymore's apparent obliviousness to Shelley's atheism (perhaps he thinks God disregarded this lapse) and his political activism in relation to his verse are in keeping with the midwestern poet's selective perceptions in general. Seymore's only real connection to the Romantic poet emerges in their record of marital infidelities, a link between the men and their moments that Glaspell percep-tively and subtly incorporates in the play.

When Seymore defines the birth control campaign for Dotty early in act 2, Glaspell simultaneously dispels any lingering uncertainty about his dismis-sive opinion of Nora's work for the movement:

> I mean a group of women banded together to keep other women from having children. Going to men and trying to change the laws so women can be told how not to have children. Isn't it dreadful, Dotty? (2.1.4)

Glaspell neatly uses Seymore's speech to point out the way the birth control issue was manipulated by a legal system totally controlled by men with a vested interest in preventing women from gaining power over their lives. Just as with her ironic use of the title "A Jury of Her Peers," Glaspell highlights how women's lack of access to real political and legal agency puts them at the mercy of men who make all the decisions about their identities and lives as women.

Through Seymore, Glaspell introduces one other element of the birth control debate that gives the lie to his social and political roots. Echoing the anti–birth control rhetoric of the period 1905–10, he comments on the act 1 office displays' potential impact "from the standpoint of the race—and all that" (1.17). The "race suicide" alarm that Roosevelt trumpeted may have still held sway for the Midwest in the 1920s, which did not face the same population problems as the eastern urban centers initially targeted by Sanger and others. Seymore's last name, Standish, echoes his WASP, Puritan heritage and points to the dominance of this group as the "American" race that Roosevelt feared would be destroyed if women were convinced to have fewer children.[6] The inclusion in *Chains* of these subtle details adds to the sense of how fully Glaspell grasped the development of arguments for and against the movement and demonstrates the dramaturgical dexterity that allowed her to write a timely and provocative work, without sacrificing theatrical strength to political diatribe.

Although Nora's public work parallels that of the Sanger campaign in the early period of the American Birth Control League, Nora's private life resembles another facet of the movement more germane to Village life. Near the close of act 1, we learn that Seymore and Nora are romantically involved, playing out the conventional scenario of a married man and a progressive single woman. Historian Caroline Ware has remarked on the perpetuation of the double standard under the era's free love philosophy in her study of Greenwich Village (258). As Linda Gordon observes, moreover, "Sexual freedom made birth control important for women. The possible impermanence of love made birth control an absolute necessity" (193).

Glaspell complicates our assumptions not only about the relationship between Nora and Seymore but also about birth control and the Midwest when, in act 3, Seymore reveals that it is their neighbor Edith, and not Nora, with whom he has been "complete" (3.4–5). We are to understand at this moment (if we have not already) the hypocrisy of the women of Bluff City, not to mention Seymore. They trumpet morality and reject the campaign, all the while duplicitously taking advantage of their privilege and knowledge of how to control their fertility. Thus, Glaspell demonstrates the significance of her major political theme for a broader contemporary American audience.

Seymore, who at the close of act 1 is about to return to his midwestern home, resents the fact that Nora should be more concerned about her work than their relationship. But Nora, thrilled at a recent donation to the cause of a thousand dollars, clearly has her priorities set. When Nora receives the call, she exclaims triumphantly, "Another thousand for birth control!" (1.34). The adjective *another* shows that, as pleased as Nora is, this success is not unique; other thousands have preceded this one. And the fact that this donation comes from a single individual demonstrates pointedly the socioeconomic bracket that bolsters the cause. Glaspell thereby indicates her understanding of the movement's shift toward the middle and upper classes.

The plot device of "fieldwork," Nora's decision to travel away from the urban center of the movement to serve its goals, also directly parallels recent tactical developments in Sanger's campaign, as does the play's move to the Midwest for the ensuing acts. Glaspell sets the stage for the arrival of the movement in Bluff City (a "city" in name but midwestern small town in attitudes and behaviors) in several ways. First, she visually contrasts the more conventional environment of the Standish home to the New York milieu of act 1 through her depiction of a painting of the Sistine Madonna, which is hanging up center in the Standish living room (2.1.1). This image obviously differs from that of the beleaguered women and excess children we have seen hanging in the Birth Control League office. Glaspell points up this symbolism by having the pictures exchanged during the remaining action. The Sistine Madonna, which hangs precariously at numerous moments in acts 2 and 3, represents conventional femininity and idealized motherhood, fragile yet enduring and revered by Seymore.

Soon after her entrance Nora asks the Standish's snooty socialite friend Mrs. MacIntyre and Dotty if they can "talk a little about birth control" (2.1.26):

Nora: . . . You'll let me show you some of our literature I know. Of course, you get the idea, you're really with it, aren't you?
Mrs. MacIntyre: I cannot say that I am. It may be true that—people of one's own sort are doing this in New York—I should have to verify the facts. . . . I have been married for twenty-two years and—
Nora: (Ingenuously) And how may children have you? . . . I wish you would take a walk with me through the East Side . . . Do you believe that women have any rights over their own lives?

(2.1.26–27)

Increasingly drifting away from *direct* involvement with the immigrant or working classes, the movement now focused on those with money and power to enact reform. These individuals could potentially help the poor indirectly, a shift echoed by the play's use of the MacIntyre figure, whose role as an employer and a possible benefactor positions her squarely in the midst of the group Sanger was now targeting through her movement. Moreover, as Nora points out to these women, birth control has become fashionable:

Birth control is the smart thing in New York this season. . . . When suffrage grew so—sort of common—the really exclusive people turned to birth control. It's rather more special, you know. (2.1.26)

The social cache of the campaign has now become as important as the cause itself, a further strategic organizational move.

Glaspell continues to embed her drama in a rich matrix of real-world activism. Nora quickly makes a convert of Dotty, naming her "first president of the first birth control league of the Mississippi Valley" (2.1.29), while Seymore's mother, who has borne seven children, volunteers to "make some dolls for birth control" (2.2.9), a gendered representation of the fusion of art and politics introduced in act 1.[7] Glaspell combines two powerful arguments for the movement in Nora's fieldwork, that of women's rights and that of children's rights. Although the former has dominated the campaign, the significance of the latter should not be underestimated. By stressing that "this is a question of babies' rights" (2.1.27), Nora is voicing an important segment of the debate: the desirability of children's being wanted to ensure their long-term health and happiness (Gordon 119). Filmmaker Alice Blaché quotes Rose Pastor Stokes's commentary on this point in her discussion of their collaboration on *Shall the Parents Decide?*

> What I advocate is that a loving couple not fear to unite, taking precautions, so that they may have children when they desire them, and can care for them, and rear them to be healthy. (88)

As Glaspell pointedly shows later in the play, Seymore's mother's conversion to the cause is directly linked to her rueful sense that access to birth control could have made a great difference in her life. A final detail adds to Glaspell's thickly rendered context of contemporary agitation. Act 3 of *Chains* opens with Dotty's inspired announcement that Seymore (a bank executive and vestryman) has been selected by her "to introduce Bluff City to birth control" and "to make the opening speech" during the "first general meeting" which is to take place in their home (3.2). This plot development exactly parallels a strategy employed regularly by the American Birth Control League: the deployment of small-town women's or charity groups that often called upon male professionals as their spokesmen to promote the campaign (Gordon 290–93).

In eschewing the propagandistic tone of the earlier birth control dramas, *Chains* uses the struggle for legalization of birth control as the impetus for a number of other debates but also as a topic with inherent dramatic appeal. More pointedly than in any of her other full-length dramatic works, Glaspell shows here the inseparability of the personal and the political for women. With birth control always part of the dialogue Glaspell also examines the power of women's love in marriage, the mother-son dynamic, and the problematic way that men construct and interpret women, especially within the family unit. Just as Nora uses the excuse of fieldwork for her trip to Seymore's home in Bluff City, so Glaspell uses the spread of the campaign for birth control as an opportunity to represent locale as a tangible force in American culture and to dramatize the resonance of a particular location with its political values, especially as they pertain to women.

Marcia Noe has written extensively on the importance of geographical place for Glaspell.[8] *Chains of Dew* highlights Glaspell's ability to render creatively the characters and social nuances of various regions of America. Although most of Glaspell's works (in all genres) choose one setting, *Chains* and its short story and novel counterparts ("The Alien" and *Ambrose Holt and Family,* respectively)[9] are distinctive. Each evokes two locations, New York City and Bluff City, the latter a composite image of midwestern settings she knew well. In *Chains* she foregrounds some of the images of the Midwest that recur throughout her writing, including conservative yet often hypocritical morality and a rigid adherence to social conventions. As in her novel *Fidelity* and her "Freeport" short stories, Glaspell uses female characters both as the repositories of these conventions and as the forces beginning to oppose them. In *Chains* she pits the converted Dotty against both Mrs. MacIntyre and Edith as representatives of midwestern ideology.

Glaspell's other political references in the play contribute to its sense of immediacy. The most obvious of these is the freedom of speech battle that had arisen during World War I and still animated the radical community who continued to feel its impact. Early in the first act Leon remarks to Nora, "I mustn't fail to get Seymore's signature to this John Maxwell protest. (*Bitterly*) The world run right—and a man in prison because he writes what he sees as the truth about things" (1.4). But Seymore refuses to sign the petition, fearing that his support could jeopardize his social and business positions. Glaspell uses this moment as an early indicator of Seymore's hypocrisy: despite assuming the mantle of self-sacrifice, he behaves thoroughly selfishly throughout the play. Moreover, this decision reveals him to be the opposite of his idol Shelley, who was expelled from Oxford for his support of a friend's atheist writings. Leon reacts angrily to Seymore's refusal, providing more details of the ongoing fight:

> The case is so flagrant a violation of constitution[al] right. It's something done to a fellow writer. I should think you would be glad to—would *have* to—Damn it. The man's in prison, you know. How can you even write another line if you refuse to lift your hand for him? (1.28)

This struggle is the same one featured even more centrally in *Inheritors* and also alluded to in *Close the Book* and *Bernice*. According to legal historian Zechariah Chafee, "almost all the convictions [under this legislation] were for expressions of opinion about the merits and conduct of the war" (51), although prosecutors often applied the legislation quite broadly to include a range of antigovernment views (104). Sentences could be extremely harsh, lasting at times to twenty-four years (79). Despite the repeal of the legislation in 1921, many convictions were not overturned for months or years, if at all.[10]

Given Glaspell's long-standing concern with free speech, its presence in yet another play should come as no surprise. While free speech struggles had most recently been linked to World War I, Glaspell perceived that the campaign to legalize the spread of information about birth control was in essence a free speech issue. The laws preventing medical practitioners and others like Sanger from educating women about reproduction fundamentally restricted their right to speak. But the reformers did not choose this angle for their revolt; Sanger's tactics instead included the infiltration of the country's power bases: the patriarchy and the government. She harnessed the rhetoric of America's evolving national identity, which, as Glaspell clearly understood, looked to the Midwest as both the geographical and the ideological core of the country.

It is within this increasingly complex political context that Glaspell establishes her picture of bohemian New York in contrast to the more conservative and conventional Midwest. Glaspell makes Seymore the spokesman for the Midwest (and thus, by extension, the nation), but Leon, contrasting Seymore to James O'Brien, sees the former's Americanness as the major problem for his artistry: "What is the matter with Ireland can make poets, but what is the matter with America is that it makes Americans. . . . Seymore, that's what's the matter with you. You're an American" (1.8). Through Seymore, Glaspell develops the opposition between eastern freedom and midwestern bondage. To his friends in New York he expounds:

> Middlewest. Not by free people will the world be set free. But by people who've grown good and sore in the middle west. . . . You see—having lived in the middle west, I want *everyone* to be free. (1.27)

Although this last comment suggests a kind of political response to Leon, it becomes clear that Seymore's ideas of freedom only encompass his metaphoric images of American culture. As he is leaving the journal office in act 1, he gives a speech that points toward the martyr role he plays at home:

> Don't despise me. I am the heart of the country. The heart can't help being the heart. . . . Well do you know that I am the backbone of this nation you run a paper about. Backbones haven't great freedom of movement. (1.34)

Glaspell imbues Seymore's diatribe with a certain comic irony derived from her knowledge of how many of her fellow bohemians hailed, as she did, from this part of the country.

When Nora arrives in Bluff City, the name of which encapsulates its hypocrisy, Glaspell has her echo Seymore's corporeal metaphors for comic effect, announcing to the women assembled in the Standish home:

> I want to get acquainted with the middle west. Seymore tells me it's the heart of the country. Also the backbone. (*To Mrs. MacIntyre, whose backbone has done no unbending*) How does it feel to be the heart and backbone of the country? (*All the while with this graceful gaiety*) The only thing we have to be in New York is the brain. (2.1.23)

The image of New York as the head of the country carries over to one of the major symbols of the play, Nora's bobbed hair, which stands synecdochically for the progressiveness and freedoms of the East. When Nora arrives on the scene, providing the living model for Seymore's recent, mysterious refashioning of one of his mother's dolls' hair into a slanted bob, Dotty is motivated to clip her locks as well. With her new hairstyle she is described as "the Dotty that never had a chance" (2.2.15), and she exclaims to Seymore, "Isn't it amazing how much you cut when you cut the hair!" (2.2.17). Glaspell connects this symbol of female liberation to women's sexuality; the bob gives its wearers allure and the promise "to be kissed a great deal" (2.1.9). The advent of the bob proves to be too great a leap, however, and by the play's end we know that Dotty will grow her hair "as long as it was before" (3.39). Yet, despite Dotty's return to midwestern norms, Glaspell provides the glimmer of hope in her request to accompany Seymore occasionally on his trips to New York (3.40). The arrival of birth control in the person of Nora and her bobbed hair prompts the first steps toward rapprochement between the convention-bound Midwest and the liberated East. Seymore's cover has been exposed, and Dotty's accompanying him to New York will preclude his philandering; the trips will also allow her a wider range of experience than is possible in Bluff City.

One of the most striking elements of Glaspell's portrait of that location is its class consciousness and snobbery, evinced by Seymore and his friends. Just before Nora arrives, Mrs. MacIntrye is gossiping with Dotty:

> I wish something could be done about laundresses having children. I had such a good laundress—and now she's going to have another. But—one doesn't like to talk to those people about—things. (2.1.20)

Not only does Mrs. MacIntyre condescend to her laundress in the matter of reproduction; throughout the second and third acts Glaspell provides further examples of the class stratification inherent to this subculture. Seymore's circle's main concerns emerge as golf, social engagements, gossip, and bridge.

Susan Glaspell at work, much as she described her drafting of *Suppressed Desires* with Jig Cook "before the grate in Milligan Place." [Cook and Glaspell papers, Berg Collection, New York Public Library]

The young and dashing George Cram ("Jig") Cook. [Cook and Glaspell papers, Berg Collection, New York Public Library]

Glaspell and companions, probably after her departure from Greece.
[Cook and Glaspell papers, Berg Collection, New York Public Library]

A more formal image of Glaspell by the famous portrait photographer Bachrach. [Cook and Glaspell papers, Berg Collection, New York Public Library]

Norman Häghejm Matson, Glaspell's companion following the death of Jim Cook. [Cook and Glaspell papers, Berg Collection, New York Public Library]

Susan Glaspell and Eva Le Gallienne. [Theatre Collection, Museum of the City of New York]

Glaspell late in life. [Cook and Glaspell papers, Berg Collection, New York Public Library]

The opening scene from an early production of *Trifles*. [Billy Rose Theatre Collection, New York Public Library]

Josephine Hutchinson and Harold Moulton in a scene from *Inheritors*. [Theatre Collection, The Museum of the City of New York]

The "thwarted tower" setting of act 2 of *The Verge*. [Billy Rose Theatre Collection, New York Public Library]

A scene from the Broadway production of *The Comic Artist*. [Photo by Van Damm. Billy Rose Theatre Collection, New York Public Library]

Eva Le Gallienne, Alma Kruger, and Donald Cameron in a scene from *Ali-son's House*. [Theatre Collection, The Museum of the City of New York]

Although Seymore presents a facade that outwardly rejects such activities in favor of weightier but unspecified concerns, it becomes clear near the end of the play how fully aligned he is with his financially privileged community. Assessing both Glaspell's political and aesthetic concerns, Veronica Makowsky observes that her

> last plays of the Provincetown years were written in the immediate aftermath of World War I and demonstrate her resistance to late modernism's calcification into a new set of constricting conventions and its disparagement of the life of the people and mass culture. ("Susan Glaspell" 50)

Although Makowsky's essay does not consider *Chains of Dew,* her comments clearly apply to Glaspell's depiction of her modernist poet and his selfishness:

Seymore: I see your idea of what my life should be. In the morning I run out to greet the newsboy. No, first the milkman. I tell him what is in my soul and ask him why he is a milkman? At the garage, in the elevator—
Leon: (*Quietly*) I don't think we made ourselves ridiculous this morning, and it is interesting to know what the cigar-man is thinking.
Seymore: Does the cigar-man know what the cigar-man is thinking?
Leon: He was so excited by this contact with his own thoughts that he wouldn't wait on his customers.
Seymore: It would no doubt be a pleasant life—if one had time and strength for it.

(3.19–20)

This last remark is typical of Seymore's beleaguered stance toward anything outside his own preoccupations. Seymore has constructed a shell of self-sacrifice into which he retreats whenever his actions or attitudes are challenged. By making others feel guilty for all he is theoretically doing for them, all he has ostensibly sacrificed on their behalf, he makes them beholden to him, ensuring the perpetuation of the only environment in which he can function. Seymore constantly complains of the bonds that hold him, but, as we realize by the last act, the titular "chains" that bind him are as ephemeral as dew.

Yet it is only within these confines of his own making that he can be an artist at all, even a lousy one (1.7). The snippets of his verse quoted in the play confirm his mediocrity:

> We need you, Shelley:
> You whose vision had the power of light,
> Seeing that gave sight.

We need the swiftness that was Shelley,
Swifter than harm; wider than falling darkness;
More sure than hate.

(1.2–3)

Glaspell tantalizes us with the notion that Seymore lacks something vital that prevents him from fulfilling his artistic potential. One is tempted to think that, if he really understood Shelley, that might have given him some much needed clarity about himself and his work. Seymore's indifferent talent makes it all the more difficult for us to accept how much influence and success he has. Glaspell will implicitly contrast the male privilege enjoyed by this middling poet to the gender-related sacrifices of the genuinely gifted female poet Alison Stanhope in *Alison's House.*

No one understands Seymore's warped mentality better than his mother, who traces his behavior back to childhood:

I don't suppose a child ever enjoyed unhappiness more. He began to write poems when I wouldn't let him go swimming in the river. Not that he would have gone swimming in the river. (*Leaning forward, voice falling*) He was afraid of the river. (2.2.12–13)[11]

The irony of Shelley's having drowned surely underscores the humor of this revelation. Through Mother we see that Seymore is enraptured by the *idea* of the romantic, poetic life, yet we also realize that he is unwilling to make the sacrifices necessary to achieve artistic greatness, even if he had the talent.

It is also Mother who makes Dotty understand what will happen if they, in conjunction with Nora, destroy the illusions that shape Seymore's existence: "You have to be a little careful about freeing people. Sometimes they like what they're freed from, and sometimes they don't know what to do about what they're freed for" (2.1.12–13). She develops this point further in act 3:

Mother: . . . Do you want to go skylarking and leave poor Seymore to his
    freedom? Perhaps you do; it depends on which we value more—our-
    selves or him. . . .
Dotty: You mean *I've* got to sacrifice.
Mother: The greatest sacrifice of all. You've got to let yourself be sacrificed
    for.

(3.31–32)

The allusion to Shelley's famous poem "To a Sky-Lark" cannot be accidental. In Shelley's lyric the poet envies and aspires to the expression of the bird, who soars above him, magnificently evoking the beauty of nature:

Teach me half the gladness
    That thy brain must know,
Such harmonious madness
    From my lips would flow
The world should listen then—as I am listening now.

(573)

While the parallel in the play is not exact, Glaspell may be pointing us to Seymore's dependence on Dotty. The strategic difference, of course, is that Seymore never acknowledges this debt.

For feminist readers of Glaspell's work Glaspell's denouement can seem disappointing, yet it must be considered in conjunction with the overall theme of gender identity the play develops. Nora, of course, represents one kind of woman, independent and self-assured, with no ties or obligations to anything other than her beliefs, a familiar female image in her Greenwich Village milieu. At the other extreme stand Edith and Mrs. MacIntyre, rigid, convention-bound midwestern women whom Glaspell virtually caricatures. Dotty and her mother-in-law are perhaps the most complex women in the drama, for, although we are at first led to believe by Seymore that they are also thoroughly midwestern, they reveal themselves as much more: women capable of growth, change, and a deep understanding of their stultifying environment.

Glaspell juxtaposes this range of female characterizations with her more limited males, chiefly Seymore and Leon. As in *Trifles*, Glaspell here shows how men both construct female identity *and* misread it, never realizing how misguided their judgment is. Early in act 2 Dotty broaches what one might call the social construction of gender with her mother-in-law:

Dotty: Do you think, mother, that it's hard to be any other way than the way you are?
Mother: Well, I suppose that depends on just how you are.
Dotty: Don't you think sometimes you are as you are—because you've *been* that way. . . . And you've been that way—well because you are supposed to be that way. When you do certain things—bridge and dancing—then you're the kind of person who plays bridge and dances. But what sort of person would you be—if you did something else? (2.1.13)

In other words, Dotty has become Dotty because she has been formed by the way her society says she should behave. Yet she also sees the potential to be different and recognizes that her identity has really been imposed on her, rather than developed organically or independently.

Much of what Dotty is has been shaped by Seymore, who explains to his mother soon after he begins to see the changes in her motivated by both Nora's arrival and her involving Dotty in political work:

> I am not going to stand by and see my wife's happiness ruined! Mother, you know what Dotty's life has been. . . . The things she grew up in. I— at no little personal sacrifice—have kept her happy in those things. She's just playing with this idea—as a child plays with a doll—a bee—a bomb. She *is* a child,—and I have not asked her to be anything else. (2.2.14)

As Marcia Noe has observed, Glaspell may well be evoking Ibsen's *A Doll House* with her use of the character name *Nora* and the central presence of the dolls (*Critical Biography* 129). But the complexity of Seymore's relationship to his mother emerges here as well. While this passage suggests that he attributes a certain level of insight to her, he also patronizes her in her absence. He reduces all she does to her maternal identity, never considering that she might think or act independently of that role. It is also patently clear that Seymore infantilizes his wife, a detail Nora quickly perceives in act 1. Through Seymore, Glaspell continues her exposure of the male construction of female identity, already explored in *Trifles* and *Bernice*. Glaspell pushes this theme even further here, by having Nora at first assume Seymore's wife is an invalid because of the way he spoke of her (1.16–17). When Seymore disabuses her of this notion, she asks him to use his wife's real name, Diantha, rather than her nickname, Dotty Dimple, that she has had since childhood (1.32–33), as a gesture acknowledging her independence and maturity.

Glaspell shows us that it is as important for Seymore to feel the martyr to his family as it is for him to generate his own image of the women close to him, no matter how mistaken we realize these images are. When Nora arrives in Bluff City, she is taken by the doll that Seymore has refashioned after her and wants to learn more about his mother who makes them.

Nora: . . . Aren't they cunning?
Seymore: You think they are cunning; I think they're—significant. They—say
    it all. Mother. They—give it all away. But you don't know what I mean.
Nora: I might if you'd tell me.
Seymore: . . . She makes them for the church, you know. They sell them at
    their bazaar. . . . You see, mother just has to go on doing things for
    people—she's got the habit.
Nora: Yes, that's what I was saying.
Seymore: (*Hastily and firmly*) Has to do her own kind of thing for them. She
    does the thing that continues her life. Brings it over into this place
    where—
Nora: Why do you speak of your mother as if she were dead. She's still alive.

Seymore: She's looking back at life. You—since we're speaking frankly—can't
   project yourself ahead and see what that means. There's something
   quite—that quite gets one, I think, mother making those dolls. Her
   children are gone, as children. She—well, she makes dolls.

                                                                    (2.2.7)

Despite Nora's suggestions of other perspectives and other interpretations,
Seymore will not let her have the power to interpret his mother, "hastily and
firmly" imposing his reading of her behavior and insisting Nora does not have
the experience to "project . . . ahead" as he apparently feels he does. As Mother
avows in act 2, Seymore "*thinks* he sees" many things (2.2.12), and by act 3 even
Dotty realizes he has "the wrong dope" about his mother (3.11), not to mention herself.

The dolls that Mother makes become central symbols in the play. Like
the quilt in *Trifles,* they hide meanings that only the empathic few can decipher. Although Seymore mistakenly sees them as sad attempts to perpetuate
maternal creativity, they are in fact powerful art for social critique whose
codes are hidden except to those with the insight to read them.

Nora: . . . Tell me—why do you make dolls? Seymore says it's because you
   have to be doing for others; but they haven't a do-for-others look.
Mother: (*With the timid eagerness of the artist*) What kind of a look have
   they?
Nora: They look to me—Perhaps I'd better not say it.
Mother: Do.—if it's like that.
Nora: I don't know that I can—exactly. But there's something *devilish* about
   those dolls.
Mother: (*With concern*) Oh, does it show?
Nora: You were getting back at something.
Mother: (*Appalled, then defiant*) Well, don't you have to—one way or an-
   other? And this isn't a way that does much harm, do you think? . . .
   The women of Bluff City—if they had any idea how funny they are—
   then it wouldn't be the kind of funniness you have to do something
   about. But after you've lived with respectability for seventy years it
   helps to make a stiff neck and a smile that doesn't know how silly
   the neck is. These dolls have kept me out of lots of trouble. Tell me
   (*Taking up the incompleted doll*) do you think this doll looks at all like
   Seymore?

                                                                  (2.2.11–12)

Glaspell may be using Mother's speech for a broader comment on one style
of women's artistry, perhaps including her own. Such artistry is an essential

outlet for its creator, and yet, for personal or social reasons, she feels she must find ways to disguise the blatancy of its political or cultural critique.

For Seymore the women are dolls, but Glaspell shows in this scene that they have a different significance. In act 1 Seymore insists that his verse be judged "by itself . . . and not by anything you may know about me" (1.24). But with this scene in act 2 Glaspell shows that the act of interpretation is more complex. Seymore does not want his works read biographically, and yet this is exactly what he does with his mother's artistry. And by misreading her biography, he consequently misinterprets the meaning of the dolls as well. Glaspell may be using these moments to reflect artists' concerns that their works are read only as reflections of their personal lives, rather than in terms of broader cultural considerations. Moreover, she points to the difficulty of determining the proper context for analysis. Nora's ability to intuit the critique crafted by Mother eschews an essentialist criticism; Nora does not understand through the shared experience of the maternal. Nora's insight suggests that Glaspell believes audiences should be careful not to impose an interpretation upon art but, instead, to let the art speak for itself through open exploration that embraces both its biographical and cultural contexts.

Finally, Glaspell's extensive focus on the meaning of the dolls puts them on a par with Seymore's verse and his friends' and family's efforts to understand it. As with her championing of women's creativity in *Trifles* and her later exploration of cartooning in *The Comic Artist*, Glaspell uses Mother's dolls to question assumptions about what qualifies as "art." Thus, she provides an immanent critique of the high culture/popular culture divide that coincided with the emergence of the male-controlled high modernist avant-garde in the United States. Misprisions about a woman's art in *Chains of Dew* exemplify the larger problems with the patriarchal construction of gender throughout the play.

Leon perpetually believes in the facade of bondage Seymore has constructed as well as the biographical interpretation of his texts that Seymore dismisses. Glaspell slips in another Shelley allusion, this time to *Prometheus Unbound*, as Leon goes to Mother to ask her to help free the poet:

Mother: Well, what do you want me to do about it?
Leon: He feels that his family binds him to this trivial life. He comes to us—
    the things he cares for—what he himself really is—and he is as a man
    let out of prison. But he knows he must return to bondage.
Mother: This is bondage, is it? . . .
Leon: He yearns to be one of the mad ones of the world. He thirsts for a
    hard life—an outlaw's life! He is goaded by this respectability into
    which he is caught. If you could hear him talk of how he hates it! *All of
    that is in his poetry—for one who can see.* Don't you feel the madness
    there—the longing for things not had?

Mother: (*As if he has expressed something for her*) Yes. The longing for things
    not had.

                                       (3.24–25; my emph.)

Mother's realization about Seymore's need for his chains, even at the expense
of her and Dotty's freedom, is enabled by this male misreading. Like the men
in *Trifles,* Leon cannot interpret signs accurately.

    Glaspell uses such scenes to expose the biases in men's perceptions of the
world. Saving one of her more humorous—and egregious—examples for act
3 of *Chains,* she has James O'Brien connect the need for birth control with the
movement for equality of the sexes:

O'Brien: I was thinking of birth control this morning. . . . I was thinking of
    the terrible inequality there is in this whole arrangement. . . . (*To*
    Leon *and* Seymore) How can there be any hope of equality between
    the sexes? It is physically impossible. . . . Why should woman have
    everything?
Dotty: Everything to bear!
O'Brien: Everything to know. What has man done that he should be ex-
    cluded from this great experience?
Seymore: Just who is it you're sorry for?
O'Brien: Me—you—men. . . . The greatest experience in human affairs and
    man absolutely excluded from it. Oh, no it's silly to talk of equality.
    Physical conditions rule it out. It's all very dispiriting—if you let your-
    self dwell upon it.
Dotty: (*To* Nora, *in excitement*) Why isn't *that* the opening speech for birth
    control?
Nora: It certainly is a new angle.
Leon: But I should say the angle was going rather than coming.
Seymore: Oh, all angles lead to birth control, if you just think long enough.
Dotty: (*As one who has had her cue*) If you just think long enough. You see,
    the great experience mustn't be too often experienced.
Nora: (*With light malice*) It wouldn't be fair to man.
Dotty: No! (*To* O'Brien, *telling him good news*) Tomorrow night you will tell
    this roomful of women that you would love to bear a child.
(O'Brien *looks around the room in alarm*)
O'Brien: (*Helplessly*) Have I been speaking for birth control?
Dotty: Absolutely.

                                       (3.20–22)

The women must seize and transform O'Brien's argument to suit their purposes, encapsulating the process by which women must support men and one

another simultaneously. They turn his naïveté to their advantage, exploiting him at the same time that they convey the appearance of admiring his stance.

Mother best exemplifies this duality by her actions at the close of the play. She gives Nora a check for $700—a symbolic $100 for each child she has borne—in support of the campaign but also urges her to leave. Birth control, and the personal and physical freedom for women it represents, become intertwined with all the other arguments about liberty in the play. As Mother asks rhetorically, "Would it be possible to think highly enough of personal liberty to feel a man had a right to keep himself in bondage if he wanted to?" (3.30). For Dotty, however, Mother's questions are even more basic: "Speaking for fundamentals, which do you love more, Dotty—Seymore or birth control? . . . If you had to choose between them, which would you take?" Glaspell makes the ultimate conflict love and marriage versus politics and activism, and Dotty "in her heart" knows how she must choose (3.31).

It is very tempting to interpret *Chains of Dew* biographically and read the sacrifices of Dotty and her mother-in-law as Glaspell's own, particularly given Cook's decision to have them both leave New York, where she had had such success, for a foreign country with which she had no connection other than through him.[12] One might look at the female characters as aspects of Glaspell's self, a playing out of the various choices she might have made. A lively, bob-haired woman like Nora, she could have stayed in New York, but, as a married woman like Dotty, she chose to put her husband first, abandoning the potential to explore her own freedom in order to safeguard her marriage, even though her husband was not a great artist. Yet, even if one didn't know the Glaspell biography, one would feel strongly the impact of that sacrifice. Glaspell's own injunction in the play to balance biographical criticism of art with a cultural reading points to this broader interpretation. One of the strengths of *Chains of Dew* is Glaspell's dramatization of each of the women's options. Dotty's and Mother's choices are realistic, if painful. Glaspell provides a note of optimism, however, through her indications that these women will continue in their creative endeavors. We grasp the cultural forces at work behind their decisions; we realize that if the Dianthas of the world are to have the freedoms of the Noras then the Seymores and Leons, and also the Ediths and Mrs. MacIntyres, must come to value that potential. They must see it and themselves objectively, jettisoning the social conventions and outdated perspectives that make such liberation impossible. Moreover, had Glaspell given the play a "happy" ending, with Dottie and her mother maintaining their liberation, Glaspell would have left her Village audience with a narrative closure that necessitated no action by them. In other words, Glaspell's calculated choice to reassert such an obviously unsatisfactory status quo was designed, in proto-Brechtian fashion, to highlight conventions of realism that demand the restitution of the social order and to force her audience to think carefully about marriage, gender roles, and American culture, very possibly with an eye to motivating social change.

Glaspell's departure for Greece with Cook rendered her incapable of overseeing any aspect of the staging of *Chains*. Glaspell ultimately chose not the publish the play, perhaps because the feedback she received undermined her confidence in the work at the time; she did, however, send a typescript to the Library of Congress, most probably before her departure, to secure the copyright. This version, compared with details from reviews and correspondence, enables speculation about the production history of the drama.

In her absence the director and cast apparently felt free to cut the script as they saw fit and to take the play in different directions from those indicated by Glaspell. The *New York Herald* review featured the secondary headline "Provincetown Players' Production Attacks Bobbed Hair and Birth Control," the verb of which suggests the balance of satire may have tipped in the opposite direction from the one Glaspell's script outlines. The satire in the play is actually quite complex, operating on multiple levels. Some of the characters within the world of the play do poke fun at birth control. But Glaspell is also careful to direct how we receive these opinions, such that by the play's conclusion we know more clearly how to evaluate each character's views. As a result, the earlier satire gives way to a more serious consideration of the significance of both personal choices and political commitments.

Given the probable directorial interventions with the script in production, it is not surprising that few critics grasped the nuances of the text. Stephen Rathbun, writing in the *Sun*, was one of the few reviewers to sense Glaspell's theme.

> Susan Glaspell's plays give one something to think about, and "Chains of Dew" is no exception to the rule. But we wonder why Miss Glaspell called the play a "comedy." To us it is tragic that a woman sacrifices her future and becomes a slave to her husband's career. It is just as tragic as though she had committed suicide. And yet, as wives are continually doing this sort of thing in real life, we might call it a grim, realistic comedy.

But some of Rathbun's other comments suggest how the production manipulated Glaspell's original text. Describing the play's denouement, he explains:

> *Dotty* has to choose between emancipating herself at the expense of her husband's inspiration or returning to the silly social life she has been leading. She makes the sacrifice, happier in making it than she was in the past when she did not know what to do to make *Seymore* happy. She becomes again the social butterfly and even lets her hair grow again to conform to

town conventions. ("Susan Glaspell's 'Chains of Dew' Is a Bright, Realistic Comedy")

Rathbun's description of Dotty's state of mind and its aftermath are the striking details here. Glaspell writes that Dotty's decision leaves her in tears for the entire conclusion of the play, although Seymore does not correctly understand their source. Glaspell gives no specific indication that Dotty will resume her former style or activities; rather, Seymore mentions his intention of joining his friend Bill in golf at the next opportunity, and encourages his wife to call their friends for a bridge party that evening (3.41). Interestingly, these differences did not seem to affect Rathbun's ultimate reading of the play's significance.

Some of the critics did at least separate Glaspell's script from the production's problems. The reviewer for the *Evening Telegram* observes:

> Miss Glaspell's "Chains of Dew" is a satire that is as delicate as gossamer. There is much that is delightful in its three acts, but the piece is so elusive that it demands perfect stage production and expert acting. Consequently, although the actors in the cast were fairly competent, several of the author's best effects missed because the players were uncertain in their lines and indeterminate in their stage business. ("Miss Glaspell's New Comedy")

Burns Mantle concurs, albeit a bit more negatively:

> It is to be regretted Susan Glaspell did not take a little more time with "Chains of Dew." It promises so well in its first act, even when it is as sluggishly played as it is at the Provincetown Playhouse, it seems a play and a theme worth working over. ("Plays of the Week")

Maida Castellun, writing in the *New York Call,* makes a similar remark: "Short and light 'Chains of Dew' may be, but length and heaviness are added by the extraordinarily long waits and the unindividualized acting" ("Plays That Pass").

Yet Castellun's review also suggests that the *Herald* critic's opinion of the play's satire may be the result of the performances:

> So subtle is the satire here and so heavy the characterization that one fears the spectator may see only the obvious theme of the martyr rejoicing in his sacrifice because he has no other claim to distinction. But there is much more implied—among other things the showing up of the male as your only true conservative in matters social and spiritual. . . . As a social iconoclast the female of the species again proves more daring than the male. ("Plays That Pass")

Such remarks indicate that a few of the critics realized not only that Glaspell had a broader political message in her play but that her work dared to take a position of critique within her own community.

The *Herald* critic noted:

> [*Chains*] was more spirited and radiant of actual life than anything she has done hitherto, and perhaps could be enjoyed by many of those living above that spiritual dead line of Washington Square which these players seem to have drawn for themselves.
>
> Actually, Miss Glaspell seems to have dared the united front of Green- wich Village by satirizing bobbed hair and birth control. One grows breathless in writing of such heresy in the Village itself. ("Susan Glaspell's 'Chains of Dew' Is Sharp Satire")

The *Evening Telegram* went even further:

> There were those in the audience who felt uneasy. Miss Glaspell was having some fun with the bob-haired, the birth controllers, the minor poets and other faddists, who are not missing on the subscription lists of the Provincetown Players. ("Miss Glaspell's New Comedy")

Glaspell calculatedly chose to create satiric portraits of personalities from her own community (at the time she wrote the piece, she probably did not know of the imminence of her departure). Her risking the ire of her audience cor- responds to her commitment to write political drama that had risked more se- rious repercussions.

Interestingly, some reviewers avoided the political content of *Chains of Dew* altogether. Alexander Woollcott, the critic for the *New York Times,* could not bring himself to discuss the presence of birth control in the play, prefer- ring instead to attack Glaspell herself in his sneering review—the only pre- dominantly negative one the play received:

> The wisp of a comedy called "Chains of Dew," which the Provincetown Players threw into the gap in their season last evening . . . is touched here and there with charming fancy. . . . Miss Glaspell does not think of it as a sketch. She calls it a play, turns it over to her Macdougal Street cohorts and sails blandly away to Greece, leaving them to struggle with it. ("Play")

In the first place Wollcott is incorrect about the mounting of the work as a last-minute production, since we know the facts surrounding her departure. Furthermore, it is also difficult to tolerate his sense of Glaspell's careless aban- donment of her drama. Most likely Woollcott knew nothing of the personal circumstances of Glaspell's departure, and thus he put his own spin on the facts. The range of opinions these reviews represent indicates that, as is true of so many productions, some critics seemed to grasp better than others the balance between a script's strengths and weaknesses and performance successes and in-adequacies. Yet they also highlight the effect of one of the key changes the Provincetown group made that may have contributed to their demise: the tran-sition from the integral involvement of authors with their own productions to the use of professional directors to help the group generate a "stronger" artistic product. The ironic impact of this change for the staging of *Chains of Dew* can best be demonstrated through the correspondence between Glaspell (and Cook) and Edna Kenton, whom Glaspell relied upon to oversee the production in her absence. The strain surrounding the rehearsals emerges from the letters they exchanged soon after Glaspell and Cook arrived in Greece.

On 5 May Kenton recounted some early problems. Not only had casting difficulties arisen, but the director had cut the script over Kenton's objections. He removed much of the comic business, including the heroine Nora's hu-morous struggles with the mimeograph machine in act 1. Kenton also inti-mated that some of the Provincetown members didn't want to stage the play at all, favoring a remounting of O'Neill's *Emperor Jones.*[13]

On 11 May Glaspell responded to the dismal news of the rehearsals. She wrote to Kenton:

> I saw there was nothing for me to do but get drunk, and so deaden the first pangs in the thought of [Edward] Reese as Standish, Blanche [Hays] as Dotty and little Marion Berry as the on-to-herself Nora. Though I admit the last may work out. There's a real idea there, anyway, whereas Reese just hasn't got the personality to suggest what Seymore must sug-gest, or Blanche the charm for Dotty. But these two I take it were tenta-tive.[14] I can only hope.
>
> However, I want the anguish of knowing the worst, so do let the bul-letins continue, if there is any worst still going on. . . . But I hate to think of *your* struggle with the damn play . . . You must have felt many times that the chains of this comedy were more than dew. (Barrett Library)

Later, after the reviews had reached her, Glaspell wrote Kenton on 29 May:

> I thought our friends the reviewers treated us very well. Giving the play pretty much all it deserved, I should say, and writing quite enter-tainingly about it. I know a Seymore equal to an impression of reserve and complexity would have helped the part a lot, but how fortunate we were to have had any Seymore at all! [one who could keep you guessing as to whether there was something there] There must have been days

when you contemplated giving the play without any of its parts. (Barrett Library)

On 22 June Edna wrote to Blanche Hays about the state of the Provincetown Players' affairs, making specific references to the *Chains* debacle: "I mailed a *cut* script to Sue—she was entitled to know, if she wanted to know—how her play went on . . . It was bad enough—remembering, but when it came to making the actual cuts in red ink—God forfend!" (Barrett Library)

On 1 July Kenton's letter to Cook contained further news for Glaspell about the publication of her plays by Small, Maynard: "They wrote to ask if "Chains" was to be included in [the] volume. I knew you would want "The Verge" alone, and told Fitzie [M. Eleanor Fitzgerald, business director for the Provincetown Players] to tell them so" (Harvard Theatre Collection). Glaspell appears to have allowed Kenton's decision on publication to stand, perhaps because of the hurdles of geographical distance, perhaps because she was too disheartened by the critics' response.

Years later, when Kenton came to write her memoir of the Provincetown, she frankly recounted her sense of the production:

> The less said of the sixth bill the better. Except this, indeed, that Susan had thrown herself to the lions, or, better simile, had cast herself, like the Roman patriot, into the gulf that yawned in our small city between [O'Neill's] "The Hairy Ape" and the close of the season. We had no other long play than hers to put on, and hers was not good—none knew it better than she. (*The Story of the Provincetown Players* 211)

Piecing these fragments together, one could conclude that Kenton's own problems, acting on Glaspell's behalf, may have colored her opinion of *Chains of Dew*. She blames the script, rather than herself, for the failed production. It is tantalizing to consider what a perceptive director and cast could do with this script were it to be produced today. We have only Kenton's word on Glaspell's opinion of the work, but here, as with her last play, *Springs Eternal*, it would appear that the less-than-favorable opinion of others, especially friends like Kenton and later Langner, whose views she valued, may have discouraged her from revising or publishing these works. But Kenton's judgments also point toward a larger problem with the historical discussion of Glaspell's dramaturgy: the tradition (particularly evident in the criticism of Bigsby) of using aesthetic criteria as the primary means of evaluating the worth of a script and of positioning a given work within a dramatic canon. As with the critical and scholarly appraisal of *Inheritors*, *Chains of Dew* demonstrates the importance of establishing additional analytic criteria with which to study Glaspell's writing. Opening discussion to incorporate such

concerns as politics and culture present two of many possible avenues for
such scholarship.[15]

Kenton's commentary highlights the fact that the script that Glaspell
wrote was not the one that was ultimately produced (a similar fate awaited
The Comic Artist). Since the production script no longer exists, there is no way
to determine the differences between the texts. The newspaper reviews, of
course, were based on that production script, with whatever cuts and changes
it included, and not Glaspell's original. Furthermore, scholars can only base
their analysis on the Library of Congress manuscript of the play, which may
or may not be Glaspell's final version or the version from which the production script developed.

This catalogue of textual problems resonates with further ironies of the
theatrical history of *Chains of Dew*. It seems clear from the reviews and the details shared by Kenton that the play's male director[16] produced a reading as
skewed in its own right as are Leon's interpretations of Seymore's verse or Seymore's understanding of his wife and mother. A similar directorial fate awaited
the New York production of her next play, *The Comic Artist*, which she cowrote
with Norman Matson. Moreover, the Players' move to remount O'Neill's *Emperor Jones*, soon followed by the breakup of the group and its reconstitution
by the triumvirate (O'Neill, Kenneth Macgowan, and Robert Edmond Jones)
that radically altered the profile of the theater, is also presciently anticipated by
the trajectory of Glaspell's play. In it male-dominated hierarchies of power sub-
sume women's creativity. Such a move reverberates with the theater's subsequent failure either to produce women's plays with any regularity or to continue the group's former dedication to developing new American dramaturgy.
Glaspell was thus extremely fortunate to have Eva Le Gallienne, an actress and
director sensitive to the integrity of the playwright's vision, stage the revival of
Inheritors and the première of *Alison's House* in New York.

The Comic Artist

In a letter probably written in 1926 to Norman Matson, Glaspell's companion following the death of Jig Cook, she shares an intimate memory of their creation of *The Comic Artist,* the play that renewed her interest in writing for the stage:

> I think of you and me, the room at Truro, the strange night, that play growing between us. Will we remember, when we sit together in a New York theatre and see those people doing the things we saw them doing that first night . . . ? Yes, we will remember.[1]

The stories surrounding the composition and production of *The Comic Artist* may well be as dramatic—even as melodramatic—as the plot of the play itself. This letter, probably the first in the collection of Glaspell's correspondence with Matson,[2] can only be read now with an ironic sense of how little of the hope and love reflected by it remained by the time the play finally opened on Broadway in the spring of 1933. By that time Glaspell's relationship with Matson was over. They had been trying to find an American producer for almost seven years, and their initial optimism about the quality of the drama had been replaced by resignation and the desire to make some much needed money from it before its inevitable, early close.

These two stories, one biographical, one theatrical, may overshadow the play itself, particularly given its weak commercial reception and its neglect within Glaspell criticism. Yet to tell only these parallel narratives of confidence turned to disillusionment would be to ignore the significant, if not entirely successful attempt by the writers to collaborate on a play not only closely engaged with major issues in American popular culture but also attempting to expand the borders of dramatic realism. *The Comic Artist* takes the phenomenon of the printed comic strip and explores it in two distinct but related ways: sociologically, by examining how commercial forces affect art and the artist in America, and dramaturgically, by pushing on the boundaries between realism and other forms of mimetic representation. *The Comic Artist* thus joins Glaspell's body of dramatic writing engaged with the exploration of both theatrical modernism and related issues of high versus mass culture.

We know, from reviews and from the correspondence, that the ending of the published version of the play (1927) differs from that of the script produced on Broadway, although most other plot details up to the final scene appear to be the same in both versions. Stephen Rolf, "a painter in his early thirties," has returned from Paris and married Eleanor, a "somewhat older" woman (5). They have settled into a quiet existence in her family home on Cape Cod. Into their peaceful lives come three additional figures: Luella, a brassy "woman of forty" whom Stephen knew in Paris; soon thereafter, Stephen's brother Karl, the title character, and Karl's new wife, Nina, daughter of Luella and former lover of Stephen in Paris. Nina, who seems to care only for material and social gain, tries to lure Stephen back into an affair. Eleanor, quickly aware of Nina's ploys, feels compelled to open Karl's eyes to his wife's true nature. In the published version Nina threatens to kill herself after she has been exposed, and Karl runs off to the beach after her, tragically (melodramatically?) drowning as he thinks he is rescuing his wife. For the Broadway production's ending, changed at the request of the director, Karl and Nina decide to try to make a go of their marriage, and Stephen and Eleanor are left with the wreckage of theirs.[3]

As this plot summary suggests, the play focused on the characters' personal lives in a hermetic way distinct from all of Glaspell's other plays to date. Percy Hammond bitingly remarked, "Miss Glaspell, one of Literature's most flaming nuns, again removes her wimple in The 'Comic Artist' and barges into . . . the battle of the sexes" ("Theatres"). But Joseph Wood Krutch more astutely observed in his review in the *Nation*, "This time Miss Glaspell has abandoned all reliance upon the topical interest of her subject matter" ("Drama" 539). In other words, this piece reflected Glaspell's post–Provincetown Players transition to a family focus in her plays. *The Comic Artist* featured no overt link to an issue of the day, such as the vogue for Freudian psychology, the campaign for birth control, the opposition to World War I, or any other of her timely concerns that the New York reviewers recalled from her earlier writing. Yet certain key lines and images from the play, noted by several reviewers, combined with some of Matson's comments in his letters on the rehearsal process, hint at subtler thematic and dramaturgical concerns that the Broadway production may not have been able to realize. Consequently, these issues also lay beyond the critics' grasp.

Emblematic of this problem is the comment made in a number of reviews that the title of the play is misleading, since Karl, the comic artist, does not seem to be the central figure in the work. Richard Dana Skinner admonishes:

> When a title is both distracting and inadequate, it can have a harmful and confusing effect on audience and critics alike. . . . This one, for nearly two

acts, distracts you from the real problem and purpose of the play, and, in the last act, fails to live up to the rich values established by the play itself. ("Play")

Rather than assume that Glaspell and Matson simply mistitled their play, I would argue that the drama represents an experiment, albeit a possibly failed one, in the fusion of theme and style (one of the hallmarks of Glaspell's dramaturgy throughout her career). From this holistic perspective the title has everything to do with the play. If one works from the assumption that a logical artistic rationale underlies both the title of the play and the character of Karl as a professional cartoonist within it, one might productively explore the significance and history of cartoon art to see how they may intersect with the drama.

Comic strips as a national medium central to popular culture, the details of their financing and publication, their generic profile, and specific, popular comic figures are all directly germane to *The Comic Artist*. Glaspell and Matson reveal here, as Glaspell had in her previous plays, a depth of understanding of their central conceit, such that both factual details and broader thematic structures work together to provide the play's texture. Starting from a basis of realistic representation, the playwrights construct Karl and his cartoons within the context of the emerging prominence of comic art in American culture. Yet the title's juxtaposition of *the comics* with *art* also points toward a central tension in the play. Karl consistently qualifies his professional status, calling himself a "funny paper artist" (28), or "comic artist," as if to separate his work from that of Stephen, whose time in Paris and preference for oils on canvas make only him worthy of the unmodified description "artist." Ironically, Karl is the one with "all the talent in the family," as Stephen "cheerfully" acknowledges (43). Yet Karl's vocation is a source of mounting stress, whereas Stephen seems little troubled by any aspect of his work. The high culture/mass culture split emblematized by the brothers' different forms of expression is one of the central themes of the play. Glaspell and Matson explore the nuances of this trope for capitalist America, specifically in terms of the evolving role of the artist in American society.

Most historians of the comic strip form agree on its origins. Dating its beginnings to the 1890s, they often position the comic strip in a tradition stretching back to cave drawings and passing through the refined technique of eighteenth- and nineteenth-century satiric artists such as Hogarth and Daumier: "Within this grand tradition of picture and poetry developed that uniquely American art form, the comics, and its special aesthetic, an aesthetic dictated by the demands of the marketplace and by the sensibilities of its readers" (O'Sullivan 9). M. Thomas Inge corroborates this view. "Along with jazz," he asserts, "the comic strip as we know it perhaps represents America's major indigenous contribution to world culture" (xi). David Manning White and

Robert H. Abel also call the comics "the oldest, most enduring popular art in America" and quote the anthropologist Geoffrey Gorer, who sees the form as "one of the few important bonds ... uniting all Americans in a common experience" (2). They position comic strips centrally within the discourse on popular culture, explaining that cartoons

> merit study as active forces in the development of the national ethos. And since their creators, in seeking to reach the widest possible audience, invariably reflect that audience and its thinking, the comics are an extraordinary cultivation of images, mirroring what we, as a people, have been like throughout the past half-century and are like today. (3)

Thus, comic strips emerge as a powerful, indigenous popular art form, closely linked with their culture and having a wide impact on American society. Glaspell may well have realized by this point in the century that Jig Cook's hopes for the theater as a central element of American culture would not materialize, and she chose to explore a popular medium that was successfully and rapidly reaching across the country.

The breadth of the comics' impact, however, is intimately tied to the financing and distribution of the strips in newspapers throughout the country. Jerry Robinson claims that "by 1906 syndicates were already in competition" for the work of popular and emerging cartoonists (36). The syndicates facilitated the countrywide distribution of cartoons and greatly enhanced the financial rewards for drawing a successful strip. By 1915 Bud Fisher, the creator of Mutt and Jeff, was earning "a $1,000-a-week guarantee plus 80% of the gross" for his strip, and within a few years his compensation had risen to $4,600 per week (Robinson 45). By the early 1920s comic artists could command million-dollar contracts, spread out over a multiyear period (Robinson 75). Glaspell and Matson show the impact of this potential level of remuneration on all aspects of Karl's life.

The financial rewards of such work led to tension, however, with the established artistic world. "Serious" artists despised the form, despite the fact that many prominent cartoonists were also notable artists and painters (Robinson 42). Public attitudes also encouraged this division. White and Abel suggest that comics, in a sense, mask their own artistry through their populism and that audiences would not be as responsive were the strips perceived as "*Art*" (11).

A similar argument could be made about their politics. While there is a lengthy tradition of political cartooning in the United States, most mass circulation daily strips, until the advent of Gary Trudeau's *Doonesbury*, did not engage politics overtly. There is a strong correlation between the subtler role of politics in Glaspell's later dramaturgy—targeted at a wider commercial audience and focused on family and relationships, with social critique as a backdrop—and its corollary role in the comics embraced by the American populace.

Questions about aesthetic attitudes toward mass versus high art recur throughout Glaspell's plays; the dramatists layer onto this theme the financial realities of strip production in *The Comic Artist*. Stephen at first worries about Karl's ability to pay for Nina's expensive tastes, which have prompted him to buy her a fur coat and a large motorcar. But, as Eleanor points out, "A man who can draw funny pictures that are funny won't starve—not in America" (23). Eleanor grasps the commercialism inherent to Karl's new career, and Karl reveals the momentum he must sustain in order to succeed: "I can't loaf now, Steve. . . . Yes, the big idea is money!" Karl also sees these rewards coming to someone who is only "almost an artist." His brother replies, "The fellow who created Mugs isn't almost an artist," but Karl still equivocates: "Funny paper artist" (28). Glaspell and Matson position Karl as a man trapped between the desire to succeed financially and to secure the respect of those whose opinions of "Art" he values. The fact that these goals are impossible to reconcile highlights the cultural division underlying the drama's exploration of art in America.

Many analysts of the strips position them in relation to other literary and narrative genres. Tying this analysis to the status of cartoons as popular culture, White and Abel, quoting Max Lerner, call them " 'not only the American's Gothic romance but also his Plutarch and his *Everyman* ' " (35). Indeed, many commentators feel the genre most closely aligned with the strip is the drama. According to Inge: "It has been suggested that the comics are closest to drama in that both rely on the dramatic conventions of character, dialogue, scene, gesture, compressed time, and stage devices" (xix–xx). Maurice Horn traces the connections back to the conventions of Aristotelian dramaturgy and makes the sweeping claim that "in the seventy-five years of their existence, [they have] accomplished much the same progression as western drama since the Middle Ages" (13). Given Matson's dabblings in cartoon art,[4] as well as Glaspell's sensitivity to American culture, we might postulate that their choices of subject (the comics) and form (the drama) were calculated for their synergy.

Many of the historians identify one type of character as key to the early success of the form: "the classic comic 'fall guys,' the little man whose roots go back to Don Quixote, and far beyond" (White and Abel 34). Judith O'Sullivan calls this "enduring and endearing" figure "the innocent" (15), and the composite profile of this personality corresponds very closely to the image Glaspell and Matson create of Mugs, the cartoon hero of Karl's strip. While there is no evidence that the dramatists were aware of this tradition, they nevertheless selected a version of this figure for their central comic icon. The parallels

between Mugs and Karl in the play are relatively overt; America's fondness for
the story of the underdog fighting tragicomically against social and personal
adversity was already entrenched.

It may or may not be a coincidence that, in the same year as *The Comic
Artist* was published, Wally Bishop created a strip featuring slightly younger
figures bearing the names Muggs and Skeeter (Robinson 92); in fact, all the
New York critics subsequently misspelled the character's name this way, with
the doubled consonant. What is ironic about this mistake is that the critics,
perhaps assuming that the play drew on the Bishop figure, spent no time exploring the role of comics in the play or in American culture. By focusing almost exclusively on the emotional lives of the human characters, they missed
the broader ramifications of the comic strip milieu for the play's dramaturgy
and social themes.

In the drama's opening scene description we learn that the first act is set
in the living room of the Rolfs's 200-year-old house. Glaspell and Matson use
each act's location strategically: while the first and third acts occur in the house,
Eleanor's ancestral home, the two scenes of the second act occur in and around
the barn/studio in which Stephen paints. These shifts suggest that we may posit
a relationship among locale, character, and action. We need to pay attention to
which figures dominate in which spaces, at which moments in the play, and
why. The Cape Cod milieu, with its established reputation as a haven for artists,
not only reminds us of Glaspell's strong ties there but also underscores the connection of setting to theme prevalent throughout her dramaturgy.

As she had done in *Inheritors* and *Chains of Dew,* Glaspell calls here for a
visual image to enhance the setting, one that synthesizes her main theme:
"There is but one picture on the walls, a drawing of Mugs, the comic little man
who is making Karl famous" (9). It is significant that this cartoon image,
rather than one of Stephen's paintings, dominates the scene. In a geographical
location closely identified with the emergence of American modernism, the
avant-garde, and high art, the dramatists announce the ascendancy of mass
culture. Just as the portrait of Abraham Lincoln reverberates thematically
throughout the action of *Inheritors,* so Mugs influences the world of *The
Comic Artist.* Not only does the cartoon create a resonance between the
(melo)drama of the human characters' lives and the world of the comic strip;
it also suggests a very different set of forces hanging over these people's lives
than what we have previously seen in Glaspell's dramatic writing: forces of
commerce, homogenized culture, and popular art. On a pragmatic level Mugs
both drives Karl's existence and makes it possible for him to provide for Nina,
almost in the style to which she would like to become accustomed.

Karl soon reveals that he is constantly torn between Nina's demands for
attention and his professional obligations. He explains "ruefully" that he is
"three weeks behind" on the strip, however, and that he'll "have to work at him

[Mugs] every day" of his visit (30). In act 2 Karl and Stephen discuss the scope of his career:

Stephen: What's the new job?
Karl: Twice as much work and a hell of a lot of money—for me, it's a
    lot. . . . My audience is growing so fast. Two hundred dailies use my
    stuff now. . . .
Stephen: Aren't you afraid you'll hurt Mugs, doing so much? If you thin your
    stuff—it'll be thin.
Karl: I am afraid of that. But what can I do? It's grow or quit. Once you've
    started serving the crowd, you've got to take orders from it.
Stephen: An artist should serve his own instincts.
Karl: A comic artist serving himself is a comic idea.

(46)

The tension in this last exchange between high art and comic art permeates the play. Stephen voices the elitist perspectives associated with high modernism: that the artist must protect his vision and not allow it to be weakened by the demands of the public. Karl sees his brother's perspective but realizes that this position is untenable for a commercial artist who needs to be part of, not separate from, his culture.

Significantly, we never see any of Stephen's work, just as we never hear any of Alison Stanhope's verse in *Alison's House.* The representation of high art is too fragile, too open to critique, in these contexts. It is better for the audience to imagine the work and engage with the world of the play through their own creative process.

The play does explore aesthetic ideas, however, and the modern attraction to surface rather than substance. *The Comic Artist* contrasts the exquisiteness of Nina's appearance with the internal beauty that she lacks but Eleanor and Karl possess. Stephen responds to Nina both sexually and artistically, whereas Karl seems almost detached from his own feelings, instead intuiting the impact of such beauty as hers on others. Glaspell and Matson seem to suggest that Karl is the true artist because he can imagine the feelings of others, not just experience his own subjectivity. Karl projects through Mugs the helplessness toward women he senses that many men feel, precisely because they are captivated by surface appearance:

Everything contributes to Mugs. Got an idea for him driving over here. Mugs running with wild flowers for some flashy mama in a big car. Looking at him she gets stuck in the sand. Can you see them? She, chic and furious: Mugs, forlornly standing in the ditch, holding out his daisies. Suddenly, she beans him with a thermos bottle! (28)

The reality that hits Mugs over the head reverberates through the play. The characters explore "what life means" through dialogue about reality versus illusion (of beauty, of love, of their self-presentation or self-conception) and its corollary, life versus art (40).

While Nina acknowledges but cannot change her behavior, she is keenly perceptive about "high" artistic endeavor of the kind that Stephen pursues:

Nina: Isn't life better than painting it?
Stephen: You've asked a question!
Nina (pleased at being taken seriously): Anyway, you can't paint what you see, can you?
Stephen: No. Not really you can't. It always gets away.

(50)

Although Glaspell and Matson do not make this point clear enough, apparently they want their audiences to understand that, ironically, the comic artist is capable of capturing the essence of the artist's observations ("Everything contributes to Mugs"): not the external "realism" of verisimilitude, given the stylized exaggeration or flatness of the cartoon style, but its internal emotional truth. The dramatists understand that it is this aspect of comic art that accounts for its huge popularity.

Thus, they make the personal conflicts Karl experiences over his work reflect larger social forces that privilege high culture over mass culture. At the same time, they expose some of the hypocrisy connected with the aesthetic value placed on Art, as opposed to the social value placed on material success at the expense of "higher" values. The dramatists selected the comic strip to demonstrate as well the self-denigrating national ethos that connects Europe only with high culture and America only with mass culture. The figure of Luella exposes these contradictions and misconceptions. The very first sound we hear in the play is her "half articulated expression of disdain" at the sight of Mugs's picture (9). She proclaims soon thereafter that she sees Karl's work as "a silly way to make a living" (15). Luella announces to her daughter in the third act that she intends to return to Paris, since "there is no culture in this country" (68), a position that she believes demonstrates her commitment to higher aesthetic values. Opportunist that she is, however, Luella is willing to modify her position on the products of culture and prefer cartoons to oils when the former's financial benefits have been assured. She intones, "Serial comic art at its best is one of the purest expressions of the American spirit. . . . Who wants painting? What can you do with them in this age. The art of the people—" (69).

Although we know the selfish motives behind Luella's new attitude—she sees the strips with dollar signs in her eyes—the line has a resonance independent of her character that adds to the nationalistic sensibility of the play.

The late 1920s era of economic boom in America, immediately prior to the financial devastation of 1929, was a moment that revealed the hierarchy of values held by our society, with monetary worth foremost among them. Karl epitomizes the individual able to reap the benefits of the American capitalist system by exploiting his talent. But, the drama asks, at what cost? The irony lies in the genuine humanity reflected through the figure of Mugs, a humanity that touches so many others caught in the same social forces as Karl. Surely the popularity of films featuring Charlie Chaplin's tramp figure can be explained in much the same way. The public's demand for Karl's work ostensibly drives the system; however, we can perceive a more complex network of power at play. The syndicates in part generate the burgeoning audience, reaping the rewards of the comics' popularity. At the same time, they transfer the onus of that demand onto individuals—the consumers—who in reality have little or no real potential to impact the system.

Despite some critics' perception that the title was out of sync with what they saw going on in the play, others perceived in various ways the playwrights' attempts to synthesize title, character, and action. The review in *Newsweek* is particularly revealing, for the critic seems to have embraced the high-culture values of individuals such as Luella that the play attempts to question and thus misconstrues the action quite distinctively:

> The comic artist of the title is Karl Rolf, a young man with great artistic potentialities, who turns out a nauseating comic strip about Muggs, a futile character forever getting knocked on the head. The artist cannot quit for more worthy work because he has a vain and extravagant wife and needs the money. ("News-Week")

Other, more insightful critics were able to understand the characterological link Glaspell and Matson were trying to make between Karl and Mugs. The *New York Times* reviewer believed the authors "settled on the idea of the artist, himself, getting hit, instead of Muggs. . . . There is the further suggestion that while they [the human characters] have lost, they will try. That is what Muggs does after he has been hit" (L. N. "Play"). Arthur Ruhl observed succinctly, "There is an obvious symbolism between Muggs's routine adventure and the experience of his creator in the play" ("Second Nights").

I would argue that the playwrights not only worked to create a parallel between Karl and his creation but that they also attempted to use this dynamic to shape the entire drama, such that the world of comic strips and the world of the play would be as strongly connected as these two characters. Two critics make specific mention of a line of Eleanor's, added for the New York production, tying the world Karl draws with the world the characters inhabit. According to Richard Dana Skinner, "the woman . . . asks at one point, 'What comes after the last picture?' and the play answers that question" ("Play").[5] Other lines throughout the play cement this concept. In act 2, for example, Stephen remarks, "Life is like Karl's comic strips. The question to ask is not What is truth? but, What is truth like? It's like a comic strip" (41). Stephen's comment suggests that he perceives the essential verity of his brother's work. Yet Stephen does not connect this to the inability of high art to capture such inner truths. Rather, he implicitly opposes philosophical abstractions ("What is Truth?") to more tangible, immediate, human lines of questioning.

This equation of comics and truth may provide a partial answer to the critics who faulted the play's title because they saw the main action revolving around Stephen and Eleanor, instead of Karl. If they had perceived the implied association between contemporary American life and its reflection in its most popular art form, the comic strip, then they might have grasped all the plot developments within the broader context of dramaturgy as comic art. It would appear that the thrust of the Broadway production precluded the reviewers making these connections. None of the critics mentions the fact that Eleanor and Stephen's baby is named Wallops—surely a cartoonlike appellation—nor that the physical appearance of Luella (whose costume of red wig and bright green silk dress trimmed with monkey fur we know from Matson's letters) conveys her character much like a line drawing would. In other words, Glaspell and Matson were trying to create a flat, two-dimensional, exaggerated cartoon world that would exist side by side with the rounded thickness of dramatic verisimilitude. The emotional pull of the plot's melodramatic rivalry threw off the precarious balance between these forms of representation.

The problem for the critics was in part that the plot of *The Comic Artist* was not comic; it held little of the humor we might expect from Mugs's antics, yet the story has the pathos a comic artist might turn to advantage, much like the idea of Mugs's presentation of flowers that results in his beaning. I believe Glaspell and Matson were trying to create a complex dramatic vehicle that would convey, with the audience's active intellectual involvement, the connection between the truth of the characters' personal lives and the small adjustment that would transform their lives to cartoon art. Clearly, they did not succeed, but the drama contains enough clues to suggest that this was one of their main intentions. The advent of sophisticated film technology, utilized in such movies as *Who Framed Roger Rabbit?* has made the pairing of cartoons and realism possible in a way that Glaspell and Matson could only stumble toward.

What seems to have disrupted their structural plan was the force of the plot mechanics, which combined the perennially compelling story of love triangles with two central and complex characters, Stephen and Eleanor, who overpowered the more ephemeral thematic structure of the drama. Furthermore, the emphasis on stage realism may have worked against the association of plot with comic strips, which, regardless of their generic link to the drama and despite their core of truth, are not usually tied to other kinds of realist art. By the time of the quite effective *scene à faire* in act 3, in which Nina and Eleanor confront Stephen to force him to choose between them, the director no doubt felt he could not undermine the dramatic tension by realizing the comic potential of this moment. Thus, Stephen's conflict among sexual passion for Nina, the desire to protect his brother, and his deeper love for Eleanor dominate; they overwhelm the figure of Karl and his alter ego, Mugs, whom it is possible to imagine in a predicament of torn desires and loyalties within a strip. Glaspell and Matson's construction of these brothers in relation to their artistry and its social connotations is not linked to their rivalry as lovers of Nina. Stephen's motivations toward Karl appear to be altruistic; when his old passion for Nina returns, we never sense that any jealousy at Karl's success underlies his actions. Even when he is forced to confront the duplicity of his behavior, Stephen only realizes he may have wanted self-gratification, mingled with his desire to make Karl see the true Nina, and not some obscure form of revenge for his brother's achievements.

Eleanor's struggle between her unwillingness to meddle in others' lives and her growing realization that only a selfish act of meddling can help to save her marriage also dominates the conclusion of the play. Her conflict adds depth and direction to the dramatists' exploration of contemporary relationships. The play clearly asks "What makes a good marriage?" contrasting the stable companionship of Stephen and Eleanor with Karl's adoration of Nina and her more confused and selfish reasons for marrying him.

Given Stephen's resemblance to Jig Cook (his physical stature and energy, his love of women and wine, his "mediocre" talent as an artist [43], etc.), it is tempting to read the play at least in part as an extension of Glaspell's biography of him, *The Road to the Temple,* or as another attempt to process Cook and their marriage in the years following his death. Luella expresses surprise at Stephen's wife being "so domestic" (13), which, however, clearly distinguishes her from Glaspell. Given the relative stability and success of these characters' marriage, one wonders how Eleanor's contented life as wife and mother should be read. It may be too easy to say that Glaspell is using Eleanor to explore the positive representation of traditional femininity. While she never personally embraced this role, Glaspell may well have wondered what impact an alternative choice might have had on her married life. Unlike most of Glaspell's central female characters, Eleanor has no strong social convictions or professional or avocational pursuits. She is dedicated to Stephen, her son, and their lives together and will fight for that alone. Like Stephen, she realizes exposing Nina is both for Karl and for herself. This both cements and complicates her bond with Stephen. Such conventional self-sacrifice goes against the grain of Glaspell's theatrical activism and her feminist sensibilities. Yet, as noted in the discussions of *Suppressed Desires* and *Tickless Time,*

Glaspell's dramatic voice undergoes a real shift when she is collaborating with a male partner. It may be too facile to account for much of the play's thrust in this way, but these three examples do point to a distinct pattern in her collaborative pieces, especially in the use of traditional gender roles, that stands in notable contrast to her other work.

Luella, though materialistic, can read others to her advantage. She perfectly understands the workings of Stephen and Eleanor's marriage. She tells Nina:

> Stephen doesn't take care of anybody, Nina. He's too helpless. . . . Eleanor entirely surrounds him, because she takes care of him—sees that he is fed and clothed and washed, that he isn't afraid at night. . . . If she didn't make a safe place for him to be brave in, he'd play anything to shut out his loneliness and uncertainty. (70–71)

We have seen a similar dynamic in the relationship of Dotty and Seymore in *Chains of Dew.* Luella senses that, despite Stephen's passion for her daughter, Nina could never provide the support that Eleanor does because she, like Stephen, is too fundamentally selfish. Karl and Eleanor's genuine altruism underlies their bond and exemplifies their close resemblance. Yet as Luella's speech indicates, the play seems to suggest that successful relationships require a pairing of altruism with selfishness. Given Glaspell's concern with extremes of behavior, however, Karl fittingly self-destructs; his excess of generosity and Nina's extremity of selfishness could not be sustained. As with *Bernice,* we sense that the title character's death will provide new direction and clarity for those he loved. The two-dimensional image of Mugs, which can only be explored in the play through language, is no match for the fully realized human lives and actions with which the audience identifies. Thus, the theme of comic artistry recedes to the background by the play's conclusion.

While the New York ending eliminates the melodrama of Karl's tragic death, maintaining a more realistic feel to the outcome of these battles, the published ending features a silhouette that perhaps more neatly captures the play's experimental trajectory, which began with the image of Luella's disdain for comic art. As the lifeguards stand helplessly by the lifeless body of Karl, brought in to the living room from the offstage beach, one of the young men catches sight of Karl's last sketch of Mugs, left behind when he dashed out to rescue Nina.[6] Unable to help himself, the youth "smiles broadly" at the final frame (87), conveying the ability of Karl's art to transcend specific tragedy and the resiliency of spirit that responds to such popular forms.

No such resiliency, however, marked the conclusion to the narratives surrounding the play and its creators. While the parallels in the story of the ultimate failure of both the play and the bond between its creators seem almost too pat, they are nevertheless valid. Ironically, the duration of the relationship (around seven years) was also about the same as the life span of its "offspring" from publication to Broadway closing. Although the time frames are staggered, the trajectory for each component of the tale is the same, with hopes and high energy giving way to recriminations and disappointment.

According to Marcia Noe, Glaspell met Norman Häghejm Matson (1893–1965) in 1924 in Provincetown, where he was staying with Mary Heaton Vorse (*Susan Glaspell* 53). Matson, sixteen years younger than Glaspell, came into her life at a critical moment. As she wrote to her friend Anna Strunsky years later:

> Norman was God's gift to me. When Jig died, and I came home from Greece, I thought of myself as the observer. I thought, I will try to be brave, and I will write. Then Norman came, and loved me and instead of seeing life from death, again I saw it from life. I was again in life.[7]

Glaspell wrote of this rediscovery of life in her 1929 novel, *Fugitive's Return*. Matson was an aspiring fiction writer, working on short stories and his first novel, *Flecker's Magic* (1926). He and Glaspell already had much in common: they had both grown up in the Middle West, shared a commitment to leftist politics, had prior experience in journalism, and knew a number of people in common, including John Reed before his death. Matson had written poetry for the *Masses* and had spent time on the "copy desk of the New York *Call*" (Matson 452).[8]

Yet Matson never achieved much prominence as a writer. His work may only be remembered for the extended discussion of *Flecker's Magic* by the British novelist and essayist E. M. Forster in his critical study *Aspects of the Novel* (1927). Forster's analysis of *Flecker's Magic,* contained in his chapter on fantasy literature, reveals its narrative and thematic parallels to Glaspell's early short fiction and provides a clue to the background plot of *The Comic Artist*: Flecker is "an American boy who is learning to paint in Paris" and encounters a witch who complicates his life with the promise of wishes fulfilled. Forster claims Matson "merge[s] the kingdoms of magic and common sense" and has "the mark of the true fantasist" (165–71).[9]

Some of Glaspell's early short fiction features a related interest in young women painters, including the stories "Whom Mince Pie Hath Joined Together" (1913), set in Paris, and "A Boarder of Art" (1912), in addition to her first novel, *The Glory of the Conquered* (1909). *The Comic Artist* also reveals parallels to Glaspell and Matson's relationship (some of them prescient), as well as to Matson's proclivity for cartoon art and to Glaspell's long-standing thematic concern with marital infidelity. Matson's penchant for fantasy seems to have given place to Glaspell's preference for realism, and the published script shows clear evidence of each writer's style, particularly in the dialogic patterns and diction that can be identified as distinctively Glaspell's. In this example from early in the play we see Glaspell's concern with tradition, reminiscent of *Inheritors*, merge with the spiritual sensitivity most fully realized in *Bernice.*

> *Eleanor:* . . . My people were here long ago. They built this house in seventeen hundred and something. I feel my great grandfather in the forgotten roads, on the beach.
> *Luella* (*in a horrified whisper*): Do you *see* him?
> *Eleanor* (*laughing*): I don't mean his ghost. But he lingers in things he made or touched, in my own imagination. . . . He is in me. After long, homesick wandering—in other countries, in New York—he has returned.
>
> (13)

Ironically, it may well have been Glaspell's penchant for abstract dialogue and realist form that undermined the writers' attempts to make the play mirror comic art.

Glaspell and Matson's correspondence provides invaluable information about their collaborative process. Apparently, the initial drafting was done together on Cape Cod, but they then spent considerable time apart during the revisions: Glaspell in Davenport, Chicago, and New York taking care of family, medical, and professional matters; Matson on several international trips connected with his journalism and creative writing. It seems they sent manuscript material back and forth, as this letter of Glaspell's, sent from Davenport in 1926, suggests:

> I didn't find a great deal to do to the play, but went over it carefully, making a few cuts and revisions, agreeing with most of yours, saving a little that you had cut, cutting a little of something else. It reads awfully well to me. I think it is a first class play . . . It seems to me a big dramatic play. The scenes stand up, and there is beauty through it, I think—something of profundity, though don't tell anybody I said so.

Within a short period of time the letters introduce possibilities for both publication and production. In the same letter quoted here Glaspell alludes to Victor Gollancz, a British publisher interested in the script. Matson tells her in a letter dated 18 October 1926, "Nice Mr. Gollancz writes: 'I am extremely excited about The Comic Artist. I hope we are going to be allowed to publish it straight away, and not to wait for performances.'" November letters indicate that these "performances" may be with Sybil Thorndike in the role of Eleanor. Thorndike had played Claire Archer in the London production of *The Verge* to acclaim and was considering this new script, although she ultimately turned down the part.

In June 1928 *The Comic Artist* received its first production by the English company the Play Actors and was revived in November 1929 at London's Players' Theatre. The British productions most likely used a script very close, if not identical, to the first published version of the play. The London *Times* reviewed both versions, determining the drama "at root a good and serious play, spoiled only by its uncomfortable and wordy traffic with vague infinities," and noting that "Miss Glaspell's is too often the flourish of a leaden sword" ("Play Actors"). For the second production the unnamed critic made a similar determination: "If only the talk did not so frequently fall away into mere word-spinning, it would be just the kind of play we should hope to see in this theatre" ("Players' Theatre"). The review of this same production in the *Era* was favorable, although the reviewer had similar reservations about its "inclination towards an exasperating type of too-literary wordiness" ("Comic Artist"), a verdict that was echoed in the American press years later. Yet not all the English critics held the same views. The writer for the *Stage* felt the Play Actors' production did not do service to Glaspell and Matson's "thoughtful and imaginative dialogue" and the "designedly fine writing" in the play ("Play Actors Say 'Au Revoir'").

One of the remarkable aspects of the critical reception of Glaspell's dramas is the consistency of their inconsistency. Throughout her career some reviewers praised her writing, while others deemed it too literary. Similarly, when finding fault with a production, the critics habitually split the blame between the director/actors and the script itself. While these patterns tell us much about the practice of theatrical criticism, they also make it difficult to determine, with any conclusiveness, how the majority of reviewers (to say nothing of audiences) appraised her career.[10]

Frederick A. Stokes, who had brought out a number of Glaspell's novels, had meanwhile published the play in New York in 1927.[11] From 1927 through 1932 Glaspell and Matson's letters refer to ongoing attempts to find a New York producer for the play. They reflect a growing disillusionment with a script with which they tinkered throughout the period, in part to try to attract interest in the work, in part because of a burgeoning sense of its dramatic unsuitability for a commercial theater geared to pure entertainment. One suspects that during this period they may have perceived the ironic parallels between the syndicates' demands placed upon their title character and the producers' upon dramatists trying to succeed on Broadway. The fact that their play contained an implicit critique of those controlling popular entertainment, as well as of audience pretensions to high culture, may have undermined their efforts to produce their play in this venue. New York producers' potential familiarity with the mixed London reviews would not have helped, either.

The script of *The Comic Artist* made the rounds of most of the major
New York producing organizations as well as a number of individuals who
might option it for Broadway. The list included the Theatre Guild, the Actors'
Theatre (Equity Theatre), and the Civic Repertory Theatre, as well as Arthur
Hopkins, Winthrop Ames, Archibald Selwyn, and, finally, Edward Goodman,
who for several years appeared their most likely prospect, except that he seems
to have been perennially incapable of raising the funds to mount the production. Glaspell and Matson even appear to have tried the theatrical gossip route
for publicity purposes: a letter from Matson, dated 5 November 1926, suggests
they attempt to get Allison Smith, who had "a daily col[umn] in the World" or
Lucy [Huffaker] to make mention of the play so that it would become known
in New York.[12] The 1933 reviews indicate they also allowed summer stock com-
panies, such as the Westport Playhouse, to produce the drama, perhaps as a
try-out or perhaps to attract further commercial interest.[13]

One of the most intriguing details of this historical context for the play
is the fact that Glaspell and Matson never seem to have considered offering it
to the newly founded Group Theatre. Glaspell clearly knew of their work,
since a letter to Matson from this period indicates that she was going to see
The House of Connelly, which the Group produced in 1931. Given the emphasis on realism that their script demands—and indeed was perhaps ultimately
overemphasized in the New York production—as well as the psychological intensity of the characters and plot, one would think it a piece the Group actors
could have handled with aplomb.

Finally, early in the fall of 1932 Matson signed a production contract with
Arthur Beckhard, a young director who had already had considerable Broadway success with Rose Franken's *Another Language* that year. Beckhard cast the
play with prominent actors of the period[14] and later lined up the noted de-
signer Cleon Throckmorton to execute the sets. In the meantime, however,
Matson had met the young Anna Walling while on a trip to France and begun
the affair that was to destroy his relationship with Glaspell. By August 1932
Glaspell had learned that Anna was pregnant and that Norman wanted to be
free to marry her.

A great deal of confusion has surrounded the exact status of Glaspell and
Matson's relationship. Most published sources say they were married, and indeed the correspondence confirms that others considered their bond in this
way. Glaspell in particular seems to have both circulated this information and
to have embraced it as fact, for Matson's letters discuss concern about a possible divorce:

> What was the sense of our not marrying—you surely remember our first
> talks?—if we couldn't separate without the disgusting mess of a divorce?
> It seems so illogical to get an illegal bond legally cut. The central fact is

that we never legally or otherwise gave our word that we would stay together for better or worse for the rest of our lives.

He entreats Glaspell, "I beg of you not to tell anybody about your divorce
plans, or that we were not legally married, or of Anna." As this letter from
Matson explains, the confusion lay in the understanding of a common-law
bond and the issue of its legal status in the various states where they lived and
worked:

> [I have been] to the public library this afternoon and there learned about
> common law marriage. I learned a number of things but only one is of
> much importance in our case. Common law marriage doesn't exist in
> Massachusetts . . . in Massachusetts we could have lived eighty years to-
> gether as man and wife . . . yet we would not be married unless we went
> through the ceremony before an accredited official or clergyman. This is
> definite, impossible of being misconstrued.

It is hard to determine if they had shared the confusion or if Glaspell alone
had expressed concern about trying to dissolve a common-law bond only after
Matson revealed his desire to part ways.

Some of Glaspell's insistence may have come from anxiety about appearances and reputations. Matson tries to reassure her, "I don't believe that your
divorce will in any manner effect [sic] your public." Although there is no correspondence to this effect, Glaspell may well have felt considerable stress
about the public response to her and this play. This was her first work to be
mounted in New York after she won the Pulitzer Prize for *Alison's House*, despite the earlier composition date for *The Comic Artist*. Several of the reviews
for the 1933 production describe Matson as Glaspell's former husband, suggesting that publicity material for the production might have contained such
information.[15] The tension surrounding the breakup reveals the ongoing
strain evident throughout both Glaspell's life and her work, between the external appearance of social conformity and a more personal drive toward independence. Particularly in matters of love relationships, Glaspell appears to
struggle in her efforts to sustain both a conventional role as supportive wife
and her independent status as a writer with feminist inclinations.

The *Comic Artist* probably began preproduction work in the late fall of
1932, although the early phase seems to have been fraught with financial complications: the proposal that Glaspell waive her advance, Matson finding that
his checks were often late or bad, and the director threatening to put off production until the following season. Soon thereafter, Matson's letters to
Glaspell narrate a series of artistic differences over the script, which at first was
only "tinkered with" but then became the source of greater friction, as Matson

reports that he has been "opposing B[eckhard]'s wilder ideas as best I can."
Matson apparently threatened to cancel their contract and close down the
production. He had heated discussions with the director, some conducted
through Glaspell and Matson's agent, over Beckhard's rewrites. Matson was
also buoyed by the rehearsal process, however, and wrote lengthy descriptions for Glaspell, who was on the Cape during this period. It is reasonable
to assume, given the state of their relationship, that she stayed away from
New York and the production because it would have been too painful. Matson's letters at this point merit quoting in full, however, for the production
details they include:

> If you see it, you may think not much toning down was done by me, but
> you'd be wrong. Our play—already announced in a large sign in front of
> the Morosco—is getting all the breaks. The theatre itself has 900 seats,
> is the most successfully "intime" theatre in town, so I am told, and is lo-
> cated on 45th—in the "block of hits," across the street from the Booth,
> where *Another Language* opened just a year ago, a couple of doors from
> *Dinner at Eight, Both Your Houses, Good Bye Again*. Throck is doing
> the sets which are very good; Beckhard's realism is meticulous, elabo-
> rate . . . Cape sounds are all to be there, steamers, surf, insects' buzz, baby
> crying, motors going, etc. etc. The cast is good; especially Richard Hale's
> Stephen; Baxter's Nina is handsome, better that [*sic*] Dorothy Gish's by
> several degrees.[16] Karl is right, and so is Luella. The last act has been
> worked on a good deal. I've managed a good deal of smoothing out of
> B.'s write-ins, the elimination of some. He's been friendly. Nobody has
> the least idea what the play will do. He said yesterday: "The public very
> well may stay away in hordes." And "Do you realize that most people
> won't know what the devil it's about?" . . . If it gets only favorable notices
> it won't last many days; if they're extravagant we might do six weeks.
> (My prediction.) . . .
>   Throck's living room is paneled to the ceiling, real cape corner cup-
> board, fireplace, and enclosed stairway right. Door back, two windows,
> two doors right. Barn is very handsome; and in the model looks much
> like Bill and Brownie's [L'Engle]. Next scene is played on back steps of
> house, glimpse of dunes, door window, etc. Nina (she's light blonde) will
> wear a scarlet silk sport dress in act one. Luella (red "windblown" wig)
> bright green silk trimmed with monkey fur; Yurka will wear a simple
> (and old) dress of Fortuni print velvet. One of her own—grayish blue.
> Nina's fur coat is of mink and worth several thousand. . . . B. is also going
> to try throwing against theatre ceiling between act enormous silhouette
> of a comic artist drawing, shadow of actual man in orchestra pit; if it
> works in dress rehearsal will stay in. He is anxious for you to come down

and see a dress rehearsal. If you decide after all to come down, let me know and there won't be the faintest risk of meeting with me.[17]

There is no mention in the reviews of the quasi-expressionistic projection Matson indicates Beckhard is considering; if he did include it in the production, it would probably have been the only gesture toward the break from realism that Glaspell and Matson attempted to incorporate in their script.

Glaspell obviously decided not to travel to New York, for Matson soon sent another letter with a report on the dress rehearsal, one that showed a marked deterioration in his opinion of the production:

> In an argument with B. in which I roughly but too gently sketched my opinion of his literary style. I told him how I had to try to think of your interests, and he said you had O.K.'d 2nd act changes. I think he lied, or exaggerated. This leads up to my opinion after dress rehearsal (last night). The play has been maltreated through the years. It still has some life in it, but it is a murky uncertain life. It cannot possibly make a hit; it will certainly be damned with faint praise; and it will run not a day over two weeks. I have wasted a dozen days looking at rehearsals because B. who is cursed with a literary itch would have otherwise written in speech after speech, all a bit arch, all bad. . . . I do not know why he likes our play; he doesn't know what it's about. Throck said, or moaned in his way, well Norman I don't know I sort of like the first ending. That ending was best but it somehow didn't work. The new ending almost does. Since last night I think less of the cast. . . . Maybe I'm pessimistic, but I wanted to write this quickly, to warn you of what you have known all along—that it will fold quickly.

Matson wrote after the opening, "*The Comic Artist* is holding on hoping for an upswing of business. It won't come, I think. You were thoroughly right about that play." His last letter about the production notes with irony, "Rubsamen [their agent] expects the play to close Saturday. It's holding on hoping for movie sale. I've never seen a performance." Matson and Glaspell's fears proved well grounded; *The Comic Artist* was received with only faint enthusiasm and lasted just twenty-one performances. Glaspell's final word on the play can be inferred from a 1939 (?) letter to her publisher, Horace W. Stokes, in Chicago, prior to the publication of her novel *The Morning Is Near Us:*

> About table of contents, my previous works should be listed as in *Ambrose Holt,* with two changes. *Fugitive's Return* got left out of that list and of course should be in; and I'd like to delete *The Comic Artist* in list of my

plays and there should be added *Alison's House,* my last play. That's the Pulitzer Prize one, and we don't want to leave it out.

The critical response to *The Comic Artist* confirmed Matson's fears about Beckhard's technique, but it also highlights the impact of directorial intervention on the assessment of the play itself. While Matson pointedly claims that Beckhard's "literary style" was undermining their script, the critics pinned the blame on the authors alone. Since the earlier British production had been similarly critiqued, it is hard to determine who was really at fault for the play's difficulties. Gilbert W. Gabriel "confess[ed] to finding it a lugubrious study, dawdling and maundering" ("Comic Artist"). John Mason Brown deemed it "undramatic," "bookish," and "a strangely stuttering play" ("'Comic Artist' Opens on Broadway"). The reviewer for *Newsweek* called it "intense and stodgy" ("News-Week in Entertainment"), while Merrill Denison maintained that it "suffer[ed] from self-conscious efforts to make it out as more important than it really is" ("Season's End" 418). Kinder appraisals came from Richard Lockridge, who pronounced it "a dignified and thoughtful study . . . entirely worthy of respect" ("New Play"), and Arthur Pollock, who called it "a sound and intelligent job" ("Theatres"). Richard Dana Skinner and Joseph Wood Krutch were the most effusive, the former determining *The Comic Artist* to be an "admirably written play" and "among the three or four finest plays of the season" ("Play"), the latter deciding it "seems to me to be in many ways the most surely as well as the most maturely written of her plays" ("Drama").[18]

Some critics, like Stark Young of the *New Republic,* chose to stress the production over the script, noting that *The Comic Artist* marked Beckhard's fourth Broadway engagement as a young director of note, quickly making his name in the commercial theater ("Mr. Beckhard's Fourth"). Robert Garland credited the director with the "touching and arresting and rightly reticent" feel of the show ("'Comic Artist' a Success on Sight"). Others took issue with his staging choices, particularly acoustical problems (Arthur Pollock, "Theatres") and his attempts at extensive realism, which seem to have worked against Glaspell and Matson's original concept. Arthur Ruhl felt that his use of realistic interior lighting effects backfired ("Second Nights"), while Merrill Denison observed, "In one scene particularly, the actors worked in so realistic a fog that they were neither visible nor intelligible" ("Season's End" 418).

The majority of reviewers, however, focused on the writing. Their comments both echo previous criticism of her dramaturgy as too literary and point to the style of Glaspell and Matson's work as being out of sync with Broadway audiences' tastes during these Depression years. Apparently, theatergoers were then favoring either sprightly comedy (such as Noel Coward's *Design for Living)* or a resurgent political drama (such as Elmer Rice's *We, the People).* Burns Mantle found fault with the lack of exposition in *The Comic*

Artist, claiming "half their play is covered before the exact relationship of their characters is known" ("'Comic Artist' Has Tragic Overtone"). John Mason Brown opined that "Miss Glaspell has never seemed to be a writer who worked happily in the dramatic form" ("'Comic Artist'"), a view taken even further by Richard Lockridge, who felt the story better suited to a novel than a play ("New Play"). The *Newsweek* critic sounded the refrain of "strained literary writing" ("News-Week in Entertainment"), and Percy Hammond dryly remarked, "Among its especial assets, in case they are to be regarded as assets, are a natural literary quality" ("Theatres"). Arthur Pollock emphasized the poetic quality of Glaspell's language—"a play of rare fluency"—but noted the problems this presented in terms of theatricality ("Theatres").

This disjunction between the play's dramaturgy and the desires of its audience was foregrounded by Robert Garland, who called the play "the modern theatre in its more enlightened aspect" but observed that "the new arrival . . . is a thing for the intelligent theatregoer to see"—reviewing code for *limited audience appeal* ("'Comic Artist'"). Joseph Krutch agreed: "The result is . . . something as far from the mere problem play as it is from melodrama which it might . . . so easily have been." Yet he observed less optimistically, "These days fortune is not usually very kind to serious plays" ("Drama"). *Variety* was frank in its view: "The writing is well done . . . but it is questionable whether the story will appeal to the average playgoer and whether the play is diversion. . . . 'The Comic Artist' should have been much more entertaining" (Ibee "Comic Artist"). These remarks suggest that on some level the reviewers were responding to the play's theme of high versus popular art, even if they were not consciously addressing or recognizing it. Moreover, it is small comfort that the difficulty in having serious drama succeed on Broadway is still an active issue for the theater today, or that Pulitzer-winning dramatists have notorious difficulty succeeding with their next production after the award.

The greatest irony of *The Comic Artist* may well be the disjunction between the populism of its theme and the intellectually sophisticated and poetic quality of its dramatic expression, trying to succeed in the unforgiving climate of entertainment-hungry Broadway. Little wonder, then, that Glaspell tried to rewrite her own theatrical history by deleting this play from her list of works in later years, linked as it was to bad personal and professional memories. Better to accentuate a triumph such as the Pulitzer Prize than to dwell on a work tied to failure and loss.

Alison's House

The year 1930 marked the hundredth anniversary of the birth of Emily Dickinson. Celebrations of her life and art occurred throughout that year, including the production of Glaspell's play *Alison's House,* a fictionalized portrait of the family of the reclusive writer that explored the impact of her artistry. The Dickinson family was notorious for its eccentricities and some outright scandals, and Glaspell must have seen in this multigenerational saga a narrative ripe for dramatization. Glaspell's poet Alison Stanhope was quickly identified with Dickinson and her legacy by audiences and critics alike.

Like many of Glaspell's plays, *Alison's House* features an absent protagonist whom she develops similarly to her title character in *Bernice.* In *Alison's House* the title character has been dead eighteen years when the scene opens on 31 December 1899. The drama chronicles her living legacy, both within her immediate family and in American culture, and debates the question of who has control over a figure who has become a cultural icon. Glaspell depicts the escalating conflict within the Stanhope family as they prepare to sell Alison's home to a couple who plan to turn it into a summer boardinghouse. This process leads to the discovery of some previously unknown work: a stash of love poems not found with her other writing after her death. These verses are a major revelation for the family and, potentially, for a wider audience as well. The light this work sheds on Alison's life makes her descendants reexamine not only their conception of their famous ancestor but also their own long-held beliefs about the individual in society, just as the twentieth century dawns with the promise of new thought and experience. Critically maligned, the play nevertheless received the Pulitzer Prize for drama in 1931.

Emily Dickinson had died in 1886, but it was only with the posthumous publication of selections of her poetry from 1890 on that she began to emerge as an author of note. Not until well after the centenary, in 1955, did a "complete" collection of poems finally appear.[1] Although her reputation as an important American poet grew steadily, comparatively little factual information was available about Dickinson's life during this early period, despite well-circulated rumors and anecdotes. The Dickinson family maintained tight control of Emily's legacy, despite—or perhaps because of—internecine family battles over her work. Dickinson's niece, Martha Dickinson Bianchi, had published the first biography of the poet only six years before the anniversary, in 1924. But Bianchi, daughter of Emily's brother, Austin, and his wife, Susan, skewed her version of Emily's life to favor her mother's biased rendition of family events. She also fostered the legend of Emily's "frustrated love affair and a broken heart" as the motivation for much of the poet's behavior and creativity (Sewall 232),[2] although she probably had little hard evidence for her hypotheses.

Others who had known Dickinson or those close to her quickly challenged the life story offered by Bianchi. In the centennial year two new competing biographies appeared: Josephine Pollitt's *Emily Dickinson: The Human Background of Her Poetry,* and Genevieve Taggard's *The Life and Mind of Emily Dickinson.*[3] Perhaps to capitalize on the centenary activity, perhaps to take advantage of a story that would enable her to explore larger questions of artistry, family, and American culture, Glaspell used elements of the Dickinson legend as the foundation for *Alison's House.* Tantalizingly, her drama reflects more accurately and perceptively than the early biographies subtle elements of the Dickinson story—details she inferred or intuited from her reading, conversations, and thinking about the poet. The play had its American premier on 1 December 1930 at Eva Le Gallienne's Civic Repertory Theatre.[4] The Civic Rep had widely publicized the drama as being based on the Dickinson story, despite its ostensible subject, the midwestern poet Alison Stanhope.

Dramaturgically, *Alison's House* adheres to the well-made form and is a typically realist, American family drama. As such, it has much in common with other plays that have won the Pulitzer Prize. How Glaspell's dramatization of the partially fictionalized Dickinson family may have won the esteem of the Pulitzer committee merits examination, especially since there was such sharp division between the adjudicators and the theater critics, a division that in large part prompted the formation of the New York Drama Critics Circle soon thereafter. While the reviewers dismissed *Alison's House* on aesthetic and dramaturgical grounds, the committee championed the piece for its conformity to the spirit of the prize, particularly in its American setting and subject, its focus on the home and family, and its concern with national values.

For purposes of the following analysis one should keep in mind Joseph Pulitzer's priorities for the award bearing his name, specifically his interest in a national theater as a locus for moral instruction. Considered from the perspectives the committee may have brought to their deliberations, *Alison's House* emerges as a philosophical exploration of individual choice; the play asks us to consider the social and personal consequences of acting within or outside established moral codes. It is this concern with foundational elements of our religious and legal systems, among other reasons, that made the play stand out for the adjudicators.

But the play's interest also lies in its foundation in the biography of Dickinson and in the form of dramatic biography. As Katherine Rodier has suggested of *Alison's House*, "Glaspell dramatizes biographical *method* as well as her own inventions and familiar Dickinson details" (209). And Sandra Gilbert and Susan Gubar see the play as participating in a "literary matrilineage," an "ambivalent act of obeisance to a female precursor" whose "eternal gifts" nevertheless come with a "monitory example of loneliness that never died" (*No Man's Land* 1.209–10). This multiplicity of purpose renders the drama a metatext: the play explores the creation of biography itself as well as unfolds a narrative into which Glaspell fits known and conjectured events from the family members' lives. Some important questions surrounding the study of *Alison's House* as biographical drama arise: what is it about the story of Emily Dickinson that so strongly struck a chord with Glaspell? Which elements of the biography seem most compelling to her, and how might one account for any digressions from this narrative?

Moreover, one must grapple with the prescient understanding Glaspell seems to have had about Dickinson and her family. While this chapter will lay out a number of the correlations between the play and the biographies, it will also explore the striking biographical parallels from the drama *not* available in the early studies of Dickinson. Only with the comparatively recent publication of authoritative, more objective Dickinson biographies, such as Richard B. Sewall's in 1974, can one see that Glaspell had a remarkably intuitive feel for the family's dynamics. In *Alison's House* she suggests more truthfully than does any Dickinson biography from the 1920s and 1930s the emotional and psychological foundations for what we now call dysfunctional family behavior. One might look to such later Pulitzer Prize–winning works as Arthur Miller's *Death of a Salesman* (1949), Eugene O'Neill's *Long Day's Journey into Night* (1956), or Sam Shepard's *Buried Child* (1978) as exemplars of the (dysfunctional) American family drama, the form that has emerged in the twentieth century as definitive for our national dramaturgy. With *Alison's House* (as with *The Verge*) Glaspell was at the forefront of explorations in dramatic style and content in the American theater. While biographical drama was not in itself new, through the fictionalized representation of a notable American family, Glaspell brought together domestic concerns with such broader issues as the construction of a national cultural heritage and the exploration of the national psyche. Arguably, this kind of dramatic innovation, more than a strict evaluation of the play's aesthetic merits, captured the attention of the Pulitzer committee; perhaps they recognized in her work the integral connection between American life and art and wanted to acknowledge her effort to use the stage to begin to explore the family structures at the core of our society.

When she came to work on this play, Glaspell had already had experience with biographical writing. She had published *The Road to the Temple*, her tribute to her late husband Jig Cook, just three years earlier. This "labor of love" may well have helped her understand how to synthesize the scattered fragments of a life; Glaspell may have discovered in this compositional process how biography can be shaped to emphasize cultural patterns and regional ethos, the tenor of a time. She may also have learned that biographical and imaginative writing have much in common, in that each must tell a story that captures and sustains interest.

The fact that Glaspell had a close, personal source for some of her information about the Dickinson family may have further spurred her creative instincts. Glaspell's engagement with the Dickinson legend was chronicled by her friend Mary Heaton Vorse in her memoir, *Time and the Town* (1942):

> Not enough has been said about Susan Glaspell and her quality of enthusiasm when a new idea absorbed her. Long after the Provincetown Players I remember when the idea of *Alison's House*, a story based on Emily Dickinson's life, first possessed her. Seeing Susan in those days when she was first plunging her mind into Emily Dickinson's story was seeing a creative force at work. (124)

Indeed, Glaspell may have gotten ideas for the play from Vorse, who had owned the Provincetown fish wharf structure that was converted into the Players' first theater. Vorse had grown up in Amherst, Massachusetts, the home of Dickinson and her family. Since all the sordid details of the family squabbles over the estate, as well as the skeletons in the Dickinson closet, seem to have become fairly common knowledge to the small Amherst community, it appears likely that Vorse could have been an important consultant for the play.[5] Genevieve Taggard certainly used her as a first-person source; in her "Acknowledgment" she thanks Vorse "for valuable memories" (ix).

Glaspell may have had other sources as well. In her 1931 novel, *Ambrose Holt and Family*, the protagonist receives a copy of Taggard's biography (262), indicating that by then Glaspell knew this work. It is impossible to determine absolutely, however, whether Glaspell had read either Taggard's or Pollitt's book (or Bianchi's, for that matter) prior to completing the play near the end of 1930. Pollitt's work had appeared early in that year, Taggard's later.[6]

Ironically, the connection between *Alison's House* and Emily Dickinson might not have been immediately obvious to all audiences were it not for the preponderance of early reviews and feature articles in which critics linked the two. Almost every review of the play featured a comment about the drama being based on Dickinson's life. Otis Chatfield-Taylor, writing in the *Outlook and Independent*, provides some tantalizing details: "[*Alison's House*] purports to deal, rumors assiduously circulated by Miss Le Gallienne's press department and others have it, with the effects on Emily Dickinson's family of the discovery, years after her death, of some of her poems previously unknown" ("Theatre"). Richard Dana Skinner alludes to the same "rumor" ("Play" 187), whereas Robert Littell flatly states, "For the Alison Stanhope of Susan Glaspell's play read Emily Dickinson" ("New Play").

While no copies of the press materials these journalists might have received appear to have survived, both the Civic Rep's souvenir program for the 1930–31 season and the November and December issues of the *Civic Repertory Theatre Magazine* confirm the biographical parallel with Dickinson ("Plays to Be Presented"; "'Alison's House' an American Play"; "'Alison's House' by Susan Glaspell").[7] In her critical biography of Glaspell, Marcia Noe explains why the foundation for the play was oblique:

> The Dickinson family refused to allow Susan to use the family name or any of Emily Dickinson's poems in the play. Susan refused to give up her project; she merely changed the setting from Amherst to Iowa and created Alison Stanhope, a Dickinson-like spinster poet who was rumored to have once loved a married man. (*Susan Glaspell* 59)[8]

Glaspell thus turned what was initially a setback in her plans for the play into a strength: the drama could now carry both the resonance of the Dickinson legend and the broader interpretive possibilities presented by fictional characters. We might even say that Glaspell joined a group of writers participating in the creation of Dickinson biography, despite the fact that her play, at least on the surface, depicted the lives of fictional characters. The fact that her version comes closer to "truth" than do the actual biographies remains one of the compelling, if ironic, aspects of its composition.

Glaspell's problems dealing with the Dickinson estate were not unique. The stories surrounding the highly contested editing, publication, and use of Dickinson's work are far too complex to detail in full here but are ably outlined in Sewall's two-volume biography. In the foreword to her 1930 biography, for example, Josephine Pollitt states that she was "not permitted by the copyright owners to make quotations" from any of the work Martha Dickinson Bianchi had published to date, namely her own biography as well as two volumes of the poetry which she had edited (xi). Genevieve Taggard seems not to have encountered quite the same difficulties with her work; she notes that she had the permission of the publisher, Little, Brown, to quote from Dickinson's poetry (v). She expresses frustration, however, at scholars' inability to explore the Dickinson oeuvre "until Madame Bianchi allows someone to study all the manuscript [*sic*] in her possession" (260).[9]

By 1930 the Dickinson legend had already reached a level of indeterminacy such that it was extremely difficult for biographers to separate fact from fiction, particularly given the family's refusal to cooperate in an objective scholarly inquiry into Emily's life and work. Indeed, Dickinson's story might serve as an exemplar of what Sharon O'Brien calls the "biography as fiction" school: the structural mode of preference for many who work in the genre and who model their studies on the nineteenth-century novel (O'Brien 124–25). When the biographical details are sketchy, there is obviously all the more impetus to augment fact with plausible additional narrative, that is, fiction. And, clearly, O'Brien's sense of the relation of biography to the novel applies equally to the drama. Although *Alison's House* is a piece of creative writing, because of its remarkable sensitivity to the behavior of the Dickinsons, it exemplifies the interesting indeterminacy, inherent to biographical writing, between fact and fiction. Glaspell seems to be using this drama to foster a debate about how to evaluate different narrative media: what are the distinctions between a medium such as biography, with its seeming access to truth, and fiction, especially when the latter is able to access other layers of reality unreached by the former?

Glaspell's dramaturgy reveals the complexity of this question through its interweaving of the Stanhope story and the Dickinson legend. At the most basic level Glaspell structures her drama around the issue of controlling a legacy, which was central to the Dickinson feud and becomes critical for the Stanhope family. Emily Dickinson had one brother, Austin, and one sister, Lavinia, both of whom survived her. Austin had married a longtime friend of Emily's, Susan Huntington Gilbert, in 1856. "Sue" bore Austin three children: Edward, Martha, and Thomas Gilbert. Starting in the early 1880s, Austin began an affair with a married woman, Mabel Loomis Todd, that lasted about thirteen years; this affair eventually became pivotal to the conflict that developed after Emily's death over who was to edit her poetry and write about her. Over the years of Austin and Sue's marriage, Sue's friendship with Emily suffered strain, and Sue seemed increasingly hostile and unstable. After Emily's death, her sister, Lavinia, who had never married, chose to entrust the poems she had found to Mabel Todd, Austin's lover, for editing.[10] Glaspell appropriated these details to construct the moral and personal struggles at the heart of her play. The early biographies of Dickinson rarely discussed these conflicts, yet they emerge as the core of Glaspell's dramatization.

The biographers, by comparison, focused on Emily's spinsterhood, obsessed over the possibility that an unrequited passion for a married man—and several possible candidates were proposed—lay behind her reclusive life and the emotional obliqueness of much of her verse. The strategic differences between the central conflict in the play and in the biographies highlight issues integral to the latter form. By focusing on the process of constructing an absent identity, rather than simply representing that identity as an end product through a combination of fact and creative supposition, Glaspell demonstrates her concern with biographical method. This project would have been impossible had she chosen to dramatize Alison/Emily herself. *Alison's House* thus expands upon dramatic techniques Glaspell refined throughout her career. The absent characters around whom she builds such plays as *Trifles* and *Bernice* share with Alison a composite identity gleaned from the memories of those present figures who touched these characters' lives, here given a further theoretical twist.

Glaspell's amplification of the theme of marital infidelity made it the structuring trope for the play. The moral struggle at the heart of both the Dickinson legend and the Stanhope story not only supplied her with a dramaturgical foundation but most likely also provided the Pulitzer committee with a compelling reason to see Glaspell's work as one reflecting the pedagogical mission of the prize. Representatives of both generations of Stanhopes from the world of the play—the elder Alison and her brother John and the younger Elsa and Eben—have been strongly affected by individual choices regarding whether to follow the heart or the conscience. Additionally, the Stanhope family struggles to shape and contain the image of Alison that the world will receive, particularly with respect to sexual morality. As we learn in the third act's climactic scene, many years earlier Alison had been dissuaded by her brother John from running off with a married man with whom she had been deeply in love. John had convinced Alison that protecting the family name and status, as well as her own reputation, outweighed any other consideration. We see in this renunciation not only the mirror image of John's own similar choice but also the refraction of generational difference: we already know that Alison's niece Elsa has made the opposite decision and has been forced to leave her family and community as a result. Her brother Eben also vaguely contemplates bucking social convention in the near future, as he is growing increasingly dissatisfied and restless in both his married and professional life.

Structurally, Glaspell replaces the figure of the Dickinson sister-in-law (Sue) with the daughter-in-law Louise, Eben's wife. Although Austin's youngest child had actually died before Emily, Glaspell retains three children for Stanhope: Eben, Elsa, and Ted. Agatha Stanhope, the elderly sister, resembles her counterpart, Lavinia Dickinson, most closely in her concern for Alison's writing, her memory, and the family secrets. Agatha's death midway through the play corresponds to the death of Lavinia in 1899 (see table 1).

Glaspell also creates several characters who have no corollary in the Dickinson legend: Ann Leslie, John Stanhope's secretary and the daughter of the woman he once loved but renounced; Richard Knowles, a reporter and aspiring poet from Chicago who is interested in Alison's story; and the Hodges, the couple who plan to buy the Stanhope estate and convert it to a summer boardinghouse for tourists. Some of the critics identified a Chekhovian flavor to this element of the plot, linking the breakup of the Stanhope estate to that found in *The Cherry Orchard*. In his 1967 study of Pulitzer dramas Thomas

TABLE 1. Comparison Chart of Dickinson Family and Corresponding Characters in *Alison's House*

DICKINSON FAMILY		STANHOPE FAMILY	
Emily Dickinson		Alison Stanhope	
Austin Dickinson,	Emily's brother	John Stanhope,	Alison's brother
Susan Dickinson,	Emily's sister-in-law	—	—
Lavinia Dickinson,	Emily's sister	Agatha Stanhope,	Alison's sister
Edward Dickinson, Martha Dickinson, and Thomas Dickinson	Austin and Susan's children	Eben Stanhope, Elsa Stanhope, and Ted Stanhope	John Stanhope's children
Mabel Todd,	Austin's Lover	—	—
—	—	Ann Leslie,	daughter of the woman John Stanhope loved but renounced

Adler comments that Glaspell's play "stands . . . like the Russian master's, as a swan song for a way of life being replaced by more commercial enterprises, though Glaspell's attitude, like Chekhov's, is ambiguous: both the old and new ways have their good and bad sides" (132). The family's chagrin over the Hodges' mercenary venture foreshadows their own ambivalence about the prospect of capitalizing on Alison's stature by publishing her newly discovered verse. These public, ethical conflicts complement the biographically based personal conflicts Glaspell develops. Through the association of family life with the physical space connected to character (Alison's *house)* and the individual life with the product of character (Alison's verse), Glaspell generates layers of moral ambivalence linking the private to the public, the personal to the social. She creates a vital link between American life and the American family reflective of the concerns with national identity shared by Joseph Pulitzer and others in the aftermath of World War I.

Juxtaposed to the three studies potentially available to Glaspell—Bianchi's, Pollitt's, and Taggard's—*Alison's House* emerges as an intertext in dialogue with the other Dickinson narratives. Given that Taggard admits to having read Pollitt (x), and both acknowledge some debt to Bianchi's study, the levels of referentiality among the works make it quite difficult to determine the exact source of Glaspell's details or, more significantly, to decide on a line separating biography from fiction. Glaspell may have conceived Bianchi herself as a structural (but certainly not characterological) model for Elsa, Alison's niece and the poet's spiritual descendant, to whom the dying Agatha entrusts the love poems. Her charge to protect a legacy also links this drama thematically to Glaspell's earlier work *Inheritors.*

Bianchi is intentionally vague in her depiction of the infamous love story of Emily and her mystery suitor, but Glaspell seems to have taken the detail of the man's picture in Alison's room from Bianchi's version (Bianchi 43–47). Glaspell adapts Emily's request that her writing be burned at her death—a scene both Bianchi and Taggard depict dramatically (Bianchi 102; Taggard 177)—to Agatha's claim that Alison demanded the love poems be destroyed. In act 2 Agatha tries to set fire to the entire house, because she cannot bring herself to fulfill her sister's last request any other way, and in the last act John almost succeeds in burning the newly discovered trove. Interestingly, this trope of the "final wish" is one Glaspell had already employed to considerable dramatic effect in *Bernice*.[11] The theatrical force of this aspect of the Dickinson legend, the fact that her poetry came so close to being lost to us forever, surely inspired Glaspell to make her climactic scenes revolve around a similar scenario.

Pollitt may have struck a further chord for Glaspell with her depiction of "the Dickinson house and grounds" as "Emily's laboratory" (237). Glaspell had already used the metaphor of a laboratory as a locus for female creativity in *The Verge;* the sense of a physical environment being inseparable from a character's essence had appeared in such works as *Trifles, The Outside,* and *Bernice.* The fact that Glaspell titled her play *Alison's **House*** cements the strong association of character and location central to this work and much of Glaspell's dramaturgy.[12] Furthermore, on a personal level Glaspell may have responded to Pollitt's version of the romance story, which posited Edward Bissell Hunt as Dickinson's lover, painting him as a mentor of the young writer. This "tutelage" of Dickinson's mind (Pollitt 136–37) reverberates with (problematic) depictions of Glaspell's own life story, the version that presents Cook as the shaper of her artistry, helping her evolve intellectually.[13] Similarly, Pollitt's claim that Dickinson's love for Hunt "gave a powerful drive to her creative faculty" (155) echoes the thematic relation between emotion and artistry evident throughout Glaspell's writing, especially some of her short fiction.

Taggard may have stood out in Glaspell's mind for other reasons. She evokes the Dickinson pioneer spirit, in their early settlement in western Massachusetts and the region's hostile relations with the Wampanoag Indians (Taggard 20). Here the Glaspell family story, set in the Midwest a century later and dramatized in part in *Inheritors,* seems to echo the portrait of Emily's ancestors and could have prompted Glaspell's decision to place the Stanhope homestead in Iowa also. Taggard diverges from Pollitt and Bianchi by rejecting the hypothesis that Emily's love was for a married man (Taggard 120), a plot element retained in *Alison's House,* however. This strongly suggests that Glaspell either must have used other sources or chose to counter Taggard by selecting a narrative shared with the other biographies.[14] On the other hand, Taggard's depiction of Emily's father as the obstacle to her plans to marry the man she loved may have influenced the creation of John Stanhope (84); the brother who keeps Alison at home like Taggard's elder Dickinson otherwise bears little resemblance to the biographers' images of Austin.

Glaspell also peppers her drama with incidents and details recollected by the Stanhope family that reflect the Dickinson legend. Eben remembers the little presents Alison would give them as children (661); Stanhope mentions a carriage (665), perhaps an allusion to the infamous carriage rides Austin and Mabel Todd took together; and Eben and Elsa both recall Alison's appearance: her white dresses, the central part in her hair, and her eyes "like golden wine" (683), all of which correspond with the Dickinson biographies, Dickinson's own writing, and the known physical image of the poet. Glaspell uses such specifics not only to enrich her dramatic world and her characterizations but also to foster the association between her drama and its biographical sources, again calling into question where biography leaves off and fiction begins.

As these connections suggest, Glaspell may have been impressed by the biographies in many ways: plot details, character profiles, elements of setting, theme, and tone. What remains tantalizing is her ability to construct the Stanhope family and its struggles without having access to the information revealed only in later biographies and critical studies. Sewall, Dickinson's 1974 biographer, for example hypothesizes that "Vinnie [Lavinia], the guardian and housekeeper, must have known more than she let on" about Emily's writing (608), a detail no earlier biographer includes yet one that is central to the development of Glaspell's plot. Many years before the play begins, Alison had enjoined Agatha to burn the unknown love poems after her death. Agatha, distraught over the fate of the Stanhope homestead, tries to fulfill Alison's wish and defeat her brother's plan through her efforts to burn down the house.

Even more significant is Glaspell's ability to convey the beauty and pathos of the hidden love poems, which correspond to the tenor of Dickinson's three "Master" letters: documents found after her death that "are among the most intense and fervent love letters she ever wrote" (Sewall 512). None of the biographies available to Glaspell provides any written evidence of the hypothesized forbidden love. Near the end of the play, as Alison's descendants read the newly discovered poems, they realize the depth of emotion and beauty she has captured in her writing:

Stanhope (*to* Elsa): Why did you say her name like that?
Elsa: Because she was telling me her story. It's here—the story she never told. She has written it, as it was never written before. The love story that never died—loneliness that never died—anguish and beauty of her love! I said her name because she was with me.

. . .

Stanhope: If I had known it was as much as this—I would not have asked her
   to stay.

                                                                     (687)

We are made to understand that Alison poured into this secret verse all the
love and loss of the relationship she gave up at her brother's behest. Dickinson's "Master" letters most strongly corroborate the early biographers' hypothesis of "a crisis, and probably a love crisis" (Sewall 513) in her life. They
were not published until 1955 (Sewall 512), however, and were obviously not
available to either Taggard or Pollitt, although Glaspell may have heard something from Vorse that led her toward this plot element.[15]

   Glaspell also made another calculated and dramatically significant choice
in the face of the obstacles presented to her by the Dickinson estate, namely,
not to try to create "great" poetry for her writer character.[16] We never hear any
of Alison's verse during the play; Glaspell leaves all the details of her writing to
the audience's imagination. We know nothing of her style, theme, or form, although the characters make allusions to subjects drawn from nature, as was
also true for Dickinson. Glaspell's decision here prevents a critique of the poet
character—and Glaspell herself—in a way that would have detracted from the
other concerns of the drama. Instead, Glaspell quotes from Emerson, whose
work Alison "loved and used" (677). Moreover, Glaspell develops part of
the significance of her title from Emerson's lyric "The House." Built on a conceit comparing architecture to poetry, Emerson's verse details how writing, in
harmony with nature, will outlast the physical structures man creates:

> There is no architect
> Can build as the muse can;
> She is skilful to select
> Materials for her plan;
>
> Slow and warily to choose
> Rafters of immortal pine,
> Or cedar incorruptible,
> Worthy of her design.
> . . .
> That so they shall not be displaced
> By lapses or by wars,
> But for the love of happy souls
> Outlive the newest star.
>   (Emerson 188–89)

Thus, Alison's house of poetry is greater than, and will remain long after, her
actual abode, which is already ceasing to exist as hers per se through the decision of her brother to sell it to the Hodges.

This absent poetry, like its absent author, is the object of interpretation within the world of the play. In important ways we might think of *Alison's House* as revisionist biography: as Glaspell's attempt to construct an alternative explication of this imagined verse through a variant on biographical criticism. The pivotal issue here is the chronology of the revelation of the love poems and the story to accompany them in relation to the rest of Alison's history. The fact that the love poems are not discovered until the *end* of the play allows Glaspell to analyze the biographical construction of identity without the singular emotional motivation for artistry posited by other biographers. At the opening of the play Alison is already an established, renowned poet. Certain details of her life story have been available to the public for some time, but there is no sense in the play that Alison's writing has been read biographically or accounted for in terms of her love life. Thus, Glaspell works to refute the reading that thwarted desire lay behind Emily's/Alison's creativity, in fact suggesting instead a preponderance of writing having no direct biographical explanation. Glaspell had begun to explore this theme in *Chains of Dew* through the characters of the poet Seymore Standish and his mother, but she refines and clarifies her response to biographical criticism in *Alison's House.* Through these works Glaspell may also be projecting a subtle refutation of the critical tendency to talk about her own work biographically, especially in regard to her relationship with Cook.

Issues with women's creativity and biography have recently been discussed by feminist critics. In her study of biographical criticism and women writers Alison Booth has remarked, "Just as women themselves have been conventionally accused of being too personal—always personal—so criticism of women's writings has been almost invariably biographical, whether or not the critic shares in the feminist revalorization of the personal as political" (86). Instead, Booth advocates "the inclusion of the author's biography and of historical context(s) as contributing, unfolding *texts,* not reified entities, in an alert intertextuality" (89). *Alison's House* exemplifies a creative demonstration of this critical practice. Glaspell constructs what we might think of as a resistant critical superstructure: the way we are encouraged to read and *not* to read Alison's verse. This superstructure surrounds the quasi-fictional case study of a poet we might otherwise evaluate using the tools of traditional biographical readings. Glaspell contains the connection of biography and writing to the love poems alone—not Alison's entire oeuvre—thereby suggesting that multiple motivations and interpretive strategies must be considered when one evaluates an author's work.

There is still another angle of this source analysis to examine. Katharine Rodier has identified numerous details from Dickinson's poetry reflected in Glaspell's text, demonstrating convincingly that Glaspell probably knew the verse well and that it influenced her playwriting. Rodier finds phrasings and rhythms in the play that closely echo Dickinson's poetry (204–5). Although

Rodier does not discuss here the additional stylistic similarities between Dickinson's writing and the poetic voice of Claire Archer in *The Verge* or the women in *The Outside,* her analysis of the links between the dramaturgy of *Alison's House* and Dickinson's artistry lends further credence to a wider-reaching stylistic association between the two authors.[17]

Rodier's reading of fragments of both the Cook and Glaspell biographies through other moments and characters in the play resembles the "persona criticism" preferred by Cheryl Walker:

> a form of analysis that focuses on patterns of ideation, voice, and sensibility linked together by a connection to the author . . . [which] allows one to speak of authorship as multiple, involving culture, psyche, and intertextuality, as well as biographical data about the writer. (109)

This kind of interpretive multiplicity appears both more provocative and, ultimately, more critically satisfying than the traditional one-on-one mapping of biography to text exemplified in such analyses as that of C. W. E. Bigsby, who calls *Alison's House* "a rather slight affair, a piece of self-justification by a woman who had, in effect, run off with a married man and who in this play offers a justification of her violation of social taboo" (*American Drama* 33). Bigsby is of course referring to the fact that Glaspell was Cook's third wife and that their relationship had become serious prior to his divorce from his second wife. But it is both biographically inaccurate to say that Glaspell "ran off with a married man"[18] and simplistic at best to reduce *Alison's House* to a therapeutic exercise to relieve feelings of guilt.

In fact, Glaspell had already explored the complex social and personal dimensions of a woman's love for a married man in her 1915 novel, *Fidelity.* *Fidelity* can be read as yet another intertext for *Alison's House,* in that the novel shares with the play thematic concerns with the individual acting against the force of a conservative, midwestern society as well as a narrative exploring the consequences of fulfilling an unsanctioned love. The title of the novel hints at the competing ideologies of faithfulness to self versus faithfulness to social strictures, frequent tropes of American literature examined in both *Fidelity* and *Alison's House.* As a character in the novel states, "One has to admit that just taking one's own happiness is thorough selfishness. Society as a whole is greater than the individual, isn't it?" (*Fidelity* 137). But, as we know, Glaspell carefully evaluates each side of complicated moral and political issues, so that such unequivocal dicta are never fully embraced in her work.

In *Alison's House* Glaspell explores the consequences of extramarital love by contrasting two generations' choices. Elsa has chosen to buck convention and live with a married man, a decision that has ostracized both. Elsa explains to her brother: "I had to go, Eben. Don't you see? That was the way I loved him." But Eben reminds her of the cost of her actions for their family, especially their father: "You made him older. Nothing ever hit him as hard" (678). Eben's wife Louise, the voice of social conformity, has already conveyed popular opinion of Elsa's behavior: "You know how they talk—it makes the whole family seem—different. . . . Oh, forgive me, but you must know how the town does talk about Elsa." Moreover, Louise establishes the idea of a generational resemblance: "They do link it up with something queer about Alison." This social perspective establishes another link between *Alison's House* and *Inheritors*: the sense of ancestry, of familial predilections passing down through the generations, informs both works. The strategic divergence in this play comes with the way each member of the family has handled passion. As Stanhope curtly observes, Alison "never lived with a man who had a wife and children" (655). The revelation of Stanhope's own renounced extramarital desire colors our understanding of his attitude toward Alison's and his children's personal choices. Ann implores him:

> You were so good to me, always. I feel as if you were my father, though I know you're not, really. You were so good to Mother. (*Low*) You loved her. And she loved you. Through years. And you denied your love, because of me, and Eben, and Elsa, and Ted. Well, here we all are—the children— Eben, Elsa, Ted, and Ann. Can't you let us, now when you are old, and sad, tell you what to do—for us? Won't you let Alison's words pass on— as a gift to all love—let them *be* here—when you are not here? (690)

Ann, the voice of the younger generation, shows an understanding of the actions of her elders but suggests that those choices may not be as viable for the present day.

From a feminist perspective one might say that the three most prominent absent figures in Glaspell's dramaturgy—Minnie Wright (*Trifles*), Bernice (*Bernice*), and Alison—are missing from their texts precisely because their patriarchal environments have enforced a conformity of image. As Karen Laughlin explains, "A basic tension in the play [*Alison's House*] exists between what women . . . *are* . . . and what they *ought to be*" (220). Upholding that patriarchal image requires that these female characters disappear from a world that cannot allow their rebellion, however slight. This more recent critical reading may help explicate the moral struggle at the heart of the play, which, though clearly delineated, is not completely resolved by the drama's conclusion. The Pulitzer committee must have been sensitive to this moral debate in the play, one that encourages the audience to consider such choices and their consequences. In the novel *Fidelity*, as in *Alison's House*, Glaspell creates women who have conformed and renounced love and others who have chosen to suffer social disgrace. Both positions represent sacrifice and emotional pain. One quits these works sensing that for Glaspell the enemy is not the individual(s) who attempts to block such relationships but the social mores that warp people's empathic response or crush their ability to rise above their own selfish adherence to their social position. Many of Glaspell's plays and novels feature a female character who represents these conservative and inflexible codes: Laura in *Bernice*, Adelaide in *The Verge*, Amy in *Fidelity*, Louise in *Alison's House*, to name just a few. Glaspell uses these figures to make an important comment on women's own complicity in perpetuating such conservative social forms. The frequency of Glaspell's use of this characterological and narrative structure suggests its compelling importance to her. Glaspell must have hoped that her audiences would observe this female type and avoid her behavior, not to mention question the codes she parrots; this in turn could improve the social climate for all men and women for whom traditional life choices may not be possible.

Ultimately, it is not the passion per se or the way that any of these individuals handle their feelings that is really important. Rather, Glaspell highlights the fact that passion, stemming from any of a number of possible motivations, can prompt great art. Poetry carries with it the resonance of deep feeling, emotion that speaks to the reader on a profound and personal level. For Glaspell this universal truth transcends the particularity of its creator's situation. John Stanhope grasps the significance of this movement from the private to the public as he comes to understand why the poetry must be shared, not destroyed:

> It isn't—what you [Elsa] said. . . . She loved to make her little gifts. If she can make one more, from her century to yours, then she isn't gone. Anything else is—too lonely. (*He holds the poems out to her.*) For Elsa—From Alison.

The details from Alison's life that lie behind the verse fade in comparison to the power of the writing to speak to her audience, to make them feel that she composed the lines for them. As her descendants observe, "I feel Alison wrote those poems for me" (691).

One senses that Glaspell wants the play to help her audiences understand the broader value in studying a life and its work. Meaningful biography should provide more than titillation; it should open a window onto a set of lives, a way of life, and we should see how and why those lives evolved as they did. Glaspell opens *Alison's House* with the entrance of the reporter character, Knowles, who has come to discover "anything about where—how—they [the poems] were written. The desk she sat at. The window she looked from" (654). Glaspell foreshadows the climactic discovery of the unknown verse with Knowles's enigmatic remark, "Alison Stanhope's room—holds something" (657). It is as if biographical minutiae will open up the writer to him and, by extension, to her broader readership. This initial dramaturgical structure, the presentation of a mystery to be solved, connects *Alison's House* with both *Trifles* and *Bernice*. The "solution" to each of the puzzles, however, is not the end point of the plays. Rather, in each instance the existence of the questions to be answered—did Minnie murder her husband? how did Bernice die and why? what prompted Alison's gift as a poet?—really serves to motivate the characters to question themselves and to come to a better understanding of their own identity and place in the world. Alison, like the other absent figures in Glaspell's plays, emerges as a foil for the rest of the characters. We only come to know her refracted by those figures we do encounter, and it is these others on whom we should focus if we are to understand the larger scope of the work.

While Alison and her poetry transcend time, Glaspell's living characters palpably reflect the tension of one era and its inhabitants giving way to the new order of the twentieth century. The trope of generational conflict that permeates the play dates to the beginning of Western drama. Yet on the American stage this antagonistic relationship between parents and children was by 1930 already emerging as *the* structure through which mainstream theater participated regularly in social critique. The family as microcosm for American society became the metaphor of choice for many of our most successful dramatists. The problems these families encountered developed through their dynamic, if not always fully articulated, relationship with their cultural moment; there was a direct correspondence between the escalating conflict within the family and the deterioration of American society, even if the drama never made that parallel explicit.

If one compares Glaspell's dramaturgy from the period of her work with the Provincetown Players to *Alison's House,* one can see how her writing evolved in tandem with this theatrical trend. The second phase of her dramatic career, which included the creation of *The Comic Artist, Alison's House,* and *Springs Eternal,* is marked by its focus on the family. While the earlier works collectively demonstrate dramatic motivation from broader social and/or political forces, the later pieces blend critique more subtly into the background of the family portrait. Many of her concerns remain the same; they are simply revealed through individualized perspectives that foreground character within the familial context.

A clear example of this shift emerges from the contrast of Alison's niece Elsa and Madeline Fejevary in *Inheritors.* Glaspell uses both characters to represent a woman's choice to stand in opposition to the beliefs of her family and her community. In *Inheritors* the cost of this stance will be legal proceedings and very possibly incarceration. In *Alison's House* the weight shifts from the community's response to the family's, although we feel and see the effects of

Elsa's decision every bit as strongly as we do Madeline's. Both women's battles are political; one may well be fought from a real prison, while the other is fought from a symbolic one, a place of isolation away from her family and friends. In each instance Glaspell indicts the society that enforces the strictures these women oppose, but in *Alison's House* we observe the censure of the family and extrapolate it to the community, seeing in John and Louise the representation of these values as well as the action of their enforcement.

The dysfunctionality social and behavioral theorists have identified as epidemic in the United States in the late twentieth century has also been traced by literary critics in cultural representations of the family dating back for decades. The breakdown in generational communication endemic to this condition operates especially poignantly in the dialogic medium of the drama. Glaspell highlights the choice characters make to remain silent, to retain secrets or refuse to connect with one another, as synecdochic of her culture's inability to act empathically and, by extension, genuinely democratically. Here, too, Glaspell shifts her emphasis from individual social examples to familial ones in the later plays while retaining her overarching sense of critique. Throughout *Alison's House* we sense that if the characters could only talk to one another, could share their feelings openly and work toward consensus, they would have been able to avoid the crises that confront them. We come to feel that John's choice not only to deny his love for Ann's mother but also to keep it a secret from his children has caused the breakdown in his relationship with others, especially Elsa; moreover, he is by extension responsible for her fate, precisely because of his silent, unquestioning endorsement of a social code with no flexibility or compassion. In *Trifles* (and even more clearly in "A Jury of Her Peers") Mrs. Hale comes to realize that her refusal to interact with Minnie Wright, to share their common struggles, is a crime against a fellow human that society may not regulate but that has serious consequences nonetheless. Whether in the spirit of communitarianism, as with *Trifles*, or within the confines of the family, as in *Alison's House*, Glaspell shows that secrets and silence only lead to isolation of both self and other. One could find many other instances in Glaspell's later plays of this transition from the early, fundamentally social critique to a critique emerging from a familial context with social corollaries, yet these two examples indicate how Glaspell accomplished this shift through characterological and narrative adjustments in her dramatic technique. These adjustments resonated not only with dramatic developments of the time but allowed for the serious consideration of her work in a theatrical environment quite different from the one she had left eight years before.

Glaspell's dramatic study in biography posed moral, social, artistic, and personal questions against a backdrop of America's cultural history. From the standpoint of theater scholars over half a century later who have seen a longer tradition of Pulitzer awards, it may be easier for us to parse the value of this play for the committee. But for critics at the time the Pulitzer decision was baffling. When *Alison's House* was awarded the Pulitzer Prize for Drama in 1931—only the second time the award had gone to a woman[19]—the announcement set off the most vociferous attack by critics of the Pulitzer committee in its then fifteen-year tradition.

In his *History of the Pulitzer Prize Plays* John L. Toohey provides a delightful anecdote on this award:

> Susan Glaspell's *Alison's House* was the rankest outsider ever to win the Pulitzer Prize. . . . Nobody gave *Alison's House* a chance; indeed, one rival producer had been so sure that his own entry would win that he ordered a fresh set of posters printed, trumpeting the expected victory. After *Alison's House* sneaked under the wire, the posters became a collector's item to rank with the *Chicago Tribune's* celebrated DEWEY DEFEATS TRUMAN headline. (90)

At the time she won the award, Glaspell had not had a new play on the New York stage for eight years, since the 1922 production of *Chains of Dew* opened following her departure for Greece with Cook.[20] But the 1927 revival of *Inheritors* at the Civic Rep had fostered the relationship of Glaspell and Eva Le Gallienne, and the playwright decided to entrust her latest work to this new ally. In her autobiography, *At 33,* Le Gallienne recalls the events:

> Our fifth season was also interesting through our production of Susan Glaspell's "Alison's House." It was cruelly treated by the press, well received by the public—and to our great jubilation—was awarded the Pulitzer Prize for 1931. (231)

Glaspell's choice of producer proved fortunate, for Le Gallienne's company scheduled work in repertory, meaning that a production not only stayed in performance for a set period regardless of initial reviews but was also kept in the repertoire for future remounting. Broadway productions, by comparison, often dissolve overnight if they fail to win early critical favor. In the case of *Alison's House* the play remained in performance on Fourteenth Street long enough to be seen by the Pulitzer committee and a good number of critics and then, following the announcement of the award, transferred uptown for a limited Broadway engagement.[21]

The disparity between the public's enthusiastic reception of the work, chronicled by Le Gallienne, and the press's dismissal of the play also merits note, since the existence of such conflicts often evaporates in subsequent commentary, unless box office or other records survive to substantiate audience response, as opposed to journalistic commentary. The 1999 production of the play by the Mint Theater, its only New York revival since the Civic Rep staging, supported Le Gallienne's reading of her audience's reaction. Viewers found the performances both entertaining and affecting; Glaspell's story retained its dramatic force more than a half-century after its premier.

The virulence of the backlash against the work and its receipt of the Pulitzer has dominated commentary on the play, overshadowing most critical analysis of the award for the 1930–31 season. George Jean Nathan remarked, "Dramatic craftsmanship is apparently not one of Miss Glaspell's talents, and, as a consequence, her plays are such in name only" ("Theatre of George Jean Nathan" 31). John Mason Brown applied such adjectives as "disappointing, wooden, and *exasperating* to the work" ("Play"). *Variety* labeled the drama "lethargic" and "suffer[ing] from anaesthesia" ("Alison's House"). Arthur Ruhl deemed it "wordy, slight, and frequently dull" ("Alison's House"). When the award was announced, Mark Van Doren observed, "Emily Dickinson has suffered many indignities from her biographers, but none so heavy-handed as this" ("Drama"). Robert Garland flatly declared the prize "undeserved" ("Cast and Miscast"), while Brown opined it represented "a sad decline in standards" by the committee ("Prize Play").[22]

Shortly after the critical furor had abated, Burns Mantle published the *Best Plays* volume for 1930–31, his annual summary of American dramatic activity. Mantle deemed the reception of *Alison's House* "unfair," remarking the reviewers' "objections in general were, to me, based largely on their disappointment in the drama as entertainment" (vii). Clearly, the critics were "entertained" by other offerings of the season, including Kaufman and Hart's *Once in a Lifetime*, the musical *Girl Crazy*, the innovative play *Grand Hotel* (on which the subsequent hit musical was based), and *The Barretts of Wimpole Street*, to name just a few (3–17). But, as Mantle suggests, the entertainment value of a piece is hardly its only measure of merit.

Mantle contextualized the critics' responses further by reminding his readers of "the usual stock company handicaps" the production had faced. Countering the majority critical view, he concluded the work was "interesting in story and sound in drama. . . . Miss Glaspell's [play was] sensitively written and honestly sympathetic" (vii). The Mantle volume is also useful for its summaries and critical appraisals of the nine other "best" competing plays; it would appear from Mantle's point of view that *Alison's House* might only have been challenged by Lynn Riggs's *Green Grow the Lilacs* (the source play for the 1943 musical *Oklahoma!*) in terms of the Pulitzer criteria (vi–vii).

An examination of the award itself, and particularly the criteria the judges used in the selection process, reveals why Glaspell's work was indeed the most appropriate piece for the prize that season. As Thomas Adler observes, *Alison's House* remains a "noteworthy" example of the group:

What continues to be most noteworthy about it is the way that so many of the subjects pursued in the Pulitzer plays over the decades here converge: the new woman whose values are a beacon for the future; the artist as quasi-mystical singer for society; and the tempering of harsh paternalism through compassion, often learned from the child. (132)

In addition to these thematic, narrative, and characterological parallels with other prize-winning dramas, *Alison's House* stood out for the judges in 1930 for very specific reasons that had much to do with their understanding of the principles of the award and what it was to signify.

When Joseph Pulitzer established the prizes to be given annually in his name through the bequest administered by Columbia University, he was specific about the type of work worthy of the honor. In drama the award would be "for the original American play, performed in New York, which shall best represent the educational value and power of the stage in raising the standard of good morals, good taste, and good manners" (qtd. in Hohenberg 19). From the outset the judges had difficulty finding drama they felt fit all the criteria. In 1917 and 1919 they made no award, and in other years felt they had somewhat compromised on the standards set by Pulitzer, particularly with regard to the moral content and value of the plays. In 1929, the year before the premier of *Alison's House,* the Advisory Board to the Pulitzer committee changed the wording of the award specifications to "the original American play 'which shall best represent the educational value and power of the stage'" (qtd in Hohenberg 102), dropping the clause about morality, taste, and manners. But the Pulitzer judges apparently favored the spirit of the original language, particularly the issue of morality. Glaspell's play represented both traditional moral choices and the rejection of conventional morality without explicitly endorsing either perspective; the ambiguity in the work—a dramaturgical technique evident in her writing from *Trifles* on—pushes the audience actively to question these values and the social structures that enforce them.

In 1944 Walter Prichard Eaton, a judge who had served on eleven Pulitzer drama committees, including that of the 1930–31 season, wrote an essay for *Theatre Annual* on the prize, revealing much of his thinking about the award and conveying his sense of responsibility as an adjudicator. Referring pointedly to the disputes between the Pulitzer committee and the New York reviewers, Eaton observed:

There is a fear, sometimes, on the part of the administrators of a trust . . . of departing too violently from conservatism in making their judgments. *That, possibly, there is a somewhat greater sense of the underlying moral responsibility of art on the part of such men as constitute the Pulitzer juries than on the part of Broadway critics.* (29; my emph.)[23]

Eaton, explaining his mission, significantly presents the original wording for the award, not the 1929 revision or others that followed. He maintains that Pulitzer, in keeping with the "canons of classic criticism" that he embraced, believed "the best drama must have a moralistic base as had the work of Sophocles and Shakespeare." Eaton wryly observes that, "as the donor of the award . . . [Pulitzer] is entitled to some consideration" (24–25).

Eaton's somewhat lengthy rationalization for the selection of *Alison's House* merits quoting in full, for it reveals the criteria underlying the committee's award extremely clearly:

> In 1930–31 we recommended *Alison's House* by Susan Glaspell for the award and by so doing brought down on our heads immediate scorn. . . . But its only real competitors among native plays were *Elizabeth the Queen* and Barry's *Tomorrow and Tomorrow,* the latter not a serious competitor.[24] The choice, really, was between a play acted with great acclaim by Lunt and Fontanne in the older fashion of romantic verse drama, and a play acted down on Fourteenth Street by Miss Le Gallienne's struggling Civic Repertory Company which plumbed the deep American love of home and family still existing outside the confines of New York cubbyhole apartments, and which also brought the strange story of Emily Dickinson to dramatic life. . . . *Alison's House* somewhat bored the critics in New York (it always bored them to have to go down to Fourteenth Street, anyhow), but it was acted for a long time by many theatre groups throughout the country, and in a production I saw only three years ago, it was still a moving and provocative play which deserved a recognition Broadway refused. (26–27)

This passage details two clear categories for evaluation. First, Eaton obviously privileges a cultural nationalist agenda, epitomized here by the native subject Dickinson rather than the British monarch. Moreover, Glaspell's historic participation in a theater committed to an agenda of cultural nationalism, the Provincetown Players, would certainly also have been known to the judges. The American domestic milieu, represented by the midwestern, familial setting of the play, furthers the cultural nationalist agenda that already had a theatrical tradition of representing home, family, and the frontier and championing the rural West over the urban East.

Second, Eaton brings to bear performative concerns. While, strictly speaking, the award goes to the *play,* it is obvious from Eaton's remarks that production considerations factored into the decision. Throughout the *Theatre Annual* essay Eaton expresses a desire to support theatrical underdogs with the prize: whether that be an aspiring playwright, a struggling theater company, or a worthy but critically dismissed play that would benefit from the award at-

tention. Eaton's sense of the future production life of plays, their potential for
theatrical longevity, emerges as a serious factor in his evaluative process as
well. But, above all, Eaton feels a sense of moral responsibility, a sacred duty
to call attention to the work best representing his sense of the moral potential
of the play itself and of the theater to instruct audiences in exemplary American values. Glaspell dramatizes the debate surrounding an unquestioning acceptance of traditional morality, specifically in her characters' choices with regard to personal integrity, social consciousness, and marital fidelity.

In granting the award, Eaton wrote the majority opinion, in which he
was joined by Clayton Hamilton (Austin Strong was the third member for that
year), highlighting "the fine sincerity of the dramatist, her choice of a theme
which is fresh, taken out of American life, and worthy of serious attention, and
her evident interest in what she had to say, quite apart from any considerations of temporal styles or box office appeal" (qtd. in Hohenberg 105). Reading between the lines of this statement, one can see the committee's response
to the critics' accusations of an overly literary style, a faulty adherence to the
traditional well-made play form, and a biographical plot of interest only to
Dickinson lovers.

Particularly with regard to the dramaturgy that the critics perceived as
old-fashioned or too conventional, we might productively recall what Glaspell
was attempting to do with the form and style of *The Verge*. By pitting more
traditional dialogue and character against experiments with expressionism,
Glaspell explored modernism as both theme and technique. With *Alison's
House* she uses the form of the well-made play to depict the moment of its
greatest popularity and theatrical strength, the end of the nineteenth century.
Precisely because Glaspell was so concerned about the relationship between
dramatic form and content, she chose a style to reflect the world she was depicting. Just as the play hints at the changes to come with the advent of the
twentieth century and at the desirabilty of some of those advances, so we
should think about what had happened over the preceding thirty years and
the profound impact of artistic and political events on American culture. It
would have made little sense for Glaspell to write *Alison's House* with the techniques of the avant-garde, despite the fact that she had the ability to do so; the
play needed to be holistically historical precisely to allow for the kind of reflection it urges us, through its central characters, to undertake. The subtlety
of her design, however, clearly eluded the critics.[25] A similar problem awaited
The Comic Artist, although, as we have seen, the critics' response was in that
instance more justified.

Two main realizations emerge from an analysis of the award itself and
Glaspell's relation to it. First, the Pulitzer Prize, even with its criteria modified
over time, always reflects a group of individuals' interpretation of the intentions of its creator, Joseph Pulitzer. Second, aesthetic as well as other shifting,

nationalistic values factor into their decision, making it necessary to contextualize the vote within the framework of its moment in the United States. These issues may, but often do not, correspond to the equally subjective criteria that the reviewers bring to bear in their evaluations of theatrical worth. For the 1930–31 season, in the post-1920s and post-crash American climate, it should come as no surprise that the Pulitzer judges favored a work itself reflecting the rapidly changing American milieu. Glaspell raises questions about the relationship between art and society, about the value of home and family, and about the codes by which we live that were already part of a nostalgic sense of our recent past; yet the ideology reflected in these questions also may have seemed precarious to those contemplating the country's future. Glaspell demonstrates an ability to encapsulate the past while simultaneously looking forward, a capacity that helped position *Alison's House* favorably. It is such dramaturgical concerns as these, rather than debates over artistic merit, that need to be remembered when contemplating this or any Pulitzer decision. Glaspell's engagement with issues of the individual and society, refracted through her concern with both the nature of biographical writing and the representation of one prominent American woman artist, gives *Alison's House* significance well beyond its immediate, conflicted theatrical reception. Still, the force of such controversy equally clearly demonstrates the ongoing power of dramatic criticism to shape and control the subsequent consideration of any work written for the stage.

Springs Eternal

After the 1933 failure of *The Comic Artist* on Broadway, Glaspell never again had a new play produced, but she did not sever her ties with the theater community, and those within it appear not to have forgotten her. She received an offer of employment from Hallie Flanagan, director of the Federal Theater Project (FTP) in Washington, DC, which had been established in 1935 as a division of the Works Progress Administration. Flanagan wanted her to move to Chicago to become the head of the project's Midwest Play Bureau. From the fall of 1936 through May 1938 Glaspell devoted herself to the Federal Theater and its goal of finding new plays to produce and theatrical artists to employ. She became an outspoken champion of her area's playwrights, actors, and directors. During her tenure the Midwestern Bureau produced such landmarks of FTP history as "the all-black *Swing Mikado, Spirochete* (Arnold Sundgaard's Living Newspaper on syphilis), and black playwright Theodore Ward's *Big White Fog*" (Noe, *Critical Biography* 196).[1] At the end of that period, however, Glaspell seems to have decided to renew her focus on her first creative medium, fiction, writing three last novels and a children's story.[2] From this point until her death, in 1948, she lived almost exclusively in her home on Cape Cod.

The eruption of World War II and the entrance of the United States into the conflict prompted Glaspell to turn to drama again, however, for what was to be her last play, *Springs Eternal*. Subtitled "A Comedy in Three Acts," the work adheres to both the classical sense of the term *comedy*, with a conclusion in proposed marriage, and to the more common notions of a humorous piece, although this second aspect of its dramaturgy is open to critique. Despite the occasional light moments and flashes of wit reminiscent of Glaspell's wryest work, especially in the first act, the play overall evinces a rather ironic feel, with philosophical dialogue and a more serious tone dominant by the play's conclusion. This movement from comedy to drama worked effectively in such earlier pieces as *The Verge* and *Chains of Dew*. Here, however, Glaspell was not so successful. The overwhelming force of the conflict abroad, which reverberates throughout the play's narrative, creates both structural and tonal problems for *Springs Eternal* that Glaspell was not able to resolve.

The play is set entirely in the "living room, which is also [the] library, in the Higgenbothem home in New York State. . . . A hospitable, open . . . room, giving the sense of a cultivated, though rather casual family, having lived there for some time" (1.1). In fact, Owen and his second wife's, Margaret Higgenbothem's, home serves as the meeting point for an entire extended clan, who either descend on the scene or check in by telephone throughout the action. Act 1 is set on the day of an emergency "family conference" (1.2–3). The meeting has been prompted by the presumed elopement of Dottie, the daughter of family friends, with Stewie Gleason, a Washington politician married to Owen's ex-wife, who is called "Harry" (short for Harriet). Dottie's father Thayer and stepmother Evelyn do not appear onstage but are nevertheless quite present through their numerous phone calls during the play.[3]

With what Marcia Noe wryly remarks is "surely the understatement of the play" Margaret Higgenbothem acknowledges, "We have entangling alliances" in the family (*Critical Biography* 224). Continuing her military conceit, she explains that they have a history of "breaking our pacts," particularly regarding marriage (1.3). These lines soon resonate with other themes in the play, including her husband Owen's seeming inability to sustain his former political convictions and visionary fervor. Owen is a linguistics scholar and philosophical writer whose book, *World of Tomorrow,* written after World War I, reflected his then-radical sympathies. Through the character of Owen and his writing Glaspell repeats some themes and narrative details she develops in her 1942 novel, *Norma Ashe.* Noe reads this novel as reflecting what "Glaspell believed to have brought about" the war. In Noe's words, "*Norma Ashe* details the failure of idealism, the slow, steady process by which youthful ideals are destroyed, perverted, buried by the tedium of daily life" (*Critical Biography* 214).[4] The novel's focus on the influence of a philosophy teacher on his students corresponds to the influence of Owen's book on the younger generation in the play. An important difference between novel and play, however, is where Glaspell puts her characterological focus. In *Norma Ashe* the plot concerns the maturation of those young people. In *Springs Eternal,* by contrast, we witness the superfluousness of the older generation, whose greatest endeavors seem to lie behind them and whose current lives seem painfully inconsequential when compared to the war effort that surrounds them. Over the years Owen has of course had a strong impact on Harold, his son by his first wife, Harry; Harold's initial stance as a conscientious objector becomes yet another kind of pact that appears to rupture during the play.

Owen's book has also deeply affected Freddie Soames, a young soldier stationed in the Pacific. Freddie is the last of Glaspell's absent yet central dramatic characters; his link to the family is through his mother, the Higgenbothem's housekeeper. Glaspell's 1946 novel, *Judd Rankin's Daughter,* develops at greater length her concern with the impact of the war on soldiers at the Pacific front. In this novel Judd Rankin, the title character, has also written influential books. Through these two late novels (as well as her 1940 children's story, *Cherished and Shared of Old,* which takes up the question of anti-German sentiments) and *Springs Eternal* Glaspell was grappling with observations of her country's complex responses to the war. Glaspell rounds out the play's cast with Dr. Bill Parks, a young local physician who is home recovering from a wound sustained in a tour of duty in Africa. Margaret has called him in to see Owen about an unspecified, but not serious, illness. The assembled characters humorously attempt to resolve multiple misunderstandings about one another as they simultaneously wrestle with the much more serious impact of the war on their country and themselves.

After drafting the work, Glaspell contacted her longtime friend and colleague, Lawrence Langner, to inquire about a possible production. Langner was an original member of the Washington Square Players and later one of the founders of the Theatre Guild and its current co–administrative director (Langner, *Magic Curtain* 158). Glaspell wrote, "I've written a play—a comedy, and I wonder if you'd care to read it; and if you think they might be interested—pass it on to the rest of the Guild?" Langner responded with kindness and careful thought, gently rejecting the play in its current form:

> I have hesitated a long time before writing you about "Springs Eternal" because it is awfully difficult to put in words my feelings about the play. If I were to try to say it in a letter, I know I would only have you hopelessly confused. I do not have so much a clear-cut intellectual conviction about the play as a feeling that most of us have gone through what these characters went through, two or three years ago and arrived at the conclusion two or three years ago. This isn't a good reason for not doing a play. Perhaps the other reason is that it is—until the middle of the second act—so much of a conversation piece.
>
> Again, I hesitate to write you about the play. You know, Susan, I think that you have one of the finest talents in America and it is an impertinence on my part to criticize anything you write. Perhaps I am too much immersed in the practical theater and you are closer to the truth than I am. I would much rather talk to you about it than write you. (Qtd. in Noe, *Critical Biography* 223–24)

Reading between Langner's lines, one can see that he felt the play was out of date and that audiences might perceive the sentiments and actions of its characters as irrelevant. Langner also seems to imply that the static dialogue in the first half of the piece simply would not play well. Moreover, he may have thought that in the midst of World War II America's theatergoers would no longer wish to reflect on how we became involved in the conflict; they would want to look to the future, when the fighting and hardship would be over. Historian Alan Brinkley sees other creative writers engaged in just such future projection. He notes that the poet and playwright Archibald MacLeish, who was working in the Office of War Information at the time, "sought to keep the public's gaze fastened on the future beyond the war" as part of his official obligations (313).

Glaspell's efforts to sustain both a comic tone and an exploration of the lives of those barely touched by the war mark the major conceptual problem that underlies the drama. As a quick survey of successful commercial productions of the era reveals, wartime audiences responded to two distinct kinds of plays: those that were distractions and those that centered on the conflict, regardless of style. Glaspell tries to bring both types together in *Springs Eternal*, but she cannot reconcile the stylistic and thematic polarities she introduces. Details of the 1942–43, 1943–44, and 1944–45 Broadway seasons may provide a comparative framework for evaluating both audience proclivities and the informed perspective of theater administrators such as Langner, who felt the piece would not conform to current tastes.

In his overview of the 1942–43 season Louis Calta stresses both the "land-office business at the box-office" and the patriotism of the theater community, which supported the war effort through the War Service's Stage Door Canteen as well as the USO–Camp Shows (938). Burns Mantle echoed these sentiments in his report on the season but felt obliged to editorialize about the poor quality of stage offerings: "While the theatre season of 1943–44 . . . may be listed with other war casualties, it had its points." For Mantle they included the "confessedly propaganda drama" *Winged Victory*, produced by the Air Force and featuring its corps. He also points to Maxwell Anderson's *Storm Operation*, which "mixed realistic war and theatrical romance" to "bring a particular phase of this war home to the American public, which needed to be told about it" ("Introduction" v). Langner's sense that *Springs Eternal* had little new to say to its audience corresponds to Mantle's belief in the public's need for Anderson's drama, which focused on action rather than philosophy. George Jean Nathan continues in a similar vein to his colleagues for 1944–45, noting "unparalleled box-office prosperity" along with "the continued poverty in drama of authentic quality." Moreover, Nathan observes the "persisting emphasis upon the lighter entertainment fare," to which the public responded enthusiastically ("Foreword" v). Mantle feels the quality of the work in the 1944–45 season has improved, however, and he maintains that audiences continued to support such war pieces as Paul Osborn's *A Bell for Adano*, which "humanized Army directives and Army directors." Mantle singles out Capt. John Patrick's *The Hasty Heart*, about "the experiences of a volunteer in the American Field Service," as well as Rose Franken's *Soldier's Wife*, which anticipated the "domestic problems" of adjustment to postwar life ("Introduction" v). He concludes his report by highlighting the kinds of diversionary pieces audiences also frequented: Tennessee Williams's "memory play" *The Glass Menagerie,* Mary Chase's gentle comedy *Harvey,* and Philip Barry's "fanciful" *Foolish Notion* (vi). Clearly, Glaspell's drama was out of step with these kinds of pieces.

After receiving Langner's response, Glaspell appears to have given up the idea of producing or publishing the play. The only extant copies of *Springs Eternal* are typed, undated manuscript drafts, part of Glaspell's papers in the Berg Collection of the New York Public Library. As the work was never presented publicly, even some Glaspell scholars seem not to know of its existence. Arthur Waterman's study has no entry on the play, and C. W. E. Bigsby also leaves it off the list of her works in his edition of her selected plays. Noe mentions it briefly in *Susan Glaspell: Voice from the Heartland* (78–79); her earlier doctoral dissertation, "A Critical Biography of Susan Glaspell," contains the only discussion of the play to date. Noe expands upon Langner's "tactful" comment on the conversational nature of the work by remarking "that the talk is neither very witty nor very profound" and that the play's attempts at humor are "tired" (224). Rather than dismiss the play with these justified observations, however, we should read it intertextually with Glaspell's other writing to see what themes, character types, and issues still consumed her at the end of her creative life. In addition to its links to her late fiction, *Springs Eternal* exhibits stylistic, characterological, and thematic ties to Glaspell's earlier dramatic work. Moreover, in its perplexing inconsistencies and reversals, her last play mirrors the complexity of the war moment during which it was written.

Throughout Glaspell's career critics compared her work to that of other leading dramatists, including O'Neill, Shaw, and Chekhov. Had a revised version of *Springs Eternal* been staged or published, reviewers might have invoked Shaw's name once again and possibly added Noel Coward or J. B. Priestley to the list of playwrights whose work resonated with Glaspell's. Langner's description of the comedy as a conversation piece aligns it with the older Shavian tradition of "disquisitory" plays, particularly his *Misalliance* (1910), set in the country home of the somewhat eccentric Tarleton family, and his *Heartbreak House* (1920; written 1913–16), which he describes as being about "cultured, leisured Europe before the war" (7). Although the latter is set at the time of World War I, its atmosphere is echoed in Glaspell's drama of America during the second. In some ways, *Springs Eternal* seems to be a play out of its time, perhaps closer in spirit to the moment of the earlier world war. It evokes the ambiance of long-established culture and leisured detachment from the world's traumas that Shaw generates. As Eric Bentley observed of Shaw's disquisitory works, their plots do not drive the plays; rather, their dialogue and ideas do (88). Much the same could be said of *Springs Eternal.* The misunderstanding surrounding what has happened with Stewie and Dottie fills act 1. As it turns out, Stew was simply assisting Dottie to track down and elope with

Harold, Owen and Harry's son. The clarification of the action sets up the younger man as a central character for the play's second half. The play then focuses our attention on Harold's ambivalence to the war, which becomes a major point for discussion.

These plot developments primarily provide opportunities for Glaspell's characters to explore their relationships to one another and to the conflict abroad. Each figure represents a distinct social stance as well as a personal perspective on national concerns, ranging from Owen's ex-wife's, Harry's, belief that all the play's events revolve around her to Owen's detached despair about the future he had once envisioned to Dr. Bill's fierce support of the soldiers he has recently left at the front. Like Shaw's war-era play, *Springs Eternal* reveals pointedly the selfish preoccupation of some segments of American society, even as, ironically, they represent what the soldiers are fighting so valiantly to protect.

Glaspell's brittle repartee within the familial environment reveals a resemblance to the work of Coward, whose popularity was at its height in the 1930s and 1940s. Glaspell's Harry, whose social standing and self-absorption seem her sole occupations, would fit well in a play like Coward's *Easy Virtue* (1925), which explores the hypocrisy behind conventional ideas of morality and social consciousness. Glaspell gives the play's strongest comic speeches to Margaret, however. In her scene with young Dr. Bill in act 1 she explains the imminent arrival of multiple family members:

> Higgenbothem is a tree of many branches, and each twig attracts to itself people who will travel hundreds of miles—sleepless and hungry—that they may finally sit in this room. With other twigs. (1.3)

Margaret reveals that she once claimed the house was infested with rats in order to get rid of a woman whom Thayer, Dottie's father, did not want to see because he had another woman there with him.

Bill: Darn shame a girl like Dottie should have a father who is no good.
Margaret: Why whatever gave you the idea he is no good? Thayer is a wonderful man. Toledo, Ohio, would collapse without him. How do you encourage rats?

(1.6)

The sharp wit Margaret demonstrates at the opening, however, is not sustained in the play. Personal complications, particularly Owen's renewed affection for his ex-wife, begin to affect her too strongly, and the war becomes too immediate to the plot to allow Glaspell to perpetuate such entertaining yet superficial dialogue.

Although the action of *Springs Eternal* takes place entirely during World War II, the ideological resonances from World War I make the play seem to exist in two time frames. J. B. Priestly used this same duality to structure his 1937 drama, *Time and the Conways,* the action of which begins in 1919, leaps forward to 1938, then returns to 1919. By taking us from the end of the "Great War" to the beginning of the latest world conflict, Priestley shows vividly how the bright hopes of the 1910s give way to a sense of hopelessness by the late 1930s. Glaspell's focus on the characters of Owen's generation allows her to depict a similar decline, while her portraits of Harold and Freddie show, perhaps ironically, how the young continue to find hope despite the record of history.

Glaspell sets the work in October 1943 (1.1). World War II hostilities date from four years earlier, specifically Germany's invasion of Poland in 1939. The United States had initially decided to maintain neutrality but began providing material support to Great Britain in its efforts against Germany in 1940. Yet the attack on Pearl Harbor on 7 December 1941 and the 8 December declaration of war against Japan ended America's noncombative status. United States forces were soon involved in the war in both the Pacific and European arenas. The invasion of North Africa by the British and Americans late in 1942 led to one of the first decisive victories for the Allies. During the summer of 1943 United States troops entered Europe, with attention focused particularly on Italy in the period immediately preceding the setting of *Springs Eternal* ("World War II" 987–1012).

Given these two distinct yet strategically related arenas of combat, the Pacific and Europe, it is noteworthy that Glaspell chooses to emphasize the Pacific conflict as the dominant locus of hostility. With only the passing reference to Africa in connection with Dr. Bill (1.7), the play foregrounds the battles in the Pacific and the attack on Pearl Harbor (1.18), where the offstage character Freddie Soames, the son of the Higgenbothem's housekeeper, is stationed. Early in act 1 we learn from his mother that Freddie is "way off on those islands. . . . A terrible place for an American boy to be—all jungles—and Japs" (1.16). In a study of *American Society in Wartime,* coincidentally published in October 1943, anthropologist Robert Redfield analyzes the attitudes of Americans toward their adversaries:

> We do not feel them [the Japanese] to be part of us as we feel the Czechs, the Poles, the Italians, and, indeed, the Germans to be part of us. . . . For, in a way which Italians and Germans do not represent, the Japanese are our enemies. . . . The pain we suffered at Pearl Harbor . . . turns again within us when we see a face or hear a name that stands for our Japanese enemies. We distinguish Nazis from Germans. Not all Italians are followers of Mussolini. . . . But the Japanese are all "Japs." (149)

Although Glaspell accurately captures this tone in the play's debates on the war, it is surprising that she should focus attention so exclusively on this aspect of the conflict, particularly to the virtual exclusion of Hitler, the Nazis, Mussolini, the Fascists, or other elements of the Axis powers.[5] One might wonder why Glaspell chose to avoid incorporating the European side to the war, especially given Americans' growing cognizance of the atrocities being committed there. Although it is impossible to determine her motives exactly, it is interesting to juxtapose her work to the issues raised in such studies as *American Society in Wartime.* In another essay from that volume sociologist Robert Park discusses the "racial ideologies" dominant during the war, comments that resonate with the analysis of the position of Japanese Americans offered by Redfield. Taken together, the two articles intimate that American hostility to the Japanese was a much more unifying force than antagonism toward other nationalities, which was harder for America to generalize, in part given its Anglo-Saxon heritage (Park 180–81).

If we consider *Springs Eternal* as one of Glaspell's contributions to the war effort, it would make sense that she would use plot and character details that she perceived as being in line with such "unifying forces" as Park identifies, even though this may suggest an acquiescence to racism. As Alan Brinkley observes, World War I depicted the enemy "as a race, a people," whereas World War II contained both racial (Japanese) and political (fascist and totalitarian) dimensions (321). According to Brinkley:

> In the 1930s, most liberals considered questions of racial, ethnic, or gender difference of distinctly secondary importance. . . . By 1945 that was beginning to change. One sign of that change was the remarkable reception among liberals of Gunnar Myrdal's *An American Dilemma,* published in 1944. Myrdal identified race as the one issue most likely to shape and perplex the American future. (317)

Glaspell may have intuited that racial concerns were generally on the ascendancy in the United States and crafted her plot accordingly.

Marcia Noe details another, more poignant contribution to the war effort, however: Glaspell's donation of the memorial plaque to her husband, Jig Cook, that Eugene O'Neill had ordered for the original Provincetown Playhouse building. Glaspell told the *Provincetown Advocate:*

> Here is twelve pounds of bronze resting in this house as a memorial when the America he loved, as we all love it, has desperate need of the metal in winning the war and shaping the better world of his old dream. (Qtd. in Noe, *Critical Biography* 213)

The visionary fervor of Owen, Freddie, and others in the play resonates with Glaspell's understanding of her late husband's own dream. Cook's belief in the chosen status of artists in shaping the future of the country meshes with the general national conviction that America was "a special moral force in the world" (Brinkley 323). Brinkley points to publishing magnate Henry Luce's 1941 book, *The American Century,* as encapsulating the country's sense of destiny and superiority in the world, which coincides directly with the belief in national mission promulgated officially during the war (323–24).

Glaspell's play is not so much about the war itself, however, as about how jaded and complacent some Americans had become in the generation since World War I. "The better world" of Cook's and his generation's "old dream" seems no longer to galvanize them; their hope for the future has given way to quotidian and narrow personal interests or a sense of despair. *Springs Eternal* also demonstrates how American ideology had evolved between the wars, such that the radical positions espoused in the 1910s and demonstrated so forcefully by Glaspell in *Inheritors,* now require serious reconsideration just twenty-five years later. One might even think that Glaspell took the complacency reflected in some of the reviews of the 1927 revival of *Inheritors* in New York as the attitudinal background for this later work.[6] Some main points for comparison between these war plays (and the eras they represent) include their depictions of conscientious objection, their characterizations of an outspoken radical, their voicing of opposition or ambivalence to the war, and their demonstrations of commitment to the principle of free speech.

Glaspell establishes the war context of *Springs Eternal* from the opening scene, drawing some faintly humorous connections between the potentially acrimonious family "pow-wow" to ensue and the campaign abroad (1.5). Margaret explains to Dr. Bill that he may be needed for "errands of mercy—blood transfusions, no doubt" (1.4), particularly since "Evelyn, the mother—the acting step-mother [of Dottie]—ranks terrifically in the Red Cross, and she's coming" (1.3). Yet Glaspell shortly continues this motif more sympathetically, with a moving depiction by Bill of the donated blood actually used in the war. The doctor describes the soldiers thinking about the donors and what they were doing at home at that moment, concluding, "It's quite a bond" (1.9). This "bond of blood" makes literal the racial/ethnic connections between Americans at home and their forces abroad, filtered through the anti-Japanese sentiments that fueled the conflict. Glaspell works throughout the play to establish the link between "over there" and "back here." She depicts both the importance of the image of America and democracy the soldiers so desperately need to sustain morale and the reality of ambivalence many at home feel whose lives have not been directly touched by the conflict. In act 3 Harry expresses a clichéd opinion that is really her rationalization for doing nothing different in wartime: "Well, the war is awful, but we do have to go on with our lives. . . . I say it is our duty to go on with our lives, so what the boys are fighting for will be right here for them when they come back" (3.9). Margaret sympathetically but frankly expresses the dilemma of her generation for the soldier-doctor:

> You want us to go out and stand in the mud when there is no mud? I'm sorry. I do see how you feel. You want us to be different. But people pretty well formed in their lives don't change overnight—not even for a war. (1.8)

Glaspell balances the seeming insensitivity of this attitude, however, with the revelation of Margaret's deep commitment to helping others.

In the last act, in a scene between her and Stew, we learn that Margaret has quietly been donating her family money to worthy causes over the years, to the point that she is no longer able to augment her husband Owen's modest income from "editorial work, the university, and of course the books and articles" with earnings from her inheritance (3.5). She has determined that she must get a job, a detail that strengthens the nexus of association among women, independence, and their own financial capabilities throughout Glaspell's work.[7]

Although Margaret emerges as the most sympathetic and insightful member of the family, many of the characters nevertheless look to Owen for answers to their questions about the war and its impact on the future. Owen, reflecting on his opus *World of Tomorrow,* reveals disillusionment with the present:

Owen: This is the tomorrow of that book. And—look at it.
Mrs. Soames: (*puzzled*) You mean it isn't *your* tomorrow. Not the one you were expecting.
Owen: Not the one I was—let us say, hoping for.

(1.15)

Owen maintains that "this home of the human race is *one.* You've got to think it as one—or be damned," a view that suggests he is opposed to the racial hatred expressed toward the Japanese (1.18). Yet Owen seems incapable of doing any further meaningful work to ensure that future. Despite the influence others tell him he still exerts, Owen sees that it is the younger generation who must act. Stew, however, feels Owen can still be a vital force for social change, and he is particularly critical of Owen in act 1:

> You have degenerated to a wise-cracking stuffed shirt of a pompous ass. But *once* you spoke the truth and I'll have you know there are a few of us

left who believe in old-fashioned American democracy and will *practice* it—at enormous sacrifice. (1.28)

Owen feels a great deal of guilt about his work, believing he "brought on the war," meaning his "generation, and particularly those people in it who were supposed to be thinking things out." But Mrs. Soames, whose son Freddie attributes his enlistment to the idealism and influence of *World of Tomorrow,* insists it is "just the *other* way. . . . Most people just made all the money they could. You thought about making the world better" (1.17).

One of the most serious problems with *Springs Eternal* is a general lack of specificity about the content or direction of the views expressed by Owen, which leads to a philosophical vagueness throughout the work, particularly for readers generations removed from life during the war. As a radical thinker who came to maturity during the period of World War I, Owen might be assumed to be sympathetic with socialist ideology and possibly to hold a utopian vision of world equality and real democracy. These kinds of idealistic projections could be embraced in turn by those feeling it was America's duty to help make that world by defeating totalitarian and repressive regimes. Yet there is also a strong current of defeatism in Owen, a sense that "he is not of this time" and that his ideas have little place in current affairs (3.6). Stew expresses this sentiment most clearly: "We *forget* so much. Forget what we were going to be" (2.33). *Springs Eternal* evokes a strong sense of generational split between the younger and older characters, an age difference Glaspell herself might well have felt at this time. In the 1910s she and her fellow radicals were at the forefront of activism, and her stage could be the site of genuine political critique. Now, however, she was part of Owen's generation, perhaps questioning both the impact of her earlier work and her potential to make any further meaningful cultural or political contributions. In *Springs Eternal* it is as if the natural distinctions between adults and youth have been magnified exponentially by the tumult of world events between the wars, making the gap between them far broader than it otherwise might have been.[8]

Glaspell oscillates between these more serious philosophical and political debates and her society-comedy plot through the device of the presumed elopement. Langner observed that the draft exhibited a structural break midway through act 2: the point at which the comedy of errors—accidental and purposive—gives way to more serious considerations of Harold, Freddie, and the war. Glaspell attempted to keep both dramatic techniques in balance throughout the work's second half, interjecting comic relief primarily through the character of Harry, Stew's inquisitive and class-conscious wife. Obsessed with her ability to control men's affections, Harry tries to make Owen love her again and cannot believe Stew would leave her for an inconsequential girl like Dottie.

   Glaspell also uses a class theme in her effort to accomplish comic continuity. Owen and Margaret decide to keep Harry as uninformed as possible
about the family developments and to portray Dr. Bill, who has already been let
in on quite a few family details, as a plumber. They know Harry will have nothing to do with the working class, a device that generates some humor until
Harry is undeceived about Bill's identity. In the second act Owen makes another attempt to keep Harry on the sidelines, by convincing her to write her
memoirs. She remains occupied with this project for quite a while, reentering
with a stack of manuscript pages and a working title, "I Wear Pink" (2.14), so
named for a childhood battle over the color of a dress that she feels trauma-
tized her for life (2.3). Glaspell's depiction of Harry and her self-absorption,
which reaches its apex in her autobiography, can be read synecdochically as an
indictment of all those fixated on the minutiae of their own lives while the battle for the democratic world raged around them.
   Glaspell puts a subtler spin on the play's theme of snobbery through the
exchanges of Owen and his housekeeper, Mrs. Soames. She depicts Owen as
condescending and intellectually arrogant, especially to the unschooled servant, whose folksy wisdom nevertheless repeatedly undercuts his rhetorical
flourishes:

Mrs. Soames: (with a sigh). Some things I just never will understand. Like
      why you would be writing in languages that are dead.
Owen: (with a little laugh, trying to regain his more usual manner). I'm not
      actually writing in them. But about them.
Mrs. Soames: And there are those—at this time—want to read about lan-
      guages that are dead?
Owen: Yes, I think so—though mostly they are old and tired.
Mrs. Soames: I should think that would be all right for a person who
      couldn't do anything else. Or in odd moments, maybe—like playing
      checkers. . . . Those boys—so many of them. They must be wondering
      and wondering why they are there—those far and heathen places. . . .
      I'm afraid lots of them don't exactly know what it's all about. They're
      good boys—they went because it was their duty. But wouldn't it be
      awful to be doing your duty, and maybe losing your life, all the time
      hardly knowing why you were doing it. Knowing in a way, but not—all
      lighted up about it. You could do that. And that's why I don't under-
      stand the dead languages—for the old and tired, at just this time. I
      should think you would want to speak to the boys, Mr. Higgenbothem.
      In a language they could understand.

                                                              (2.8–9)

Glaspell portrays Mrs. Soames sympathetically and vividly. Although her son
Freddie commands much of our attention, as the symbolic, representative sol-

dier, his mother also emerges as an important figure in the play, not only for her position as the mouthpiece for the average American but also as a strong, independent woman who has triumphed over considerable odds. Soon after we learn that Freddie has been captured by the Japanese and is now a prisoner of war, we also hear more about their family background:

Mrs. Soames: [Freddie has] not had a father—not since he was three years old.
Bill: You—supported him, I suppose?
Mrs. Soames: (*with surprise for such a question*) Certainly I supported him. What would you expect me to do?
Harry: How did you do it, Mrs. Soames? I always say a woman is at such a disadvantage.
Mrs. Soames: Why, I never thought I was at a disadvantage. I just did things there were to be done. Sometimes it was sewing—then again it might be washing. Or just helping out—like I've done here.

(2.34)

Mrs. Soames's matter-of-fact countering of both the classist and sexist assumptions behind the others' questions epitomizes the way Glaspell imbues all her dramas with a range of political themes on both the societal and personal levels. Mrs. Soames's achievements as a single mother, providing financial security for her son as well as raising him successfully in her working-class environment, exemplify the playwright's feminist and democratic sympathies. Ironically, of course, Glaspell shows us that the good mothers are just as likely to lose their sons as any other mother in such times of national crisis. Nevertheless, the late plot point of Margaret's need to enter the workforce allows Glaspell to transcend class divisions to form an important alliance between women in the play who are making significant contributions to society as workers, wives, and mothers.

In the play's most affecting scene Dottie suggests that Mrs. Soames "introduce us to Freddie" so that they all can have a better sense of the captured soldier (2.35). His mother then creates a vivid image of the youth by sharing both physical and personal details about him: what he looks like, what sports he played as a boy, how he came to have a girlfriend. Amazed at the power of this seance-like summoning, she exclaims, "Why—we almost did it. Almost brought Freddie into this room" (2.37).

Yet Glaspell also complicates Mrs. Soames's character by making her the voice of conventional decorum in the play, much as she had done with Madeline's loving aunt in *Inheritors*. Mrs. Soames expresses dismay at the Higgenbothem's tacit approval of the affair between Stew and Dottie. She contrasts such loose behavior to her own innocent romantic past and her son's more proper relationship with the young woman named Esther, who works in

Oswego (2.35–37). She threatens to leave their employ due to "the morality" (or lack thereof) the family displays. Owen counters with an argument based on the doctrine of free speech, one of Glaspell's primary concerns in earlier works such as *Inheritors:*

> I question the morality of a statement you made a little while back. . . . [U]nder the Constitution you have a right to your mistaken opinions. But there is a certain rigidity in you, Mrs. Soames, which to my mind does not evoke morality. . . . Now you said, Right is right and wrong is wrong. Where did you ever get that idea? . . . And who is to hand down the decisions? . . . There is conflict. Always there are decisions to be made, and when you do one thing that is right it may be at the expense of something far more important. Thus in doing right you do wrong. (2.5–7)

Glaspell soon juxtaposes these issues of free speech to another related moral question: Harry reveals that her son Harold has been incarcerated for his stance as a conscientious objector (2.15–16), a form of imprisonment she links to Freddie's status as a prisoner of war.

One major contrast between *Inheritors* and *Springs Eternal* emerges through the depiction of Harold's decision to take a formal stance against the conflict. Fred Jordan, the conscientious objector who is the absent center in *Inheritors*, is made a martyr figure for his beliefs, but in the later play Freddie, a soldier, is the idealized individual, and not Harold. Glaspell suggests that such choices cannot be viewed in the same light for World War I as for World War II. Margaret observes of Harold, "He must believe it—it's not a very popular stand," and Harry concludes, "Well, anyway, he won't be shot" (2.16), attitudes quite different from those expressed in the earlier drama.

As with the portrait of conscientious objection in *Inheritors*, Glaspell here also uses factual details to add to the realism of the milieu. Harry explains that her son is currently in New Hampshire chopping trees, an indication that he may be in one of the Civilian Public Service camps, established by legislation in 1940 so that "objectors who could not accept noncombatant service under military authority . . . [could] perform work of 'national importance'" (Schlissel 215). According to historian Lillian Schlissel:

> Of the first twenty-five camps set up, twelve were under the Forestry Service, eleven under the Soil Conservation Service, and two under the National Park Service. Between May, 1941, and March, 1947, 11,950 objectors worked at sixty-seven camps on such projects as soil erosion control, reforestation, and agricultural experimentation. (215)

Harry has already accused Owen of converting their son to communism, a detail that also has bearing on the new government attitude to conscientious objectors (1.13). Between the wars much more understanding seems to have developed in Washington on this issue, as demonstrated in this transcript of testimony before the Congressional Subcommittee on Conscientious Objectors, held immediately after Pearl Harbor (Schlissel 225).

Mr. Fitzpatrick: Suppose we get a man who does not belong to any of these religious orders but he is just an ordinary man, and he is a conscientious objector?

General Hershey: Well, that is where the problem comes up. Now, 70 percent of these fellows belong to the so-called historical creeds. The other 30 percent belong to about 140 different "collections" and "noncollections." The law does not give any consideration whatsoever to the conscientious objector unless his objection is founded on religious training and belief. . . . What is religion? is a difficult thing to say. A man perhaps has read, and whether it is religion—if he comes up and says, "I am a Communist" or "I am a Socialist" . . . A man perhaps has been something, in his past, and we have tried to be rather open-minded on what is "religion."

(Qtd. in Schlissel 227–28)

Although not a communist, as Harry fears, Harold seems to fit within the parameters, outlined in such testimony, of a man following his private convictions. Unlike the situation Glaspell depicts in *Inheritors,* however, there is no evidence in this play of his mistreatment or details involving any other objectors. Harold's choices appear much more personal, with little political force; it does not seem that his stance emerged from a broader set of convictions or principles. The consequences of his actions involve his family exclusively, rather than having repercussions on others or on his community. Glaspell repeats this turn toward the personal and familial, with social and political concerns in the background, in all three of her post–Provincetown Players dramas. The extremity of the war as a backdrop for this play, however, throws her change of dramaturgical focus into relief; despite the play's other weaknesses, she is more able here to integrate the shift with her theme, characterizations, and dialogue. Harold must develop from a young man making unexamined personal choices to one who takes action from a socially conscious perspective.

At the end of act 2 Glaspell unravels the Higgenbothem's confusion about the activities of Dottie and Stew, whom they believe have tried to elope on two occasions, inexplicably to no avail. The only result of their efforts appears to have been the exhaustion of Stew's gasoline rations for the month. Stew and Dottie have actually been tracking Harold, however, who has apparently been moved around from camp to camp by the government. Dottie, who had left a cryptic note concerning her intention to elope and imminent departure with Stew, had actually planned to marry Harold with Stew's assistance. These details conveniently resolve the questions of morality.[9]

Harold, who enters near the end of the second act, is an artist. Glaspell may have made this choice as a gesture toward her relationship with Norman Matson and the play they wrote together, *The Comic Artist*, or, it may be another Cowardesque coincidence, as his plays often feature an artist figure out of place in the larger world of the play. Harold reveals:

> I never had the feeling anybody believed in me. I thought this was kind of funny—because I believed in myself. But it made me feel—well, there was me—by myself—and then there were the rest of you with each other—or that was the way it seemed to me. I liked you—loved you, I guess—but I never felt right there with you. I suppose that's why I love my pictures—feel right there with them. (*Pausing to enjoy this*) It's a nice feeling. (3.20)

Harold is seen painting as act 3 opens, an activity his father despises, as he links it to the cowardice he feels his son's objector stance thinly masks. Entering the room and seeing Harold's easel on his own work table, Owen explodes:

> He's been here, I see. So this is what my books are for! My papers—! (*roaring*) Chaos! And for *what?* (*Snatching the picture*) Sunflowers!—is that what I see? How beautiful! Sunflowers against the woodshed—*that's* how we'll win the war. We'll free Freddie with a nice picture of—It's an infernal daub! (*Tearing it*) *That* for your pictures—you little coward! Confounded impertinent—(*Tearing it again—again*) (3.7)

But Margaret disagrees, incorporating Harold's passion into the "over there" / "back here" schema of the drama:

> Do you know what Freddie was fighting for?—one of the things got him in the hands of the Japanese? He was fighting for Harold's right to paint sunflowers against a shed—if that was what he wanted to do! If *anything* you ever said was true—a man has a right to be the thing which in an honest heart he is. He doesn't *have* to be—what Hitler or his own dear father tells him to be! (3.7)

Moving toward a resolution between Harold and his father, as well as toward a conclusion for the play, Glaspell gives Harold a series of speeches explaining his initial decisions:

> I think it was because I felt all by myself that I never could kill any-
> thing. . . . So then the war came and how could I go to the war and kill men?
> Maybe the man I would kill had something like my pictures—something
> he loved—all by himself. So I became a conscientious objector. (3.20)

But Harold continues with his narrative, showing how his views have recently
evolved:

> Dottie began sending me the telegrams—how she believed in me and we
> would stand together against the world. But when she believed in me I
> didn't have to stand against the world—because I was in it. . . . Now I'm
> in the Army. (3.20–21)

With this surprising about-face, we realize how Harold could actually be
at the Higgenbothem home—a question that has remained unasked throughout the act but would certainly have been in the minds of an audience. He is
not AWOL, as we might have assumed, but, rather, en route to begin his training as an enlisted soldier. Harold finishes his explanation by revealing the conclusions he has reached about this startling change of mind:

> I don't think I'm abandoning my principles. Isn't there a difference be-
> tween principles and just hating to do a thing? You see, all the time I
> knew it had to be done by somebody. So would it be right for somebody
> else to do it for me—when maybe he wouldn't like it any better than I
> did? (3.22)

Harold thereby unknowingly echoes his father's statement from act 2, which
was intended to rebut Harry's accusation of Owen's having influenced their
son: "I have *always* said we had to fight this war" (2.16). This acknowledgment
reveals the critical philosophical shift Owen and other radicals who opposed
World War I have undergone since that prior conflict. Glaspell appears to have
felt it was very important to convey this new perspective, to demonstrate that
her central characters support the war effort, but she may not have accomplished this as clearly or forcefully as she had wished.

These developments soon resolve one set of conflicts in the play: the immediate fate of Harold and his relationship with his parents. This move allows
Glaspell to focus all the characters' attention on the play's other concerns.
Harold, realizing Dottie does not really love him, but has simply been a true
friend in her commitment to him and his ideals, suggests that she marry Dr.
Bill,[10] the fitting conclusion to the romance that has been developing between
them throughout the work.

Harold urges his father to write another book, not about the dead languages with which he has recently been occupying himself but another visionary work such as *World of Tomorrow* that "ought to fix it so there won't be any more wars" (3.22). In *Bernice* Glaspell also had the father character involved in ancient languages. He explains that his deceased daughter "laughed at my spending the whole time of the war studying Sanscrit. . . . [I]n a world that won't have visions—why not study Sanscrit while such a world is being made over—into another such world" (163). It would seem that, in revisiting this character trope, Glaspell wanted to provide a clearer vision for Owen to express, perhaps by emphasizing the connection between ideas and the history of the language used to convey them. Sadly, however, she was not able to capture this dramatically. Harold's suggestion of another book reintroduces the theme of generational contrasts that has dominated the play; we sense that Harold may be the character who will someday be able to articulate the hopes of his own generation. But his plea also demonstrates Glaspell's (naive?) faith in the power of the written word, an impact that would soon give way to the force of other media on American society.

In addition to noting the distinctions between the older and younger characters and the values they represent, Glaspell extends these differences to issues facing the culture at large. If the attitude of Harold toward his participation in the war is only the most obvious of changes separating the period of World War I from the play's moment, there are also subtler elements of that evolution threaded throughout the work. *Springs Eternal* seems to imply the necessity of change, with an acknowledgment of the value of the past. In Mrs. Soames's words, "There's so much we're used to and wouldn't want to lose" (3.26). Still, at the end of the play all the characters are focused on the future and the bright potential it holds, the only viewpoint that will help them get through this most difficult of times. While Bill leads the group in a toast to the "Brave Old World," he also encourages them to look ahead, and the curtain falls on the titular line, "But hope springs eternal as I give you—" (3.34).

Bill's voicing of the title's missing word *hope*—an absent force as central as a character—draws our attention to its talismanic nature in the play and perhaps to Glaspell's sense of its importance for America in the middle of war. It is difficult at this remove to know whether Lawrence Langner's contention that "most of us have . . . arrived at the conclusion [the characters and the play reach] two or three years ago" was indeed an accurate appraisal of current opinion. We know now, of course, that many American writers were at work during this same period generating major works of fiction, poetry, and drama in an effort to process the tumultuous and devastating impact of the war and that the conflict continues to affect both global cultural production and world affairs.

Yet, as Langner observed, "This isn't a good reason for not doing a play."

When a dramatist has written strong and provocative pieces that have had great impact in the theater, it is saddening to realize that her last work is not of that same caliber. We don't know if Langner ever had the conversation with her he proposed; I suspect he did not. It seems fairly clear that he saw the work was not stageworthy, and obviously Glaspell decided against trying to make it so. The play holds echoes of her earlier, more powerful work, however, in its attempt to capture a range of opinions on a compelling political issue and in its balance of character types, including the strong female figures of Margaret and Mrs. Soames. Its moments of wry humor and its efforts to capture the current ethos both dialogically and situationally remind us in brief flashes of what she could accomplish for the stage. Although *Springs Eternal* may not enhance, it confirms Glaspell's position as an important American playwright.

Afterword

Rather than bring this book to a conclusion by rendering exactly the kind of mastery-assuming synthetic summations or totalizing aesthetic judgments of Glaspell's dramaturgy that I have resisted throughout this study, I prefer simply to leave this project with a reiteration of my original goal: to establish some of the historical and critical contexts for her theatrical writing. In doing so, I hope that this ending can mark a beginning for others' scholarship and staging of Glaspell's still fascinating and complex dramas. Many questions remain, and many avenues of inquiry lie uncharted.

I do want to linger, however, on two cruxes—one of style and one of content—that recurred throughout my readings of Glaspell criticism. Precisely because of their prominence, these issues merit if not resolution then at least some final consideration. While it would be misleading to highlight these critical quandaries as alone the most salient for Glaspell studies, they are nevertheless germane to any exploration of how and why she wrote as she did.

The first of these we might deem the bête noir of her theatrical reviewers: what they called the overly "literary" quality of her plays. Even Glaspell's most glowing reviews often make this accusation, although the literary tendency in her writing clearly bothered some journalists more than others. Perhaps because of the constraints placed upon their commentary by strict word limits or perhaps because they assumed their readership shared their sensibilities, Glaspell's reviewers never quite defined or illustrated what they meant by the term *literary*. Nevertheless, they intoned it like a mantra at the première of each new piece. In his overview of *Alison's House*, in *The Best Plays of 1930–31*, Burns Mantle finally provides one explanation of his colleagues' complaint:

> Alison's House is what drama critics most frequently describe as a literary play. Meaning, usually, that it is burdened with intelligence, a generally undramatic story and a superabundance of stiff dialogue. ("Alison's House" 223)

Mantle's wry gloss neatly exposes what he believes are the shallow preferences of many reviewers: they don't want to think; they want to be entertained by a ripping plot; and they want easy—perhaps colloquial or at least more succinct and straightforward—stage speech. Glaspell, of course, resisted all of this, maintaining her commitment to the new American theater that she, Cook, and their group envisioned at the inception of the Provincetown Players. Theirs was to be a theater of ideas and exploration, of commitment and purpose, of challenge. The slim record we have of her cohorts' responses to her plays, such as the exchanges over *Bernice* in the *Little Review* and the analyses of *The Verge* by Ruth Hale in the *New York Times,* by her fellow bohemians in the *Greenwich Villager,* and from the Heterodites, confirms the success of her efforts to counter the vacuous quality of the commercial stage. Yet these colleagues, too, sometimes gesture toward a concern with lengthy speeches and abstract diction in her plays. Nevertheless, their ringing endorsements of her themes and dramaturgical style suggest that she played a vital role in their battle to place the theater at the center of national culture.

Veronica Makowsky attributes the subsequent erasure of Glaspell's importance to the development of the American theater to the trajectory of high modernism. Makowsky states ringingly that the theater "incorporated her . . . innovations, and proceeded to ignore their creator. It made her reputation, but only to repudiate it" ("Susan Glaspell" 49). We might ask, virtually rhetorically, if there are not connections among this history of American modernism, the coding of Glaspell's dramaturgy by the mainstream press as too literary and her role as a woman playwright at a time and in a place that were, outside the confines of her bohemian community, less than welcoming of female, let alone feminist, incursions? It seems reasonable to pose some basic questions: How many other women playwrights of Glaspell's era attempted to dramatize women's speech and women's lives so adventurously or successfully? How many confronted national concerns and risked prosecution in the effort to publicize burning political issues? Might not the struggle to find the right language, or the outpouring of language in the urgency of expression, accompany the compulsion to represent what had not been represented—to dare to say what was elsewhere being either politically or institutionally suppressed? It is, perhaps, too easy to suggest that the appraisal of Glaspell's dramaturgy has been caught between the Scylla of the historical dismissal of women playwrights and the Charybdis of more recent performance theory that has narrowly defined what theater can be called "feminist." Between these critical maelstroms may lie a place for a measured evaluation of Glaspell's theatrical writing.

Contextualizing Glaspell's feminism thus emerges as the second crux for this closing discussion as well as a more compelling element of the revaluation of her dramaturgy. While a number of critics have, over the years, questioned whether Glaspell was a feminist, or the extent of her feminism, the work of Marcia Noe most clearly exemplifies the debate. Noe, whose dissertation and subsequent monograph, *Susan Glaspell: Voice from the Heartland,* made early, invaluable contributions to Glaspell studies, asserts, "First and foremost, Susan Glaspell was not a feminist" (*Susan Glaspell* 10). She bases this statement in part on her correspondence with Glaspell's stepdaughter, Nilla Cook, who wrote of Glaspell:

> She subordinated herself completely, always to the man of the moment, was *anything* but a feminist, and was always sad when work of her own succeeded more than my father's. (Qtd. in *Susan Glaspell* 10)

Noe further maintains:

> It would be . . . a distortion to portray her as a socialist or even a liberal activist. . . . Her sympathy with liberal causes rarely moved her to political action; her one sustained venture into left-wing politics was her work for the Federal Theater Project as Director of the Midwest Play Bureau, a position she held for less than two years. (*Susan Glaspell* 9–10)

Instead, Noe accounts for Glaspell's creativity by identifying her as an "idealist" (10), a rubric that must support all the various positions Glaspell seems to project through her writing. But Noe never clarifies how she can claim that *Trifles,* for example, was then "written from a feminist point of view" (33).

This apparent contradiction of her denial of Glaspell as a feminist may stem from an incomplete exploration of the relationship among Glaspell's narrative voice and technique, her biography, and her cultural moment. If Noe means that Glaspell employed perspectives in her writing that were distinct from her own politics, personal or social, she does not say so explicitly. Noe separates Glaspell's creativity from her other activities, such as her connection with the Federal Theater Project, deeming only the latter "political." But, if we look at her pursuits more holistically, we may conclude that Glaspell chose her writing, particularly her drama, as her political platform, her form of activism. Admittedly, she was not directly involved in many of the protest activities of her colleagues in Greenwich Village. Still, the public presentation of her concerns in a widely viewed arena such as the theater must be seen as a political act. Furthermore, it seems illogical to separate the political content of her writing in such works as *Inheritors* from the act of writing itself, somehow emptying only the latter of its agency.

To call Glaspell a political dramatist is not, however, the same as deeming her a feminist playwright. As scholarly debates of the past two decades demonstrate, there is no longer a sense of a monolithic "feminism" but, rather, multiple "feminisms" that emanate from a range of subject positions in their social and historical contexts. They may indeed conflict with one another. One of the problems with Noe's analysis, and her use of Nilla Cook's appraisal, is Noe's omission of her own (or any questioning of Nilla Cook's) definition of *feminism*. For Nilla Cook it seems that Glaspell's "subordinate" relations with men contradicted the stepdaughter's sense of feminism. Noe seems to have accepted this view yet nevertheless proposes Glaspell's ability to write from a feminist perspective. A review of the historical context for early-twentieth-century feminism may help reconcile this seeming contradiction.

If one considers the conflicts faced by middle-class, heterosexual women in the late Victorian and early Modern eras, who struggled between the social roles conveyed to them and their emerging sense of individuality and potential, one may better understand Glaspell's personal and professional decisions as well as her concern with women in that cultural moment.[1] In other words, the fact that Glaspell gave priority to her husband's needs, desires, and creativity does not automatically exclude her from being considered a feminist, given the historical dynamics of feminism for women in the United States. The tensions one perceives between the politics of her writing and her life choices are indeed endemic to her era. In her analysis of the absent female characters in Glaspell's dramaturgy Susan Kattwinkel reads these figures as projections of Glaspell's own "battle" between "nineteenth-century Victorianism" and "modern feminism" (41), in essence the opposition of women's selflessness and selfishness. Kattwinkel sees this conflict played out in such critical statements as those of Noe and Nilla Cook, who may have equated feminism with this sense of independence and selfishness. Furthermore, Kattwinkel suggests, the inconclusive endings of Glaspell's plays can be linked to her awareness of the indeterminacy in women's lives at this transitional cultural moment (53).

The issue of Glaspell's "point of view" introduced by Noe raises interesting theoretical questions. *Trifles,* for example, clearly exemplifies Glaspell's attempt to make readers and audiences perceive a situation from both the women's and men's perspectives, as opposed to the exclusively male perspective that feminist criticism has identified as the putative norm. But does redressing this balance qualify Glaspell as feminist? Or do Glaspell's attempts to present both "sides" of an argument qualify her as feminist? Is introducing the female perspective the strategic point for the definition, especially given her efforts to embody both positions theatrically? Or are her subtle subversions of the conventions of realism the all-important distinction?

Rather than privilege some of Glaspell's plays, such as *The Outside* or *The Verge,* as feminist, we may more productively consider Glaspell's feminism as part of her strongly held political convictions. All of Glaspell's dramaturgy is political, particularly as seen within Greenwich Village culture of the early twentieth century. One could argue that to call her a political writer is just as reductive as to call her an idealist, as does Noe, or to say that each play questions "life's meaning," as does Gerhard Bach (37). I would suggest, however, that a construction of Glaspell as a political writer allows for greater flexibility in the critical and theatrical exploration of her work. Moreover, it holds the potential for readers to see important connections between her theater and other components of American history, especially those that may not traditionally have included the arts as part of their discursive arena.

Glaspell's commitment to women is a strong—arguably the strongest—element of her politics. As many of her critics have observed, she places a female character (absent or present) at the center of every play she wrote. Within socialist circles in that era women's concerns were one of many that formed a background to the workers' issues that theoretically dominated the foreground. Significantly, Glaspell rarely dramatized either the problems of the urban working class or the ethnic Other in American culture. Glaspell's embracing of women's concerns is thus a strategic point for positioning her dramaturgy as well as her politics. The women's perspective she highlights in *Trifles*, for example, arises from economic and social considerations that are integral to the entire cultural moment under examination. Moreover, Glaspell's sense of place—of the midwestern, bohemian, and East Coast subcultures among which she traveled—figures strongly in all her writing. We must examine a matrix of regional forces to understand the political configuration of each of her works. Examined collectively, Glaspell's dramas reveal the politics of gender and the politics of place that not only define her writing but also exemplify the status of the American woman writer throughout the first half of the twentieth century.

✧ Notes

Introduction

1. Throughout this introduction I consciously employ the terms *America* and *American* as they have come to be used in a range of disciplines that predate current concern with the imperialist connotations of designations that, in most cases, actually refer exclusively to the United States of America and those living here while nevertheless subsuming a much larger geographical area.

2. Linda Ben-Zvi presents a similar trajectory for Glaspell's career and its critical standing in her essay "Susan Glaspell's Contributions to Contemporary Women Playwrights" (147–48).

3. Veronica Makowsky admirably surveyed tropes in her fiction central to concerns with women's writing in *Susan Glaspell's Century of American Women: A Critical Interpretation of Her Work* (1993).

4. A lengthier discussion of the relationship between Glaspell's writing and her biography appears in the chapter on *The Verge*.

5. Gay Gibson Cima has written recently of the professional and personal obstacles facing professional women critics in nineteenth-century England. Many of her observations can, by extrapolation, be applied to the climate of theater reviewing in both New York and London in the first decades of the twentieth century. See Cima, "'To Be Public as a Genius and Private as a Woman': The Critical Framing of Nineteenth-Century British Woman Playwrights."

6. For a fuller discussion of Glaspell's relationship to the Heterodoxy Club, see the chapter on *Bernice*.

7. See, for example, Christine Dymkowski, "On the Edge: The Plays of Susan Glaspell"; and Susan Kattwinkel, "Absence as a Site for Debate: Modern Feminism and Victorianism in the Plays of Susan Glaspell."

The One-Act Play in America

1. A complete set of the subscription circulars, although unsigned, was most likely written by Cook and resides in the Cook and Glaspell papers in the Berg Collection of the New York Public Library.

2. See, for example, John Corbin, "The One-Act Play"; and Montrose J. Moses, *American Dramatist*.

3. In addition to Cook's championing of the Players' dramas in the season

circulars, see also Maurice Brown, *The Temple of a Living Art.* Brown cofounded the Chicago Little Theatre and writes eloquently of his theatrical vision.

4. For a detailed explanation of their amateur status, see the annual Province-town subscription circulars, probably penned by Cook, in the Cook and Glaspell papers in the Berg Collection of the New York Public Library. In the 1916–17 issue, for example, Cook wrote, "The impelling desire of the group was to establish a stage . . . without submitting to the commercial manager's interpretation of public taste."

5. Many of the Little Theatres dispensed with the class-based seating structure linked to ticket price altogether, partly for democratic reasons and/or their status as amateur enterprises and partly due to the intimate size of their performance spaces, which rendered such distinctions fiscally inappropriate.

6. The contemporary American playwright Sam Shepard has complained of this very critical tendency in the evaluation of his own body of theatrical writing, a large percentage of which is in the one-act form.

7. See Ben-Zvi, "Susan Glaspell and Eugene O'Neill"; and "Susan Glaspell and Eugene O'Neill: The Imagery of Gender"; Larabee, "Meeting the Outside Face to Face."

8. See "Susan Glaspell—Provincetown Playwright."

9. For a longer discussion of this adjudication process, see the section on *The People.*

10. See my essay "The Provincetown Players' Experiments with Realism."

11. In the context of the emerging modern theater in the United States it is hard to separate out these forms and stylistic categories, unlike the situation in Europe, where many elements of the modern theatrical movement began as direct responses to extant stage forms.

Suppressed Desires

1. While Davenport, Iowa, was known for its pockets of advanced views at the time, Glaspell always depicted the Midwest as a generally conservative area.

2. In the chapter "Talking about Sex," in *American Moderns,* Christine Stansell claims that "the theater of sex" in the Village "had little to do with Freud" and that "American habits of talking about sex were, at their inception, derived from other sources," especially before 1920 (302). Based on the writings of Glaspell, Kenton, Eastman, Dell, and others, however, it would appear that the Freudian influence by 1915 was stronger in the Village than Stansell believes and that the bohemians were indeed linking ideas about sexuality to Freudian theory by this time.

3. The play has rarely been viewed politically; in an editorial a few years after its initial production, however, Bobby Edwards remarked, "It is the only blot on the record of the little theater movement that this most foul and insidious of German propaganda [i.e., psychoanalysis] should have been innocently distributed by them" (qtd. in Hoffman 75, *Freudianism and the Literary Mind*).

4. See Larabee, "Death in Delphi: Susan Glaspell and the Companionate Marriage"; and Fishbein, *Rebels in Bohemia: The Radicals of* The Masses, *1911–1917.*

5. For a list of works produced that season by the Washington Square Players, see appendix 2 of the first volume of Bigsby, *Twentieth-Century American Drama,* 300.

6. In this first performance Glaspell took the role of Henrietta Brewster, and Cook played the husband, Stephen.

7. For a sampling of the brief commentary typical of the early New York revivals, see the listings by play title in the bibliography.

8. There is a tradition in theatrical criticism of anonymous or pseudonymous reviewing, sometimes with abbreviations as code names for the critics. In the United States the latter practice was common, for example, in *Variety*. Examples of such pen names for critics can be found throughout this study.

9. Similar sets occur in Rita Wellman's *The Rib Person* and *Funiculi Funicula,* Floyd Dell's *The Angel Intrudes,* Eugene O'Neill's *Before Breakfast,* and Pendleton King's *Cocaine,* among others.

10. The name suggests that Glaspell may have been thinking of either the Irish poet George William Russell (1867–1935), who used the initials *A.E.* as a pseudonym and whose dramas were in the repertoire of the Irish National Theatre, or the British poet A. E. Housman (1859–1936), whose collection of verse, *A Shropshire Lad,* was hugely popular in the early twentieth century.

11. See Kuttner, "A Note on Forgetting." Brill was a New York psychiatrist who had been Freud's American translator since 1908 (Wertheim, *The New York Little Renaissance: Iconoclasm, Modernism, and Nationalism in American Culture, 1908–1917,* 70).

12. It is interesting that Anderson directly continues this discussion with his own thoughts on homosexuality and his ambivalence toward gay men, as if the "psyching" in which Dell and others engaged were intimately connected in his memory with issues of male sexual orientation (339 ff.). Margaret Anderson, editor of the *Little Review,* claims she and her lover/coeditor, Jane Heap, "spent their evenings searching for 'the Achilles heel in everybody's psychic set-up'" (qtd. in Hoffman, *New York Little Renaissance,* 69). Bobby Edwards, a writer and editor of the short-lived Village periodical the *Quill,* included this verse, with its overt reference to gay life, in his longer work, *The Village Epic:*

> Way down south in Greenwich Village
> > In the Freud and Jung and Brill age
> People come with paralysis
> > For the balm of psychoanalysis
> Here the modernist complexes
> > And the intermediate sexes—
> Fairyland's not far from Washington Square.
> > (qtd. in Watson, *Strange Bedfellows* 225)

According to historian George Chauncey, "In the 1920s, Greenwich Village hosted the best-known gay enclave in both the city and the nation" (*Gay New York* 227). Nevertheless, the Provincetown Players principally dramatized heterosexual concerns, and Cook and Glaspell's figuration of Freudian psychology makes no reference to its concern with "intermediacy."

13. See *Inheritors* for Glaspell's engagement with the war and *The Verge* for the connection of the war with psychoanalysis, specifically posttraumatic stress.

14. These parallels also appear quite like the explications provided by Alfred Kuttner, who had written about Freud for the *New Republic* in 1914: "The unconscious, according to Freud, is simply a vast repository, located in some parts of our psychic structure, in which we store the disagreeable" ("Note on Forgetting" 15).

15. The coincidence of both the author of this essay from *McClure's Magazine* and the couple in *Suppressed Desires* having the same last name—Brewster—is tantalizing.

16. Dell, whose essay appears a bit more tongue-in-cheek than Eastman's, also depicts this procedure, adding a list of "popular association or test words":

> purple, sweetheart, floating, crash, velvet, lily, pistol, lead, swan, despair, wound, bugle, hair, foot, thunder, dress, teeth, baby, etc., etc. ("Speaking of Psycho-analysis" 53)

17. See, for example, Hapgood, *A Victorian in the Modern World;* Luhan, *Movers and Shakers;* Dell, *Homecoming.*

18. See, for example, Mabel Dodge Luhan, *Movers and Shakers;* Hutchins Hapgood, *A Victorian in the Modern World;* and Floyd Dell, *Love in Greenwich Village.* Stansell has a lengthy discussion of these issues in section 4 of *American Moderns.*

19. Both pieces deal with issues of infidelity, and are barely disguised biographical pieces. *Constancy* dramatizes the relationship of Mabel Dodge with John Reed; *Enemies* chronicles the stormy relationship of the Neith Boyce and Hutchins Hapgood.

20. This reading, of course, assumes that Stephen is truthfully reporting the analysis; thus, Russell becomes a proponent for the masculine sexual freedom embraced by many Village figures such as Hapgood and Eastman. Glaspell will later consider the darker side of the movement toward modernism and scientific advancement in *The Verge.*

21. See, for example, Floyd Dell's *Homecoming* for a description of his abandonment of open marriage.

Trifles

1. The title referred to a local euphemism for pregnancy, as being "not smart" (Steele, *"Not Smart,"* 254).

2. Glaspell originally drafted, "because my husband . . . made me," but crossed that out and wrote in "forced me to." It is difficult to determine exactly how to interpret these remarks, somewhat humorously or seriously. My instinct is to see them as humor masking real and somewhat difficult memories: the record of Cook and Glaspell's life together shows a pattern of Cook's manipulation of Glaspell and others and Cook's demands that others support his vision.

3. There is a tantalizing connection between Glaspell's narrative of forced dramatic creativity and that of another woman playwright of her era, Mary Macmillan, whose work was first produced in Cincinatti. In the preface to her collection *Short Plays* Macmillan remarks, with a wittily ironic echo of Malvolio: "Some are born dramatists—like Shakespeare, some achieve dramatic construction—like Ibsen, some have drama thrust upon them—like me. . . . I was locked up alone in a room with a crust of bread and a tincup of water and commanded to write a drama that could be produced by five or six women in forty-five minutes without scenery on a stage as big as a good-sized book" (n.p.). Macmillan's volume was published by Stewart and Kidd, which was also Glaspell's publisher, in 1913. While there is no evidence of Glaspell's knowing of Macmillan or her work, the similarities in the depiction of both women's dramatic beginnings are striking. I am grateful to Anne Beck for bringing the work of Macmillan to my attention.

4. I am grateful to Veronica Makowsky for suggesting this latter interpretation.

5. In a letter written from Greece in 1922 to her mother, Glaspell remarks on her return to her "real" vocation, after the "detour" of the theater.

I am glad for myself too [in addition to being glad for Jig's sake that they were in Greece now]; the theatre has always made it hard for me to write, and now I will have a better chance for my own writing. I would like to write another novel, though perhaps I will do some short stories first. (Glaspell Papers, Berg Collection)

6. A more detailed examination of Glaspell's one-acts appears in the opening chapter of this study.

7. For a comparative analysis of the narrative in both genres, see Leonard Mustazza's "Generic Translation and Thematic Shift in Susan Glaspell's *Trifles* and 'A Jury of Her Peers.'" Mustazza argues that, despite their similarities, the story version is superior to the drama.

8. Mary Papke's *Susan Glaspell: A Research and Production Sourcebook* provides a comprehensive overview of criticism on *Trifles* and "Jury" through 1992 and is an invaluable resource for Glaspell scholarship. For readers unfamiliar with this body of writing, I provide the following summary: One of the earliest and strongest streams of Anglo-American feminist criticism champions women authors whose understanding of the realities of women's lives finds compelling representation in their writing. In this vein "Jury" received praise from Elaine Hedges for its "truth about the lives of rural women" (59). She applauds Glaspell's rendering of women in the Midwest for its clarity and accuracy; Marcia Noe makes similar observations in her essay "Region as Metaphor in the Plays of Susan Glaspell."

Other critics focus on the presumed action of the absent Minnie Wright, invoking instead the context of women's commission of serious crime, especially murder. Susan Gubar and Anne Hedin, for example, have used the play as a teaching tool for women in prison, while Ruth Nadelhaft and Linda Williams each read the play against the conventional, patriarchal literary tropes of feminine passivity belied by such violence. Phyllis Mael uses feminism and psychoanalysis to explore the play and its 1981 film adaptation by Sally Heckel, which was nominated for an Academy Award. Drawing on the writing of such influential feminist theorists as Nancy Chodorow and Carol Gilligan, Mael examines Glaspell's evocation of "gender and moral development" ("*Trifles*: The Path to Sisterhood" 283), looking at Mrs. Hale's and Mrs. Peters's responses to the evidence they discover.

A more overtly political and historically oriented group of readings uses the pieces to discuss the inequities in such institutions as the American judicial system and traditional marriage. Karen Alkalay-Gut speaks strongly of "Glaspell's need . . . to empower women to rectify . . . unjust situation[s]" through her "criticism of the legal system" and her "indictment of the social and romantic conventions of society" ("Jury of Her Peers: The Importance of Trifles" 71). Alkalay-Gut also emphasizes the strategic role women's bonding plays for Glaspell in accomplishing these goals. Like many critics, Richard Clarke Sterne sees Glaspell's writing as part of influential, larger cultural trends in the twentieth century; he focuses on the works' sense of injustice as representative of a major movement away from "lucid idealism" in both European and American literature (*Dark Mirror* 243).

Close readings of Glaspell's symbolism and imagery inform virtually every piece on the works. Beverly A. Smith's "Women's Work—*Trifles?*" stands out in this regard and is often mentioned by other scholars. Similarly, Elaine Showalter's discussion of "Piecing and Writing" has been highly influential for its identification of quilting "as a metaphor for the difference between male and female discourse" (241). Feminist scholars have produced a wealth of interpretations of the "trifles"—as the male characters see them—that define Minnie's existence in the Wright household. Her unfinished bread, her frozen preserves, her broken birdcage, her erratic sewing all hold great significance, both within the world of the play and for their larger importance to the imagery of women's literature. Scholars read in these symbols commentary on gender and class, geography and history. In a recently published essay Veronica Makowsky adds to these interpretations, positioning *Trifles* amid other Glaspell plays contributing to the development of American modernism.

9. Seeley Regester was the pseudonym for Mrs. Metta Victoria Fuller Victor (Rahn, "Seeley Regester: America's First Detective Novelist" 49).

10. This tradition includes such prominent women authors as Dorothy Sayers, Agatha Christie, and P. D. James, among many others.

11. For a discussion of mystery theater, see Marvin Carlson, *Deathtraps: The Postmodern Comedy Thriller*. Carlson's is to date the only book-length study of this theatrical subgenre, although his focus is, as his title implies, on contemporary theater. As I do in this chapter, Carlson in his study draws heavily on the criticism of detective fiction. Clearly, this is an area in need of further theater scholarship from both historical and theoretical perspectives.

12. Actress and playwright Elizabeth Robins makes a similar point for British audiences in her suffrage play *Votes for Women* (1907). Her heroine Vida Levering, speaking to a crowd at a suffrage rally in Trafalgar Square, connects the inequities in the English judicial system with the fact that women cannot vote to change those laws: "Men boast that an English citizen is tried by his peers. What woman is tried by hers?" (72).

13. See, for example, Dymkowski, "On the Edge: The Plays of Susan Glaspell"; and Kattwinkel, "Absence as a Site for Debate: Modern Feminism and Victorianism in the Plays of Susan Glaspell."

14. Mustazza ("Generic Translation and Thematic Shift in Susan Glaspell's *Trifles* and 'A Jury of Her Peers'") also believes the works should be considered separately, but for generic, stylistic, and aesthetic reasons.

15. For details of the Brechtian style of performance and its distinction from the Stanislavskian system, see Willett, *Brecht on Theatre: The Development of an Aesthetic;* and Wiles, *The Theater Event: Modern Theories of Performance.*

16. See my essay "The Provincetown Players' Experiments with Realism."

17. A similar experience might be remembered by many readers in the phenomenon of the "school play," in which parents, friends, and classmates are acutely conscious of their relations with and knowledge of those onstage.

18. A similar argument could be made for seeing Aphra Behn's *The Rover* (1678) as a (proto)feminist text precisely through its audience's perception of the work as a revision of the tropes of Restoration comedy. For a detailed analysis of Behn, see Diamond, *Unmaking Mimesis: Essays on Feminism and Theatre.* Moreover, as discussed in my first chapter, Glaspell's comic technique, with its feminist revisions of traditional structures, provides another parallel to the dramaturgy of detection she deploys in *Trifles.*

Other One-Act Plays

1. The premiere performance at the Provincetown was on 9 March 1917.

2. There is also an echo here of Lambert Strether in Henry James's *The Ambassadors* (1903): "Live! Live all you can—it's a mistake not to."

3. Anthony Comstock (1844–1915) was an influential reformer who succeeded in convincing the government to pass legislation prohibiting the mailing of obscene material. He voluntarily worked for the U.S. Postal Service up till the time of his death to enforce this legislation, and his subjective determinations of the morality of written and artistic materials, including works that have since become literary classics, significantly influenced their dissemination in the States at this time. The impact of Comstock on free speech will also be a concern of Glaspell's play *Chains of Dew*, while other forms of government censorship during World War I form the backdrop to *Inheritors*.

4. Linda Ben-Zvi has established the close creative relationship of O'Neill and Glaspell, and, while she points to the connections of such plays as *The Hairy Ape* and *The Verge* as demonstrations of their artistic reciprocity, I would suggest that we might expand the arena of influence to include some of Glaspell's earlier one-act plays as well. See "Susan Glaspell and Eugene O'Neill: The Imagery of Gender."

5. See, for example, Arthur Hornblow, "Mr. Hornblow Goes to the Play" (June 1918); and "A Quadruple Bill."

6. See Stansell, *American Moderns*, chap. 3.

7. Cf. the character of Felix Fejevaray in *Inheritors*.

8. I am indebted to Veronica Makowsky for having pointed out this parallel to me.

9. Jhansi is a town in northern India perhaps best known as the site of a massacre of British officers and civilians during the 1857 Indian Mutiny, details that further connect this play to *Inheritors* and its theme of Indian independence from British colonial rule ("Jhansi" 548). Glaspell may also have known that Gypsies "had their origin in India" (Singhal, *Gypsies: Indians in Exile* 13) and thus chose her name to foreground this connection. Glaspell may also have known the Village resident "Romany Marie," a woman of Jewish extraction who ran a tearoom and claimed Gypsy heritage to exoticize herself, and used her self-transformation as background for her play. For information on Romany Marie, see Stansell, *American Moderns* 97–98.

10. Although Glaspell never clarifies this, it seems safe to assume that the *Torch* is the campus or local paper, its title indicative of the enlightened positions it prints. It may also be an allusion to the British publication of the same name that championed anarchism and communism from the 1890s through the early 1900s. I am grateful to Allan Hepburn for this information.

11. This perspective will find fuller expression in *Inheritors*, in which Glaspell again contrasts the concepts of academic freedom and the open-mindedness education should promote with the jingoism and censorship that were actually the norm at the time of the war. Peyton, an instructor of American literature, prefigures the character of Professor Holden in the later play in terms of both plays' threats to suppress the teachers' pedagogical views and the accusations or assumptions of sedition that surround them.

12. See, for example, such stories as "Contrary to Precedent," *Booklovers Magazine* 3.2 (Feb. 1904): 234–56.

13. This bill featured verse drama by Kreymborg and Edna St. Vincent Millay as well as Rihani's "Static Dances," modern dance choreography set to music by Grieg and Cui (Sarlós, *Jig Cook and the Provincetown Players* 88–89, 174).

14. It is indeed a pity that there appear to have been no reviews of the third bill of the Provincetown Players' 1917–18 season. Dell's *Angel Intrudes* featured "the New York acting debut of Edna St. Vincent Millay" (Sarlós, *Jig Cook* 84), while Glaspell's paired the playwright, in the role of Allie Mayo, with "the Duse of MacDougal Street,"

Ida Rauh, as Mrs. Patrick. To have seen three such compelling women performing in one evening must have been remarkable.

15. For a comprehensive overview of the evolution of the modern theater in Europe and America, see J. L. Styan, *Modern Drama in Theory and Practice,* vols. 1–3. See also Wainscott, *Emergence of the Modern American Theater 1914–1929,* chap. 6, on American expressionism.

16. The setting closely mirrors the real edifice near Peaked Hill Bars that was once decorated by Mabel Dodge and later occupied by Eugene O'Neill (Sarlós, *Jig Cook* 85; Ben-Zvi, "Susan Glaspell and Eugene O'Neill" 26).

17. There are fascinating parallels between the plot of *The Outside* and an incident recounted by Mabel Dodge Luhan, a member of the Provincetown group, who wrote extensively of her experiences with them in her memoir, *Movers and Shakers.* In the section devoted to her relationship with the artist Maurice Sterne, she describes his near drowning and rescue by the crew of the lifesaving boat, who take him to the rescue station for resuscitation (400–405). In the memoir Luhan provides not only graphic details of the lifesaving process but also describes its emotional impact on her. It is tantalizing to think how this accident—or others like it that Glaspell knew of— may have influenced her creation of a play about the station.

18. For a discussion of liminality in the play, see Larabee, "'Meeting the Outside.'"

19. There seems to be no record of the design team for this production. As Ann Larabee has pointed out, O'Neill seems to have borrowed much of this scenic imagery for the setting of his 1920 *Emperor Jones* ("'Meeting the Outside'" 79). O'Neill makes Glaspell's upstage scenic environment the totality of his setting for scene 2, however, thereby removing the gendered spatial connotations inherent to Glaspell's design. The description of the doors upstage is strongly reminiscent of the doors at the rear of the Wharf Theatre (Sarlós, *Jig Cook* 17), the converted fishhouse on Cape Cod the Players used in their first two summers. It could well be that Glaspell had this theatrical space in mind when she composed the play, constructing this drama spectatorially as she had earlier with *Trifles,* as discussed earlier.

20. Glaspell will use a similarly evocative physical gesture in *Inheritors,* when Madeline raises her hands to emulate the imprisonment of her friend Fred.

21. At one point Allie is drawn to the door behind which is the body of the victim (108). Glaspell will use this scenic image to even greater effect in *Bernice.*

22. Glaspell's Cape Cod stories frequently feature Portuguese characters who serve as foils for the central figures of her fiction, providing "local color" marked by class and linguistic difference from the focal characters.

23. I am grateful to Veronica Makowsky for this reading.

24. In an unpublished short story version of this work, "Ellen Paxton," Glaspell introduces an orphaned child to foreground the issue of assumed female nurturance. Glaspell also included details that seem to be drawn from *The Outside* in her later novel, *Fugitive's Return* (1929), which features a Cape setting, an abandoned wife, and a character named Allie Meyer.

25. See for example, Ben-Zvi, "Susan Glaspell and Eugene O'Neill: The Imagery of Gender"; and Larabee, "'Meeting the Outside Face to Face': Susan Glaspell, Djuna Barnes, and O'Neill's *The Emperor Jones.*"

26. For a discussion of Glaspell and modernism, see Makowsky, "Susan Glaspell."

27. This same concept underlies Glaspell's *Chains of Dew.*

28. I am grateful to Veronica Makowsky for pointing out the Bergsonian link to the play.

29. For a detailed study of this group, see Blake, *Beloved Community*.

30. James Oppenheim was also connected with the Provincetown Players during this period. His play *Night* appeared on the same bill as Glaspell's *Close the Book* in November 1917.

31. Glaspell describes the sundial Cook built in their own garden in *The Road to the Temple* (281).

32. Similarly, one is tempted to see a parallel, in terms of relative dominance, between their collaborative process and the relationship of Cook and Glaspell, particularly in the detail of Cook's decision that they should leave the States for Greece at a time when Glaspell's writing career was so successful.

33. Cook considered himself a socialist, which would suggest that he might have been more sensitive to class position. Critics of Greenwich Village bohemian culture have observed, however, that there was a disjunction between the politics espoused by the group and their social practice along these lines.

34. *The Comic Artist* is equally unquestioning of gender (class is a less prominent issue; all the characters appear comfortable, despite the fact that financial drive and the desire for wealth are important elements of plot and character) and similarly conservative in its presentation of conventional roles and attitudes.

Bernice

1. Rohe, like Glaspell, was a member of the important Greenwich Village women's group, Heterodoxy, discussed later in this chapter. I attribute the candor Glaspell displays in this interview to her knowledge of Rohe through this organization.

2. Internal evidence in the play suggests either western Massachusetts or perhaps southern New Hampshire, given references to "hills" (179), a train station (159), and a few hours' remove from Boston (166).

3. See Kattwinkel, "Absence as a Site for Debate"; Friedman, "Bernice's Strange Deceit"; and Makowsky, "Susan Glaspell," for some of the only detailed analyses of this play.

4. See Glaspell's letter to Anna Strunsky, qtd. in Noe, *Critical Biography* 183.

5. See, for example, the autobiographical sketch written around the time of her publication of the novel *Judd Rankin's Daughter* in the Glaspell papers, Berg Collection, New York Public Library.

6. See, for example, "The Boycott on Caroline," *Youth's Companion*, 22 Mar. 1906, 137–38.

7. Liza Nelligan makes a similar claim for the influence of Heterodoxy on Glaspell's creation of *The Verge*.

8. All information about Heterodoxy, unless otherwise noted, is from Schwarz, *Radical Feminists of Heterodoxy*. For a different slant on the organization, see Stansell, *American Moderns*.

9. This diary resides among Glaspell's papers in the Berg Collection of the New York Public Library.

10. There are some striking parallels in these aspects of Glaspell's plot and that of another piece produced at the Provincetown in 1918, Rita Creighton Smith's *The Rescue*. In this earlier drama a servant figure is pivotal in the communication of a lie, the lie itself ultimately meant to save, to "rescue."

11. Critics routinely praised Glaspell's acting, and Edwin Björkman observed

that she often performed the "drab and superficially expressionless female figures that seem so curiously characteristic of her art" ("Theatre" 518).

12. Dee Garrison's description of the marriage between Hutchins Hapgood and Neith Boyce, replete with Hapgood's infidelities and his "infantile fervor to absorb her very soul," resonates closely enough with the exposition and characters in *Bernice* that the relationship could well have served as an influence on the drama (*Mary Heaton Vorse* 81).

13. Cook had a history of infidelity, both before and after his marriage to Glaspell. Steven Watson believes Cook had an affair with Ida Rauh (*Strange Bedfellows* 220) during their time with the Players. It is grimly ironic that Glaspell ultimately made a wifely sacrifice much like that in her plays to such little effect, given Cook's untimely death in Greece.

14. For information on the Free Speech League, see Stansell, *American Moderns*.

15. Glaspell alludes to the recent war in *Bernice* (169), and a sense of postwar despair hangs over the play. One can see Glaspell's projection of the futility of such conflict microcosmically reflected in the impotence Craig and Margaret feel about the state of their world. A dramatization of political struggle linked to the war, however, does not find full expression until her next drama, *Inheritors*.

16. The theme of marital infidelity clearly obsessed Glaspell, no doubt for both societal and personal reasons. One of her finest novels, *Fidelity* (1915), explores the hypocrisy of the double standard, changing sexual mores, and related issues at length.

17. I am extremely grateful to Allan Hepburn for bringing this material from the *Little Review* to my attention. For detailed discussions of the magazine, Anderson, and Heap, see Watson, *Strange Bedfellows;* Stansell, *American Moderns;* and Biggs, "From Harriet Monroe to *AQ*: Selected Women's Literary Journals, 1912–1972."

18. Referring generally to such exchanges in this periodical, Christine Stansell remarks, "The fights in the letters columns turned the *Little Review* into something of a free-speech soapbox" (*American Moderns* 201), an observation that neatly underscores the connections between Glaspell's works and her community.

19. Glaspell, *Plays,* contains the cast list for the original productions of each of the works collected.

20. For a discussion of these conflicting artistic views, see Bach, "Susan Glaspell— Provincetown Playwright."

Inheritors

1. Many reviews describe the play as being in three acts, although it was published in four. I suspect that in performance, acts 2 and 3 were combined as the second act, and act 4 thus became the third.

2. Marcia Noe states, "*Inheritors* takes place in the Iowa of Susan Glaspell's birth, in a town on the Mississippi River . . . that once was the hunting ground for Black Hawk" (*Susan Glaspell: Voice from the Heartland* 42). The historical details of the Black Hawk War, however, suggest that this can not be possible, as the war was not fought in the Iowa territory. It seems reasonable to hypothesize that the town Glaspell envisioned for *Inheritors* was like that of her birth but across the river. It may be significant that she does not call it "Freeport" here, the name she often used as the fictional equivalent of Davenport in her stories.

3. Historian Dan Clark relates very similar details in his account of the war but

dates the original treaty disputed by Black Hawk to 1804, with subsequent government confirmation in 1816 and 1825 (*Middle West in American History* 65).

4. See Riley, *The Female Frontier, Women and Indians on the Frontier 1825–1915;* and *Frontierswomen: The Iowa Experience.*

5. For additional details on frontierswomen's experiences with Indians, see Riley, *Frontierswomen: The Iowa Experience* 177–81.

6. See, for example, her book *In a Different Voice.*

7. Glaspell's Darwinian interest and some of her scientific confusion may well date to her early association with Cook and Floyd Dell in the Monist Society, which the men founded in Davenport, Iowa, in 1906. The philosophy of the Monists can be traced to the influence of Ernst Haeckel (1834–1919), a German zoologist who championed social Darwinism beginning in 1863 and helped to create the Monist League there between 1904 and 1906 (Gasman, *Scientific Origins of National Socialism* 1–23). Glaspell's depiction of Cook's philosophy in "the Monist Society" chapter of *The Road to the Temple* strongly echoes the rhetoric of Haeckel. Cook had spent the year 1894 in Germany preparing for an academic career, and his interest in German literature, culture, and thought stayed with him long after his return to the United States.

8. See, for example, her novel *Ambrose Holt and Family* and the short story "Pollen."

9. Linda Ben-Zvi notes that the character of Jordan may have been based on Fred Robinson, who was prosecuted for his opposition to the war ("Susan Glaspell's Contributions" 164).

10. Christine Stansell identifies Columbia as a "nest of patriotic zeal" that its president "restructured . . . along military lines" (*American Moderns* 315) in this period.

11. Her most obvious examples are Minnie Wright in *Trifles* and the title characters in *Bernice* and *Alison's House.*

12. For a fascinating, if rather religiously biased, study of foreign students, including Indian, in the United States in the 1920s, see *The Foreign Student in America,* commissioned by the Friendly Relations Committees of the Young Men's Christian Association and the Young Women's Christian Association.

13. Probably a reference to the American Legion, founded in 1919, and known for its support of American nationalism following the war (Preston, *Aliens and Dissenters* 192).

14. For a discussion of the opposition to American imperialism, see Beisner, *Twelve Against Empire.*

15. A famous event of 1913 had been the Paterson Strike Pageant at Madison Square Garden in New York, directed by John Reed, designed by Robert Edmond Jones, and funded in part by Mabel Dodge. The pageant was a reenactment of the IWW-supported strike against the management of a silk factory in nearby Paterson, NJ. Cook and Glaspell had attended the event, which she called "the first labor play" (*Road* 250).

16. This designation of one of the Hindus as an "anarchist" cements the connection between them and the Red scare of the postwar era. Horace's calling the student "Bakhshish"—which means "tip," "gratuity," or "bribe"—may well be another racist slur.

17. The gender issues raised here are also subtle elements of the feminist theme in the play. The implication that the older, wiser, and more savvy uncle can help the naive and headstrong niece is expressed not only by Emil but by Horace and Fejevary himself, who also enlists Holden, another older male authority figure, to aid in guiding

Madeline. That Horace should think the only reason Madeline supports the Hindus is that she has a crush on one of them is equally sexist and demeaning (147). Madeline, of course, ultimately proves herself to be stronger in principles than any of the men and eminently capable of following her own course of action with full knowledge of its consequences. Glaspell's critique of the gender inequities of the American judicial system finds evidence in both *Trifles* and "A Jury of Her Peers."

18. Glaspell had begun to develop this theme of family, racial, and moral solidarity in *Close the Book,* her early one-act that anticipates many of the concerns of *Inheritors.*

19. Ira's experimentation with corn parallels Claire Archer's plant breeding in *The Verge.* Both plays use this motif to demonstrate the instability of characters who engage in this kind of genetic manipulation and, by extension, seek to control nature.

20. The actresses in the role were: Ann Harding (New York, 1921), Murial Randall (Liverpool and London, 1925–26), and Josephine Hutchinson (New York, 1927).

21. N. G. Royde-Smith intimated that some of the audience in London left before the play's conclusion ("Drama: The American Play" 25). None of the New York critics on either production mentioned walk-outs.

22. Bigsby's analysis of the play may also be colored by his own position as a British, rather than an American, reader of Glaspell.

23. While Bigsby's specific commentary on *Inheritors* was not published until 1987, a comparison of these remarks with his views of Glaspell and her work found in his 1982 *Twentieth-Century American Drama* indicates that he did not change his perspectives on her writing in the intervening five years.

The Verge

1. Julie Holledge was probably the first scholar to note the humor in Glaspell's choice of these "generic" men's names (*Innocent Flowers* 147).

2. For a more detailed description of this period of the Provincetown Players' history, see Sarlós, *Jig Cook* chap. 6.

3. Noe claims both were drafted during the sabbatical year, but, as *The Verge* was not produced until the fall of 1921, it seems likely that she was still working on it beyond that period. In her article on Glaspell and Eugene O'Neill, Linda Ben-Zvi quotes a letter from Cook to Glaspell, dated 27 August 1921 that implies the play still needed approval by the executive committee before production, further evidence that *The Verge* may have been finished after the couple's leave of absence from the theater ("Susan Glaspell and Eugene O'Neill" 24).

4. C. W. E. Bigsby argues convincingly that *The Verge* resembles Cook's 1911 novel, *The Chasm* ("Introduction" 21).

5. See Ben-Zvi, "Susan Glaspell and Eugene O'Neill"; and "Susan Glaspell and Eugene O'Neill: The Imagery of Gender"; Larabee, "'Meeting the Outside Face to Face.'"

6. These ideas derive from Ben-Zvi's keynote address at the First International Susan Glaspell Conference, University of Glasgow, May 1996.

7. See Baritz, *Culture of the Twenties;* and Hoffman, *Freudianism and the Literary Mind.* I am grateful to my colleague Joel Porte for suggesting these works to me.

8. See Diamond, *Unmaking Mimesis* pt. 1.

9. Glaspell drew on similar stage conventions of farce in her earlier one-act *Woman's Honor*.

10. See Sanford Gifford, "The American Reception of Psychoanalysis, 1908–1922"; and the chapter on *Suppressed Desires* in this study. Glaspell may also have gained knowledge of Freud through contact with Grace Potter, a psychoanalyst who was also a member of Heterodoxy (Schwarz, *Radical Feminists of Heterodoxy* 14).

11. See, for example, Eric Leed, *No Man's Land: Combat and Identity in World War I;* Sandra Gilbert and Susan Gubar, *No Man's Land,* vol. 2: *Sex Changes;* Elaine Showalter, *The Female Malady: Women, Madness and English Culture, 1830–1980;* and Mark S. Micale, *Approaching Hysteria: Disease and Its Interpretations.*

12. There is, of course, much scholarly debate about the beginnings of modernism. Many drama scholars see the plays of German playwright Georg Büchner (1813–37) as launching theatrical modernism in Europe; modernism arrived later in America, around the end of the first decade of the twentieth century. For many scholars World War I marked the beginning of the "high modernist" era associated most strongly with canonized male artists and writers; this is the moment to which Gilbert and Gubar allude. For discussions of American modernism, see Stansell, *American Modern;* and Watson, *Strange Bedfellows.* For Glaspell and modernism, see Makowsky, "Susan Glaspell."

13. See especially his essay "Susan Glaspell—Provincetown Playwright" (36).

14. See, for example, Kenneth Macgowan, "The New Play," *Commercial Advertiser.*

15. See, for example, Watson, *Strange Bedfellows;* and Gilbert and Gubar, *No Man's Land.*

16. For a description and interpretation of the case of "Anna O.," see Showalter, *Female Malady* 154–57.

17. I am grateful to Katharine Rodier for sharing these insights with me in our correspondence on *Alison's House.*

18. Arthur Waterman suggests the de Vries link (*Susan Glaspell* 82), while the parallel to Burbank was proposed in a letter to the editor of the *New York Times* at the time of the play's New York premier (Hale, "Concerning 'The Verge'"); as well as in Stephen Rathbun's review (4).

19. Although Glaspell was raised in a churchgoing household, her affiliation with the Monists distanced her from organized religion. Ernst Haeckel, the founder of Monism, saw his work as directly in opposition to the hold Christianity had over Germany and its social and political structures (*Road* 191; Gasman, *Scientific Origins of National Socialism* 22).

20. See, for comparison, *The Church Hymnal,* edited by the Reverend Charles L. Hutchins (1906) for versions of this hymn no. 344. In his study *New York 1913* Martin Green provides a fascinating historical tidbit that may also have relevance for Glaspell's choice of this particular hymn for Claire. According to Green, "Nearer, my God, to Thee" was one of the favorite hymns parodied by the IWW—in this case as "Nearer My Job to Thee" (157). Glaspell's knowledge of this group, especially through her close friendship with Jack Reed, could have both made this a familiar song to her and suggested its suitability as a melodic message for resistance.

21. For a more detailed discussion of Glaspell and Heterodoxy, see the chapter on *Bernice.*

22. Ruth Hale was at that time the wife of Heywood Broun, theater critic for the *New York Tribune* and a supporter of both Glaspell and the Provincetown Players. Hale

founded "the Lucy Stone League in support of married women who preferred to keep their maiden names" (Schwarz, *Radical Feminists of Heterodoxy* 14).

23. For a synthetic breakdown of critical response to all of Glaspell's work, see Papke, *Susan Glaspell: A Research and Production Sourcebook*.

Chains of Dew

1. For a fuller discussion of these works, see my essay "*Chains of Dew* and the Drama of Birth Control," in *Susan Glaspell: Essays on Her Theater and Fiction*, ed. Linda Ben-Zvi. Unfortunately, due to an editorial error, this version of the essay omits the discussion of Sada Cowan's *The State Forbids* (1915), a birth control drama with overt political connections to World War I.

2. For a fuller discussion of these facets of the history of the birth control movement in America, see Gordon, *Woman's Body, Woman's Right: Birth Control in America* 84–93.

3. Sanger's arrest stemmed from violation of section 211 of the Criminal Code of the United States, which "was part of the so-called Comstock law" that prohibited the mailing, transporting or importing of "'obscene, lewd, or lascivious'" material (Kennedy, *Birth Control in America: The Career of Margaret Sanger* 23–24). For a detailed discussion of the laws relating to birth control and their implications at the time, see Dennett, *Birth Control Laws*.

4. Note the parallel here between the more recent decision to separate off the abortion rights division of the American Civil Liberties Union (ACLU) and Sanger's tactics.

5. This conflict found expression at the Playwright's Theatre when Alfred Kreymborg championed the aesthetic importance of verse drama, resulting in the experiment of the Other Players' Bill of the 1917–1918 season. On a more personal level it also underlay the tension between Hutchins Hapgood and Max Eastman over the sufficiency of their radicalism. See Hapgood, *Victorian in a Modern World*, and O'Neill, *Last Romantic*.

6. The name suggests lineage to Myles Standish, one of the leaders of the *Mayflower* pilgrims who landed in Plymouth, MA, in 1620.

7. Glaspell's choice of name for Seymore's wife, Dotty, combined with her mother-in-law's work with dolls, might have made her Village audiences think of Dolly Sloan, wife of *Masses* artist John Sloan, who was active in the birth control campaign (Stansell, *American Moderns* 250).

8. See, for example, her essay "Region as Metaphor in the Plays of Susan Glaspell."

9. For a discussion of Glaspell's reworking of the plot of *Chains* in these different genres, see Noe, *Critical Biography* 127–28.

10. For a fuller discussion of Glaspell's concern with this issue, see the *Inheritors* chapter.

11. The idea of an exaggerated childhood trauma affecting adult behavior recurs in *Springs Eternal* with the character of Harry and may reflect Glaspell's early interest in popularized psychology.

12. Coincidentally, Margaret Anderson, editor of the Village magazine the *Little Review*, emigrated to Europe at about this same time. Historian Christine Stansell reads her departure as "an early sign of a general retreat of the American avant-garde

from a politics that had grown too narrow to interest them" (*American Moderns* 328). It is tempting to speculate that Cook decided to leave New York for this as well as his other reasons.

13. The complete text of this manuscript letter is in the Provincetown Players Collection of the Harvard Theatre Collection.

14. Louise Treadwell took over the role before the opening and received solid notices.

15. I am grateful to Peggy Phelan for crystallizing this aspect of Glaspell scholarship for me at the 1993 Association for Theatre in Higher Education (ATHE) meeting, where I presented the initial research for this chapter.

16. Kenton refers to "Stewart" the director in her letter of 5 May. Unfortunately, none of the reviews mentions the director (as was customary for the time), and, as there is no archival copy of the program, I have not been able to determine the last name of this individual.

The Comic Artist

1. All correspondence concerning *The Comic Artist* resides with Glaspell's unpublished papers in the Berg Collection of the New York Public Library. The resemblance of this passage to Glaspell's description of the composition of her first play with Cook, *Suppressed Desires,* is notable. See *The Road to the Temple* 250.

2. Very few of the letters in this part of the collection have the year dated. In many cases, however, the approximate date of composition can be deduced from internal theatrical or biographical references, and in some cases there are accompanying envelopes with postmarks that provide more exact information.

3. Several reviewers of the New York production seemed well aware of the play's production history as well as the changes in its script from published to produced versions. See, for example, "News-Week in Entertainment"; and Gilbert W. Gabriel, "Comic Artist."

4. Matson's letters to Glaspell are filled with marginal drawings of cartoon characters and cartoonlike sketches, some of which are self-caricatures.

5. John Mason Brown talks in similar fashion of the thematic idea of what happens after the last frame in "'The Comic Artist.'"

6. This ending echoes Glaspell's early one-act, *The Outside,* with its lifesaving station setting and action of rescue of a doomed man.

7. Manuscript letter, 1932. Berg Collection, New York Public Library. Anna Walling was the daughter of Anna Strunsky and William Walling, who were part of the radical bohemian circles in which Glaspell traveled. Anna was the younger woman for whom Matson left Glaspell.

8. Most of the published details of Matson's background and early writing experiences are contained in a biographical essay he wrote for the *American Review* in 1934, "The Shortest Way Out Was to the Left."

9. It is, somehow, perfectly fitting that there would be a popular culture coda to this story. Matson's novel would, years later, go on to inspire the creation of one of the best-loved situation comedies in the history of American television, *Bewitched* (Makowsky, *Susan Glaspell's Century* 27).

10. For further discussion of Glaspell's critical reception, see the Afterword.

11. The British publication of the same year appeared under the E. Benn imprint.

12. The correspondence also reveals that Glaspell and Matson collaborated on another play during this time, *The Good Bozo,* which Glaspell felt "has a chance to be more popular" than *The Comic Artist.* Their letters, however, contain no information about the work or whether any serious efforts were made to have it produced. There seem to be no extant copies of the script.

13. The Westport Playhouse had been founded by Glaspell's longtime friend Lawrence Langner. For details on summer productions, see Gabriel, "The Comic Artist"; "The News-Week in Entertainment" indicates that, in addition to the summer productions, the play had been announced several times in New York before it actually made it on the boards.

14. The cast included Lea Penman as Luella, Blanche Yurka as Eleanor, Richard Hale as Stephen, Robert Allen as Karl, and Lora Baxter as Nina.

15. See, for example, Robert Garland, "'Comic Artist' a Success on Sight."

16. Dorothy Gish was an actor and the sister of the more famous performer Lillian Gish. There is no record of Dorothy's connection with the production; it is possible that she was initially cast in the role and then replaced in rehearsal for some reason.

17. Matson's spelling and punctuation have been regularized throughout; all the correspondence contains numerous misspellings and abbreviations that warrant standardization for the general reader.

18. This quotation exemplifies one interesting detail of the critical reception of the play. Most of the reviewers acknowledged the collaboration with Matson but essentially treated Glaspell as the sole author, no doubt because of her established position as a playwright.

Alison's House

1. For a complete chronology, see Sewall, *Life of Emily Dickinson.*

2. For a complete description of the disputes surrounding the Bianchi biography, see Sewall, *Life of Emily Dickinson.*

3. A third study of Dickinson also appeared that year, MacGregor Jenkins's *Emily Dickinson: Friend and Neighbor,* which, according to Rodier, is a more personal reminiscence than an attempt at a complete biography ("Glaspell and Dickinson: Surveying the Premises of *Alison's House*" 202).

4. The world premier actually occurred in England in November 1930 and was then remounted there in 1932 to greater critical attention. A letter from Glaspell to Barrett H. Clark, dated April 1930, intimates that the Theatre Guild had previously turned down the play (Beinecke Library, Yale University).

5. I am grateful to Katharine Rodier for sharing a copy of her essay "Glaspell and Dickinson: Surveying the Premises of *Alison's House,*" prior to its publication, which enabled me to draw on her research into Glaspell's sources for the play.

6. Assuming a standard four-week rehearsal period, Glaspell would have had to have finished her script by early September at the very latest, to allow sufficient time for mailing, casting, and script duplication for the British production in November. Le Gallienne would have had to have seen a draft some months prior to that in order to place the drama on her schedule for the 1930–31 season. According to Katharine Rodier, Pollitt's book was published in January, giving Glaspell ample time to consult

it for her play. Taggard's work appeared in May, which makes for a much tighter but not impossible consultation schedule (Rodier, "Glaspell and Dickinson" 215 n. 5).

7. Extensive files on the Civic Repertory Theatre are in the Billy Rose Theater Collection of the New York Public Library.

8. In correspondence with Noe, 28 Jan. 1993, I learned that the source of her information on this matter was Arthur Waterman's study for the Twayne series. In subsequent correspondence with Waterman (10 Feb. 1996), he explained that he had learned about the conflict with the Dickinson estate from Harl Cook, Jig Cook's son from his second marriage. No documentation of the exchanges exist, however. I am grateful to both scholars for their assistance.

9. Dickinson's verse continues to be at the center of publication struggles. The *Chronicle of Higher Education* ("Hot Type," 17 Nov. 1995, A10) reported that Harvard University Press, which owns the rights to Dickinson's poetry, denied a scholar's request to publish a new edition of the verse focusing on Dickinson's composition process by examining a selection of the poems in various drafts.

10. The details of the Dickinson family are developed in the first volume of the Sewall biography.

11. In this way Agatha mirrors Abbie in *Bernice*. Both are entrusted with a secret they cannot quite keep, the revelation of which, however, ultimately aids rather than hurts the other characters.

12. For a reading of the setting of *Alison's House,* see Czerepinski, "Beyond *The Verge:* Absent Heroines in the Plays of Susan Glaspell" 150.

13. For further discussion of this aspect of Glaspell's life and her work, see the chapter on *The Verge.*

14. The object of Alison's unrequited love is an English teacher at Harvard University (688). Glaspell creates irony with this revelation late in act 3, as Ted has been harping throughout the play on his Harvard English professor's demands that he convey information about Alison in order to pass his class successfully. Harvard has an almost mythic resonance for Glaspell, who uses it as a touchstone throughout her writing, very possibly because Cook revered the institution and had attended it for a year.

15. More recently, Dickinson criticism has focused on the thesis of her lesbian identity. In his 1992 biography of Eva Le Gallienne, *Shattered Applause,* Robert Schanke links Le Gallienne's lesbianism to Dickinson in his discussion of the Civic Rep's production of *Alison's House,* calling the poet's sexuality "widely known by this time" (90). There is no indication in the play, however, that Glaspell was aware of this; Alison's hidden poems were written about her love for a married man, and Glaspell constructs all the thematic and characterological links in the play through heterosexual relationships.

16. Glaspell repeatedly avoids demonstrating true art in her plays, although she has no compunction about creating the second-rate verse of a character such as Seymore Standish in *Chains of Dew,* for example.

17. Rodier does extrapolate from the drama, however, a series of biographical parallels between Jig Cook and Alison (211), extending a connection she traces not only within the play but also through other work such as Glaspell's edition of Cook's own poetry and her biography of him. Projecting Cook as a partial model for Alison, Rodier hypothesizes that Glaspell's treatment of the artist "crosses genders" (211), noting that her next novel, *Ambrose Holt and Family,* features a male poet. While this novel's narrative is arguably much more closely tied to Glaspell's earlier drama *Chains of Dew,* Rodier's thesis merits consideration. The critical issue of the interpretation of women's writing through biography would have been a compelling and vexed matter

for Glaspell; this may counter Rodier's notion that Glaspell was, even in part, projecting a male artist through a female persona in this play.

18. For details of the development of Glaspell and Cook's relationship, see *The Road to the Temple,* esp. chap. 25–29.

19. The first Pulitzer award to a woman occurred in 1921, Zona Gale's *Miss Lulu Bett.*

20. Glaspell's dramatic collaboration with Norman Matson, *The Comic Artist,* had been published in 1927 but was not produced in New York until 1933.

21. For a full list of performance dates for *Alison's House,* see the *Civic Repertory Theatre Magazine.*

22. When the play was remounted in London in 1932, the English reviewers also had serious reservations about the play itself, although some of the critics seemed to feel the fault lay with the production. See "Entertainments: Little Theatre"; Ivor Brown, "Alison's House"; "Little: 'Alison's House'"; Leslie Rees, "Where Are Our Senior Dramatists?"; and, for a particularly delicious, if biting, response, James Agate, "Second-Hand Ibsen."

23. An essay by John Anderson in the *Theatre Annual* for 1942 portrayed the Pulitzer controversy more from the perspective of the critics, who by 1935 felt the prize had lost any critical merit it might once have had. The essay charts the beginning of the New York Drama Critics Circle, which subsequently established its own annual award. See Anderson, "Circle."

24. The list of plays the jury considered included, additionally, *Once in a Lifetime, Green Grow the Lilacs,* and *Five Star Final* (Toohey, *History of the Pulitzer Prize Plays* 93).

25. Veronica Makowsky reads the dramaturgy of the play and its relationship to modernism quite differently; see her essay "Susan Glaspell and Modernism."

Springs Eternal

1. For more details of Glaspell's work with the Federal Theater Project in Chicago, see Noe, *Critical Biography.*

2. The novels were *The Morning Is Near Us* (1939), *Norma Ashe* (1942), and *Judd Rankin's Daughter* (1945); the children's story was *Cherished and Shared of Old* (1940).

3. These two characters, despite their absence from the stage, should not, however, be grouped with Glaspell's other absent characters such as Minnie Wright, Bernice, Alison Stanhope, and Fred Jordan. Thayer and Evelyn have very little impact on plot or theme and thus are not central forces in *Springs Eternal.*

4. Since the manuscripts of *Springs Eternal* are undated, it is impossible to determine exactly when Glaspell drafted it. We know that it was completed by 1945 because of the dates on the Langner correspondence. We might assume that the play postdates the composition of *Norma Ashe,* which Noe proves was written while Glaspell was still in Chicago (*Critical Biography* 213), and precedes that of *Judd Rankin's Daughter,* but, pending the publication of the fuller Glaspell biographies, these must remain conjectures.

5. There is a passing reference to Hitler late in the play (3.7), quoted later in this chapter.

6. For a summary of the reviews of this revival, see especially the latter part of the *Inheritors* chapter.

7. The fact that Glaspell would re-use the character's name—Margaret—for another woman of independent spirit and conviction is significant. See the discussion of Margaret Pierce in the chapter on *Bernice*.

8. One might contrast this sensation to that created by Caryl Churchill between the acts of *Cloud 9*, in which she demonstrates how little changes over history by collapsing almost a century to the span from childhood to adulthood.

9. Given the pervasiveness of the theme of marital infidelity in Glaspell's work, often with the championing of extramarital love over the ties of an unhappy marriage, this resolution seems more designed for the exigencies of a rather complicated plot of comic misunderstanding than a statement of transition in Glaspell's own longstanding attitude.

10. Bill, echoing lines in *Chains of Dew*, lovingly observes: "Such nice words go with Dottie. We'll omit the dimple but sometimes we might have the dumpling" (3.29).

Afterword

1. See, for example, Martha Vicinus, ed., *A Widening Sphere: Changing Roles of Victorian Women.*

✧ Bibliography

A comprehensive listing of Glaspell's published works in all genres can be found in Mary Papke, *Susan Glaspell: A Research and Production Sourcebook*. Additional unpublished works are held primarily in the Cook and Glaspell papers in the Berg Collection of the New York Public Library. Papke also lists most reviews and feature articles on Glaspell productions; those I have found that she does not include are listed herein. Information on published and archival versions of plays produced by the Provincetown Players from 1915–1922 can be found in the bibliography of Robert Károly Sarlós, *Jig Cook and the Provincetown Players*.

Works Cited

Adler, Thomas P. *Mirror on the Stage: The Pulitzer Plays as an Approach to American Drama*. West Lafayette, IN: Purdue UP, 1987.

Agate, James. "Second-Hand Ibsen." *Sunday Times*, 16 Oct. 1932, 4.

"Alison's House." *Variety*, 3 Dec. 1930, 63.

"'Alison's House,' an American Play by Susan Glaspell Scheduled for Early December Opening." *The Civic Repertory Theatre Magazine* 1.2 (Nov. 1930): 1.

"'Alison's House' by Susan Glaspell." *The Civic Repertory Theatre Magazine* 1.3 (Dec. 1930): 5.

Alkalay-Gut, Karen. "Jury of Her Peers: The Importance of Trifles." *Studies in Short Fiction* 21.1 (Winter 1984): 1–9.

———. "Murder and Marriage: Another Look at *Trifles*." In *Susan Glaspell: Essays on Her Theater and Fiction*. Ed. Linda Ben-Zvi, 71–81.

Anderson, John. "The Circle." *Theatre Annual* (1942): 17–28.

Anderson, Margaret. "Susan Glaspell's New Play." *Little Review* 5.11 (Apr. 1919): 58–59.

———. "Neither Drama nor Life." *Little Review* 6.1 (May 1919): 59–62.

Anderson, Sherwood. *Sherwood Anderson's Memoirs: A Critical Edition*. Ed. Ray Lewis White. Chapel Hill: U of North Carolina P, 1969.

Atkinson, J. Brooks. "Pioneer Traditions." *New York Times*, 20 Mar. 1927, 8:1.

———. "The Play." *New York Times*, 6 Mar. 1927, 23.

Bach, Gerhard. "Susan Glaspell—Provincetown Playwright." *Great Lakes Review* 4.2 (Winter 1978): 31–43.

Bargainnier, Earl F. "Introduction." In *10 Women of Mystery*. Ed. Earl F. Bargainnier, 1–7. Bowling Green: Bowling Green State UP, 1981.

Baritz, Loren, ed. *The Culture of the Twenties*. Indianapolis: Bobbs-Merrill, 1970.

Mr. Barnes. "A Great Drama." *Little Review* 6.1 (May 1919): 53–55.

Barzun, Jacques. "Detection and the Literary Art." In *Detective Fiction: A Collection of Critical Essays*. Ed. Robin W. Winks, 144–53.

Beisner, Robert L. *Twelve Against Empire: The Anti-Imperialists, 1898–1900*. New York: McGraw-Hill, 1968.

Beneš, Václav L. "Land of the Free." In *The Heritage of the Middle West*. Ed. John J. Murray, 121–51. Norman: U of Oklahoma P, 1958.

Ben-Zvi, Linda. "Introduction." *Susan Glaspell: Essays on Her Theater and Fiction*. Ed. Linda Ben-Zvi. 1–14.

———. "'Murder, She Wrote': The Genesis of Susan Glaspell's *Trifles*." *Susan Glaspell: Essays on Her Theater and Fiction*. Ed. Linda Ben-Zvi. 19–48.

———. "Susan Glaspell and Eugene O'Neill." *Eugene O'Neill Newsletter* 6.2 (Summer–Fall 1982): 21–29.

———. "Susan Glaspell and Eugene O'Neill: The Imagery of Gender." *Eugene O'Neill Newsletter* 10.1 (Spring 1986): 22–27.

———. "Susan Glaspell's Contributions to Contemporary Women Playwrights." In *Feminine Focus: The New Women Playwrights*. Ed. Enoch Brater, 147–66. New York: Oxford UP, 1989.

———, ed. *Susan Glaspell: Essays on Her Theater and Fiction*. Ann Arbor: U of Michigan P, 1995.

Bianchi, Martha Dickinson. *The Life and Letters of Emily Dickinson*. Boston: Houghton Mifflin, 1924.

Biggs, Mary. "From Harriet Monroe to *AQ*: Selected Women's Literary Journals, 1912–1972." *13th Moon* 8.1–2 (1984): 183–216.

Bigsby, C. W. E. "Introduction." Susan Glaspell. *Plays by Susan Glaspell*, 1–31.

———. "Susan Glaspell." *A Critical Introduction to Twentieth-Century American Drama*. Vol. 1: *1900–1940*, 25–35. Cambridge: Cambridge UP, 1983.

Björkman, Edwin. "The Theatre." *Freeman*, 11 Aug. 1920, 518–20.

Blake, Casey Nelson. *Beloved Community: The Cultural Criticism of Randolphe Bourne, Van Wyck Brooks, Waldo Frank, and Lewis Mumford*. Chapel Hill: U of North Carolina P, 1966.

Booth, Alison. "Biographical Criticism and the 'Great' Woman of Letters: The Example of George Eliot and Virginia Woolf." In *Contesting the Subject*. Ed. William H. Epstein, 85–107.

Brabazon, James. *Dorothy L. Sayers: A Biography*. New York: Charles Scribner's Sons, 1981.

Breuer, Josef and Sigmund Freud. *Studies on Hysteria*. Vol. 3 of *The Standard Edition of the Complete Psychological Works of Sigmund Freud*. Trans. and ed. James Strachey. London: Hogarth Press, 1973.

Brewster, Edwin Tenney. "Dreams and Forgetting." *McClure's Magazine* 39 (May–Oct. 1912): 714–19.

Brill, A. A. "The Introduction and Development of Freud's Work in the United States." *American Journal of Sociology* 45.3 (Nov. 1939): 318–25.

Brinkley, Alan. "World War II and American Liberalism." In *The War in American Culture: Society and Consciousness During World War II*. Ed. Lewis A. Erenberg and Susan E. Hirsch, 313–30. Chicago: U of Chicago P, 1996.

Brockett, Charles. "The Theatre." *New Yorker*, 19 Mar. 1927, 33.

Brooks, Van Wyck. "The Culture of Industrialism." In *Van Wyck Brooks: The Early Years*. Ed. Claire Sprague, 192–202. New York: Harper and Row, 1968.

Broun, Heywood. "Best Bill Seen at the Comedy." *New York Tribune,* 14 Nov. 1916, 7.

———. "Drama." *New York Tribune,* 23 Dec. 1918, 9.

———. "In Wigs and Wings." *New York Tribune,* 18 Mar. 1917, iv:3.

———. "Realism Has Special Thrills of Its Own." *New York Tribune,* 30 Mar. 1919, n.p.

Brown, Ivor. "Alison's House." *Observer,* 16 Oct. 1932, 17.

Brown, John Mason. "'The Comic Artist' Opens on Broadway." *New York Evening Post,* 20 Apr. 1933, 17.

———. "The Play." *New York Evening Post,* 2 Dec. 1930, 12.

———. "This Bad Showmanship." *Theatre Arts Monthly* 11 (May 1927): 325–35.

Calta, Louis. "The Theatre." In *The American Year Book: A Record of Events and Progress.* Ed. William M. Schuyler, 938–43. New York: Thomas Nelson, 1944.

Carb, David. "Inheritors." *Vogue,* 1 May 1927, 138.

Carlson, Marvin. *Deathtraps: The Postmodern Comedy Thriller.* Bloomington: Indiana UP, 1993.

Castellun, Maida. "The Plays That Pass" *New York Call,* 30 Apr. 1922, 4.

———. "The Stage." *New York Call,* 16 Nov. 1921, 4.

Chafee, Zechariah, Jr. *Free Speech in the United States.* Cambridge: Harvard UP, 1941.

Chatfield-Taylor, Otis. "The Theatre." *Outlook and Independent,* 31 Dec. 1930, 711.

Chauncey, George. *Gay New York: Gender, Urban Culture, and the Making of the Gay Male World, 1890–1940.* New York: Basic Books, 1994.

Chinoy, Helen Krich, and Linda Walsh Jenkins, eds. *Women in American Theatre.* 1981. Rpt. New York: Theatre Communications Group, 1987.

Churchill, Caryl. *Cloud 9.* 1984. Rev. American ed. New York: Routledge, 1995.

Cima, Gay Gibson. "'To Be Public as a Genius and Private as a Woman': The Critical Framing of Nineteenth-Century British Woman Playwrights." In *Women and Playwriting in Nineteenth-Century Britain.* Ed. Tracy C. Davis and Ellen Donkin, 35–53. Cambridge: Cambridge UP, 1999.

"Claire—Superwoman or Plain Egomaniac? A No-verdict Disputation." *Greenwich Villager,* 30 Nov. 1921, 1, 4.

Clark, Dan Elbert. *The Middle West in American History.* New York: Thomas Y. Crowell, 1966.

"The Comic Artist." *Era,* 27 Nov. 1929, n.p.

Conover, Roger L. "Textual Notes." Mina Loy, *The Last Lunar Baedeker.* Ed. Conover, 323–329.

Cook, George Cram. "The Provincetown Players: 'The Playwrights' Theater' Season of 1916–17." Season circular, Berg Collection, New York Public Library.

———. "The Provincetown Players: 'The Playwrights' Theatre' 1917–18." Season circular, Berg Collection, New York Public Library.

———. *The Spring: A Play.* New York: Frank Shay, 1921.

Cook, George Cram, and Frank Shay, eds., *Provincetown Plays.* Cincinnati: Stewart Kidd, 1921.

Corbin, John. "The One-Act Play." *New York Times,* 19 May 1918, iv:8.

———. "Seraphim and Cats." *New York Times,* 30 Mar. 1919, 4:2.

Coward, Rosalind, and Linda Semple. "Tracking Down the Past: Women and Detective Fiction." In *From My Guy to Sci-Fi: Genre and Women's Writing in the Postmodern World.* Ed. Helen Carr, 39–57. London: Pandora, 1989.

Czerepinski, Jackie. "Beyond *The Verge*: Absent Heroines in the Plays of Susan Glaspell." In *Susan Glaspell: Essays on Her Theater and Fiction.* Ed. Linda Ben-Zvi, 145–54.

Dell, Floyd. *Homecoming: An Autobiography.* New York: Farrar and Rinehart, 1933.

———. *Love in Greenwich Village.* New York: George H. Doran, 1926.

———. "Speaking of Psycho-analysis." *Vanity Fair* (Dec. 1915): 53.

———. *Women as World Builders.* Chicago: Forbes and Co., 1913.

Denison, Merrill. "Season's End." *Theatre Arts Monthly* (June 1933): 415–21.

Diamond, Elin. *Unmaking Mimesis: Essays on Feminism and Theatre.* London: Routledge, 1997.

Dolan, Jill. *The Feminist Spectator as Critic.* Ann Arbor: UMI Research P, 1988.

Downer, Alan S. *Fifty Years of American Drama, 1900–1950.* 1951. Gateway Edition. Rpt. Chicago: Henry Regnery, 1966.

"Drama." *Greenwich Villager,* 16 Nov. 1921, 7.

Dubois, P. C. *Les psychonévroses et leur traitement moral.* Paris: Masson, 1904.

Dymkowski, Christine. "On the Edge: The Plays of Susan Glaspell." *Modern Drama* 31.1 (Mar. 1988): 91–105.

Eastman, Max. *Enjoyment of Living.* New York: Harper and Brothers, 1948.

———. "Exploring the Soul and Healing the Body." *Everybody's Magazine* 32.6 (June 1915): 741–50.

———. "Mr.—er—er—Oh! What's His Name?" *Everybody's Magazine* 33.1 (July 1915): 95–103.

———. "A New Journal." *Masses* (Apr. 1914): 9.

Eaton, Walter Prichard. "Introduction." *Washington Square Plays,* v–xvi. Garden City, NY: Doubleday, Page and Co., 1919.

———. "The Pulitzer Prize." *Theatre Annual* (1944): 24–30.

Emerson, Ralph Waldo. "The House." *Representative Men [and] Poems.* Vol. 2 of *American Authors in Prose and Poetry,* 188–89. New York: P. F. Collier and Son, n.d.

"Entertainments: Little Theatre." *Times,* 12 Oct. 1932, 10.

Epstein, William H., ed. *Contesting the Subject: Essays in the Postmodern Theory and Practice of Biography and Biographical Criticism.* West Lafayette, IN: Purdue UP, 1991.

"Everyman." *Sunday Times,* 9 Oct. 1921, 4.

"The Everyman." *Stage,* 6 Oct. 1921, 16.

Farjeon, Herbert. "The Theatre." *Weekly Westminster,* 11 Apr. 1925, 708.

———. "The Theatre." *Weekly Westminster,* 9 Jan. 1926, 242.

Ferguson, Mary Anne, ed. *Images of Women in Literature.* Boston: Houghton Mifflin, 1973.

Fetterley, Judith. "Reading about Reading: 'A Jury of Her Peers,' 'The Murders in the Rue Morgue,' and 'The Yellow Wallpaper.'" In *Gendered Reading: Essays on Readers, Texts, and Contexts.* Ed. Elizabeth A. Flynn and Patrocinio P. Schweickart, 147–64. Baltimore: Johns Hopkins UP, 1986.

Firkins, O. W. "Drama." *Weekly Review,* 13 Apr. 1921, 344–45.

Fishbein, Leslie. *Rebels in Bohemia: The Radicals of* The Masses, *1911–1917.* Chapel Hill: U of North Carolina P, 1982.

Flannery, James W. *W. B. Yeats and the Idea of a Theatre: The Early Abbey Theatre in Theory and Practice.* New Haven: Yale UP, 1976.

Forster, E. M. *Aspects of the Novel.* New York: Harcourt, Brace and World, 1954.

Freud, Sigmund. *The Interpretation of Dreams.* Trans. A. A. Brill. New York: Macmillan, 1913.

Friedman, Sharon. "Bernice's Strange Deceit: The Avenging Angel in the House." In *Susan Glaspell: Essays on Her Theater and Fiction.* Ed. Linda Ben-Zvi, 155–64.

Gabriel, Gilbert W. "The Comic Artist." *New York American*, 20 Apr. 1933, 9.

Gainor, J. Ellen. "*Chains of Dew* and the Drama of Birth Control." In *Susan Glaspell: Essays on Her Theater and Fiction.* Ed. Linda Ben-Zvi, 165–93.

——. "The Provincetown Players' Experiments with Realism." In *Realism and the American Dramatic Tradition.* Ed. William W. Demastes, 53–70. Tuscaloosa: U of Alabama P, 1996.

——. "A Stage of Her Own: Susan Glaspell's *The Verge* and Women's Dramaturgy." *Journal of American Drama and Theatre* 1.1 (Spring 1989): 79–99.

Garland, Robert. "Cast and Miscast." *New York World-Telegram*, 12 May 1931, 16.

——. "'The Comic Artist' a Success on Sight." *New York World-Telegram*, 20 Apr. 1933, 24.

Garrison, Dee. *Mary Heaton Vorse: The Life of an American Insurgent.* Philadelphia: Temple UP, 1989.

Gasman, Daniel. *The Scientific Origins of National Socialism: Social Darwinism in Ernst Haeckel and the German Monist League.* London: Macdonald, 1971.

"The Gate Theatre Salon." *Era*, 4 Nov. 1925, n.p.

Gibbs, Clayton E. "The One Act Play." *Theatre Magazine* 23 (Mar. 1916): 143, 156.

Gifford, Sanford. "The American Reception of Psychoanalysis, 1908–22." In *1915: The Cultural Moment.* Ed. Adele Heller and Lois Rudnick, 128–45.

Gilbert, Sandra M., and Susan Gubar. *No Man's Land: The Place of the Woman Writer in the Twentieth Century.* Vol. 1: *The War of the Words.* New Haven: Yale UP, 1988.

——. *No Man's Land: The Place of the Woman Writer in the Twentieth Century.* Vol. 2: *Sexchanges.* New Haven: Yale UP, 1989.

——, eds. *The Norton Anthology of Literature by Women: The Tradition in English.* New York: Norton, 1985.

Glaspell, Susan. *Alison's House.* In *The Pulitzer Prize Plays, 1918–1934.* Ed. Kathryn Coe and William H. Cordell, 649–91. New York: Random House, 1935.

——. *Ambrose Holt and Family.* New York: Frederick A. Stokes, 1931.

——. *Bernice. Plays*, 157–230.

——. *Chains of Dew.* Transcript, Library of Congress.

——. *Close the Book. Plays*, 61–96.

——. "Contrary to Precedent." *Booklovers Magazine* 3.2 (Feb. 1904): 234–56.

——. "Ellen Paxton." Short story draft, Berg Collection, New York Public Library.

——. "Faint Trails." Transcript, Berg Collection, New York Public Library.

——. *Fidelity: A Novel.* Boston: Small, Maynard, 1915.

——. *Fugitive's Return.* New York: Frederick A. Stokes, 1929.

——. *Inheritors.* In *Plays by Susan Glaspell.* Ed. C. W. E. Bigsby. 103–57.

——. "A Jury of Her Peers." In *Images of Women in Literature.* Ed. Mary Anne Ferguson, 370–85.

——. Letter to Edna Kenton, 11 May 1922. Barrett Library, U of Virginia.

——. *The Outside. Plays*, 97–118.

——. *The People. Plays*, 31–60.

——. *Plays.* Boston: Small, Maynard and Co., 1920.

——. *Plays by Susan Glaspell.* Ed. C. W. E. Bigsby. Cambridge: Cambridge UP, 1988.

——. *The Road to the Temple.* New York: Frederick A. Stokes, 1927.

——. *Springs Eternal.* Transcript. Berg Collection, New York Public Library.

——. *Trifles. Plays by Susan Glaspell*, 1–30.

——. *The Verge.* In *Plays by Susan Glaspell.* Ed. C. W. E. Bigsby. 57–101.

——. *Woman's Honor. Plays*, 119–56.

Glaspell, Susan, and George Cram Cook. *Suppressed Desires*. Glaspell. *Plays*, 231–71.
———. *Tickless Time*. Glaspell. *Plays*, 273–315.
Glaspell, Susan, and Norman Matson. *The Comic Artist: A Play in Three Acts*. New York: Frederick A. Stokes, 1927.
Godfrey, Harry. "The Mews." *Greenwich Villager*, 3 Dec. 1921, 3.
Goldberg, Isaac. *The Drama of Transition: Native and Exotic Playcraft*. Cincinnati: Stewart Kidd, 1922.
Goldman, Arnold. "The Culture of the Provincetown Players." *Journal of American Studies* 12.3 (1978): 291–310.
Goodman, Edward. "Why the One Act Play?" *Theatre Magazine* 25 (June 1917): 327.
———, ed. *Washington Square Plays*. Garden City, NJ: Doubleday, Page, 1919.
Gordon, Linda. *Woman's Body, Woman's Right: Birth Control in America*. Rev. ed. New York: Penguin, 1990.
Gray, Madeline. *Margaret Sanger: A Biography of the Champion of Birth Control*. New York: Richard Marek, 1979.
Green, Martin. *New York 1913: The Armory Show and the Paterson Strike Pageant*. New York: Collier, 1988.
Grella, George. "The Formal Detective Novel." In *Detective Fiction: A Collection of Critical Essays*. Ed. Robin W. Winks, 84–102.
Griffith, Hubert. "The Week's Theatres." *Observer*, 5 Apr. 1925, 11.
Gubar, Susan, and Anne Hedin. "A Jury of Our Peers: Teaching and Learning in the Indiana Women's Prison." *College English* 43.8 (Dec. 1981): 779–89.
Hale, Nathan G., Jr. *Freud and the Americans: The Beginnings of Psychoanalysis in the United States, 1876–1917*. New York: Oxford UP, 1971.
Hale, Ruth. "Concerning 'The Verge.'" *New York Times*, 20 Nov. 1921, 6:1.
Hamilton, Cicely. "The Theatre." *Time and Tide*, 17 Apr. 1925, 379.
Hamilton, Clayton. "The One-Act Play in America." *Bookman* 37 (Apr. 1913): 184–90.
Hammond, Percy. "The Theatres." *New York Herald Tribune*, 30 Apr. 1933, 7:1.
Hapgood, Hutchins. *A Victorian in the Modern World*. New York: Harcourt, Brace and Co., 1939.
Hartman, Geoffrey H. "Literature High and Low: The Case of the Mystery Story." *The Fate of Reading and Other Essays*, 203–22. Chicago: U of Chicago P, 1975.
h[eap], j[ane]. "The Provincetown Theatre." *Little Review* 6.1 (May 1919): 62–63.
Hedges, Elaine. "Small Things Reconsidered: 'A Jury of Her Peers.'" In *Susan Glaspell: Essays on Her Theater and Fiction*. Ed. Linda Ben-Zvi, 49–69.
Heller, Adele, and Lois Rudnick, eds. *1915: The Cultural Moment: The New Politics, the New Woman, the New Psychology, the New Art and the New Theatre in America*. New Brunswick: Rutgers UP, 1991.
"Heterodoxy to Marie." N.p. Schlessinger Library, Harvard University.
Hohenberg, John. *The Pulitzer Prize: A History of the Awards in Books, Drama, Music and Journalism, Based on the Private Files of Six Decades*. New York: Columbia UP, 1974.
Hoffman, Frederick J. *Freudianism and the Literary Mind*. Baton Rouge: Louisiana State UP, 1945.
———. *The Twenties: American Writing in the Postwar Decade*. New York: Viking, 1955.
Holledge, Julie. *Innocent Flowers: Women in the Edwardian Theatre*. London: Virago, 1981.
Holms, J. F. "Drama." *New Statesman*, 4 Apr. 1925, 746.
Horn, Maurice. "Introduction." *75 Years of the Comics*, 7–16. Boston: Boston Book and Art, 1971.

Hornblow, Arthur. "Mr. Hornblow Goes to the Play." *Theatre* 25 (Jan. 1917): 21–24, 64.

———. "Mr. Hornblow Goes to the Play." *Theatre Magazine* 27 (June 1918): 355–58.

"How Experimental Theaters May Avoid the Pitfalls of Professionalism." *Current Opinion* (July 1918): 28–29.

Hutchins, Rev. Charles L., ed. *The Church Hymnal*. Edition A. Boston: Parish Choir, 1906.

Ibee. "The Comic Artist." *Variety*, 25 Apr. 1933, 50.

"India." *The New Enclyclopaedia Britannica*. 15th ed. Chicago: Encyclopaedia Britannica, Inc. 1991. 21:1–164.

Inge, M. Thomas. *Comics as Culture*. Jackson: U of Mississippi P, 1990.

"Inheritors." *Era*, 6 Jan. 1926, 1.

"Inheritors." *Stage*, 31 Dec. 1925, 13.

"Inheritors." *Times*, 28 Sept. 1925, 12.

"'Inheritors' a Triumph in Critics' Opinion." *New York Times*, 28 Sept. 1925, 24.

"'Inheritors' by Susan Glaspell." *Christian Science Monitor*, 5 Apr. 1921, 12.

R. J. "The Theatre." *Spectator*, 16 Jan. 1926, 80–81.

James, Henry. *The Ambassadors*. 1903. Ed. S. P. Rosenbaum. New York: Norton, 1964.

"Jhansi." *The New Encyclopaedia Britannica*. Vol. 6. 15th ed. Chicago: Encyclopaedia Britannica Inc., 1991. 548.

Johnston, Denis. "Director's Notes." *Trifles* Program. Shaw Festival. Niagara-on-the-Lake, Ontario, 1999.

Kattwinkel, Susan. "Absence as a Site for Debate: Modern Feminism and Victorianism in the Plays of Susan Glaspell." *New England Theatre Journal* 7 (1996): 37–55.

Kennedy, David M. *Birth Control in America: The Career of Margaret Sanger*. New Haven: Yale UP, 1970.

Kenton, Edna. Manuscript letter to George Cram Cook, 1 July, 1922. Provincetown Players Collection, Harvard Theatre Collection.

———. Manuscript letter to Susan Glaspell, 5 May 1922. Provincetown Players Collection, Harvard Theatre Collection.

———. Manuscript letter to Susan Glaspell, 29 May, 1922. Barrett Library, University of Virginia.

———. Manuscript letter to Blanche Hays, 22 June, 1922. Barrett Library, University of Virginia.

———. "The Story of the Provincetown Players: The Playwrights' Theatre 1915–1922." Transcript. Fales Collection, New York University.

Kolodny, Annette. "A Map for Rereading: Gender and the Interpretation of Literary Texts." In *The New Feminist Criticism: Essays on Women, Litearature, and Theory*. Ed. Elaine Showalter, 46–62. New York: Pantheon Books, 1985.

Krutch, Joseph Wood. *The American Drama Since 1918*. New York: George Braziller, 1957.

———. "Drama." *Nation*, 10 May 1933, 539–40.

Kuttner, Alfred. "A Note on Forgetting." *New Republic*, 28 Nov. 1914, 15–17.

Langner, Lawrence. *The Magic Curtain: The Study of a Life in Two Fields, Theatre and Invention*. New York: E. P. Dutton, 1951.

Larabee, Ann. "Death in Delphia: Susan Glaspell and the Companionate Marriage." *Mid-American Review* 7.2 (1987): 93–106.

———. "First-Wave Feminist Theatre, 1890–1930." Ph.D., State University of New York—Binghamton, 1988.

———. "'Meeting the Outside Face to Face': Susan Glaspell, Djuna Barnes, and O'Neill's *The Emperor Jones*." In *Modern American Drama: The Female Canon*. Ed. June Schleuter, 77–85.

"Last Subscription Performance." Unidentified clipping. Cook and Glaspell Papers. Berg Collection, New York Public Library.

"Last Week's Theatrical Hurricane." *The Lady.* Unidentified clipping. Cook and Glaspell Papers. Berg Collection, New York Public Library.

Laughlin, Karen. "Conflict of Interest: The Ideology of Authorship in *Alison's House.*" In *Susan Glaspell: Essays on Her Theater and Fiction.* Ed. Linda Ben-Zvi, 219–35.

Leach, Eugene R. "The Radicals of *The Masses.*" In *1915: The Cultural Moment.* Ed. Adele Heller and Lois Rudnick, 27–47.

Leed, Eric J. *No Man's Land: Combat and Identity in World War I.* Cambridge: Cambridge UP, 1979.

Le Gallienne, Eva. *At 33.* New York: Longmans, Green, 1934.

Lewis, B. Roland. *The Technique of the One-Act Play: A Study in Dramatic Construction.* Boston: John W. Luce and Co., 1918.

Lewisohn, Ludwig. "Drama." *Nation,* 6 Apr. 1921, 515.

———. "Drama." *Nation,* 14 Dec. 1921, 708–9.

———. *Expression in America.* New York: Harper and Bros., 1932.

Littell, Robert. "The New Play." *World,* 2 Dec. 1930, 11.

"The Little." *Stage,* 13 Oct. 1932, 14.

Little, Judy. "Humoring the Sentence: Women's Dialogic Comedy." In *Women's Comic Visions.* Ed. June Sochen, 19–32.

Lockridge, Richard. "The New Play." *New York Sun,* 20 Apr. 1933, 18.

Loving, Pierre. "Introduction." In *Fifty Contemporary One-Act Plays.* Ed. Frank Shay and Pierre Loving, n.p.

Loy, Mina. "Feminist Manifesto." *The Last Lunar Baedeker,* 269–71.

———. "Gertrude Stein." *The Last Lunar Baedeker,* 26.

———. *The Last Lunar Baedeker.* Ed. Roger L. Conover. Highlands: Jargon Society, 1982.

Luhan, Mabel Dodge. *Movers and Shakers.* Vol. 3 of *Intimate Memories.* New York: Harcourt, Brace and Co., 1936.

Macfarlane, Peter Clark. "Diagnosis by Dreams." *Good Housekeeping* 60 (1915): 125–33, 278–86.

Macgowan, Kenneth. "Broadway Bows to By-Ways." *Theatre Arts Monthly* 5 (July 1921): 175–83.

———. "The New Play." *Globe and Commercial Advertiser,* 15 Nov. 1921, n.p.

Macmillan, Mary. *Short Plays.* Cincinnati: Stewart and Kidd, 1913.

Mael, Phyllis. "*Trifles:* The Path to Sisterhood." *Literature/Film Quarterly* 17.4 (1989): 281–84.

Makowsky, Veronica. "Susan Glaspell and Modernism." *The Cambridge Companion to American Women Playwrights.* Ed. Brenda Murphy, 49–65. Cambridge: Cambridge UP, 1999.

———. *Susan Glaspell's Century of American Women: A Critical Interpretation of Her Work.* New York: Oxford UP, 1993.

Malpede, Karen. "Reflections on *The Verge.*" In *Susan Glaspell: Essays on Her Theater and Fiction.* Ed. Linda Ben-Zvi, 123–27.

Mantle, Burns. "Alison's House." *The Best Plays of 1930–31 and the Year Book of the Drama in America.* Ed. B. Mantle, 222–53. New York: Dodd, Mead, 1931.

———. "Introduction." *The Best Plays of 1930–31 and the Year Book of the Drama in America.* Ed. B. Mantle v–ix.

———. "Introduction." *The Best Plays of 1943–44 and the Year Book of the Drama in America.* Ed. B. Mantle, v–vii. New York: Dodd, Mead, 1951.

————. "Introduction." *The Best Plays of 1944–45 and the Year Book of the Drama in America*. Ed. B. Mantle. v–vii. New York: Dodd, Mead, 1946.

————. "Plays of the Week." *New York Mail*, 29 Apr. 1922, 7.

————. "'The Comic Artist' Has Tragic Overtone." *New York Daily News*, 20 Apr. 1933, 41.

————, ed. *The Best Plays of 1930–31 and the Year Book of the Drama in America*. New York: Dodd, Mead, 1931.

Marx, Leo. *The Machine in the Garden: Technology and the Pastoral Ideal in America*. New York: Oxford UP, 1967.

Matson, Norman Häghejm. "The Shortest Way Out." *American Review* 3.4 (1934): 448–53.

Matthews, Fred. "The New Psychology and American Drama." In *1915: The Cultural Moment*. Ed. Adele Heller and Lois Rudnick, 146–56.

Micale, Mark S. *Approaching Hysteria: Disease and Its Interpretations*. Princeton: Princeton UP, 1995.

Middleton, George. "The Neglected One-Act Play." *Dramatic Mirror*, 31 Jan. 1912, 13–14.

"Miss Glaspell's Long Play." *Evening Transcript* (Boston), 31 Mar. 1919, n.p.

"Miss Glaspell's New Comedy." *Evening Telegram*, 28 Apr. 1922, 7.

Mitgang, Herbert. "Theater: 'Inheritors,' with Geraldine Page." *New York Times*, 14 Dec. 1983, 3. 26.

Mock, James R. *Censorship, 1917*. Princeton: Princeton UP, 1941.

Moeller, Philip. "An Important Play." *Little Review* 6.1 (May 1919): 56–59.

Moi, Toril. *Feminist Theory and Simone de Beauvoir*. London: Basil Blackwell, 1990.

Morley, Sheridan. *Sybil Thorndike: A Life in the Theatre*. London: Weidenfeld and Nicolson, 1977.

Moses, Montrose J. *The American Dramatist*. Boston: Little, Brown, 1925.

Munt, Sally. *Murder by the Book? Feminism and the Crime Novel*. London: Routledge, 1994.

Mustazza, Leonard. "Generic Translation and Thematic Shift in Susan Glaspell's *Trifles* and 'A Jury of Her Peers.'" *Studies in Short Fiction* 26.4 (Fall 1989): 489–96.

L. N. "The Play." *New York Times*, 20 Apr. 1933, 20.

Nadelhaft, Ruth. "Domestic Violence in Literature: A Preliminary Study." *Mosaic* 17.2 (1984): 243–59.

Nathan, George Jean. "Foreword." *The Theatre Book of the Year, 1944–45: A Record and an Interpretation*, v–xv. New York: Knopf, 1945.

————. "The Theatre of George Jean Nathan." *Judge*, 27 Dec. 1930, 16, 31.

Nelligan, Liza Maeve. "'The Haunting Beauty from the Life We've Left': A Contextual Reading of *Trifles* and *The Verge*." In *Susan Glaspell: Essays on Her Theater and Fiction*, ed. Linda Ben-Zvi, 85–104.

"The News-week in Entertainment." *Newsweek*, 29 Apr. 1933, 20.

Nichols, Carroll Leja, M.D. "War and Civil Neuroses—A Comparison." *Long Island Medical Journal* 13.8 (Aug. 1919): 257–68.

Noe, Marcia. "A Critical Biography of Susan Glaspell." Ph.D. diss., Department of English, U of Iowa, 1976.

————. "Region as Metaphor in the Plays of Susan Glaspell." *Western Illinois Regional Studies* 4.1 (1981): 77–85.

————. *Susan Glaspell: Voice from the Heartland*. Macomb: Western Illinois UP, 1983.

————. "*The Verge: L'Écriture Féminine* at the Provincetown." In *Susan Glaspell: Essays on Her Theater and Fiction*. Ed. Linda Ben-Zvi, 129–42.

O'Brien, Sharon. "Feminist Theory and Literary Biography." In *Contesting the Subject.* Ed. Willaim H. Epstein, 123–33.

Ogburn, William Fielding, ed. *American Society in Wartime.* 1943. Rpt. New York: De Capo, 1972.

O'Neill, William, ed. *Echoes of Revolt:* The Masses, *1911–1917.* Chicago: Quadrangle Books, 1966.

———. *The Last Romantic: A Life of Max Eastman.* New York: Oxford UP, 1978.

Oppenheim, James. "Art, Religion and Science." *Seven Arts* (June 1917): 229–34.

O'Sullivan, Judith. *The Great American Comic Strip.* Boston: Little, Brown, 1990.

Ozieblo, Barbara. "Rebellion and Rejection: The Plays of Susan Glaspell." In *Modern American Drama: The Female Canon.* Ed. June Schleuter, 66–76.

Papke, Mary E. *Susan Glaspell: A Research and Production Sourcebook.* Westport, CT: Greenwood P, 1993.

Park, Robert E. "Racial Ideologies." In *American Society in Wartime.* Ed. William Fielding Ogburn, 165–84.

Parry, Albert. *Garrets and Pretenders: A History of Bohemianism in America.* New York: Covici Friede, 1933.

Peterson, H. C., and Gilbert C. Fite. *Opponents of War, 1917–1918.* Madison: U of Wisconsin P, 1957.

"Philosophers Wrestle with 'The Verge' While Bread Burns." *Greenwich Villager,* 23 Nov. 1921, 1.

"The Pioneer Players." *Daily Telegraph.* Unidentified clipping. Cook and Glaspell Papers. Berg Collection, New York Public Library.

Pirandello, Luigi. "Preface to *Six Characters in Search of an Author.*" *Naked Masks.* Trans. Eric Bentley, 363–75. New York: E. P. Dutton, 1952.

"The Play Actors." *Times,* 25 June 1928, n.p.

"The Play Actors Say 'Au Revoir.'" *Stage,* 28 June 1928, 19.

"Players' Theatre." *Times,* 23 Nov. 1929, 10c.

"Plays to Be Presented at the Civic Repertory Theatre during 1930–31." Civic Repertory Theatre Souvenir Programme. 1930.

Pollitt, Josephine. *Emily Dickinson: The Human Background of Her Poetry.* New York: Harper and Bros., 1930.

Pollock, Arthur. "The Theatres." *Brooklyn Daily Eagle,* 20 Apr. 1933, 22.

Preston, William, Jr. *Aliens and Dissenters: Federal Suppression of Radicals, 1903–1933.* Cambridge: Harvard UP, 1963.

"The Provincetown Players Third New York Season 1918–1919." Season Circular. Cook and Glaspell Papers. Berg Collection, New York Public Library.

P. F. R. "Inheritors." *New York Evening Post,* 23 Mar. 1921, 9.

"A Quadruple Bill." *Era,* 20 July 1927, 1.

Rader, Barbara A., and Howard G. Zettler, eds. *The Sleuth and the Scholar: Origins, Evolution, and Current Trends in Detective Fiction.* New York: Greenwood Press, 1988.

Radner, Joan N., and Susan S. Lanser. "The Feminist Voice: Strategies of Coding in Folklore and Literature." *Journal of American Folklore* 100 (Oct.–Dec. 1987): 412–25.

Rahn, B. J. "Seeley Regester: America's First Detective Novelist." In *The Sleuth and the Scholar: Origins, Evolution, and Current Trends in Detective Fiction.* Ed. Barbara A. Rader and Howard G. Zettler, 47–61.

Rathbun, Stephen. "Spanish Operetta, Musical Comedy and Two Dramas Arrive Thanksgiving Week." *New York Sun,* 19 Nov. 1921, 4.

———. "Susan Glaspell's 'Chains of Dew' Is a Bright, Realistic Little Comedy." *Sun,* 29 Apr. 1922, 4.

Reddy, Maureen. *Sisters in Crime: Feminism and the Crime Novel.* New York: Continuum, 1988.

Redfield, Robert. "The Japanese-Americans." In *American Society in Wartime.* Ed. William Fielding Ogburn, 143–64.

Rees, Leslie. "Where Are Our Senior Dramatists?" *Era,* 19 Oct. 1932, 21.

Reinelt, Janelle. "Feminist Theory and the Problem of Performance." *Modern Drama* 32.1 (Mar. 1989): 48–57.

Riley, Glenda. *The Female Frontier: A Comparative View of Women on the Prairie and the Plains.* Lawrence: UP of Kansas, 1988.

———. *Frontierswomen: The Iowa Experience.* Ames: Iowa State UP, 1981.

Roberts, R. Ellis. "A Great Playwright." *Guardian,* 17 July 1925, n.p.

Robins, Elizabeth. *Votes for Women.* 1907. In *How the Vote Was Won and Other Suffragette Plays.* Ed. Dale Spender and Carole Hayman, 35–87. London: Methuen, 1985.

Robinson, Jerry. *The Comics: An Illustrated History of Comic Strip Art.* New York: Berkeley Publishing, 1974.

Rodier, Katharine. "Glaspell and Dickinson: Surveying the Premises of *Alison's House.*" In *Susan Glaspell: Essays on Her Theater and Fiction,* ed. Linda Ben-Zvi, 195–218.

Rohe, Alice. "The Story of Susan Glaspell." *Morning Telegraph,* 18 Dec. 1921, sec. 2:4.

Royde-Smith, N. G. "The Drama." *Outlook,* 9 Jan 1926, 25.

Ruhl, Arthur. "Alison's House." *New York Herald Tribune,* 2 Dec. 1930, 18.

———. "Audience Stirred By 'Inheritors' at Civic Repertory." *New York Herald Tribune,* 8 Mar. 1927, 17.

———. "Second Nights." *New York Herald Tribune,* 23 Apr. 1933, vii:1.

E. O. S. *Hungary and Its Revolutions: From the Earliest Period to the Nineteenth Century with a Memoir of Louis Kossuth.* London: Henry G. Bohn, 1854.

W. H. S. "Another Play." *New York Evening Post,* 8 Mar. 1927, 14.

Sarlós, Robert Károly. *Jig Cook and the Provincetown Players: Theatre in Ferment.* Amherst: U of Massachusetts P, 1982.

Schanke, Robert A. *Shattered Applause: The Lives of Eva Le Gallienne.* Carbondale: Southern Illinois UP, 1992.

Schleuter, June, ed. *Modern American Drama: The Female Canon.* Cranbury, NJ: Associated UP, 1990.

Schlissel, Lillian, ed. *Conscience in America: A Documentary History of Conscientious Objection in America, 1757–1967.* New York: Dutton, 1968.

Schmidt, Albert. "Blazing a Trail to Higher Education." In *The Heritage of the Middle West.* Ed. John J. Murray, 234–54. Norman: U of Oklahoma P, 1958.

Schwarz, Judith. *Radical Feminists of Heterodoxy.* Revised ed. Norwich, VT: New Victoria Publishers, 1986.

Sewall, Richard B. *The Life of Emily Dickinson.* 2 vols. New York: Farrar, Straus and Giroux, 1974.

"Shall Women Have Families like These—Or Shall We Let Them Control Births?" *Birth Control Review* (Apr. 1919): 10–11.

Shaw, Bernard. *Heartbreak House: A Fantasia in the Russian Manner on English Themes.* 1919. Rpt. New York: Penguin, 1977.

Shay, Frank. "Drama." *Greenwich Villager,* 23 Nov. 1921, 7.

———. "Introduction." *Fifty More Contemporary One-Act Plays,* v–vi. New York: D. Appleton, 1928.

Shay, Frank, and Pierre Loving, eds. *Fifty Contemporary One-Act Plays.* New York: D. Appleton, 1925.

Sheppard, Alice. "Social Cognition, Gender Roles, and Women's Humor." *Women's Comic Visions.* Ed. June Sochen, 33–56.

Shipp, Horace. "The Language of Drama." *English Review* 17 (Jan.–June 1926): 267–69.

Shortridge, James R. *The Middle West: Its Meaning in American Culture.* Lawrence: U of Kansas P, 1990.

Showalter, Elaine. *The Female Malady: Women, Madness, and English Culture, 1830–1980.* New York: Pantheon, 1985.

———. "Hysteria, Feminism, and Gender." In *Hysteria Beyond Freud.* Ed. Sander L. Gilman et al., 286–344. Berkeley: U of California P, 1993.

———. "Piecing and Writing." In *The Poetics of Gender.* Ed. Nancy K. Miller, 222–47. New York: Columbia UP, 1986.

Sievers, W. David. *Freud on Broadway: A History of Psychoanalysis and the American Drama.* New York: Hermitage House, 1955.

Singhal, D. P. *Gypsies: Indians in Exile.* Berkeley: Folklore Institute, 1982.

Sinor, Denis. *History of Hungary.* London: George Allen and Unwin, 1959.

Skinner, R. Dana. "The Play." *Commonweal,* 30 Mar. 1927, 582–83.

———. "The Play." *Commonweal,* 17 Dec. 1930, 187.

———. "The Play." *Commonweal,* 12 May 1933, 49–50.

Smith, Beverly A. "Women's Work—*Trifles?* The Skill and Insights of Playwright Susan Glaspell." *International Journal of Women's Studies* 5.2 (Mar.–Apr. 1982): 172–84.

Smith, Cynthia D. "'Emasculating Tom, Dick, and Harry': Representations of Masculinity in Susan Glaspell's *The Verge.*" *Journal of American Drama and Theatre* 11 (Spring 1999): 60–77.

Smith, Rita Creighton. In *The Rescue. Plays of the Harvard Dramatic Club.* Ed. G. P. Baker, 51–72. New York: Brentano's, 1918.

Sochen, June, ed. *Women's Comic Visions.* Detroit: Wayne State UP, 1991.

"Social Darwinism." *The New Encyclopaedia Britannica.* 15th ed. Chicago: Encyclopaedia Britannica, Inc. 1991. 10:919–20.

Stansell, Christine. *American Moderns: Bohemian New York and the Creation of a New Century.* New York: Metropolitan Books, 2000.

Stasio, Marilyn. "A Sweep through the Subgenres." In *The Sleuth and the Scholar: Origins, Evolution, and Current Trends in Detective Fiction.* Ed. Barbara A. Rader and Howard G. Zettler, 69–75.

Steele, Wilbur Daniel. In *"Not Smart." Provincetown Plays.* Ed. George Cram Cook and Frank Shay, 241–72.

Stein, Karen F. "The Women's World of Glaspell's *Trifles.*" In *Women in American Theatre.* Ed. Helen Krich Chinoy and Linda Walsh Jenkins, 251–54.

Sterne, Richard Clark. *Dark Mirror: The Sense of Injustice in Modern European and American Literature.* New York: Fordham UP, 1994.

Styan, J. L. *Modern Drama in Theory and Practice.* Vol 1. Cambridge: Cambridge UP, 1981.

Sundgaard, Arnold. "Susan Glaspell and the Federal Theatre Revisited." *Journal of American Drama and Theatre* 9 (Winter 1997): 1–10.

"Susan Glaspell's 'Chains of Dew' Is Sharp Satire." *New York Herald,* 28 Apr. 1922, 10.

Sweeney, S. E. "Locked Rooms: Detective Fiction, Narrative Theory, and Self-Reflexivity." In *The Cunning Craft: Original Essays on Detective Fiction and Contemporary Literary Theory.* Ed. Ronald G. Walker and June M. Frazer, 1–14.

Taggard, Genevieve. *The Life and Mind of Emily Dickinson.* New York: Alfred A. Knopf, 1930.

Tarn. "The Theatre." *Spectator,* 15 Oct. 1921, 494–95.

Tatla, Darshan Singh. *Sikhs in North America: An Annotated Bibliography.* New York: Greenwood P, 1991.

Toohey, John L. *A History of the Pulitzer Prize Plays.* New York: Citadel Press, 1967.

Tuttle, William M., Jr. *Race Riot: Chicago in the Red Summer of 1919.* New York: Atheneum, 1970.

Van Doren, Mark. "Drama: The Pulitzer Prize Play." *Nation,* 27 May 1931, 591–92.

"The Verge." *Times,* 30 Mar. 1925, 12.

"The Verge." Unidentified clipping. Cook and Glaspell Papers. Berg Collection, New York Public Library.

Vorse, Mary Heaton. *Time and the Town: A Provincetown Chronicle.* New York: Dial Press, 1942.

Wainscott, Ronald. *The Emergence of the Modern American Theater, 1914–1929.* New Haven: Yale UP, 1997.

Walker, Cheryl. "Persona Criticism and the Death of the Author." In *Contesting the Subject.* Ed. William H. Epstein, 108–22.

Walker, Kenneth R. *A History of the Middle West: From the Beginning to 1970.* Little Rock: Pioneer, 1972.

Walker, Nancy. "Toward a Solidarity: Women's Humor and Group Identity." In *Women's Comic Visions.* Ed. June Sochen, 57–81.

Walker, Ronald G. and June M. Frazer, eds. *The Cunning Craft: Original Essays On Detective Fiction and Contemporary Literary Theory.* Macomb: Western Illinois UP, 1990.

Walton, Priscilla L., and Manina Jones. *Detective Agency: Women Rewriting the Hard-Boiled Tradition.* Berkeley: U of California P, 1999.

Ware, Caroline. *Greenwich Village, 1920–1930: A Comment on American Civilization in the Post-War Years.* Boston: Riverside Press, 1935.

Waterman, Arthur. *Susan Glaspell.* New York: Twayne, 1966.

Watson, Steven. *Strange Bedfellows: The First American Avant-Garde.* New York: Abbeville Press, 1991.

Wertheim, Arthur Frank. *The New York Little Renaissance: Iconoclasm, Modernism, and Nationalism in American Culture, 1908–1917.* New York: New York UP, 1976.

"What 'The Verge' Is About, Who Can Tell?" *New York Herald,* 15 Nov. 1921, 15.

Wheeler, W. Reginald, Henry H. King, and Alexander B. Davidson, eds. *The Foreign Student in America: A Study by the Commission on Survey of Foreign Students in the United States of America, under the Auspices of the Friendly Relations Committee of the Young Men's Christian Association and the Young Women's Christian Association.* New York: Association Press, 1925.

White, David Manning, and Robert H. Abel. *The Funnies: An American Idiom.* New York: Free Press of Glencoe, 1963.

Wilde, Percival. *The Craftsmanship of the One-Act Play.* Boston: Little, Brown, 1923.

Wiles, Timothy J. *The Theater Event: Modern Theories of Performance.* Chicago: U of Chicago P, 1980.

Willett, John, ed. *Brecht on Theatre: The Development of an Aesthetic.* New York: Hill and Wang, 1964.

Williams, Linda. "A Jury of Their Peers: Marlene Gorris's *A Question of Silence.*" In *Postmodernism and Its Discontents.* Ed. G. A. Kaplan. 107–215. London: Verso, 1988.

Williams, William Carlos. *Paterson.* New York: New Directions, 1963.

Winks, Robin W., ed. *Detective Fiction: A Collection of Critical Essays.* 1980. Rpt. Woodstock: Countryman Press, 1988.

Woods, Robin, "'His Appearance Is Against Him': The Emergence of the Detective." In *The Cunning Craft: Original Essays on Detective Fiction and Contemporary Literary Theory.* Ed. Ronald G. Walker and June M. Frazer, 15–24.

Woolf, Virginia. *A Room of One's Own.* New York: Harcourt Brace Jovanovich, 1957.

Woollcott, Alexander. "The Play." *New York Times,* 15 Nov. 1921, 23.

———. "The Play." *New York Times,* 28 Apr. 1922, 20.

———. "Second Thoughts on First Nights." *New York Times,* 27 Mar. 1921, 7:1.

———. "Second Thoughts on First Nights." *New York Times,* 20 Nov. 1921, 6:1.

Worthen, W. B. *Modern Drama and the Rhetoric of Theater.* Berkeley: U of California P, 1992.

Young, Stark. "After the Play." *New Republic,* 7 Dec. 1921, 7.

———. "Mr. Beckhard's Fourth." *New Republic,* 10 May 1933, 365–66.

Zorach, William. *Art Is My Life.* Cleveland: World Publishing Co., 1967.

Works Consulted

Abrahams, Edward. *The Lyrical Left and the Origins of Cultural Radicalism in America.* Charlottesville: UP of Virginia, 1986.

Abramson, Doris, et al. "Women in the Theatre." *Centerpoint* 3 (Fall–Spring 1980): 31–37.

"'Alison's House' Is Brought up to the Ritz Theatre." *New York American,* 12 May 1931, 9.

"Ancient Poetess Chief Character in 'Alison's House.'" *New York American,* 2 Dec. 1930, 15.

Anderson, John. "The Circle." *Theatre Annual* (1942): 17–28.

"Arts Theatre." *Stage,* 3 Nov. 1927, 15.

A. S. "Another New Play." *New York World,* 8 Mar. 1927, 13–14.

Atlas, Marilyn J. "Harriet Monroe, Margaret Anderson, and the Spirit of the Chicago Renaissance." *Midwestern Miscellany* 19 (1981): 43–53.

Bach, Gerhard. "Susan Glaspell (1876–1948): A Bibliography of Dramatic Criticism." *Great Lakes Review* 3.2 (Winter 1977): 1–34.

———. "Susan Glaspell: Supplementary Notes." *American Literary Realism* 5.1 (Winter 1972): 71–73.

Baskin, Alex. "Margaret Sanger, the *Woman Rebel* and the Rise of the Birth Control Movement in the United States." In *Woman Rebel.* Ed. A. Baskin, i–xxii. New York: Archives of Social History, 1976.

"Barnard Girls Vote on Pulitzer Prizes." *New York Times,* 15 May 1931, 27.

Baym, Nina. *Women's Fiction: A Guide to Novels by and about Women in America, 1820–1870.* Ithaca: Cornell UP, 1978.

Beard, Rick, and Leslie Cohen Berlowitz, eds. *Greenwich Village: Culture and Counterculture.* New Brunswick: Rutgers UP, 1993.

"The Bookshelf: Some American Plays." *Era,* 17 Sept. 1924, n.p. Clipping. Cook and Glaspell Papers. Berg Collection, New York Public Library.

Brackett, Charles. "The Theatre." *New Yorker,* 19 Mar. 1927, 111.

Brown, Maurice. *The Temple of a Living Art: Being a Plea for an American Art Theatre in a Letter to Theodore B. Hinckley, Esq., Editor of "Drama."* Chicago: Chicago Little Theatre, 1914.

Bruner, Jerome S. *Mandate from the People.* New York: Duell, Sloan and Pearce, 1944.

Bryce, Mary. "'Alison's House.'" *Leveller*, n.d., n.p. Clipping. Billy Rose Theatre Collection, New York Public Library.

Carne, Rosalind. "'Alison's House.'" *Fiancial Times*, n.d., n.p. Clipping. Billy Rose Theatre Collection, New York Public Library.

Chauncey, George, Jr. "Christian Brotherhood or Sexual Perversion? Homosexual Identities and the Construction of Sexual Boundaries in the World War I Era." In *Gender and American History Since 1890.* Ed. Barbara Melosh, 72–105.

Cheney, Sheldon. *The Art Theater.* 1917. Rev. ed. New York: Knopf, 1925.

Clark, Barrett H. "Success and Failure on Broadway." *Drama Magazine* (Jan. 1931): 11–14.

Cook, George Cram. "The Provincetown Players Third New York Season 1918–1919." Season circular. Cook and Glaspell Papers. Berg Collection, New York Public Library.

———. "The Provincetown Players Sixth Season 1919–1920." Season circular. Cook and Glaspell Papers. Berg Collection, New York Public Library.

———. "The Provincetown Players Season of 1920–21." Season circular. Cook and Glaspell Papers. Berg Collection, New York Public Library.

Corbin, John. "Village Morality." *New York Times*, 23 Feb. 1919, sec. 4.2.

Deighton, Lee C., ed. *The Encyclopedia of Education.* Vol. 3. New York: Macmillan, 1971.

de Jongh, Nicholas. "'Alison's House.'" *Guardian*, n.d., n.p. Clipping. Billy Rose Theatre Collection, New York Public Library.

Dennett, Mary Ware. *Birth Control Laws: Shall we Keep Them, Change Them or Abolish Them?* New York: Frederick H. Hitchcock, 1926.

Deutsch, Helen, and Stella Hanau. *The Provincetown: A Story of the Theatre.* New York: Farrar and Rinehart, 1931.

Dickinson, Emily. "Emily Dickinson's Letters." *Atlantic Monthly* (Oct. 1891): 444–56.

Dickinson, Thomas H. *Playwrights of the New American Theater.* 1925. Rpt. Freeport, NY: Books for Libraries P, 1967.

D. L. M. "The Drama." *Nation and Athenaeum,* 15 Oct. 1921, 119–20.

———. "The Drama." *Nation and Athenaeum* 22 July 1922, 576.

Duffey, Bernard. *The Chicago Renaissance in American Letters: A Critical History.* Lansing: Michigan State UP, 1954.

Eaton, Walter Prichard. "Realistic Drama and the Experimental Theatre." *Theatre Arts* 2 (1918): 18–20.

Edminston, Susan, and Linda D. Cirino. *Literary New York: A History and Guide.* Boston: Houghton Mifflin, 1976.

Ervine, St. John. "The Week's Theatres." *Observer,* 3 Jan. 1926, 9.

"Everyman." *Sunday Times,* 23 July 1922, 4.

"Everyman Theatre: Inheritors." *Daily Telegraph,* 29 Dec. 1925, n.p. Clipping. Cook and Glaspell Papers. Berg Collection, New York Public Library.

Finney, Gail. "Theater of Impotence: The One-Act Tragedy at the Turn of the Century." *Modern Drama* 28.3 (Sept. 1985): 451–61.

"The First Reader." *World,* 23 Dec. 1930, 9.

Fosdick, Raymond B. "Our Machine Civilization—A Frankenstein Monster?" *Current Opinion* (Sept. 1922): 365–67.

France, Rachel. "Susan Glaspell (1882–1948)." In *A Century of Plays by American Women.* Ed. France, 49. New York: Richards Rosen P, 1979.

Frank, Waldo. "Concerning a Little Theater." *Seven Arts* (Dec. 1916): 157–64.

Friedman, Sharon. "Feminism as Theme in Twentieth-Century American Women's Drama." *American Studies* 25.1 (Spring 1984): 69–89.

Garland, Robert. "Drama-Wise Say Poetess of Sorrow Is Not Fictional." *New York World Telegram*, n.d., n.p. clipping. Glaspell File. Theatre Collection, Museum of the City of New York.

———. "Opening Stanza Powerful Tribute to One's America." *New York Telegram*, n.d., n.p. Clipping. Glaspell File. Theatre Collection, Museum of the City of New York.

Gassner, John. "Pioneers of the New Theater Movement." *American Theater Today*. Ed. Alan S. Downer, 15–24. New York: Basic Books, 1967.

Gelb, Arthur, and Barbara. *O'Neill*. New York: Harper and Row, 1973.

Goldman, Michael. "The Dangerous Edge of Things." *Times Literary Supplement*, 5–11 Feb. 1988, 139.

Gould, Jean. *Modern American Playwrights*. New York: Dodd, Mead, 1966.

"The Greatness of the Little Theater Movement Explained by Its Champions." *Current Opinion* (Dec. 1917): 389–90.

G. W. B. "The Comic Artist." *Era*, 27 June 1928, 1.

Harrington, Fred Harvey. "Literary Aspects of American Anti-Imperialism, 1898–1902." *New England Quarterly* 10 (Dec. 1937): 650–67.

Hedges, Elaine. "The Nineteenth-Century Diarist and Her Quilts." *Feminist Studies* 8.2 (Summer 1982): 291–99.

Hedges, M. H. "Miss Glaspell's Vision of Life." *Nation*, n.d., n.p. Clipping. Cook and Glaspell Papers. Berg Collection, New York Public Library.

Henderson, Mary C. *The City and the Theatre: New York Playhouses from Bowling Green to Times Square*. Clifton, NJ: James T. White, 1973.

H. G. "Suppressed Desires." *Observer*, 23 July 1922, 9.

H. H. "A Triple Bill." *Observer*, 15 Jan. 1933, 13.

"Hope for the Movies Seen in the Little Theater Movement." *Current Opinion* (Dec. 1921): 762–63.

Hopkins, Arthur. "Our Unreasonable Theatre." *Theatre Arts* 2 (1918): 79–84.

"How Experimental Theaters May Avoid the Pitfalls of Professionalism." *Current Opinion* (July 1918): 28–29.

"'In The Zone.'" *Times*, 19 July 1922, 12.

"Inheritors." *Drama Calendar*, 14 Mar. 1927, 3–5.

"Inheritors." *Manchester Guardian*, 28 Sept. 1925, n.p. Clipping. Cook and Glaspell Papers. Berg Collection, New York Public Library.

Jones, Margaret C. *Heretics and Hellraisers: Women Contributors to "The Masses," 1911–1917*. Austin: U of Texas P, 1993.

Kenton, Edna. "Provincetown and Macdougal Street." George Cram Cook. *Greek Coins*, 17–30. New York: George H. Doran, 1925.

Kessler, Carol Farley, and Gail Rudenstein. "Mothers and Daughters in Literature: A Preliminary Bibliography." *Women's Studies* 6.1 (1978–79): 223–34.

Kolin, Philip C. "Therapists in Susan Glaspell's *Suppressed Desires* and David Rabe's *In The Boom Boom Room*." *Notes on Contemporary Literature* 18.5 (Nov. 1988): 2–3.

Kozlenko, William, ed. *The One-Act Play Today: A Discussion of the Technique, Scope and History of the Contemporary Short Drama*. New York: Harcourt, Brace, 1938.

Lasch, Christopher. *The New Radicalism in America, 1889–1963: The Intellectual as a Social Type*. New York: Knopf, 1966.

Leonard, Martha. [Letter to the editor.] Clipping. Cook and Glaspell Papers. Berg Collection, New York Public Library.

Lippmann, Walter. *A Preface to Politics*. 1914. Rpt. Ann Arbor: U of Michigan P, 1962.

Macgowan, Kenneth. *Footlights across America: Towards a National Theater.* New York: Harcourt, Brace, 1929.

———. "The New Play: 'The Spring.'" Clipping. Cook and Glaspell Papers. Berg Collection, New York Public Library.

———. *The Theatre of Tomorrow.* New York: Boni and Liveright, 1921.

Malone, Andrew. "Susan Glaspell." *Dublin Magazine* 2 (1924–25): 107–11.

Mantle, Burns. "'Alison's House.'" *New York Daily News,* n.d., n.p. Clipping. Glaspell File. Theatre Collection, Museum of the City of New York.

———. *Contemporary American Playwrights.* New York: Dodd, Mead, 1938.

———, ed. *The Best Plays of 1919–20 and the Year Book of the Drama in America.* Boston: Small, Maynard, 1920.

———, ed. *The Best Plays of 1920–21 and the Year Book of the Drama in America.* Boston: Small, Maynard, 1921.

———, ed. *The Best Plays of 1921–22 and the Year Book of the Drama in America.* Boston: Small, Maynard, 1922.

———, ed. *The Best Plays of 1932–33 and the Year Book of the Drama in America.* New York: Dodd, Mead, 1933.

Mantle, Burns, and Garrison P. Sherwood, eds. *The Best Plays of 1909–1919 and the Year Book of the Drama in America.* New York: Dodd, Mead, 1943.

Maxwell, Perriton. "Another Hat in the Ring." *New York Times,* 19 Apr. 1931, 2:2.

May, Henry F. *The End of American Innocence: A Study of the First Years of Our Own Time, 1912–1917.* New York: Knopf, 1959.

McKnight, Jeannie. "American Dream, Nightmare Underside: Diaries, Letters and Fiction of Women on the American Frontier." In *Women, Women Writers, and the West.* Ed. L. L. Lee and Merrill Levis, 25–44. Troy, NY: Whitson Publishing, 1979.

Melosh, Barbara, ed. *Gender and American History Since 1890.* London: Routledge, 1993.

Meyerowitz, Joanne. "Sexual Geography and Gender Economy: The Furnished Room Districts of Chicago, 1890–1930." *Gender and American History Since 1890.* Ed. Barbara Melosh, 43–71.

Miller, Jordan Y., and Winifred Frazer. *American Drama Between the Wars: A Critical History.* Boston: Twayne, 1991.

Moody, Richard. "Theatre U.S.A., 1909–1919: The Formative Decade." In *Contributions in Drama and Theatre Studies.* No. 5. Ed. L. W. Conolly, 113–33. Westport, CT: Greenwood Press, 1982.

"Mr. Belasco's Quarrel with the Experimental Theatres." *Current Opinion* (Mar. 1917): 184.

"News of the Theater." *New York Herald Tribune,* 11 May 1931, 10.

Noe, Marcia. "'A Romantic and Miraculous City' Shapes Three Midwestern Writers." *Western Illinois Regional Studies* 1 (1978): 176–98.

Olauson, Judith. *The American Woman Playwright: A View of Criticism and Characterization.* Troy, NY: Whitston Publishing, 1981.

"One Bright Playlet in Comedy's Bad Bill." *World,* 24 Jan. 1918, 7.

"Our Little Theater Movement Has a Meaning All Its Own." *Current Opinion* (June 1919): 372.

Parsons, Louella O. "State Labor Federation Fights Film Censorship." *Morning Telegraph,* 16 Dec. 1921, 5.

Peavy, Linda. "A Bibliography of Provincetown Players' Dramas, 1915–1922." *Bibliographical Society of America* 69.4 (1975): 569–74.

Perkins, Bradford. *The Great Rapprochement: England and the United States, 1895–1914.* New York: Atheneum, 1968.

Pfister, Joel. *Staging Depth: Eugene O'Neill and the Politics of Psychological Discourse.* Chapel Hill: U of North Carolina P, 1995.

Phelps, William Lyon. "Introduction." In *The Pulitzer Prize Plays, 1918–1934.* Ed. Kathryn Coe and William H. Cordell, vi–ix. New York: Random House, 1935.

"The Pioneer Players." *Stage,* 2 Apr. 1925, 19.

Ramirez, Jan Seidler. *Within Bohemia's Borders: Greenwich Village, 1830–1930. Interpretive Script Accompanying an Exhibition at the Museum of the City of New York.* New York: The Museum of the City of New York, 1991.

Rapp, Rayna, and Ellen Ross. "The 1920s: Feminism, Consumerism, and Political Backlash in the United States." In *Women in Culture and Politics: A Century of Change.* Ed. Judith Friedlander et al., 52–61. Bloomington: Indiana UP, 1986.

Reed, James. *The Birth Control Movement and American Society: From Private Vice to Public Virtue.* 1978. Rpt. Princeton: Princeton UP, 1983.

Riley, Glenda. *Women and Indians on the Frontier, 1825–1915.* Albuquerque: U of New Mexico P, 1984.

Rivers, W. H. R. *Instinct and the Unconscious: A Contribution to a Biological Theory of the Psycho-Neuroses.* 2d ed. Cambridge: Cambridge UP, 1924.

Rollins, John W. "The Anti-Imperialists and Twentieth Century American Foreign Policy." *Studies on the Left* 3.1 (1962): 9–24.

Ruitenbeck, Hendrik M. *Freud and America.* New York: Macmillan, 1966.

Sarlós, Robert K. "The Provincetown Players' Genesis or Non-Commercial Theatre on Commercial Streets." *Journal of American Culture* 7.3 (Fall 1984): 65–70.

Sayler, Oliver M. *Our American Theatre.* New York: Brentano's, 1923.

"The Science of the Soul." *Masses* 8 (July 1916): 30–31.

Shay, Frank. "Introduction." *Fifty More Contemporary One-Act Plays.* Ed. F. Shay, v–vi. New York: D. Appleton, 1928.

———. *The Plays and Books of the Little Theatre.* New York: Theatre Crafts Exchange, 1919.

———, ed. *Contemporary One-Act Plays of 1921.* Cincinnati: Stewart Kidd, 1922.

———, ed. *A Treasury of Plays for Women.* Boston: Little, Brown, 1922.

Showalter, Elaine. "Rivers and Sassoon: The Inscription of Male Gender Anxieties." In *Behind the Lines: Gender and the Two World Wars.* Ed. Margaret Randolph Higonnet et al., 61–69. New Haven: Yale UP, 1987.

Sochen, June. *Movers and Shakers: American Women Thinkers and Activists, 1900–1970.* New York: Quadrangle Books, 1973.

———. *The New Woman: Feminism in Greenwich Village, 1910–1920.* New York: Quadrangle Books, 1972.

Spencer, Benjamin T. *Patterns of Nationality: Twentieth-Century Literary Versions of America.* New York: Burt Franklin, 1981.

Stocking, George W., Jr. "The Ethnographic Sensibility of the 1920s and the Dualism of the Anthropological Tradition." In *Romantic Motives: Essays on Anthropological Sensibility.* Ed. George W. Stocking Jr., 208–76. Madison: U of Wisconsin P, 1989.

Stokes, Rose Pastor. *The Woman Who Wouldn't.* New York: G. P. Putnam's Sons, 1919.

"Suppressed Desires." *Era,* 12 Oct. 1921, 9.

"Susan Glaspell: New American Dramatist." *Daily Telegraph,* 19 June 1924, n.p. Clipping. Cook and Glaspell Papers. Berg Collection, New York Public Library.

"Susan Glaspell, 'Born' at Provincetown, Has Yet to Go from 14th St. to Broadway." *New York World-Telegram*, 6 May 1931, 3.

"Susan Glaspell's Play 'Bernice': A Great Drama." *Little Review* 6.1 (May 1919): 53–55.

Sutherland, Ann. *Gypsies: The Hidden Americans*. London: Tavistock, 1975.

Sutherland, Cynthia. "American Women Playwrights as Mediators of the 'Woman Problem.'" *Modern Drama* 21.3 (Sept. 1978): 319–36.

Sway, Marlene. *Familiar Strangers: Gypsy Life in America*. Urbana: U of Illinois P, 1988.

"Three One-Act Plays." *Era*, 15 Nov. 1933, 8.

Törnqvist, Egil. "The Modern(ist) One-Act Play." In *Facets of European Modernism: Essays in Honour of James McFarlane Presented to Him on His 65th Birthday, 12 December 1985*. Ed. Janet Garton, 175–98. Norwich: U of East Anglia P, 1985.

"Two Pulitzer Prizes Are Won by Women." *New York Times*, 5 May 1931, 1:6.

Umphlett, Wiley Lee. *Mythmakers of the American Dream: The Nostalgic Vision in Popular Culture*. Lewisburg: Bucknell UP, 1983.

Valgemae, Mardi. *Accelerated Grimace: Expressionism in the American Drama of the 1920s*. Carbondale: Southern Illinois UP, 1972.

"The Verge." *Era*, 4 Apr. 1925, 8.

"The Verge." *Sunday Herald*, n.d., n.p. Clipping. Cook and Glaspell Papers. Berg Collection, New York Public Library.

Von Blon, Katherine T. "'Alison's House' Presented." *Los Angeles Times*, 22 Feb. 1933, 5.

Vorse, Mary Heaton. *A Footnote to Folly*. New York: Farrar and Rinehart, 1935.

Waterman, Arthur E. "Susan Glaspell (?1882–1948)." *American Literary Realism* 4.2 (Spring 1971): 183–91.

———. "Susan Glaspell and the Provincetown." *Modern Drama* 7.2 (Sept. 1964): 174–84.

Williams, Gary Jay. "Turned Down in Provincetown: O'Neill's Debut Re-Examined." *Eugene O'Neill Newsletter* 12.1 (Spring 1988): 17–27.

Wilson, Rob. "Producing American Selves: The Form of American Biography." In *Contesting the Subject: Essays in the Postmodern Theory and Practice of Biography and Biographical Criticism*. Ed. William H. Epstein, 167–92.

"The World of the Theatre." *Illustrated London News*, 11 Apr. 1925, n.p. Clipping. Cook and Glaspell Papers. Berg Collection, New York Public Library.

Yeats. W. B. *Explorations*. London: Macmillan, 1962.

Z. "The Provincetown Players." *Seven Arts Chronicle* (Aug. 1917): 522–24.

✧ Index